JUSTICE CURTIS IN THE CIVIL WAR ERA

Constitutionalism and Democracy

Gregg Ivers and Kevin T. McGuire, Editors

JUSTICE CURTIS
IN THE CIVIL WAR ERA

At the Crossroads of American Constitutionalism

STUART STREICHLER

UNIVERSITY OF VIRGINIA PRESS
CHARLOTTESVILLE AND LONDON

University of Virginia Press
© 2005 by the Rector and Visitors of the University of Virginia
All rights reserved
Printed in the United States of America on acid-free paper

First published 2005

1 3 5 7 9 8 6 4 2

LIBRARY OF CONGRESS CATALOGING-IN-PUBLICATION DATA

Streichler, Stuart, 1957–
Justice Curtis in the Civil War era : at the crossroads of American
constitutionalism / Stuart Streichler.
p.   cm. — (Constitutionalism and democracy)
Includes bibliographical references and index.
ISBN 0-8139-2342-5 (cloth : alk. paper)
1. Constitutional history—United States—19th century. 2. Slavery—Law and
legislation—United States—History—19th century. 3. Judicial process—United
States—History—19th century. 4. Curtis, Benjamin Robbins, 1809–1874.
5. United States—History—Civil War, 1861–1865. I. Title. II. Series.
KF4541.S73   2005
342.7302'9—dc22
2004026763

Frontispiece
Benjamin R. Curtis, engraving by J. H. Daniels.
(Courtesy of the Library of Congress)

For my mother and father

CONTENTS

PREFACE

THIS BOOK PRESENTS a constitutional history of the Civil War era by focusing on Justice Benjamin Robbins Curtis (1809–1874). A Harvard-trained Boston attorney, Curtis served on the U.S. Supreme Court in the 1850s. He is best known for dissenting in the *Dred Scott* case, where he disputed the Court's ruling that no black person could ever qualify for U.S. citizenship. His arguments there had a singular effect on public opinion, and in the wake of that decision, Curtis resigned from the bench.

More than anything else, Justice Curtis's dissent in *Dred Scott* led me to consider writing this book. My interest grew as I realized the full extent of his role in a succession of constitutional crises. Although later judges and scholars have ranked him as one of the most brilliant justices in the nation's history, only one book has been written about him previously, and that was a memoir by his brother published in the nineteenth century.

What attracted me from the start was not Curtis's life story so much as what his actions might tell us about constitutional developments in the age of the Civil War. It has seemed to me that debates surrounding the Constitution were an important aspect of the political and cultural history of that period. With that in mind, I did not set out to write a traditional biography. This book is organized around the constitutional problems Curtis engaged from 1850 to 1868. It examines the justice's constitutional principles, interpretations, and arguments in the context of his times.

In following the issues Curtis addressed, this study does not analyze every constitutional problem that arose in the Civil War era. Secession is briefly discussed, for example, because Curtis contributed little on that point: he thought it obvious that the southern states had no right to secede. The topics covered in this book vary in emphasis. Some chapters concern historically important events like the *Dred Scott* case. Others explore critical stages in long-running developments in constitutional law. Only one chapter deals with wartime issues. That said, this book's contents are to my mind brought together by the idea suggested in its subtitle. Justice Curtis was not simply involved in a number of discrete questions concerning the Constitution. He was at the center of a contest over American constitutionalism that was waged not in abstract terms but in actual controversies over power and individual rights.

That contest was not shaped by slavery alone, but the peculiar institution had a pervasive effect on constitutional developments in the mid-nineteenth century. The relationship between slavery and the Constitution is an ongoing theme of this book. Frankly, it has been difficult to evaluate Curtis's positions on this subject from a twenty-first-century perspective. In my own view anything short of abolitionism suffers by comparison. Justice Curtis was no abolitionist, nor always as high-minded as he appeared in the *Dred Scott* case. Yet as I reviewed Curtis's efforts to deal with the constitutional problems posed by slavery, I was struck by their complexity, and I have tried in this book to picture how events appeared 150 years ago, notwithstanding my personal judgments.

Many people have assisted me in the course of this project. I am particularly indebted to J. Woodford Howard Jr. for his dedication, perspective, and insights. It is a pleasure to thank those who have read and commented on the manuscript in whole or in part: Eve Darian-Smith, Tony Freyer, Benjamin Ginsberg, Mark A. Graber, Lisa Hajjar, Dirk Hartog, Timothy S. Huebner, Michael Johnson, Harold J. Krent, J. G. A. Pocock, Juliet Williams, and Larzer Ziff. At an early stage in my thinking, I was fortunate to have the opportunity to discuss my work with Herman Belz, John Ely, Allen Grossman, and Fred D. Miller Jr. For research and administrative assistance, I must single out Nicole Alvarado, Amber Hawk, Michelle Lee, John Lopez, Bianca Roig, Erika Ruiz, Shiry Tannenbaum, and Kevin Scott Willen among the students whom I enlisted. I am also grateful to numerous archivists and librarians around the country, especially at the Harvard Law School Library, Harvard University Archives, Library of Congress, and Massachusetts Historical Society. An earlier version of chapter 5 appeared as "Justice Curtis's Dissent in the *Dred Scott* Case: An Interpretive Study," © 1997 by University of California, Hastings College of the Law, *Hastings Constitutional Law Quarterly* 24:2 (Winter 1997): 509–44, used by permission.

CHRONOLOGY

1809   Born, Watertown, Massachusetts, November 4.
1825–29   Harvard College.
1829–32   Dane Law School, Harvard University.
1832   Admitted to the bar, Northfield, Massachusetts.
1833   Married Eliza Maria Woodward, May 8
            (deceased 1844).
1834–51   Law practice with Charles P. Curtis, Boston.
1836   Argued *Commonwealth v. Aves.*
1844   Published "Debts of the States."
1846   Married Anna Wroe, January 5 (deceased 1860).
1848   Elected to the House of Representatives of the
            Massachusetts General Court (also elected in 1850).
1850   Speech on fugitive slave law in Faneuil Hall.
1851   Appointed associate justice of the Supreme Court.
1852   Opinion in *Cooley v. Board of Wardens.*
1856   Opinion in *Murray's Lessee v. Hoboken Land
            and Improvement Co.*
1857   Dissented in *Scott v. Sandford.*
1857   Resigned from the Court, September 1.
1857–74   Law practice, Boston.
1861   Married Maria Malleville Allen, August 29.
1862   Published *Executive Power.*
1868   Argued in President Andrew Johnson's impeachment trial.
1874   Died, Newport, Rhode Island, September 15.

JUSTICE CURTIS IN THE CIVIL WAR ERA

INTRODUCTION

THE CIVIL WAR was a turning point in U.S. history. Some historians consider it the second American Revolution.[1] Those who lived in that time sensed the radical break with the past, a feeling summed up perfectly by Harvard professor George Ticknor. There was a "great gulf" between what happened before and "what has happened since, or what is likely to happen hereafter," Ticknor wrote in 1869. "It does not seem to me as if I were living in the country in which I was born."[2]

The same could have been said of the constitutional world Americans inhabited. Whatever the continuities, the Constitution was transformed by three amendments adopted during Reconstruction. The Thirteenth Amendment abolished slavery. The Fourteenth recognized all native-born Americans, black and white, as citizens. It also declared that no state shall deny any person due process or equal protection of the law. The Fifteenth Amendment extended voting rights to black men.[3]

Although progress toward racial equality stalled, this marked the beginning of a new phase in American constitutional development. The Fourteenth Amendment in particular set the stage for the Constitution that Americans are familiar with today: a charter of individual rights in which leading questions concern free speech, protections for the criminally accused, and civil rights, with federal judicial power regularly deployed against the states. Constitutional change on a large scale would occur again, with the New Deal, for example. Yet so many of the political struggles after the Civil War played out within the constitutional framework put in place then, it is tempting to view that period as a watershed in American constitutional history.[4]

Perhaps it is not surprising, then, to find that the Constitution occupied a central place in the nation's political discourse during the Civil War era. How the Constitution should be interpreted was often the subject of popular discussion. Newspaper editorials, preachers' sermons, and abolitionist tracts examined constitutional questions in detail. Union soldiers staged formal debates over complicated constitutional propositions. One sergeant recorded that he took "part on the affirmative of Resolved that the Constitutional relations of the rebel states should be fixed by Congress only." Another debate topic, reported by a private, was more expansive: "Resolved that the present struggle will do more to establish and maintain a republican form of government than the Revolutionary war."[5]

The significance of the Constitution to the Civil War is illustrated by Abraham Lincoln's first inaugural address, delivered shortly before fighting broke out. With all of the possible things to say under the circumstances (seven states had already seceded), the president focused on the Constitution to a remarkable degree. He referred to the charter over a dozen times, quoted a fifty-two-word constitutional provision, acquiesced in a proposed constitutional amendment, and discussed the precedential effect of Supreme Court decisions. Lincoln said that "all" of "our constitutional controversies" derived from questions the Constitution "does not expressly" answer. The Union was vulnerable, he suggested, because opposing sides refused to compromise over the divergent interpretations the Constitution seemed to permit.[6]

The constitutional controversies Lincoln identified had one other feature in common. Each concerned slavery. The Constitution was naturally drawn into the discussion of liberty or the rights of person and property. The relationship between slavery and the Constitution was more extensive than that, however. Americans then displayed an uncanny ability to convert the terms of debate over slavery into constitutional form, whether involving federal power, states' rights, congressional authority, or the president's wartime powers. It is no wonder the country's most famous fugitive slave, Frederick Douglass, felt compelled to "study with some care" the "just and proper rules of legal interpretation."[7]

No wonder, too, that given the Constitution's open-ended language, rival interpretations emerged. Proslavery constitutionalism prevailed on the U.S. Supreme Court; its high point was the decision in *Dred Scott v. Sandford* (1857). Purportedly following the framers' original intent, Chief Justice Roger B. Taney held that blacks did not belong to the American political community. He made it clear that no black person, whether slave or free, could ever be a U.S. citizen. Taney also strictly construed national power so that Congress could not prevent the spread of slavery.[8]

Different views of the Constitution's possibilities circulated in antislavery quarters. Some abolitionists, following William Lloyd Garrison's lead, renounced the Constitution as a proslavery "covenant with death." Others offered creative if not fully developed interpretations to show that slavery was flatly unconstitutional, as Douglass argued in a speech called "The Constitution of the United States: Is It Pro-Slavery or Anti-Slavery?"[9] Still other opponents of slavery, notably Salmon P. Chase, mixed constitutional principle with practical politics. Conceding that the Constitution did not require immediate abolition in the slave states, he argued that it did not permit the federal government to support slavery either. While gaining ground in the political arena (with the Free-Soil and Republican parties), such views of the Constitution made little headway in the courts.[10]

Enter Lincoln, who like many abolitionists looked upon the Constitution as one founding document that must be read in conjunction with another, the Declaration of Independence. The Declaration's principle of universal liberty was the "apple of gold," Lincoln suggested in an extended metaphor. The Constitution was the "picture of silver, subsequently framed around it," made to preserve the apple. At first reluctant to commit Union troops to end slavery, President Lincoln took a more radical position as the war progressed, paving the way to a "new birth of freedom" by word (the Gettysburg Address) and deed (the Emancipation Proclamation). It was left to the postwar Congress to inscribe the result in the nation's fundamental law, with Republican legislators pushing through the Reconstruction amendments.[11]

With all that, it is easy to see why scholars would classify the Civil War as a "constitutional war" leading to the "greatest constitutional revolution in our history."[12] Just as the Constitution figured significantly in the conflicts of the Civil War era, this period was a critical juncture in the development of American constitutionalism.

One of the most important figures in these constitutional contests was Supreme Court justice Benjamin Robbins Curtis.[13] He was born in Watertown, Massachusetts, in 1809. His father, a sea captain who traded in slaves on the African coast, died when Curtis was five. Although his mother struggled to make ends meet, Curtis went on to graduate from Harvard College and its law school. It was not long before he distinguished himself as a member of Boston's competitive bar, noted for his expertise in evolving areas like commercial, maritime, and patent law. Yet Curtis remained aloof from the political controversies roiling Massachusetts over slavery and the Mexican War, even after his election to the state legislature in 1848, where he headed an effort to reform the state's antiquated legal procedures.[14]

The sectional crisis two years later drew him beyond the strict confines of the law, and in a series of events, Curtis emerged as a leading spokesman for the conservative Whigs of Massachusetts. He publicly defended Daniel Webster when many New Englanders were dismayed by the senator's role in the Compromise of 1850. In response to widespread opposition to the fugitive slave law, Curtis delivered an influential speech in Faneuil Hall justifying its enforcement. And after an unusual bargain among state legislators put Charles Sumner in the U.S. Senate—a resounding victory for antislavery forces—Curtis wrote a pamphlet declaring the election a criminal conspiracy.[15] President Millard Fillmore appointed Curtis to the Supreme Court a few months later, a reward, abolitionists claimed, for services rendered the "Slave Power."[16]

The new justice had an auspicious start. Tackling a problem that had divided the justices for a generation, Curtis in his first term issued a landmark opinion in *Cooley v. Board of Wardens* (1852). He crafted a doctrine to reconcile state and federal powers over interstate commerce. In doing so, the justice recognized an implied judicial authority to invalidate state laws affecting the country's rapidly growing economy. Curtis also wrote the first opinion for the Court analyzing the due process clause, in a case called *Murray's Lessee v. Hoboken Land and Improvement Co.* (1856). No one then could have anticipated all the meanings due process would be given over the years. Yet Curtis's explicit statement that this constitutional guarantee empowered judges to nullify legislation in some sense inaugurated the use of due process as a fundamental protection of individual rights.[17]

Justice Curtis is remembered most of all for dissenting in the *Dred Scott* case. In response to Taney's claim that "the negro race" was "a separate class of persons" not considered "a portion of the people or citizens of the Government," Curtis argued that black persons were "in every sense part of the people of the United States." He produced compelling evidence from the statute books, which abolitionists had overlooked, that black Americans had voted to ratify the Constitution. Lincoln said Curtis made this point "with so much particularity as to leave no doubt of its truth."[18] Curtis further suggested that the federal courts provided an appropriate forum for free blacks to confirm their civil rights. As for the right of property in slaves, strenuously maintained by southerners, the justice insisted that chattel slavery was not a form of property protected under the Constitution. He argued that Congress had plenary power to block any further expansion of slavery. In a statement that had immediate political impact, Curtis declared the Supreme Court's decision illegitimate. For many northerners Curtis's arguments undermined the constitutional foundations of proslavery thought. Justice Curtis added to the notoriety surrounding the case when, disgusted with "the state of the court," he resigned.[19]

That did not stop Curtis from speaking out on major constitutional issues. During the war he wrote a pamphlet entitled *Executive Power* that challenged the Lincoln administration for relying on military tribunals to try civilians. Seemingly at odds with his *Dred Scott* dissent, he denied that the president had constitutional authority to issue the Emancipation Proclamation.[20] Curtis argued several appeals before the Supreme Court during Reconstruction, but his most celebrated case then was the impeachment trial of President Andrew Johnson. As Johnson's attorney, Curtis delivered a two-day opening argument that marked the turning point in the Senate proceedings. "Judge Curtis gave us the law," explained one senator who voted to acquit, "and we followed it."[21]

Through all of this, Curtis acquired a reputation for extraordinary skill in constitutional argument. Samuel F. Miller, one of the leading justices in the late nineteenth century, thought that in legal reasoning Curtis "never had an equal in this country." Curtis's interpretive talents were given special notice by his critics, who repeatedly complained that he carried artfulness too far. The "public know how to appreciate legal subtilty and ingenuity," declared the *New York Tribune* before castigating Curtis for "so many exhibitions" of "adroitness" on "the side of tyranny and injustice."[22]

Justice Curtis obviously had a different perspective. He presented himself to the public as an advocate for constitutionalism, an idea which was in his view under considerable pressure. The threat to constitutional government posed by secessionists was for Curtis only one aspect of a larger problem. He saw a need to defend the Constitution against extreme and destructive positions wherever they arose, whether from Boston abolitionists, southern justices, a wartime president, or radical congressmen. "Of all the causes of alarm which now distress the public mind," Curtis said in 1862, "there are few more terrible than the tendency to lawlessness which is manifesting itself in so many directions."[23]

Curtis's constitutionalism was grounded above all else in the common law. Practically all American lawyers then had at least a rudimentary understanding of this legal system, built up over centuries in England and adopted throughout the United States. Curtis excelled in its case-by-case method of reasoning, but what set him apart was the extent to which the common-law style of thought was interwoven into his constitutional jurisprudence. This was evident in his craftsmanlike approach toward interpreting the Constitution, his philosophy of evolutionary growth in the law, his emphasis on pragmatic problem solving, his conviction that judges could play a central role in governing, and his sensibility to the customary practices of the people and their political institutions. A remark Curtis once made about Daniel Webster might well have been said of the justice himself. "His mind was imbued" with the "logic" of the common law, and its "fundamental principles had become a part of the structure of his mind."[24]

With that mind-set Curtis was convinced that questions elsewhere resolved by "mere force" could be addressed within the "staid, settled, and regular course of judicial procedure."[25] He did not think that courts could solve every political issue on their own. Yet the justice recognized that constitutional cases often presented political problems, and he had a faith in the judiciary's capacity to handle such questions, first, by focusing on concrete disputes between parties in court and, second, by moving from one case to another with the expectation that a fuller solution would emerge over time. The common-law approach, in short, provided judges with a way to translate political conflict into legal terms. Justice Curtis made no secret of his strategy for confronting potentially explosive questions. "It is safer," he wrote in a case implicating the rights of citizenship one year before *Dred Scott*, "and more in accordance with the duty of a judicial tribunal" to leave the Constitution's "meaning to be determined, in each case, upon a view of the particular rights asserted and denied therein." This was especially true "with so broad a provision, involving matters not only of great delicacy and importance, but which are of such a character, that any merely abstract definition could scarcely be correct; and a failure to make it so would certainly produce mischief."[26]

These comments provide a glimpse into Curtis's conception of the Constitution. One of its "excellencies," Curtis once declared, was "that it did not attempt too much." The Constitution was "neither a treatise nor a code, but a simple enumeration of the great powers and principles necessary to constitute the government of our country." To say, as Taney had, that the Constitution has not only the "same words" but the "same meaning and intent" as "when it came from the hands of its framers" missed the point from Curtis's perspective. For Justice Curtis the Constitution was not fixed in meaning. It was an adaptive and flexible instrument of self-government. While he did not believe it appropriate to contradict the framers' intent, he recognized that they had left many key points open to interpretation.[27]

Not surprisingly, Curtis saw the judiciary as critical to making the Constitution work. When he joined the Supreme Court at midcentury, it was still an early point in that tribunal's history. The scope of judicial review—the power to declare unconstitutional acts of the legislature and executive—was unsettled. No statute had been found in violation of the Bill of Rights, an event today considered a hallmark of judicial review. The Court had ruled an act of Congress unconstitutional only once, in *Marbury v. Madison* (1803). In addition, the justices held conflicting views of their authority to invalidate state laws.[28]

Early on it was clear that judicial review, a power the Constitution does not expressly describe, did not simply involve technical questions of federal jurisdiction. That the doctrine had political consequences was well understood, and prominent officials contested the Supreme Court's authority throughout the antebellum period. The Constitution was the nation's fundamental law, Chief Justice John Marshall had reasoned in *Marbury*, and it was naturally the "province" of the courts "to say what the law is." Thomas Jefferson resisted any implication that the Court had the final say, what has become known as judicial supremacy. Having judges serve "as the ultimate arbiters of all constitutional questions" was "a very dangerous doctrine," he wrote. Congress and the president had "co-equal" authority to interpret the Constitution, according to Jefferson, a view reiterated by Andrew Jackson and Lincoln.[29]

For his part Justice Curtis viewed judicial power along the lines Marshall had taken. Curtis broadly described the Supreme Court's "duty" to declare "void all legislative acts not in conformity with the Constitution." He believed the Court had a vital role to restrain the states "within their appropriate limits of power."[30] What is noteworthy about Curtis is not so much his judicial philosophy in the abstract but how he applied it under the pressure of events. Secession had been a real threat one year before his appointment. Indeed, the whole constitutional system was in a state of crisis and had been for some time before any state had seceded. In these circumstances Curtis displayed a sense of both the delicate task judges faced and the stakes involved.

With his brand of constitutionalism, Curtis addressed a variety of issues that the Constitution touched on. Slavery was critical in all this, of course, and more broadly race. So too was the extraordinary economic development of Curtis's day, which in turn was shaped by the nationalization of free-labor capitalism. Yet that was only part of an even larger cultural transformation. There was a wholesale change in perspective, reflected, for example, in the everyday understanding of the nation that can be seen in the postwar reference to "the United States" as a singular rather than a plural noun. It was also a pivotal point in the conduct of public affairs. The founding reflected a commitment to resolving conflict through a deliberative political process instead of the use of force. Yet for all the attention paid the Constitution in the antebellum period, Americans had not completely figured out how to do that, as the very fact that there was a civil war indicates.

1. IN THE WHIG TRADITION

THE ISSUES CONFRONTING the country in 1861 did not spring full-blown that year, nor did Curtis's views. His constitutional thought as it found expression then was rooted most of all in what might be called the Whig tradition, a political culture that revolved round the party that went by that name. For roughly twenty years starting around 1834, the Whigs comprised one of the two major parties in the United States; the Democrats were the other. The Whig Party was home to a diverse group of politicians and voters, initially drawn together in opposition to Andrew Jackson. Its national leaders included Henry Clay of Kentucky and Daniel Webster from New England. Abraham Lincoln was a Whig, along with future Republicans like Charles Sumner and William H. Seward. So too was Georgia's Alexander Stephens, destined to become vice president of the Confederacy. Often noted for its economic program, the Whig Party backed protective tariffs on imports to promote the development of the young nation's industries. Whigs supported government-financed internal improvements such as roads, canals, and turnpikes. They defended the banking system, especially the Bank of the United States, against the Democrats' sustained attack.[1]

Whiggery involved more than policy positions and party politics, however. Daniel Walker Howe has suggested that American Whigs brought to life a political culture with a system of beliefs, social customs, and habits of thought.[2] Along these lines, Curtis can be identified with a political and intellectual culture which was essentially Whig, but to be precise the cultural setting was both broader and narrower than the label Whig suggests. It was broader because the Whigs were a part of a larger tradition of thought stretching back to the Federalists of the early nineteenth century;[3] narrower as Curtis was a Massachusetts Whig, and the Whigs from the Bay State, particularly Boston's elite, were distinctive. Closer to the Civil War, what it meant to be a Whig in Massachusetts—what the Whig tradition stood for—was itself contested. The divisive question was what should be done about slavery, and in the 1840s a group of mostly young Whigs, including Sumner and Charles Francis Adams, broke ranks with the old guard. Styling themselves Conscience Whigs, they derided those who disagreed with their antislavery views as

Cotton Whigs, "lords of the loom," in Sumner's memorable phrase, allied with "lords of the lash."[4]

Where Curtis fit within all of this provides the background for understanding his actions in the Civil War era. At its most basic level, Curtis's early life and career is the story of his rise to prominence among Boston's elite Whigs. More complex was the Whiggish conceptual framework—his political, legal, and economic thought—that he brought to bear on constitutional questions. Add to that assumptions Curtis held about slavery, and the sum total is an image of Curtis's inner frame of mind, so far as that might be possible to ascertain.

I

Benjamin Robbins Curtis was born on November 4, 1809, in Watertown, near Boston. His family had roots in America from 1632. According to his brother's account, their father, named Benjamin Curtis, was a ship's captain in the merchant marine. It appears that Curtis's father was involved in the African slave trade. In the early 1800s a person named Benjamin Curtis was sued in the Massachusetts courts for breaking a contract to deliver slaves. The published judicial opinion recited the terms of the contract: "I promise to pay . . . nine four-foot slaves, thirty-seven prime slaves . . . for value received. . . . Benjamin Curtis." It is possible that this defendant was not the justice's father, but that seems unlikely.[5]

Curtis's father died abroad in 1814, leaving his wife, Lois Robbins Curtis, to care for two young sons. The family's circumstances, modest to begin with, became more difficult. Curtis was blessed with a valuable connection, however. His uncle was George Ticknor, a professor of French and Spanish languages and literatures at Harvard College. Ticknor, whose position in Boston's salon culture led ranking Bostonians to call the city Ticknorville, was a phenomenon in the intellectual and social life of nineteenth-century New England. He had a list of acquaintances which read like an honor roll of literary giants, including Byron, Goethe, and Wordsworth. Jefferson tried unsuccessfully to entice Ticknor to teach at the University of Virginia.[6]

What he owed Ticknor, Curtis once said, was "not to be measured."[7] Yet it was Curtis's mother who encouraged him to enroll in Harvard College, a move which Ticknor initially questioned. Curtis entered Harvard at the age of fifteen.[8] He was recalled years later by his schoolmate Oliver Wendell Holmes as the boy in the class "with a three-decker brain/That could harness a team with a logical chain."[9] Curtis found the niche for such talents in law. He started his legal studies in 1829, a propitious moment in the life of the law school at Harvard. That was the same year that the university appointed Supreme Court justice Joseph Story to head the school, which had been declining. (He reported that no students had attended the year before, though no official record exists). Story, one of the leading jurists in the early nineteenth century, came with the intention of creating a bastion of conservative thought in order to counter the rising power of Jackson Democrats.[10]

Although Curtis regarded the law school as the best place "for getting the theory of the law," in 1831 he cut short his coursework for a legal apprenticeship in Northfield, a small town in northern Massachusetts. Curtis professed dissatisfaction with "the influence of Boston and its society upon young men."[11] Hidden beneath this dour exterior was Curtis's real motivation. He wanted to court his cousin Eliza Woodward of Hanover, New Hampshire, whom he married two years later.[12] Continuing to study law on his own, Curtis returned to Harvard, received his law degree, and was admitted to the bar in the Northfield area in 1832. After two years of an uneventful country practice, Curtis, frankly declaring that he was "worthy of a wider field," joined the established Boston law office of Charles P. Curtis, an older cousin.[13]

Their practice on Court Street placed the young lawyer in the midst of New England's economic transformation. By 1835 Massachusetts had chartered seventeen railroad lines (the first only nine years before); the changeover to the factory system in the region's textile industry had vastly increased production; New England had become a center for technological innovation (a disproportionate number of the most significant patents were granted to its residents). Add to that Boston's position as a major port of international shipping, the growth in the state banking system, and the rise of the corporation as a preferred form of business organization, and all the ingredients were in place to spawn novel legal questions. Technical issues at the bar often reflected broad economic concerns and political divisions. Patent law became a battleground between Jackson Democrats, who objected to the monopoly characteristics of patents, and Whigs, who generally favored making them easier to obtain. Likewise, while Whigs supported using the corporate form to organize private enterprise, Jacksonians remained suspicious of the growing power of corporations. Wide-ranging economic activity brought to the fore questions concerning the scope of the state government's regulatory powers. As this issue took shape, Whigs, solicitous of rights in private property, generally differed with Democrats, who were more willing to find public interest overriding private right.[14]

With cases ranging from maritime insurance to railroad liability, Benjamin Curtis was in the vanguard of various legal developments.

Recognizing that patent law had "great practical consequence," he was among the earliest group of lawyers known for expertise in this area. His most famous client in that field was Samuel F. B. Morse, whom Curtis represented in litigation over the telegraph.[15] Before the Massachusetts Supreme Judicial Court, Curtis argued several important cases. He prevailed in *Cary v. Daniels* (1844), which opened the way for new textile factories to use scarce water resources unencumbered by the property claims of older mills. In *Smith v. Hurd* (1847), Curtis successfully argued that a chartered bank's shareholders could not sue the firm's directors for negligence and malfeasance. Shortly before his appointment to the U.S. Supreme Court, Curtis lost an appeal in *Commonwealth v. Alger* (1851), a foundational case which established the state's regulatory power over private property rights.[16]

While engaged in his practice, Curtis was not, as he put it, "in the habit of writing any thing but bills in equity, & such like." There was one exception, an article entitled "Debts of the States" which was published in the *North American Review*, a leading Whig journal. In this article Curtis addressed a seemingly esoteric question—whether states could repudiate debts incurred to finance public works. This issue had significant policy implications in the wake of the panic of 1837, one of the deepest economic depressions in American history. In the course of explaining why states could not disavow their debts, Curtis articulated several Whig themes: the sanctity of contractual obligations and private property, the role of the government in promoting economic development, and the importance of the banking system.[17]

As Curtis rose among the "eager community of the bar," he solidified his social position in Boston.[18] He was involved in several elite institutions in the area, often in a position of distinction. When the Harvard alumni organization was formed in 1840, Curtis was elected secretary, joining a set of eminent officers who included John Quincy Adams as president and Justice Story and the noted Whig orator Edward Everett as vice presidents.[19] In 1846 Curtis became a fellow on the Harvard Corporation, which governed the school's affairs. At that time the corporation's seven members included Everett, then serving as Harvard's president, and Chief Justice Lemuel Shaw of the Supreme Judicial Court of Massachusetts.[20] Outside Harvard, Curtis acted the part of a leading figure in the community. He was a vestryman of Kings' Chapel, whose laity was overwhelmingly upper-class; a proprietor of the Boston Athenaeum, the exclusive private library; and a trustee of Mount Auburn Cemetery.[21] For several years Curtis belonged to the Wednesday Evening Club, organized around weekly suppers that brought the up-and-coming together, including Robert C. Winthrop Jr. and the historian Francis Parkman.

In 1848 Curtis was elected to the House of Representatives of the state legislature (called the Massachusetts General Court). His chief interest was in judicial reform. Curtis had previously joined other lawyers petitioning the legislature to investigate the backlog in the courts. As a representative from Suffolk County, Curtis introduced resolutions supporting such an investigation, and Governor George N. Briggs appointed him to chair a three-member commission. Curtis's commission recommended various procedural reforms—to enable parties to discover facts before trial, to deter baseless pleadings, and to require clear statements of claims and defenses, for example—which accord with the motivating principles underlying modern civil procedure. Over the opposition of some members of the bar, the legislature incorporated the commission's suggestions in the Massachusetts Practice Act of 1851.[22]

Benjamin Curtis started "with nothing but his profession and strong powers of mind," reported a directory of *The Rich Men of Massachusetts*, but by 1852 he was included in its list. A resident of Beacon Hill, he also bought 300 acres near Pittsfield, Massachusetts, to build a summer home.[23] More than that, as a protégé of Webster, Story, and Ticknor, Curtis moved easily within Boston's unique inner circle where law, politics, and society intersected.

II

No one, it seems safe to say, would look to Curtis for his political theories as one might turn to Jefferson, Madison, or Lincoln. Nevertheless, the justice had a rudimentary political philosophy which formed the basis of his constitutional thought. He articulated the background assumptions of his political philosophy in a speech he delivered in Deerfield, Massachusetts, when he was twenty-two, as part of the small town's celebration of the centennial anniversary of George Washington's birthday. Curtis used the occasion to discuss "the origin and history of the principles of government."[24]

In commemorating Washington, it was open to Curtis to focus on the newness of the nation this founder had led into being, to consider the American Revolution a decisive break with the past and, with the Constitution, a rejection of English institutions and practices. The emphasis in Curtis's account was on continuity, however. He saw American political developments as part of a progression of events reaching back into English history. Above all else, what emerges from his Deerfield speech is Curtis's intellectual debt to Edmund Burke. Curtis found in Burke a classic justification for traditional institutions, an explanation for the gradual development of individual rights, and a logic for assessing the legitimacy of political change. Without mentioning the British statesman by name, Curtis restated central themes of Burke's most famous work, *Reflections on the Revolution in France.* Curtis's reliance on Burke was characteristic of Massachusetts Whigs who, according to Daniel Walker Howe, "enshrined" the Britisher in their "political pantheon."[25]

The foundational point of Curtis's political understanding can be drawn from his view of how governments should be formed. In his mind this came down to a choice between two alternatives; in some form these could be traced back to Plato and Aristotle. Governments could be forged out of experience (by which Curtis meant the customary practices people develop over time) or out of some abstract conception of an ideal state. This antithesis runs throughout Curtis's speech, and his disdain for idealism and preference for experience is clear. He denigrated the "ideal world of dreaming speculators" and the "pathless wilds of political speculation." The French Revolution provided a model of how badly this kind of thinking could end up; the revolutionary government there was built on the visionary theory of Jean-Jacques Rousseau and was grounded in a "pompous declamation about the abstract rights of man," according to Curtis. In this judgment he echoed Burke, who dismissed the French revolutionaries' "political metaphysics" and their "false claims" about the rights of men.[26]

In Curtis's view the relative merits of experience and idealism were vividly demonstrated in the development of colonial governments in Massachusetts and Carolina. He praised the Puritan settlers for indulging "in no splendid theories"; instead, "they drew their ideas of government from observation and experience; from observation of the character and relations of their society, from experience of the necessities and wants to which those relations gave rise." Carolina was by contrast a ripe target for Curtis, its constitution having been written by John Locke, who never set foot there. This had, Curtis argued, "served as a proof in all succeeding times how utterly absurd and inconsistent, are the political theories, formed by the philosopher in his closet, for the direction and government of affairs with which he has no practical acquaintance."[27]

Curtis's preference for experience over idealism rested upon his view of government as a fundamentally human arrangement. "Human institutions," Curtis noted, "cannot be wholly constructed on principles of science, which is proper to immutable objects." Underlying this was a basic assumption of the complexity surrounding political and social developments. The idea was that people, in whatever circumstances they found themselves, developed customary practices to meet their needs. Customs developed over time by an untold number of persons operating in countless ways throughout their lives. No one, no matter how brilliant, was capable of comprehending these developments—let alone doing better—by simply thinking things through. Burke was explicit on this point. He explained that the "objects of society are of the greatest possible complexity" and that, as a result, the "science of constructing a commonwealth" is "not to be taught à priori" but is rather a practical matter which requires experience. As Curtis put it, there was a "practical wisdom" derived from experience which could not be matched by abstract reasoning alone.[28]

Curtis went so far as to say that "expediency" was the "only true foundation of human government." By expediency he meant simply what was appropriate under the circumstances. The mark of a good government was that it was "adapted to the character and wants" of the people. To start with the ideal was bound to make matters worse, in Curtis's view; the aim in political affairs was to construct the "best possible" government.[29]

Curtis's view of political development—the value he placed upon gradual change and continuity—grew out of this understanding of experience. He believed that as each generation adapted social and political practices to meet the needs of its day, the institutional arrangements that emerged over time reflected the collective experience of successive generations. Because the political knowledge of any single generation was limited by its own experience, it followed that no present generation was likely to understand fully the merits of the institutions that had evolved to that point. For Curtis, as for Burke, there was a general presumption in favor of traditional institutions that reflected past experience. If it was difficult to articulate reasons to justify particular customs and practices, it was possible to state an overall rationale for presuming their worth.[30]

Once Curtis took hold of this idea, there was no limit to his efforts to fit American political history into a pattern of gradual progress. To explain the development of individual rights in America, Curtis used the idea of inheritance, which figured prominently in Burke's *Reflections*. Burke had suggested that the English people transmitted their government and their rights just as a family transmitted property from one generation to the next. The English, Burke noted, regarded their liberties "as an *entailed inheritance* derived to us from our forefathers, and to be transmitted to our posterity." Along with other English jurists (Edward Coke and William Blackstone, for example), Burke saw inheritance as the key to unravel an involved series of English political developments: "The antient charter, the Magna Charta of King John, was connected with a more positive charter from Henry I, and . . . both the one and the other were nothing more than a re-affirmance of the still more antient standing law of the kingdom. . . . In the famous law of the 3d of Charles I. called the *Petition of Right*, the parliament says to the king, 'Your subjects have *inherited* this freedom.' . . . The same policy pervades all the laws which have since been made for the preservation of our liberties."[31]

Curtis endorsed this version of English political history; indeed, he repeated this passage practically verbatim in his Deerfield address.[32] The "English people were accustomed to look upon their rights and liberties, as hereditary," Curtis said, and "our ancestors brought this feeling with them to America."[33] He suggested that Americans, armed with this idea of inheritance, "looked for the origin of their rights" not "to the ideal world of dreaming speculators, but to their own past history, where experience was ever waiting to teach them wisdom and caution."[34]

With this in mind, Curtis offered a skewed version of American political history with the emphasis on continuity with England. It struck an odd tone to celebrate Washington. In sketching the development of the principles of American government, Curtis did not discuss the Constitutional Convention over which Washington presided, the ratification debates, or *The Federalist Papers*. Instead, Curtis highlighted the role New England Puritans played in the development of American constitutional principles. Curtis found in the Massachusetts Bay Colony the "distinguishing features of our government" that "every one must recognize": the principle of separation of powers, the idea that power resides in the people, and the utility of a bill of rights. While acknowledging the contribution of other colonists to American political thought, Curtis suggested that they were not "at heart republicans" as the Puritans were.[35]

For Curtis the American Revolution was the natural outgrowth of English political traditions. He turned to the Puritans again to establish continuity as he traced the "great causes" of the Revolution to their "ideas of political liberty." Having credited the Puritans with preserving liberty at a crucial point in England's history, Curtis then suggested that they brought to America a "habit of free thought." As for the liberties claimed by American colonists, Curtis praised their "temperate and dignified assertions" of "the rights which had come down to them from their fathers," while condemning the "pompous declamation" in France "about the abstract rights of man."[36] This description of the colonists' efforts to secure the rights of Englishmen finds adherents in various quarters, past and present. Yet in his willingness to show continuity with

England, Curtis relegated the Declaration of Independence to mere background. His speech gave no indication of the intricacies of the political arguments of the American revolutionaries, the extent to which broad claims of natural rights were in the mix, or the radical character of at least some aspects of the Revolution.

Curtis's Deerfield address was, taken altogether, a Whig performance, in line with the views expressed by other Massachusetts elites. The American Revolution represented "a change of forms, but not of substance," according to Jared Sparks, who served as editor of the *North American Review* and then became Harvard's president. More broadly, Webster emphasized that American liberty had an English "ancestry, a pedigree, a history."[37]

On the other side, Curtis's Burkean mode of thought differed at its core from the philosophies of individualism that emerged in the antebellum period. Generally speaking, transcendentalists (and abolitionists too) saw the individual pitted against society, and for the most part they believed that one must prevail over the other. Their answer, seemingly for any question, could be found in the primacy of the individual. As Ralph Waldo Emerson put it, "the growth of the Individual" provided the "antidote" to the "abuse of formal Government." These thinkers issued such a powerful critique of institutions—the church, the bar, the state—that some scholars have been led to view this period as an age of "anti-institutionalism."[38] "I am ashamed," Emerson said, "to think how easily we capitulate" to "large societies and dead institutions."[39] His distrust of the state (a "trick") and society (a "conspiracy") was palpable enough, yet it paled in comparison to Henry David Thoreau's views. In *Walden,* Thoreau complained that everywhere "men will pursue and paw" the individual "with their dirty institutions." Antislavery leader Wendell Phillips believed that the basic problem confronting abolitionists was that they were "bullied by institutions."[40]

While Emerson objected to existing institutions because they were "already made," it was precisely for that reason that institutions attained legitimacy in Curtis's view. In his speech Curtis described the "sacred" duty to transmit "the noble institutions" that "have come down to us . . . unimpaired to our posterity." He also suggested that the history he recounted makes "us understand and feel *the spirit* of our institutions, and that the precious rights, which we have inherited, do not belong to us as individuals, but as component parts of a great people." Curtis opened his address by suggesting that there were ties to past and future generations which "unite us into a people which does not die; whose existence is as real, in its different parts and periods as dependant on each other, as the life of an individual."[41] As Curtis perceived the community across time (rights were inherited), the historical process had claims on his attention just as the particular rights asserted by the individual had. Implicit in his speech was a view which he elaborated more fully over time: it was through institutions, not in spite of them, that individual rights were preserved and developed.

III

As for the place of law in American political society and the role that judges could play there, Curtis looked mainly to the common law as a model. He made some scattered remarks that, when placed in the context of a public debate over the common law in the antebellum period, throw light on his views.

The common law at this time was generally understood to refer to the body of legal principles developed in English courts, as distinct from the systems of civil law based on the Roman code adopted elsewhere in Europe. The common law also was taken to mean the unwritten law declared by judges in contrast with statutes enacted by legislatures. One important feature of the common law was its customary quality. Judicial rulings were supposed, in the mind of the common lawyer, to reflect the community's customs and practices concerning a whole range of social activities.[42]

Following the Declaration of Independence, most states adopted so much of English common law considered applicable to American conditions. It was not long before the common law became a political bone of contention, roughly though not exclusively along party lines. Jeffersonian Republicans, suspicious of the Federalist-dominated judiciary, backed various legal reforms. Among the most radical were codification proposals to replace the common law with legislative codes.[43] This was the prelude to the debate about the law and the judiciary in the Jackson era.

Articulate spokesmen appeared on both sides of this issue in Massachusetts during the 1820s and 1830s. Democrat Robert Rantoul Jr. saw the common law as "sprung from the dark ages," with its "origin in folly, barbarism, and feudality." Frederick Robinson charged that the bar was a "privileged order" controlling an incomprehensible system of law. As this unwritten law was "deposited only in the head of the judge," Robinson said, the law was whatever the courts pronounced it to be.[44] The central point of their arguments was that the common law was undemocratic: its mysterious workings allowed the judiciary to act arbitrarily. Codification held out the promise of a Jacksonian solution by displacing judicial power with that of elected legislatures.[45]

Whigs generally opposed codification. In the face of mounting public pressure, Massachusetts Whig leaders pursued a middle course in an attempt to block more wide-ranging legal reform. In 1836 Governor Edward Everett appointed Justice Story to lead a commission to explore the merits of codification. The justice had previously supported codification in some limited form, although he, like Webster, dismissed wholesale codification as incapable of handling the immense variety of questions brought before the courts. Story's attraction to codification differed markedly from the concerns motivating Jacksonian Democrats. Interested in promoting uniformity in the rules governing business transactions, he believed that a commercial code was desirable in light of growing uncertainty over legal principles in that area, stemming in part from the rapidly increasing number of judicial decisions and the difficulty of obtaining reports of them. Story advocated moderate codification without undercutting judicial authority. Codification worked best, he thought, for common-law principles that the courts had already developed; the legislature could perform a useful service by restating these established principles. The commission also suggested that courts remain free from legislative interference in applying the law, "exactly as they now do." The Story commission reported favorably on codification in specified areas, including commercial transactions, evidence, and criminal law.[46]

Governor Everett then invited the state legislature to enact a code following the commission's recommendations. Going beyond what Everett had in mind, a legislative committee sought to replace the common law entirely with written statutes reduced to "concise, chaste and elegant language in a volume or two." The committee report expressed the desire to enable "the mass of the community" to represent themselves without attorneys.[47]

At this point Curtis revealed to Ticknor his own concerns over the "wild theories" circulating in the state legislature. Curtis ridiculed the idea that "the whole body of the law" could be compressed into "a pocket volume, so that any man may carry about with him his own lawyer." He said that "a good system of law must be at the same time so extensive as to apply to and govern all the existing relations between men in society; so stable and fixed, in all important principles, as to furnish *a certain* guide; and so flexible as to be capable of adaptation to the ever-changing forms into which property is thrown by the unwearied enterprise and all-absorbing love of gain which distinguish our people."[48]

When Curtis closed with his point on adaptability, he touched on a theme familiar to leading jurists. One of the "peculiar excellences" of the common law, Justice Story said, consisted in its "adaptation to all circumstances, and, in a general sense, to all the exigencies which civil society may present." Written codes were inherently defective because they lacked this capacity to adapt. The "great objection" to codification, according to Chancellor James Kent of New York, was that legislative rules were "not malleable; they cannot accommodate to circumstance."[49]

Proponents of codification conceded that the common law was adaptive. The problem, they suggested, was that adaptability came with a price: vesting judges with unfettered discretion. "It is because judge-made-law is indefinitely and vaguely settled," Rantoul stated, "that it possesses the capacity of adapting itself to new cases." He believed that this natural tendency of the common law was made worse by the nation's "rapidly advancing state," which placed a large number of unsettled questions before the courts, thus magnifying the scope of judicial power. Even one of Story's students recognized "the whole body of common law" as "*Judicial Legislation*" made "from first to last by *Judges*."[50]

Whig defenders of the common law had a different view of the judicial process, which they saw as the outgrowth of reason. A tradition had grown up that judges, by recognizing preexisting rules through the human faculty of reason and historical understanding, served as oracles of the law. Judges were merely engaged in the task of discovering what the law was.[51] Some legal thinkers in the glow of the Enlightenment looked upon the common law as a science, by which they meant that legal principles were susceptible to logical ordering and classification.[52] Precedent was considered binding, with judicial decisions rendered by drawing analogies from earlier cases. In defense of the common law, Justice Story argued that precedent controlled "the arbitrary discretion of judges" and put decisions "beyond the peculiar opinions and complexional reasoning of a particular judge." Reflecting on the common law in 1860, Curtis said that the progress made by American courts was achieved "not under a claim of right to alter the law, but by treating ancient rules, established under very different circumstances, with the strictness which is appropriate to them, and by admitting exceptions which changes in the affairs of men have both assumed to exist and have rendered necessary."[53]

But when, using Curtis's words, was strictness appropriate and exception necessary? The tensions in the Whig line of thought—the incantation that reason governed in cases where seemingly reasonable minds differed, the difficulty in harmonizing certainty with adaptability—did not go unnoticed. Rantoul delivered some of the most slashing attacks on common-law methodology. "The common law is the perfection of human reason,—just as alcohol is the perfection of sugar," he said. Explicitly recognizing the human factor in judicial decision making, he put little stock in the process of legal reasoning. "The judge is human, and feels the bias which the coloring of the particular case gives." Precedent, rather than curbing discretion, was in his view easily manipulated. "The judge makes law, by extorting from precedents something which they do not contain." A lawyer himself, Rantoul proceeded from the assumption that in practically every case the judge could draw "plausible analogies" from "the great storehouse of precedent" to support either side. From that he argued that the law was nothing more than the judge's "will."[54]

With these arguments, Rantoul appears to have anticipated twentieth-century legal realism, and Whig pabulum about judges discovering antecedent rules suffers by comparison. While Curtis spoke blandly about law as a science, he also projected a more sophisticated understanding. All law, he said, "should be derived, not created; deduced by experience and careful observation from the existing usages, habits, and wants of men, and not spun out of the brains even of the most learned." The accent in Curtis's conception, as this statement indicates, was on law as custom.[55] This understanding went hand in hand with his Burkean philosophy. By an intricate process, he thought, people collectively but imperceptibly tried out various solutions to numerous problems until they settled on customary responses. Custom embodied the experience of many generations working out the details of life's activities, and human relations had a level of complexity which defied the power of the individual mind to understand fully. From that perspective it was difficult to conceive how the members of a single generation could construct a comprehensive legal code; certainly no individual could. The common law, on the other hand, had a built-in mechanism to integrate the complexity of experience into the law. Curtis's comment that the law should be derived from experience tapped into this crucial aspect of common-law thought, that the law embodied the "accumulated wisdom of the ages," as William Blackstone had described it.[56]

If this notion was carried far enough, it was possible to see custom as a genuine constraint on judicial decision making. Judges did not decide cases based solely on abstract reasoning; they engaged in an effort to understand customs and apply them to cases presented. Rather than create legal principles from whole cloth, judges operated within a framework growing out of the people's customary practices.

This appears to have been the way in which Curtis viewed the common law. In his judicial opinions he explicitly recognized the existence of customary law, more than once describing his actions in terms of deriving a rule from customary practices.[57] Whether Curtis's understanding was accurate is debatable,[58] but he carried this over to his constitutional jurisprudence. This was particularly evident in his use of what he called "practical construction." By this he meant that the judiciary, in interpreting the Constitution, was obliged to give substantial weight to the practices of the elected representatives of the people.[59]

Yet this line of thought was also subject to question. Perhaps there was a republican component to the common law in Britain, where it was plausible to see written law as "imposed upon the Subject" and the unwritten common law as a consensual production derived from the people's customs and interposed by judges against royal prerogative.[60] The case was different in America, suggested some Jacksonian Democrats, as here "we have neither king nor aristocracy to dread," and written laws "speak the public voice."[61]

While Democrats saw the judiciary as an aristocratic institution at odds with republican theory, Curtis's response, as it may be reconstructed, took the form of partly conceding the premise but wholly rejecting the conclusion. Like other Federalists and Whigs in his day, he entertained an elitist notion of lawyers and judges as a sort of natural aristocracy.[62] It was precisely for that reason—lawyers were among the best men who should govern—that Curtis believed they had an indispensable role in reconciling the competing forces of American political society.[63]

IV

Curtis's economic thought, which underlay much of his constitutional jurisprudence, is revealed most clearly in "Debts of the States," an article published in the *North American Review* in 1844.[64] There, Curtis addressed a major question of public policy stemming from the panic of 1837. When this economic depression began, Curtis reported to Ticknor on the "most gloomy" state of affairs. "We are thus reduced in a day to a state of universal bankruptcy, at a time when the commercial engagements of the country are vast beyond all former precedent."[65]

As the depression engulfed the country, some states found themselves unable to pay debts incurred for the most part to finance public works like canals and railroads.[66] Mississippi repudiated its financial obligations in 1842, spawning a national debate. Unwilling to be cornered on this issue, Democrats joined Whigs in condemning Mississippi's action.[67] Even so, several other states threatened to follow Mississippi's lead. The prospect of widespread debt repudiation naturally frightened creditors. Foreign lenders had much at stake. In fact, Curtis's article was part of a public relations effort by Baring Brothers & Company, a London banking house, although not all of his arguments conformed to the company line.[68]

In his article Curtis characterized debt repudiation as a "naked" act of "arbitrary power, prompted by no motive except a base love of money." In outlining the problem and its solution, he mixed age-old concepts of contract and property with unconventional legal solutions and progressive economic ideas. Curtis took a traditional tone when discussing the "legal and moral obligation" of contracts. The "binding force of a contract depends" upon God and his law, which "neither kings nor people" can repeal. Curtis classified debts as property "in form and in substance." It followed for him that when the states repudiated their debts, they confiscated private property. More in the nature of adoration than analysis, Curtis recited the virtues of property in civil society, which he linked to "all our ideas of justice, of social order, of personal security, and of the peaceful pursuit of happiness." He wrote that "the absolute security of property" was "one principle of policy which can be considered as settled, and as essential to all tolerable government." In his view Americans honored property for its uses, not out of a "blind and sordid love of wealth." Curtis emphasized the public purposes of property—charities, churches, and education—and he also tied property to the independence of the individual.[69]

To Curtis's way of thinking, the concepts of contract and property provided sufficient reason to oppose debt repudiation. He supplemented those points with a theory of the nation's economy. As Curtis analyzed Mississippi's action, he portrayed a country divided into two sectors: agrarian and commercial. Curtis believed that different conceptions of contractual obligations prevailed in each. "To pay debts punctually is *the* point of honor among all commercial people. But the planters in Mississippi do not so esteem it."[70]

While Curtis understood that the agrarian and commercial economies were distinct, he also perceived that the nation was, to borrow Joyce Appleby's phrase, "commercially integrated." He noted that Mississippi's action had consequences beyond its borders, a ripple effect impairing the credit of other states as well as the national government. After Mississippi disavowed its obligations, European lenders were not only reluctant to extend credit to any state, they refused to finance a congressionally authorized loan. The upshot of all this for Curtis was that the agrarian society must play by the rules of contract of the commercial society.[71]

The continental market economy envisioned by Curtis depended on the construction of public works financed by the government, whether state or federal. He argued that such government support was not only "legitimate" but "absolutely necessary." Curtis made this point by responding to an argument receiving attention in Maryland, one of the states threatening repudiation. There a constitutional objection had been raised against proposals to levy taxes in order to pay off the state's outstanding debt. It was said that the Maryland constitution limited the state's taxing power to providing support for the government. Building canals and railroads were not "legitimate objects of government," so the argument ran, and the legislature therefore had no authority to tax in order to satisfy debts incurred for public works.[72]

Curtis considered this objection frivolous, revealing a "lamentable ignorance of the nature and objects of all social institutions." He pointed to "the universal practice of all civilized governments" of constructing public works, but he thought that the United States presented a special case. Americans, he said, "have not much taste for cathedrals and palaces, but 'the useful magnificence of roads and bridges' excites their admiration." Curtis had no difficulty connecting these public works, designed "to facilitate and promote internal communication," to the nation's economic development.[73]

Curtis's proposed solution to the problem of state debt repudiation was twofold. First, while acknowledging the danger of running "too close a parallel between public and private duties," he applied an idea from private law concerning contractual relationships between individuals to this question of public law involving government debt.[74] He recognized that some states were in such poor financial condition that they could not pay their debts promptly. As between individuals, he explained, insolvency was a legitimate excuse for delaying payment, although the contractual obligation remained intact.[75] He saw no reason why the same rule should not apply to the states. The law, then, afforded a remedy short of the extreme action of repudiating debts. As for creditors who might object, Curtis thought they shared responsibility with the debtor states. The states "have been rash," he said, "but it was a time when rashness was epidemic." If "a State has been led astray partly by the insane confidence of its creditors, those creditors must bear some of the blame."[76]

Second, Curtis suggested that the U.S. Supreme Court was the appropriate forum to adjudicate questions between foreign creditors and the states. Mississippi's action had exposed the vulnerability of the federal system, where the actions of a part (Mississippi) affected the whole (the nation). In that context Curtis thought the Court was the only institution that could provide a remedy. He described the Court in glowing terms, as "our own ark of safety," to which "offended Europe may come confidently, and obtain such justice as war and reprisals never gave, and never can give."[77]

The constitutional problem was in figuring out how the Court could take jurisdiction of these cases. Originally the Constitution gave the Court power to entertain suits between states and "foreign States, Citizens or Subjects," but the Eleventh Amendment removed from federal jurisdiction cases against states "by Citizens or Subjects of any Foreign State." As a result, foreign banks and individuals could not bring lawsuits. Curtis came up with an inventive solution derived from the common law. Pointing to the English rule that "the king might take an assignment of a debt, and sue therefore in his own name," he proposed that foreign states bring lawsuits in behalf of these private parties. Curtis's suggestion was eventually taken up, though the Supreme Court did not decide the jurisdictional question for another ninety years. Contrary to Curtis's position, the Court declared states immune from suits by foreign states.[78] In any event, Curtis's article was well received in Whig circles. Justice Story congratulated his former student for his "sound constitutional views."[79] Curtis's analysis foreshadowed a fundamental theme in his work: the creative development of practical, legal solutions to handle difficult political problems.

V

Curtis, the justice who galvanized public opinion in the North with his dissenting opinion in the *Dred Scott* case, drew sharp criticism from antislavery quarters early in his career. Abolitionists vilified him. In Theodore Parker's view "no lawyer in New England had laid down such southern 'Principles' for foundation of law" or "rendered such service to the Slave Power." Modern scholars have found Curtis's record on slavery contradictory at best, deplorable at worst. Leonard W. Levy suggested that Curtis launched his career "arguing for the right of property in human flesh." According to Robert M. Cover, Curtis was willing to sacrifice the rights of blacks "on racist grounds" as he publicly "upbraided" Bostonians who valued "the liberty of a mere black to the unity and security of a white man's country."[80]

Judging from these remarks, Curtis was far removed from antislavery thought. Whatever moral judgment he deserves in retrospect, his positions reflect the complexities surrounding slavery as he saw them. The basic assumptions underlying his constitutional views on slavery are best illustrated in a legal argument he made in 1836. *Commonwealth v. Aves*, an early test of the capacity of the courts to address issues surrounding slavery, presented the question whether a slaveholder visiting Massachusetts had the right to keep slaves while in that free state.[81] Curtis represented the slaveholder's interest before the Massachusetts Supreme Judicial Court in this case. While an advocate's statements in court may not necessarily reveal personal views, Curtis's argument provides a lens for examining his way of thinking about slavery: how he balanced the personal rights of the slave against national unity and, most tellingly, how he defined law and morality in this context.

As important as the common law was in antebellum America, from the standpoint of legal theory, natural law was the focal point in the debate over slavery.[82] The idea of natural law contained the seeds of a powerful antislavery argument: that there were universal and eternal principles of justice and that every person had natural rights in life, liberty, and property. Blackstone's *Commentaries* stated that slavery was "repugnant" to "the principles of natural law."[83] As American colonists relied on natural law to contest British rule, the inconsistency with slavery became apparent.[84] In the years preceding the Civil War, natural law became an increasingly important weapon in the abolitionist arsenal. The founding declaration of the American Anti-Slavery Society, written by William Lloyd Garrison, labeled laws supporting slavery "a daring infringement on the law of nature." In less polemical fashion the antithesis between slavery and natural law was standard doctrine among Massachusetts Whigs. Echoing Blackstone, Justice Story stated that "slavery, under any shape, is so repugnant to the natural rights of man" that "it seems difficult to find for it any justification."[85]

Some southern jurists agreed in principle. Early in the nineteenth century, St. George Tucker, a law professor at the College of William and Mary in Virginia, wrote that it was "hard to reconcile" slavery with the law of nature unless "we first degrade" blacks "below the rank of human beings, not only politically, but also physically and morally." He concluded that as a "moral truth," blacks were "equals." The Kentucky court of appeals declared that slavery was "without foundation in the law of nature." Meanwhile, proslavery advocates cobbled together various explanations, often based on racial difference, to show why slavery was consistent with the law of nature. Their defense of American slavery was essentially based upon two premises: inequality was a natural human condition, and blacks were inferior to whites. In an essay published in 1832, Thomas R. Dew, another professor at William and Mary, wrote that blacks were "entirely unfit for a state of freedom among the whites," as he crudely described skin color as "the indelible symbol" of the "inferior condition" of blacks. Three years later South Carolina's Governor George McDuffie said that blacks were "in all respects, physical, moral, and political, inferior" and "destined by providence" to be enslaved. This line of thinking culminated in the assertion that slavery was not an "evil" but a "positive good." As Senator John C. Calhoun argued, slavery raised blacks from the "low, degraded, and savage condition" in which they had lived in Africa.[86]

In light of the racism running through proslavery theory, it may be tempting to credit Curtis and the Massachusetts Whigs with a comparatively progressive outlook. In *Commonwealth v. Aves* he said that slavery was inconsistent with natural right. "If this cause, or any cause required me to maintain that slavery was not a violation of the law of nature, I would abandon it." Speaking of fugitive slaves in 1850, Curtis reiterated this position. "I admit" their "natural rights to their fullest extent."[87]

Standing alone, such statements were potentially far-reaching. Against the background of the increasingly explicit racist tone taken by southern apologists, Curtis's use of the language of natural law seemed to recognize the humanity of blacks. To say that slaves had natural rights to their fullest extent controverted the basic premise of American slavery, that the slave was not a person but property without rights. On the other hand, what Curtis said had implications for his views of the law. For "to speak of slavery as against natural law," as Robert Cover has suggested, "was to admit the moral blemish on the legal system."[88]

How far, then, was Curtis willing to take the natural law position? Did he believe that principles of natural justice provided a source for judicial decision making in cases involving slavery? If slavery violated natural right, were laws supporting slavery unjust? Were citizens obliged to obey unjust laws? Was, in the formulation known from ancient Greek times, an unjust law not a law at all?

Somersett v. Stewart (1772), an English judicial opinion widely known in antebellum America, furnished a starting point for analysis. A slave, James Somersett, was taken by his owner from the American colonies to England. While there, Somersett escaped, only to be recaptured and locked up in a ship bound for Jamaica, where he was to be sold. In the hope of obtaining a broad antislavery declaration, British abolitionists brought Somersett's case to the attention of Lord Mansfield, chief justice of the highest common-law court of England. The case put Mansfield in a dilemma. He was not about to emancipate the 14,000 slaves he believed to be in England at that time. Yet he also recognized that many of the "consequences" of slavery were "absolutely contrary" to English law. To get around this, Mansfield ruled that slave owners could not force their slaves to leave English soil. "So high an act of dominion must be recognized by the law of the country where it is used," the lord chief justice stated. Mansfield was also reported to have said that slavery, "so odious" and "incapable of being introduced on any reasons, moral or political," was supported only by "positive law." It remains unclear whether Mansfield really made this statement, or if he did, what exactly he had in mind. In any event, the court freed Somersett.[89]

On the authority of this case, the idea that slavery depended on positive law entered American legal thought. It was generally agreed that the relationship between master and slave was derived from local law, often referred to as the municipal law of the state. The difficulties surrounding this deceptively simple construction came to view in *Commonwealth v. Aves*. A woman from Louisiana visiting her father, Thomas Aves, in Boston brought with her a slave, a six-year-old girl named Med. The Boston Female Anti-Slavery Society decided to press Med's interests in court. Abolitionists understood the relevant legal history, as shown by the name they gave the child: Maria Somersett.[90]

Strange as it may seem, the case presented a question not settled under the law of Massachusetts. The state constitution, adopted in 1780, declared that "all men are born free and equal, and have certain natural, essential, and unalienable rights." The judiciary had construed this provision to mean that slavery was "effectively abolished." When Med's case came before the Supreme Judicial Court of Massachusetts, the law of the commonwealth did not expressly prohibit southern slaveholders from taking up temporary residence in the state with their slaves. The rule in Britain for such cases, as restated by Justice Story in 1834, was unequivocal: "The law of England abhors, and will not endure the existence of slavery within the nation; and consequently, as soon as a slave lands in England, he becomes *ipso facto* a freeman."[91] Story's language, taken from Blackstone, was reinforced by the interpretation of *Somersett* given by some English judges. Justice Story believed that the same principle undoubtedly "pervades" the common law of the free states.[92]

Commonwealth v. Aves brought to light these issues under the rubric of conflict of laws, a technical branch of law of some importance in the American federal system. What rules governed the choice between the law of the forum (Massachusetts in this instance) and the law of domicile (Louisiana)? The answer was derived from a principle known as comity, which was explained and popularized by Story and Kent in influential legal commentaries. Under their suggested mode of analysis, the forum state was not required to recognize the laws of another jurisdiction. However, it was expected that states would choose to enforce another state's laws out of "mutual interest" and convenience, unless those laws ran counter to the public policies, laws, morals, or rights of the forum state.[93]

The abolitionists promoting Med's case considered a decision freeing the child "of greater importance than any within the last half century." They were taken aback by the legal strategy employed by Benjamin Curtis and his partner, Charles P. Curtis, on the other side. Lydia Maria Child, a member of the Boston Female Anti-Slavery Society, believed that these "pro-slavery lawyers" broke "new and extraordinary ground" when they argued that "Southern masters had a legal right to hold human beings as slaves while they were visiting here in New England." With so much at stake, the abolitionists had asked Daniel Webster to argue their side. He was willing to do so, according to Child, but needed a delay in the proceedings which was not forthcoming.[94] Rufus Choate served in his stead, joined by Ellis Gray Loring, the abolitionist lawyer who later represented the Africans from the slave ship *Amistad*. All four lawyers delivered arguments before the Supreme Judicial Court, but the case mostly turned into a contest between the two junior counsel, Benjamin Curtis and Loring.

One of the principal difficulties Curtis faced had to do with the most basic fact of the case. Here was a slave in Massachusetts. Curtis preemptively noted Lord Mansfield's observation in *Somersett* that the "difficulty of adopting the relation" of slavery "without adopting it in all its consequences, is indeed extreme; and yet, many of those consequences are absolutely contrary to the municipal law of England." Curtis tried to narrow the question before the court to whether the slaveholder had a "qualified and limited" right to "restrain" the slave "for the purpose of carrying him out of the state." It was unnecessary, in Curtis's mind, to give "full effect to the foreign law concerning master and slave."[95]

This argument had a fictive quality which did not escape the notice of opposing counsel. "No," Loring argued, "all the learned counsel's ingenuity could not shew an English or a Massachusetts Court, how to adopt the relation without adopting its most abhorrent consequences." By spelling out the details that Curtis had avoided, the abolitionist lawyer demonstrated why this purportedly limited right to take the slave from the state was not easily cabined. Loring raised the possibility of the master resorting to "the cogent aid of the whip or the fetter" if the slave was unwilling to leave Massachusetts. Even before the moment of departure, Loring suggested that the slave owner, having the right to remove the slave, would also retain the power "to confine his person" while in the state. Loring also produced a list of questions concerning the "anomalous" circumstances of slaves in Massachusetts. Could slaves enter into contracts or testify in court? Could slaves have legally recognized marriages? In short, could slaves enjoy any of the rights and duties traditionally denied them in slave states? In effect, Loring suggested that Curtis turned a blind eye to the realities of the practice. "Slavery is an abuse," Loring argued. "Take away its incidents of oppression and baseness, and it is all gone."[96]

Counsel for both sides openly discussed the question of law and morality. That issue arose as part of the debate over comity, as the general preference to respect another jurisdiction's laws evaporated when the forum state considered those laws immoral. "To prove that slavery is not immoral," Curtis did not try to reconcile slavery with natural right. He stated unambiguously that slavery was inconsistent with natural right. To get around nature's dictates, Curtis used a definitional ploy. Starting with the assumption that morality had "very wide and various meanings," he thought it "perfectly clear, that the standard of morality by which courts of justice are to be guided, is that which *the law* prescribes." Curtis said that the opinions of judges "as men" or "moralists" were irrelevant.[97]

By invoking what the law prescribes as the standard of morality, Curtis touched upon a timeless question of political philosophy concerning the relationship between law and justice. He developed this position from materials close at hand, though, relying mainly on a case called *The Antelope* (1825), in which the U.S. Supreme Court declined to declare the slave trade in violation of international law. There, Chief Justice John Marshall conceded the inconsistency between the slave trade and natural law, but he added that whatever "the answer of a moralist to this question, a jurist must search for its legal solution" in "usages" and "national acts." His opinion was grounded in a distinction between the "feelings" a judge may have about the traffic in slaves and his "path of duty" under the "mandate of the law." Such an approach laid the groundwork for lawyers and judges to deflect one of the basic points of antislavery jurisprudence. The principles of natural justice were not, Marshall suggested, a legitimate source of law, at least for cases involving the slave trade. Not only were judges duty-bound to put aside their internal compass of natural justice, they were in theory also cut off from the community sense of morality, as Marshall suggested when he acknowledged that "public feeling" may outpace "strict law."[98]

An alternative view had been suggested by Justice Story in a circuit opinion also involving the slave trade, in which he said that courts could enforce "moral obligation."[99] Yet Curtis extended Marshall's line of reasoning to the factual situation presented in *Commonwealth v. Aves*. Applying the standard of what the law prescribed, Curtis argued that "slavery is not only recognized as a valid institution" under Massachusetts law "but to a certain extent is incorporated into our own law." His principal evidence for this was the fugitive slave clause of the U.S. Constitution, which provided for the return of slaves from one state who escaped into another. That was the "supreme law" of Massachusetts, Curtis suggested, as he cited commonwealth precedent that this constitutional provision embodied "*an agreement that slaves should be considered as property*." The "court will hardly declare in this case, that slavery is immoral," he said, "when, before you rise from your seats, you may be called upon, by the master of a fugitive slave, to grant a certificate, under the constitution, which will put the whole force of the commonwealth at his disposal, to remove his slave from our territory." [100]

Loring accepted that there was a "legal standard" for morality, but he outmaneuvered Curtis by suggesting that the argument about morality depended upon legal categories. Perhaps the judges would have to concede Curtis's morality argument for fugitive slave cases, but outside of that specific category, the morality of slavery was open for the court to consider. [101]

In addition to denying the relevance of natural law in this setting, Curtis broadened what was at stake in *Commonwealth v. Aves*. This was not a case, in his view, that merely concerned the rights of two people. While it is difficult today to fathom that anything could offset the injustice of slavery, what emerges from Curtis's account was a series of countervailing moral imperatives: to honor a promise, to respect the consensual production of the body politic, and to keep the Union intact.

Focusing on the constitutional bargain struck at the nation's founding, he suggested that slavery was one of the "chief obstacles" to forming the Union. According to Curtis, this obstacle was overcome by a constitutional commitment to protect slavery. He described this in the language of contractual obligation. The protection of slavery was "guaranteed," with the "faith" of the northern states "pledged thereto" by their "own free will." The North agreed willingly, Curtis argued, having made the determination that forming the Union outweighed reservations over slavery. His point was vulnerable to attack, and again Loring suggested that the constitutional compromise did not extend beyond fugitive slaves. [102]

Curtis was most effective when he gestured to what he thought was really at stake—national unity—and what that implied. He pointed out that slavery had become "incorporated" into southern culture, "infused into their agriculture, their commerce, their mechanical arts, their domestic relations." Curtis explained that to permit southerners to bring slaves into Massachusetts during temporary stays was a natural consequence of the Union as it existed. In Curtis's view there was a need to increase ties between the different sections of the nation. It was "extremely desirable," he said, to "promote harmony and good feeling," to "encourage frequent intercourse, and soften prejudices by increasing acquaintance." All of this would be made more difficult if free states prohibited southerners from traveling north with their slaves.[103]

The driving force behind Curtis's argument was a practical conception of the Union. He did not detail what the Union meant to him, though he noted its "inestimable" value, "upon the preservation of which no man doubts that our own peace and welfare depend." Daniel Webster's influence is evident in Curtis's remarks. No one cultivated the ideal image of the Union any better than Webster at this time. Webster's Union—exceptional in human history, inextricably linked to liberty— was a test of the capacity of free government to survive anywhere. In the decade preceding *Aves*, this view was contested. While Webster believed that the Union "makes us one people," Calhoun dismissed the "very idea of an *American People*, as constituting a single community," as "a mere chimera."[104] These competing theories of the Union had a prominent place in disputes over public policy in this period, ostensibly concerning federal policies over tariffs and public lands but with slavery an ever-present consideration. Only three years before *Commonwealth v. Aves*, Calhoun advanced the doctrine of nullification, which South Carolina used to declare the federal tariff law void, threatening secession in the process. This was the context about which Curtis's audience needed no reminder.

Curtis also indicated that as *Aves* presented a question of "voluntary comity," northern states "might be unwilling to be bound through all time, and amidst all changes," to "enforce" claims presented by slave owners.[105] The potential significance of this passage is undercut by the vagueness surrounding Curtis's suggestion. In light of the stress Curtis laid upon developing a national community (increasing communication, lessening prejudice), it is difficult to guess what conditions he believed would justify such a reversal of policy by the free states. Perhaps he thought that southerners were working in good faith to end slavery. Possibly he had in mind the well-publicized debates in Virginia of a few years before (following Nat Turner's slave rebellion of 1831), when that state's legislature came surprisingly close to abolishing slavery. Those legislative debates were a watershed event, but rather than spawning open discussions in the South, they marked the last serious effort by moderates in the region to push for the gradual elimination of slavery. Moreover, Curtis's own observations that slavery had become increasingly intertwined in southern society belied such wishful thinking. At best the lawyer's argument was grounded in the assessment that the issue presented in *Aves* was important but collateral to the underlying problem of slavery in the South; thus to deny comity would do little to get at the root of the difficulties and would only serve to aggravate southerners.

In the end, the Massachusetts Supreme Judicial Court freed Med. Chief Justice Shaw's opinion was elegant in its simplicity compared with Curtis's argument. One can feel the weight of Shaw's several premises drawn together: the state constitution abolished slavery "upon the ground that it is contrary to natural right and the plain principles of justice"; slavery was "founded in force, not in right"; the right to hold property in slaves existed only where established by positive local law; slavery was contrary to Massachusetts laws that "secure the liberty and personal rights of all persons"; blacks as well as whites were entitled to various privileges under state law, including provisions banning forcible detention and removal. It was "wholly repugnant to our laws, entirely inconsistent with our policy and our fundamental principles," Shaw concluded, to permit a slave owner to exercise in Massachusetts the powers that a master wielded over his slaves. The chief justice was not drawn into Curtis's train of thought. It was taking comity too far to allow slaveholders to bring their slaves to Massachusetts for periods that might last several months. As for the fugitive slave clause, Shaw declined to draw any inference favorable to the slave owner's case on the theory that its language must be strictly read to reflect accurately the constitutional agreement reached.[106]

The result in *Commonwealth v. Aves* was publicized throughout the nation. The abolitionist newspaper, the *Liberator*, hailed the decision as "rational, just and noble." Boston abolitionists, vindicated in their reliance on the law, celebrated Shaw's ruling with work-bags that on one side depicted a slave "kneeling before the figure of Justice." Southern reaction was mixed, including at one extreme the view that the decision was an "outrage upon southern rights." A Georgia newspaper asked whether southerners were "willing to sustain forever a confederation" with northern states producing such opinions.[107]

The case of *Commonwealth v. Aves* arose at an interesting juncture in the struggle over slavery. With the rise of a more radical form of abolitionism—the formation of the American Anti-Slavery Society in 1833, the emergence of Garrison as a leading spokesman, and the insistent calls for the immediate end of slavery—the public debate focused on abolitionists' goals and tactics. Exactly one year before *Aves*, Curtis described the Anti-Slavery Society as the "topic which engrosses the public attention, to the exclusion of almost every other." A national controversy had grown out of abolitionists' efforts to distribute antislavery publications in the South. Curtis believed newspaper reports that the Anti-Slavery Society sought "to excite the slaves to insurrection," a charge which Garrison denied. Though obviously unhappy with the abolitionists' methods, Curtis expressed concern over the reaction of whites in the South. "Dreadful scenes have already occurred in Mississippi," Curtis reported to Ticknor. "The mob have hung numerous persons, *suspected* of being emissaries of the Society, without legal trial." He felt that southerners who were "enemies to the Union" had exploited the situation. Extremism, Curtis suggested, bred extremism and could come to no good result. Meetings in the North called to counter abolitionism appeared to end the crisis. "We are all glad it is so *well* over," Curtis wrote. "Would that the whole subject could be as easily and as safely disposed of!" [108]

VI

Even though Curtis did not discuss slavery in public again until 1850, his appointment to the Supreme Court the following year was due to his loyalty to Whiggery's longtime champion, Daniel Webster, whose stand on slavery had become the center of controversy in New England. [109]

Massachusetts Whigs had never looked with favor on slavery. Webster had once maintained that it was "one of the greatest evils, both moral and political." He expressed hope that southerners would end the practice on their own over time. Webster opposed the westward expansion of slavery, the annexation of Texas, and the war with Mexico. The Whigs of Massachusetts were in general agreement on these points. The events of the mid-1840s exposed underlying differences in the party's ranks, however. As some considered further opposition on Texas and Mexico futile, others like Charles Sumner, Charles Francis Adams, and Henry Wilson were unwilling to put aside their antislavery convictions, giving rise to the so-called Conscience Whigs. They opposed the Cotton Whigs, the faction named for textile industrialists such as Abbott Lawrence and Nathan Appleton, whose tepid response to slavery revealed to the Conscience wing a willingness to sacrifice principle for economic interest. Conscience Whigs considered themselves the true heirs of the Whig tradition. The "essence of Whig principles," Sumner said, was "the idea that all men were created free and equal." The Whigs "are, or ought to be, the party of Freedom."[110] As the Massachusetts Whig Party split apart, Webster occupied his own ground. He was certainly not a Conscience Whig, nor was he firmly in the Cotton Whig camp, as he was willing to work with both sides for his own political purposes.[111]

The appearance in 1848 of the Free-Soil Party, dedicated to keeping slavery out of the western territories, created a new outlet for antislavery politics. Despite the party's limited showing in the presidential election that year, the campaign marked the start of a "moral & political revolution," according to one Free-Soiler.[112] Indeed, events seemed to coincide with the worst of southerners' fears. The new Whig president, Zachary Taylor, supported efforts to block slavery from the territories, contrary to what southerners had expected of the slave owner from Louisiana. As the 1840s drew to a close, Congress was the scene of stalemate, passionate debate, and fistfights. Southern lawmakers openly discussed disunion. The extent of the crisis remains open to debate, though some historians have concluded that many Americans genuinely believed some states might secede. In this setting Senator Henry Clay offered several resolutions which formed the basis of the Compromise of 1850. He suggested that California be admitted as a free state with no bar against slavery in the other territory ceded by Mexico. In an attempt to get a comprehensive settlement, Clay proposed strengthening the fugitive slave law while ending the slave trade in the District of Columbia.[113]

In New England discussion about the compromise legislation revolved around Daniel Webster, then representing Massachusetts in the U.S. Senate, and his Seventh of March speech. The gist of this famous address was a call to preserve the Union: both sections had grounds for complaint, the interests of the whole nation must be served, secession would inevitably bring war, and the questions were complex and would take time to resolve. Webster saw no need for an express prohibition against slavery in the new territories; he thought the terrain could not sustain southern plantation agriculture. In the belief that southerners had legitimate grievances concerning runaway slaves, the senator indicated that he would support tougher legislation on this subject "to the fullest extent."[114]

Although Webster considered himself the statesman in this time of crisis, most of his native New England opposed him. The speech did not reflect "the sentiments of the Whigs of New England," reported the *Boston Atlas*, a proadministration Whig newspaper. Everett kept his distance, and Winthrop thought "the speech would have killed" any other politician in the North. Not one member of the Massachusetts congressional delegation rallied behind Webster. Outside the Whig Party, Webster was the target of no-holds-barred attacks. Wendell Phillips branded him a traitor for giving aid and comfort to the enemy. There was among the literati a recurring metaphor of Webster's fall, as in John Greenleaf Whittier's poem "Ichabod": "A fallen angel's pride of thought / Still strong in chains."[115]

In this climate of opinion, Curtis, whom Everett counted among Webster's "fastest friends," came to the senator's defense.[116] At a rally honoring the senator upon his first return to Boston after March 7, Curtis delivered the welcoming speech. Echoing Webster's central theme, Curtis said that the only solution to the crisis was "under the Constitution, and in the Union." He took a hard line against dissent. The "friends of the Constitution are our friends," Curtis stated; "its enemies, whether open or secret, wilful or blind, are our enemies also." The implication was that Webster spoke for the Constitution and that even moderate differences with his policies were defections from the constitutional process. Faith in the Constitution had become rigid orthodoxy.[117]

How far Curtis was willing to take this position, and to use law as a political instrument, was demonstrated when he challenged Charles Sumner's election to the U.S. Senate in 1851. For some time Sumner had been Boston society's gadfly, not only for the stands he took on international peace, prison reform, and abolitionism but also for his intemperate attacks on those with whom he disagreed. What alienated Beacon Hill brought him to prominence among reformers.[118]

In the 1850 election none of the three major parties—Whig, Free-Soil, or Democrat—won a clear victory at the polls in Massachusetts. As a result, the state legislature had to fill several offices, including that of U.S. senator. Free-Soilers and Democrats patched together an agreement to vote as a bloc. This coalition quickly pushed through its candidates with the exception of Sumner, who was unable to get a majority in the state House of Representatives, as some Democrats refused to vote for him. Lacking the numbers to elect one of their own, Whig lawmakers embarked upon a strategy of postponing the decision on Sumner "indefinitely," as Curtis reported to Webster. After four months of wrangling, the lower house selected Sumner on the twenty-sixth ballot. Evidently, one Whig broke ranks with his party, though the voting remained secret.[119]

After Sumner was elected, Everett urged Curtis to prepare a public statement of the Whig position.[120] The result was a short pamphlet entitled an *Address to the People of Massachusetts*. While Whigs had from the start condemned the coalition as immoral and unprincipled, Curtis's argument was remarkable for the specificity with which he charged the Democrats and Free-Soilers with criminal offenses. He characterized the coalition agreement as a *"factious conspiracy to violate a public trust, and as such, criminal, not only in morals, but in the law of the land."* The basic reason Curtis offered for this conclusion was simple: the agreement required legislators to support candidates with whom they disagreed on fundamental issues, in effect, to vote against their own principles. He found an obscure Virginia case concerning two justices of the peace to show that the Democrats and Free-Soilers had committed misdemeanors under common law. In good Whig style Curtis asserted his belief that "public morals are essential to public order; that absolute fidelity to public trusts is the only secure basis of republican government; and that no people is safe which passes over in silence even questionable acts of its servants."[121]

Curtis's *Address*, signed by all Massachusetts Whig legislators, was given to several senators in Washington. Everett advised Henry Clay that Curtis's arguments provided the grounds for the U.S. Senate to remove Sumner from office.[122] Of course, Sumner withstood these attacks and went on to a distinguished, if controversial, career.

As for Curtis, in little more than a year he had become a rising star among the so-called Webster Whigs. When Levi Woodbury, the U.S. Supreme Court justice from New England, died in September 1851, President Millard Fillmore wrote Webster, now serving as secretary of state. Mindful of putting a Whig on the Supreme Court, Fillmore sought "as long a lease and as much moral and judicial power as possible from this appointment." He had "formed a very high opinion of Mr. B. R. Curtis. What do you say of him?" Coincidentally, Webster sent a letter to Fillmore that same day from Boston to recommend Curtis's "immediate appointment." The "general, perhaps I may say the almost universal, sentiment here is, that the place should be filled by the appointment of Mr. B. R. Curtis."[123] As Congress was out of session, Fillmore gave Curtis a recess appointment; (the usual confirmation process was completed when the Senate met in December. It was revealing that Curtis, in his gracious acceptance, instructed the president to fulfill a statutory requirement assigning the new justice to the U.S. circuit court for New England. Alluding to cases involving the rescue of a fugitive slave, Curtis noted that his "presence" would be "very desirable" at the upcoming term in Boston.[124]

2. THE FUGITIVE SLAVE CONTROVERSY

OF ALL THE QUESTIONS surrounding slavery, the one that produced the most uproar in the North during the 1850s had to do with the capture and return of escaped slaves. The Constitution provided that runaway slaves "shall be delivered up" to their owners. Early on, Congress enacted implementing legislation known as the Fugitive Slave Act of 1793. This federal law was a source of continuing conflict. While northerners expressed concern over the act's procedures, which they believed had enabled slave catchers to kidnap free blacks, slave owners pushed for stronger federal enforcement. In the Compromise of 1850, Congress adopted a new fugitive slave law as a concession to the South. Although the compromise measures were hailed as a "final settlement" of sectional differences, the Fugitive Slave Act of 1850 actually galvanized antislavery sentiment in the North.[1]

Nowhere was opposition more intense than in Boston. In the space of a few years, a small number of fugitive slave cases in that city gave rise to an extraordinary set of events. There were efforts to rescue slaves held in custody. The first ended in a dramatic midday escape from the courthouse; the last left a deputy marshal dead. At one point armed guards carried bayonets at the ready in Boston's Court Square after city officials had roped off the courthouse to prevent the public from entering. One captured fugitive slave, Anthony Burns, was taken to the wharf for his journey south by hundreds of troops (marines, infantry, artillery, and cavalry) while as many as 50,000 people milled about the streets. In protest, Bostonians covered buildings in black and hung U.S. flags upside down.

Above all else, though, Boston stood out for its robust debate over the fugitive slave law. Not only was this legislation constitutionally suspect, it also proved vulnerable to attack on moral grounds. This was one of those moments when events gave clarity to abstract ideas about law and justice. These were matters of public concern in Boston, as suggested by local newspaper headlines like "Conscience and the Law."[2] The debate there was a model of lucid expression, with Emerson, Thoreau, and Frederick Douglass among the roster of speakers, and there arose a frank exchange over when resistance to government was justified.

Both as a lawyer and as a judge, Benjamin Curtis was deeply involved in the controversy. While still an attorney, he furnished the U.S. marshal in Boston with a legal opinion arguing that the 1850 act was constitutional. Curtis also delivered a speech in Faneuil Hall to counter resistance. His arguments, published in Boston newspapers, were influential. Abolitionist preacher Theodore Parker held Curtis responsible for "coming to the rescue of despotism when it seemed doubtful which way the money in Boston would turn." The antislavery *New York Tribune* acknowledged that Curtis's constitutional defense of the 1850 act, which "reechoed from so many quarters, was the only one which legal ingenuity has been able to make for such an atrocious enactment."[3]

Once on the bench, Curtis engaged in intermittent battles with abolitionists. His various actions earned him the reputation as a "slave-catching Judge," even though he never ordered the return of any fugitive slave. As a newly appointed justice, Curtis instructed the federal grand jury that forcible resistance to the 1850 act was treason.[4] Later he directed grand jurors to consider whether speeches given by leading abolitionists were indictable offenses. Curtis also presided over trials of persons charged with participating in the successful fugitive slave rescue. In one trial Curtis delivered a judicial opinion denying that jurors were entitled to determine questions of law based upon their personal views of morality. This was significant in its own right as one of the earliest judicial opinions on jury nullification.[5]

Curtis's encounter with the Fugitive Slave Act was not only or even primarily about constitutional interpretation in the narrow sense of the term. The controversy surrounding this law represents the classic case of law versus morality in American legal history. It was also an important phase in thinking about civil disobedience. Ironically, while Curtis's legal analysis on the 1850 act was open to criticism, he developed a comparatively sophisticated moral justification for enforcing this law. How Curtis addressed the moral as well as legal issues, and the effect his position had on subsidiary constitutional questions, illustrates the complexities surrounding slavery and the Constitution in the decade before the war.

I

In full, the Constitution's fugitive slave clause stated: "No Person held to Service or Labour in one State, under the Laws thereof, escaping into another, shall, in Consequence of any Law or Regulation therein, be discharged from such Service or Labour, but shall be delivered up on Claim of the Party to whom such Service or Labour may be due." The Fugitive

Slave Act of 1793 recognized significant rights of slave owners throughout the nation. It specifically "empowered" slaveholders to arrest black persons and bring them before federal judges or local magistrates in the state where they were captured. Without affording the alleged runaway the opportunity to present evidence, the statute mandated that upon satisfactory proof of ownership (oral testimony was sufficient), the presiding official issue a certificate enabling the slave owner to take the supposed slave to his own state. Framed in this way, the act made it possible for slave catchers to kidnap free blacks with judicial imprimatur based upon flimsy evidence. Some northern states adopted personal liberty laws, sometimes called antikidnapping laws, which afforded procedural protections like the writ of habeas corpus and the right of jury trial to blacks claimed as fugitive slaves.[6]

In *Prigg v. Pennsylvania* (1842), the U.S. Supreme Court declared the 1793 act constitutional on the view that Congress had implied power to enact such legislation under the fugitive slave clause. While the opinion, written by Justice Story, recognized the slaveholder's right to recapture his slaves, it did not directly address the question of whether the act violated the rights of persons claimed as fugitive slaves, although counsel had raised that concern in the proceedings. Among the opinion's most consequential points was its double-edged analysis of state power. On the one hand, Story thought that states had no authority to "interfere" with the slave owner's rights; he struck down Pennsylvania's antikidnapping statute on that basis.[7] On the other hand, the justice suggested that states could not be "compelled" by federal law to assist in fugitive slave rendition, though he did not have a majority for that point. Only Justice John McLean dissented. He did not contend that the 1793 act was unconstitutional but rather that the states had power to prevent the use of force and to require rendition by legal process.[8]

Notwithstanding gaps in reasoning, *Prigg* had the effect of closing off any serious reconsideration by the federal courts of the constitutionality of the 1793 act.[9] The Supreme Court could not cut off public debate, however. This was demonstrated in Boston a few months after the decision, in the fugitive slave case of George Latimer. Following *Prigg*, Chief Justice Shaw invalidated the state's personal liberty law. Story, sitting as federal circuit judge, was prepared to order Latimer's return to slavery. In the end, Latimer was saved by abolitionists who pressed his owner to give up his claim in a forced sale.[10]

Latimer's case marked a critical turn in the development of abolitionist theory. The positions taken by these notable judges crystallized the views of Garrison's followers that the Constitution was unalterably proslavery and that disunion was necessary.[11] Speaking in Faneuil Hall while Latimer's fate was still in doubt, Wendell Phillips memorably stated the Garrisonian position: "I say, my CURSE be on the Constitution of these U. States!" There "stands the bloody clause," Phillips said of the fugitive slave provision; "you cannot fret the seal off the bond. The fault is in allowing such a Constitution to live an hour." Garrison saw no difference between Shaw's action and "that of the slave pirate on the African coast." The Massachusetts Anti-Slavery Society put itself on record for the first time in favor of disunion.[12]

Antislavery forces added legislative remedies to moral indignation, as northerners applied Justice Story's dictum from *Prigg*. After receiving a petition with over 60,000 signatures, the Massachusetts state legislature adopted a new personal liberty law. It prohibited the use of state judges, officers, or jails in fugitive slave rendition. Aiding in the capture and return of runaway slaves was an offense punishable by one year's imprisonment. Several other states enacted similar statutes. Southern dissatisfaction with this state of affairs gave impetus to strengthening the federal law, a movement which reached fruition with the Fugitive Slave Act of 1850.[13]

While the 1793 act discomfited northerners, many regarded this new legislation as an even more egregious assault by the "Slave Power."[14] Supplementing the older federal statute, the 1850 act put in place enforcement machinery lacking to that point. This law conscripted federal marshals and made them criminally liable for refusing to enforce its provisions. More than that, Congress commanded all citizens to assist in returning fugitive slaves to their owners. Any person helping escaped slaves was subject to imprisonment for six months. In the attempt to secure the rights of the slave owner, the act lost all semblance of procedural fairness: rendition hearings were summary; persons claimed as fugitive slaves were barred from testifying; presiding commissioners had their fees doubled when they issued certificates of removal (supposedly because of added paperwork).[15]

Given the draconian procedures employed, the constitutionality of the 1850 act was at least open to question, notwithstanding *Prigg v. Pennsylvania*.[16] After Congress passed this legislation, antislavery meetings around Boston produced various resolutions declaring, in essence, that the 1850 act violated the Constitution and that any attempt to enforce the law would be resisted. Calling for a League of Freedom, "A Declaration of Sentiments of the Colored Citizens of Boston" stated that any fugitive slave commissioner "would have delivered up Jesus Christ for one third of the price that Judas Iscariot did." At a crowded meeting in Faneuil Hall, Frederick Douglass, Wendell Phillips, and Theodore Parker denounced the Fugitive Slave Act. Charles Francis Adams, presiding over the assembly, responded directly to suggestions that the statute merely put into effect the constitutional requirement of the fugitive slave clause. "God forbid!" That argument, "whilst it does nothing to justify the barbarous provisions of the law itself, does a great deal to sap the foundations of our regard for the noble" Constitution. Richard Henry Dana Jr., an up-and-coming Free-Soil lawyer, introduced resolutions asserting that the 1850 act contravened the constitutional rights of due process, habeas corpus, and protection against unreasonable seizures. A vigilance committee was formed to protect Boston's black community. The meeting ended with a portentous declaration: "Constitution or no Constitution, law or no law, we will not allow a fugitive slave to be taken from Massachusetts."[17]

Within days, antislavery resolve was put to the test with the first attempt to enforce the 1850 act in Boston. Two men from Georgia came seeking William and Ellen Craft, who had made an heroic escape from slavery two years earlier. Ellen, able to pass as white, had disguised herself as a sick old man, while William had pretended to be her slave. Abolitionist newspapers had celebrated their escape, and the Crafts had spoken publicly, lecturing in England as well as Boston. Unfortunately for them, their former owner was able to keep abreast of their whereabouts. With the new law in place, he sent two men to bring the Crafts back south. "Slave-hunters in Boston!!" headlined the *Liberator*. The Vigilance Committee swung into action, moving Ellen Craft from one safe house to another, while lawyers filed actions in court to harass the slave catchers, who were charged with conspiracy to kidnap, among other things. Meanwhile, William Craft prepared to fight, joined by friends in his neighborhood armed with swords, guns, bayonets, and gunpowder.[18] Justice Woodbury issued a warrant for the arrest of the Crafts, and an overwrought directive was given to U.S. Marshal Charles Devens to confront resistance with force, "to break open dwelling-houses, and perhaps take life." In the end, the slave catchers gave up, and abolitionists spirited the Crafts away to England.[19]

In these circumstances Curtis, still a private attorney, prepared a legal opinion for Marshal Devens. With good reason, Theodore Parker viewed Curtis's opinion as contrived to influence the public.[20] The opinion became part of Daniel Webster's ongoing public relations campaign. Curtis's "reputation is high," and his arguments were "well drawn," Webster informed President Fillmore; "his opinion will silence the small lawyers." Webster, in Boston "to put this business of the attempt to arrest Crafts into a better shape," asked the *Boston Courier* to publish Curtis's opinion.[21]

Interestingly, Curtis skirted the unsettling question about the use of force, which apparently concerned Devens. Suggesting instead that what the marshal really wanted to know was whether the act was constitutional, Curtis returned a detailed constitutional defense of it.[22]

A good case could have been made that *Prigg* was not dispositive of the constitutional questions raised by the 1850 act, not only because Story's opinion skipped over questions concerning blacks' personal rights but also because the statute employed novel procedures.[23] Curtis seemed to sense the need for careful reexamination. Admitting that Congress had made "very important changes," he picked up the argument where Justice Story had left off. Curtis also recognized the antislavery arguments as "ingenious."[24]

At stake, according to the 1850 act's opponents, was one of the most basic rights in the American legal system: the Seventh Amendment right of jury trial in suits at common law. They argued that federal commissioners improperly exercised judicial power that should have remained in the hands of judges appointed under Article III of the Constitution (with the independence that accompanied life tenure in office). Curtis countered these arguments with a simple classification, which echoed the position taken previously by Webster. Proceedings for fugitive slave rendition were neither suits at common law nor cases under Article III, Curtis said, but rather among the "summary" class of judicial inquiries conducted for a "special and limited object." The object was not "to try and finally settle" the rights in question. According to Curtis, extradition was the goal, just as with cases involving fugitives from justice. The expectation, Curtis insisted, was that "justice would be done under the laws of the State to which the fugitive should be restored."[25]

If Curtis's logic was appealing on its face, it was nonetheless deficient. To begin with, the analogy to extradition was strained. Horace Mann, then serving as a Whig congressman, had previously noted that persons claimed as fugitive slaves were not placed in the "custody of the law" but in "private hands." There was no assurance of further legal proceedings following rendition.[26] In fact, southerners had opposed a proposed amendment to the fugitive slave bill that would have required slave owners to post bonds in order to ensure recaptured slaves access to southern courts.[27]

Even if black persons seized as runaways could get a hearing in the South, there were reasons to doubt that "justice would be done."

There was a significant difference in how blacks were treated in southern and northern court systems. In slave states every black person was presumed under the law to be a slave; the opposite was the case in free states.[28] That was a potentially decisive legal presumption for anyone who was claimed as a fugitive slave.

Moreover, Curtis sidestepped the question of how the statute affected free blacks. To a considerable degree the constitutional objections to the 1850 act, like those lodged against the 1793 act, hinged on the idea that persons claimed as fugitive slaves might well be free. Senator John P. Hale of New Hampshire raised this issue during congressional debate. The fugitive slave bill "proceeds on the assumption that the man who is seized in a free State is of course a slave," said Hale. Suppose that assumption was mistaken. Where, then, the senator asked, "is the protection which the Constitution guaranties to the meanest citizen living under the law?"[29]

Curtis refused to look at the Fugitive Slave Act in that way. He saw the "class of persons now in question" as slaves (not as persons claimed as slaves) who were "not parties to the constitution, nor under its protection." The fact that Curtis excluded slaves from constitutional protection was noteworthy, although there was judicial precedent for that position.[30] From that premise Curtis suggested that any discussion about free blacks was irrelevant to assessing the constitutionality of the 1850 act. It "can never be" a legitimate objection that a law, valid when applied to cases to which it was intended to apply, "may by accident or malice be applied to others, not within its terms or meaning." That was, however, exactly the point in contention. Abolitionists argued that the statutory procedures were so lax that they invited mistake and malice. In Wendell Phillips's words, the 1850 act was a "wide-open gate for avarice and perjury."[31]

Curtis let serious questions about constitutional rights slip from view. More than most of his contemporaries, he understood the significance of procedural protections under the common law and the Constitution. Yet in his rush to defend the Fugitive Slave Act, Curtis construed the Constitution so that blacks—whether slave or free—were effectively shut out from any legal protection. It is difficult to believe that Curtis would have readily defended a law allowing free white citizens to be carted off to slavery. Although he portrayed his opinion as comprehensive, Curtis conveniently overlooked one important antislavery argument, that the 1850 act deprived persons of their liberty without due process of law in violation of the Fifth Amendment.[32] This was a conspicuous omission on his part, given his later efforts to develop due process.

The opinion, in the final analysis, was a politically inspired piece of advocacy. One of Curtis's most interesting lines came in closing. "It is nothing to you as an executive officer nor to me as your legal adviser, what the law ought to be. What it is, being the only rule for your action and my consideration." This reiterated the position Curtis had taken years before in *Commonwealth v. Aves.* The relevant standard of morality in court, he had said, was what the law prescribes. Curtis offered no signposts to show how to bridge what is into what ought to be. Instead, he gave officials a way of looking at the law so that they could shed personal responsibility for their actions. One imagines that Webster would have been gratified by this particular passage, as federal officers in Boston had been reluctant to enforce the act against the Crafts. Curtis's motive seems clear: keep at a distance the arguments roiling Boston—that the 1850 act was unjust—so that the authorities would get on with enforcing the law and the public would view their actions as a necessary part of the Compromise of 1850.

II

Curtis offered a more compelling argument when he considered the underlying moral issues. Privately recognizing "the moral duty which we owe to the fugitive slave," he said that he blamed "no one for arriving at the opinion, either by reasoning or impulse, that fugitive slaves ought not to be restored to their masters." There was always "another step" to take in Curtis's mind, however. As he put it, the "true issue" was whether "the moral duty which we owe to the fugitive slave, when in conflict with the moral duty we owe to our country and its laws, is so plainly superior thereto, that we may and ought to engage in a revolution on account of it." Here was an exact statement of the "moral-moral" dilemma legal scholar Robert M. Cover described years later, between the "substantive moral propositions relating to slavery and liberty and the moral ends served by the formal structure as a whole."[33] There was really no question of how Curtis would resolve the dilemma; of more interest were the arguments he advanced.

Curtis presented his views to the public in a speech he delivered in Faneuil Hall one week after his legal opinion was published. The event in this historic building, billed as a Constitutional Meeting, was part of the Webster Whigs' public relations efforts. Several large assemblies (sometimes called Union meetings) were held around the country to garner support for the Compromise of 1850 and to allay southern concerns over resistance to the Fugitive Slave Act.[34] Webster, still under attack in New England, thought his own appearance would detract from the proceedings in Boston. Besides, he wrote Fillmore, it would be "expedient to bring out new men. Mr. Gray, Mr. B. R. Curtis, &c." In fact, Boston's Constitutional Meeting became a Curtis family enterprise. Curtis's brother, George Ticknor Curtis, was one of its organizers, and a cousin, Thomas Buckminster Curtis, called the meeting to order. Benjamin Curtis was the first of four featured speakers; the most notable other orator was Rufus Choate.[35]

The call for the meeting, signed by several thousand, set the tone: Constitution and Union on one side; the "spirit of disobedience to the laws of the land" on the other. But there were strong grounds for that "spirit of disobedience," which had coalesced around a religious justification for resistance to the law. This argument, which could be stated as simply as the idea that the 1850 act violated the Golden Rule, reflected a more complex line of reasoning: this act of Congress was a human law, the product of earthly powers; the statute conflicted with the will of God; each individual was bound to examine this statute as a matter of conscience, and upon reflection, it should be clear that the usual obligation to obey laws was suspended; indeed, each person had the duty to resist this legislation.[36] This became condensed in the popular shorthand expression that there was "a higher law than the Constitution."[37] As many northerners had an instinctive reaction that the Fugitive Slave Act was fundamentally wrong, antislavery leaders had a ready-made platform to exert a powerful appeal when they pointed to conscience as the guide for individual action.

"It is a moral question," Curtis stated at the outset of his speech, and "I shall endeavor to state, as well as I can, that course of reasoning which has satisfied my own mind."[38] He proceeded to string together a series of propositions which amounted to one of the most plausible explanations of why it was necessary to obey the 1850 act, as much as it was despised.

Curtis's analysis was based on one basic assumption: there would always be a need to have agreed-upon principles between slave and free states concerning fugitive slaves. To show "the necessity of some such provision, in some form," Curtis noted seemingly unrelated historical cases. He cited the arrangements among the New England colonies in the seventeenth century for the return of runaway servants. Curtis also pointed to the agreement between Spain and the United States regarding slaves escaping from Georgia to Spanish Florida. The picture that emerged from Curtis's account was that fugitive slave rendition was inevitably a source of conflict between governments permitting slavery and those that did not. The premise underlying Curtis's argument, not fully articulated, was that in any economic and social system built upon slavery, slave owners would have concerns over escaped slaves.

Turning to the fugitive slave clause itself, Curtis explained what he thought the framers had in mind. At first Curtis reiterated the position taken by Justice Story in *Prigg v. Pennsylvania*.[39] It is "certain," Curtis said, "that the Union could not be formed and the Constitution adopted, without this article." Although this view was widely held in the antebellum period, historians have cast doubt on it.[40] As Curtis developed his argument, however, he set out a more complex explanation. He did not rest his claim on the idea that the fugitive slave question had been a pressing problem during the founding. Instead, Curtis suggested that the framers recognized the issue as potentially divisive and, for that reason, established guiding principles.

In Curtis's view the events of 1850 had demonstrated the framers' foresight. Nobody "in this age," he asserted, could seriously believe it possible "to live in peace, side by side, with the slaveholding States, without some effectual stipulation." Curtis suggested that the conflict over fugitive slaves would remain if the Union was dissolved. "You may break up the Constitution and the Union to-morrow; you may do it by a civil war," Curtis said. "You may draw the geographical line between slaveholding and non-slaveholding *anywhere*; but when we shall have settled down, they will have their institutions, and we shall have ours. One is as much a fact as the other. One engages the interests and feelings and passions of men as much as the other. And how long can we live in peace, side by side, without some provision by compact, to meet this case? Not one year."[41]

No doubt constructed for rhetorical effect, this passage combined melodrama with a Madisonian political theory. Curtis's reference to interests, feelings, and passions calls to mind the language of *Federalist* no. 10. The real world, James Madison there suggested, was full of "local prejudices," "clashing interests," and "unfriendly passions." It would remain so, in his view. According to Madison, people in a free society naturally divide into factions, serving their own particular interests, sometimes opposed to the good of the whole. He believed that the government designed by the framers offered the best chance of promoting the public good over factional interests. Madison noted two basic reasons for this: first, it would be difficult for factions to control policy in such a large republic because they would counterbalance one another; second, this representative government enhanced the possibilities for wise elites to clarify and promote the public interest. Underlying this was one of *The Federalist*'s central themes. Reason over passion was the key to self-government, according to Madison, who envisioned a deliberative process in which opposing sides engaged in argument instead of "violent conflicts."[42]

In his speech Curtis did not say that he had *The Federalist* in mind, but it is difficult to read his argument without detecting its Madisonian perspective. Slavery posed especially difficult problems, Curtis suggested, "so connected with the interests and sentiments and passions of our countrymen" that it was "difficult for the wisest and coolest on either side, to restrain themselves within the limits of prudence and moderation." Southerners did not escape criticism. Some clearly lacked that "excellent virtue called moderation." Curtis was mainly concerned with actions closer to home, however. He recognized that resistance in Massachusetts grew out of a "love of human liberty." These local passions had a "certain dignity and power," Curtis conceded, but they were "bad passions" nonetheless.[43]

With that, it is possible to reconstruct more precisely what the Fugitive Slave Act signified to Curtis and why he believed it had to be enforced. He identified this law with the overall public interest not because of the substantive content of this legislation but rather because of the governing process it represented. There was in his view a constitutional mode for regulating differences over slavery, and he saw the 1850 act as a product of that process. Congress, where it was possible to air opposing views from around the country and to mold conflicting opinions into law, was the appropriate place to settle the fugitive slave question.

The rendition of runaway slaves had grown in Curtis's mind as a test of the vitality of republican government. The founders "anticipated," Curtis stated, that through the Constitution and "in no other way could we become an example of, and a security for, the capacity of man, safely and peacefully and wisely, to govern himself, under free and popular Constitutions." At stake was the idea that people could govern themselves and resolve their most intractable political conflicts by reason rather than force. Reminding his audience of Shay's Rebellion, an "insurrection against the laws *in this State*," Curtis quoted George Washington: "It is but the other day we were shedding our blood to obtain the Constitutions under which we live—Constitutions of our own choice and making—and now we are unsheathing the sword to overturn them."[44] The parallel to 1850 was clear, at least to Curtis's way of thinking.

Thus, whether the 1850 act was flawed was not the overriding question for Curtis. It appears that Curtis was able to disregard its deficiencies based upon his practical conception of law. Opponents of the Fugitive Slave Act required an identification between law and justice (an unjust law was not a law). A "statute contrary to natural right" is "null & void," wrote Emerson. Possibly he had Curtis in mind when he wrote, "I am surprised that lawyers can be so blind as to suffer the principles of law to be discredited."[45] Curtis operated from a different perspective. The question at hand was not whether "this or that law be wise or just," Curtis said, "but to declare that there *is* law, and its duties and power."[46] As Curtis had indicated in his Deerfield speech years before, he viewed law as a fundamentally human arrangement. To hold man-made laws to the standard of natural justice would make government practically impossible. Proceeding directly to forcible resistance was in his mind fatal to constitutional government as an ongoing enterprise.

All of these ideas led Curtis to take an inflexible view of the act's opponents. To spell out for Bostonians what he thought resistance entailed, Curtis used Theodore Parker as a foil for his argument. In a sermon called *The Function and Place of Conscience, in Relation to the Laws of Men*, the Unitarian clergyman had argued that every fugitive slave had a right of self-defense. The slave catcher "alienates his right to life" at the moment of attack, Parker explained. If "I were the fugitive, and could escape in no other way, I would kill" the slave catcher "with as little compunction as I would drive a mosquito from my face." Parker also embraced a position gaining currency that posed a serious if less dramatic challenge to enforcing the law. Jurors, he said, were not obliged to follow their oaths in trials of persons resisting the law.[47]

Curtis responded directly in his speech. "I should like to ask the Rev. Preacher," Curtis said, what he expected in the afterlife for violating a "vow to render a true verdict according to the law and the evidence." A brief sideshow ensued when Parker, who was in the audience in Faneuil Hall, shot back, "Do you wish me to answer it?" Shouts followed: " 'Put him out'—'hear him'—'let him be heard'—hisses—'go on'—order—order." The exchange closed quickly, and Curtis continued. Parker later said that Curtis "refused me the opportunity to reply!" According to the *Atlas*, Curtis acknowledged Parker's right to speak at a proper time but expressed his desire to continue without interruption.[48]

Parker's zealotry was useful to Curtis's purpose. One of Curtis's aims was to reach those drawn to the path of resistance yet unaware of the implications of their position, as he understood them. He classified resistors in two groups: one, mainly Free-Soilers, who did not picture themselves subverting the government; the other, Garrisonian abolitionists, who "openly" claimed that this was "a case for revolution." Curtis recounted the Garrisonian position that the fugitive slave clause was "a fundamental error in the Constitution" and that Massachusetts

49

had the duty "to withdraw itself instantly" from the Union and "thus revolutionize the Government." According to Curtis, the Free-Soilers, "apparently not at all aware of the direction in which they are moving," had taken an equally extreme position. They did not simply object to the 1850 act as an aberrant use of legislative power; they were in fact unwilling to fulfill the constitutional commitment to return fugitive slaves under any circumstances.[49]

Curtis suggested that there was "no middle ground" between obedience and revolution. Today, civil disobedience would appear to be an obvious alternative. As Robert Cover has interpreted Curtis, the Boston lawyer refused to "concede the middle ground of civil disobedience" in the belief that "conscience against law implied revolution."[50] This is a tempting reading, which should nevertheless be qualified in an important respect. Although one of the 1850 act's opponents specifically argued for disobeying a particular law, accepting the punishment, and permitting "the wheels of Government to roll on,"[51] civil disobedience was not so clearly defined in 1850. By the end of the twentieth century, this kind of resistance to oppression had a pedigree. Particularly with the examples of Mahatma Gandhi and Martin Luther King Jr., civil disobedience has become a legitimate, even glorified way to secure change against an unjust system of government. Nonviolence is widely recognized as one of its hallmark characteristics.

The case was different at the midpoint of the nineteenth century. That was a moment of original thinking about resistance to government in America, prompted largely by the question of slavery. Henry David Thoreau's essay on civil disobedience, a formative step in the development of this concept, was first published in 1849. (He entitled this article "Resistance to Civil Government"; the title "Civil Disobedience" was given after his death.) Significantly, there was no consensus on the use of nonviolent means. While Charles Francis Adams said that resistance should be peaceful, Frederick Douglass and Parker specifically endorsed violence, which, interestingly, Thoreau did not rule out.[52]

Whatever the duty to abide by the law in the abstract, for Curtis the threat of disunion colored resistance to the fugitive slave law. "For I understand we have come here," he said, "not to consider particular measures of government, but to assert that we *have* a Government . . . not to consult whether this or that course of policy is beneficial to our country, but to say that we yet *have* a country, and intend to keep it safe." Curtis believed that northern resistance fueled southern extremism and the fate of the Union hung in the balance. He was "seriously alarmed for the safety of the Union," Curtis told the attorney general of Massachusetts. "I fairly believe that if the moderate" and "stable men of all parts of the country do not bestir themselves we shall soon be on the brink of a precipice."[53]

The extent of the danger was a matter in dispute. On the day Curtis delivered his speech, the *Boston Advertiser* claimed "abundant evidence from the South that the spirit of resistance" to the 1850 act, particularly in Massachusetts, "has given great encouragement to the cause of disunion." Meanwhile, the *Boston Atlas* considered such talk a ploy to "gag the mouths of the people." Perhaps Curtis's fears were overblown. The most tangible moves to unite southerners to secede had come to nothing. The Nashville Convention, called to gather representatives of all slave states, failed to garner widespread support. Its second session in November 1850 was marked by a "sense of futility." In state elections in the South, hard-line secessionists lost to moderate Constitutional Unionists. Yet there was an ominous tone throughout the South: the grudging acceptance given the Compromise of 1850, the understanding that no further concessions could be wrung from the slave states, and the assertion of southern rights and particularly the right of secession. Some southerners looked upon the Fugitive Slave Act as a crucial test. The Georgia Platform, adopted by a convention in that state in December 1850, stated its "deliberate opinion" that "the preservation of our much beloved Union" depended upon a "faithful execution of the *Fugitive Slave Law*."[54]

Curtis's arguments, however sophisticated they might have been, were sullied by the scare tactics and diatribe at the close of his speech. He called runaway slaves "foreigners" who were, by their mere presence in Massachusetts, "rebels against our law." Reminding his listeners of the Irish immigration, which he characterized as "pouring upon our shores a tide of pauperism and disease," Curtis wondered whether slave states would enact "retaliatory legislation" to send "aged, diseased, or infirm slaves" to Massachusetts. While Curtis said he recognized the natural rights of fugitive slaves without qualification, he insisted that Massachusetts "has nothing to do" with their rights. It is hard to imagine a more insular set of remarks: "It is enough for us that they have no right to be *here*. Our peace and safety they have no right to invade. . . . Whatever natural rights they have, and I admit those natural rights to their fullest extent, *this* is not the *soil* on which to vindicate them. This is *our* soil—sacred to *our* peace—on which we intend to perform *our* promises, and work out, for the benefit of ourselves and our posterity and the world, the destiny which our Creator has assigned to us." Curtis concluded in a more charitable vein: "So far as He has supplied us with the means to succor the distressed, we, as Christian men, will do so, and bid them welcome, and thank God that we have the means to do it."

Yet this expression of compassion seemed empty. Curtis offered no specific recommendation of what could be done to help the slaves. Instead, he reiterated the actions he considered out of bounds: violating a "solemn compact," forswearing a juror's oath, plunging into "civil discord," and shedding blood.[55]

Curtis closed to "hearty cheers," according to the *Advertiser*, which commended him for considering the moral as well as the political questions. The editors expressed "full confidence that few readers who wish to be enlightened in their duty cannot fail to concur" in his "course of reasoning." The anti-Webster *Atlas* conceded that "every one will give grave consideration" to the "able legal argument." Curtis was "a lawyer of the highest grade," the *Atlas* noted, while adding that "there were gentlemen equally respectable, equally learned in Constitutional Law who believed the law to be unconstitutional." Wendell Phillips described Curtis as the "only one of the speakers entitled to much influence or consideration." Others were not so diplomatic. The *Liberator* called the speech "detestable." Abolitionists responded to Curtis's exclusionary views. The *Boston Republican* accused Curtis of pandering "to the prejudices, and lowest and basest sentiments of the meanest portion" of our population. "Can anything be more heartless, cold-blooded, or selfish?" The *Liberator*, not satisfied with publishing a point-by-point rebuttal of Curtis's argument, promised "we have not quite done with him."[56]

III

Nor was he done with the abolitionists. Only the battleground had shifted, from Faneuil Hall to Boston's courthouse. In this day every member of the U.S. Supreme Court served as circuit justice for a particular region of the country. When riding the circuit, as it was known, the justices traveled from one federal judicial district to another. They heard appeals taken from the lower federal district courts and conducted trials, sometimes jointly with U.S. district judges. Circuit riding provided the opportunity for the justices to educate the public on their views of federal law, not only in trials but also in grand jury charges, which were often published in newspapers.

Curtis had the New England circuit, which covered Massachusetts, New Hampshire, Maine, and Rhode Island. In his first term he continued his battles against abolitionists in proceedings growing out of the rescue of a fugitive slave named Shadrach Minkins.

In February 1851 U.S. deputy marshals arrested Minkins and brought him to the courthouse before one of the federal commissioners, who happened to be George Ticknor Curtis. As antislavery lawyers sought to delay the proceedings, a crowd gathered in Court Square and in the stairwell leading into the U.S. Court Room. At some point—whether by prearranged signal or not was later disputed—several men rushed into the courtroom, got hold of Shadrach, and carried him off. No shots were fired, although one deputy marshal yelled, "Shoot him!" Shadrach was shepherded out of the city. He eventually made his way to Montreal.[57]

Reaction was noteworthy for its emphasis on race. The *Boston Advertiser* portrayed the city under the "dominion of a colored mob." A New York newspaper noted the "sensation" created in the nation's capital by news of "the negro insurrection." Senator Henry Clay demanded to know "whether we shall have a government of white men or black men."[58]

Arrests were made within two days of the rescue, even before the president issued a proclamation ordering the prosecution of all "aiders or abettors" for "this flagitious offense." The War Department took the significant step of directing federal troops to aid the U.S. marshal in Boston. Secretary of State Webster released a public letter pronouncing the rescue a "case of treason." Curtis, not yet appointed to the Court, appeared more sanguine at this point. "I hope you will not think too seriously of the breach of the laws here," he wrote Webster. The rescue had a positive effect, Curtis believed, as it had "startled" moderates who had been drawn to the doctrines espoused by "fanatics."[59]

Through the rest of February, Bostonians were treated practically every day to news of additional arrests and an ongoing inquiry. Within two months the federal grand jury had indicted several men for complicity in the rescue. Webster, seeking the "best talent" at the bar, authorized George Lunt, the U.S. district attorney for Massachusetts, to secure the services of Rufus Choate or Benjamin Curtis. Preoccupied with his legislative activities (including the contested senatorial election), Curtis declined. He was willing to discuss "Administration matters" publicly later, Webster reported to the president.[60]

Just as it appeared that there would be some respite from controversy as the trials were delayed, another fugitive slave, Thomas Sims, was arrested. Sims's case, taken together with the Shadrach rescue, shows the intensity with which opposing forces contended in Boston. To avert another rescue city officials put iron chains around the ground floor of the courthouse. The sight of northern judges ducking under chains furnished abolitionists with the perfect metaphor: "the Southern chain on the neck of the Massachusetts court." Armed guards posted around the courthouse created a "warlike" scene, according to the *Boston Courier*. In the face of these measures, abolitionists devised equally extraordinary plans to rescue this runaway slave. In one, Sims was supposed to jump from the third-floor window.[61] Wendell Phillips suggested an alternative: "Block the wheels of Government." He urged Bostonians to "fill their pockets with pistols, to tear up the rails on the railroads, to crowd the streets and surround the Court-House, so that if the fugitive should be taken away, it must be over their dead bodies."[62]

For several days Sims's lawyers, including Richard Henry Dana Jr., Robert Rantoul Jr., and Sumner, engaged in an unremitting but unsuccessful effort to save him. They argued before Commissioner George Ticknor Curtis, tried to get Chief Justice Shaw to grant a writ of habeas corpus, and sought various forms of relief from U.S. District Judge Peleg Sprague. Perhaps the most ingenious idea was to place Sims in state custody under a criminal warrant charging him with assault (Sims had used a knife while trying to resist arrest). This would have cut off the rendition proceedings, a federal civil action, because state criminal process had priority. To ensure that the fugitive slave remained in the hands of federal marshals, U.S. Commissioner Benjamin F. Hallett issued a criminal warrant against Sims. In a last-ditch effort, Sims's counsel brought this matter before U.S. Supreme Court justice Levi Woodbury, then sitting in Boston. Benjamin Curtis had a minor part in this drama, as he defended the U.S. marshal in this hearing. In the end, Commissioner George Ticknor Curtis issued a certificate of removal, and three hundred guards marched Sims to a waiting ship at the wharf before dawn. Upon his return to Savannah, he was given thirty-nine lashes in a public whipping.[63]

In this state of affairs—one fugitive slave safely in Canada, another returned to slavery in the South, no lessening of commitment on either side—Curtis took office in the fall of 1851. He wasted no time before issuing a grand jury charge that laid down a chilling interpretation of the law of treason. If taken seriously, Curtis's charge put several prominent abolitionists at risk for this capital offense.

The Constitution defines treason to include "levying War." Webster had previously outlined how Shadrach's rescue satisfied this definition; Curtis filled in the details. According to the new justice, levying war was not restricted to making war to overthrow the government. Treason included "any combination, or conspiracy" formed "to prevent the execution" of federal law by force. Although Justice Curtis acknowledged that force must be used, he diluted this requirement. Actual use of force could be found in the "presence of numbers who manifest an intent to use force." Curtis insisted that it was not necessary that anyone fire shots or strike any officers; there was no need for a "military array" or weapons. Significantly, the grand jury charge made persons criminally liable for treason for performing "any part, however minute, or however remote from the scene of action, and who are actually leagued in the general conspiracy." That could include speech, in Curtis's view, "when discussion passes into direct and urgent incitement to crime, when ignorant men are stirred up to form combinations to resist the law by violence."[64]

There was precedent for much of what Curtis said; Dana conceded that the charge was done "in the technical Curtis-like style."[65] Yet in attempting to quell resistance, Curtis lost sight of the lessons of English history, which illustrated how easy it was for the government to exploit the crime of treason in order to eliminate political opposition. The pattern in England was so clear, with judges beholden to the Crown giving arbitrary interpretations to elevate lesser crimes into treason, that the term *constructive treason* came into use to describe it. Aware of the English experience, the framers of the American Constitution defined treason in the charter (the only crime for which this was done).

Curtis understood the danger to individual liberties. He distinguished between political discussion and criminal activity, but he seemed to be of two minds on what that entailed. On the one hand, he suggested that speech was outside the purview of the criminal process until it passed into "direct and urgent incitement to crime." On the other hand, Curtis indicated that incitement, "however remote" from the scene of action, was treasonable.[66] Although Curtis's message was clear—be careful if you speak out strongly against the Fugitive Slave Act—it did not stifle dissent in Boston. No one there was indicted for treason.

Shortly after charging the grand jury, Curtis (sitting with Judge Peleg Sprague) presided over the trial of Robert Morris, an activist black lawyer who had been indicted for helping Shadrach escape. All of the so-called rescue cases in Boston had political overtones, but this trial was distinctive as the force of the law was concentrated upon the head of a black member of the Massachusetts bar. As Morris's counsel stated in his opening statement, recent events had produced "an irritation" approaching "hostility" against "this race." One of the original members of Boston's Vigilance Committee, Morris had been active in the antislavery cause. He was among several lawyers working on Shadrach's defense while the fugitive slave was in custody. Before his own arrest, Morris represented another supposed rescuer during a preliminary inquiry before U.S. Commissioner Hallett.[67]

Morris's trial turned into a contest over the jurors' authority to decide the case based upon their own moral views. Senator John P. Hale and Richard Henry Dana Jr., the two prominent Free-Soilers defending Morris, argued that any juror who conscientiously believed the Fugitive Slave Act unconstitutional was bound by his oath to disregard any contrary instruction from the bench. Thus the moral argument that had been circulating in the public debate—reflected in the exchange between Parker and Curtis in Faneuil Hall—found its way into court. Justice Curtis responded with an opinion denying that the jury had authority to decide questions of law.[68]

Thanks to Justice Curtis, there exists a blow-by-blow account of Morris's trial. Curtis kept detailed records of his circuit cases, and his bench notes of Morris's case look comprehensive. The justice recorded prospective jurors' responses during jury selection, the witnesses' testimony, and the lawyers' arguments; all in all, he kept an unofficial transcript of an important criminal trial from the nineteenth century.[69]

The factual disputes in the case boiled down to two issues. The first concerned Morris's part in the courthouse rescue. The defense claimed that there was "no concerted attempt" to rescue Shadrach. His escape was "sudden" and "unexpected," Dana said. The prosecution's witnesses told a different story. One described what he heard at the courthouse door shortly before the rescue: "Men stand by—don't leave—something must be done now or never," with the reply "We are ready." The government produced evidence that Morris was not only aware of the rescue plans but that as one of the few persons moving freely about the courtroom, he provided vital information to the crowd outside. Perhaps the prosecution's most devastating testimony on this point came from a fifteen-year-old boy. He said that outside the courtroom shortly before the crowd rushed in, a black man asked Morris how many were inside and that the lawyer said seven or eight and added, "A good time" or "good chance." The prosecutor also left the impression that Morris conveyed the rescue plans to Shadrach. A deputy marshal said he saw Morris whisper to the prisoner, who then loudly proclaimed, "If I die I die like a man." The defense portrayed Morris as an attorney engaged in legitimate activities. According to their witnesses, the crowd questioned Morris when he emerged from the courtroom, but he responded with an innocuous remark indicating that the case was postponed.[70]

The other major factual question had to do with what happened shortly after the escape from the U.S. courtroom. At a stable a quarter mile from the courthouse, with a crowd all around, Shadrach got in a cab with some others. The prosecution called a carpenter who identified Morris as one of those in the cab. In his notes Curtis underlined the testimony: "*I am sure I saw him in the cab.*" Another witness singled out Morris "walking side by side" with Shadrach with "his arm laid on the fugitive's back." The defense produced several witnesses who contradicted these statements.[71]

While both sides gave no quarter contesting the facts, all of the lawyers apparently believed that the outcome hinged upon the jurors' views of the fugitive slave law. The question of the jury's prerogative was a theme running throughout the trial. Before jury selection, Hale signaled the defense team's basic strategy: "If the Court tells the whole truth it must tell the jury they have the *right* to pass on the laws" and "can not be questioned upon it." The first words in the prosecutor's opening were that the "jury are not to judge of the law"; "they have sworn to take it from the court"; the "expediency of the law" was "not in question." Meanwhile, in his opening, Dana argued that the Fugitive Slave Act was unconstitutional. "This is not extradition," Dana emphasized (as Curtis jotted down what appears in his notes as an unspoken rejoinder: "What is it?").[72] In his closing argument Hale stated that the jury could judge the law as well as fact and that any juror who believed the Fugitive Slave Act was unconstitutional was obliged under oath to ignore any contrary direction from the bench. This time Justice Curtis interrupted in order to hear argument on this issue without the jury present.[73]

The defense touched upon a significant question with a long history. Indeed, Hale asked the court to recur to the "earliest fountains of the law," a reference to the development of the jury in England.[74] As the English legal system evolved, the distinction between law and fact became the official dividing line between the powers of judge and jury in criminal trials. Supposedly the judge decided questions of law; the jury those of fact, and the jury accepted the law given by the judge and applied it to the facts. In practice, dispensing criminal justice was never so simple. The jury's decision-making process was largely insulated from outside review; its decision usually was rendered in the form of a general verdict of guilty or not guilty. A tradition developed around cases that may be termed political trials, like those of William Penn in England and John Peter Zenger in the American colonies, where defendants appealed directly to the jury to check the government's abuse of power. In a case from the middle of the seventeenth century, the defendant John Lilburne, an opponent of Oliver Cromwell's government, claimed for the jury the right to judge the law. The sitting judges resisted this request, but the case set a benchmark nonetheless.[75]

In America the issue was neatly stated by Justice Story. The jury had the "physical power" to "disregard the law, as laid down to them by the court," a recognition that the general verdict masked how the jury reached its decision, but the real issue was whether to acknowledge that jurors had "the moral right" to determine the law "according to their own notions." The U.S. Supreme Court did not resolve this question until the end of the nineteenth century, in *Sparf and Hansen v. United States* (1895). Denying the criminal jury's authority to decide questions of law, the justices relied on Curtis's opinion in *United States v. Morris*. Writing for the majority, Justice John Harlan noted that the question, "in all of its aspects, was examined by Mr. Justice Curtis with his accustomed care" in a "great opinion." Curtis "gave reasons which appear to us entirely conclusive," Harlan added.[76]

In his circuit opinion Curtis indicated that he would have preferred that a question of "so much importance" go before "the highest tribunal," but he felt he had "no right to avoid a decision on it." Curtis ruled that the judge in a criminal trial had the duty to decide every question of law while the jurors were required to apply the law given by the court to the facts. Precedent could be found supporting both sides on this question. The justice appears to have relied on an earlier opinion by Chief Justice Shaw for some points, but Curtis was the first to offer a detailed constitutional analysis.[77] "The true question," he said, centered on the meaning of the constitutional provision that "the Trial of all Crimes, except in Cases of Impeachment, shall be by Jury." This language may appear unavailing to Curtis's position, perhaps even liable to an opposite construction, if the emphasis is placed on the idea that the trial shall be by jury. Yet by framing the issue as a constitutional question, the justice was able to bring a broader view of the Constitution to bear on this particular problem. He specifically stated that he would look at the "whole" of this charter to construe this "part" of it. There was "no sounder rule of interpretation," according to Curtis.[78]

Curtis followed with what may seem to be an inconsequential line: the "object" of the Constitution "was to create a government for a great country, working harmoniously and efficiently through its several executive, legislative, and judicial departments." In fact, this was a critical move in his argument. He suggested that the founders faced a basic problem of how to set up a workable government over a vast expanse of territory. The constitutional solution was reflected in the supremacy clause, which established the Constitution and the laws of the United States as "the supreme Law of the Land." Curtis deduced a principle of uniformity from this: "whatever was done" by the federal government "should be by standing laws, operating equally in all parts of the country, binding on all citizens alike."[79]

For Curtis the correlate responsibilities of judge and jury in federal criminal trials followed naturally. He singled out the judiciary as the branch of the federal government best suited "to secure a uniform and consistent interpretation of the laws, and an unvarying enforcement of them." If the jury had the acknowledged right to decide the law, uniformity would be undermined. The justice called to mind the fears expressed in *The Federalist* over the "hydra in government" that would result if each state's highest court interpreted national laws without being subject to review.[80] How much the worse, Curtis wondered, if every criminal jury had the right to pass on the constitutionality of federal legislation. Although the justice refrained from openly ridiculing the idea, the image he conveyed was that it would be absurd to authorize an indefinite number of tribunals, whose members were selected without any thought of their qualifications for deciding legal questions, to deliver unreviewable decisions on the law, with the reasons behind those decisions shielded from view. He expressed concern that juries with such broad discretion might wrongly convict the innocent. Judges, by contrast, were "obliged to express their opinions publicly," to provide reasons in their opinions that were subject to appeal, and "to stand responsible for them, not only to public opinion, but to a court of impeachment."[81]

At bottom, the positions taken by the justice and the defense reflected fundamentally different perspectives, and more could be said for both sides than appears in the record of this case. Defense counsel argued that the jury's right to decide the law was essential to the preservation of individual liberties. Hale and Dana looked upon the jury as a counterweight to abuse of power in government. They saw the criminal jury as a vehicle for the expression of popular attitudes, with the jury's authority to decide the law skewed in direction of acquittal. Certainly that was the situation with the rescue cases, where there was little risk of an erroneous conviction. The Fugitive Slave Act was widely considered unjust; the jury was an institution which could inject a popular conception of justice into the criminal process.

For Justice Curtis there was a principle at stake which overshadowed the immediate context. His view was based on the principle of uniformity and the rule of law. The goal was "to enforce the laws uniformly and impartially, without respect of persons or times, or the opinions of men." To that end, having judges rather than juries decide the law was "one of the highest safeguards of the citizen." Justice Curtis underscored the judiciary's relative independence from popular feeling. "To enforce popular laws is easy," he said. "But when an unpopular cause is a just cause, when a law, unpopular in some locality is to be enforced there, then comes the strain upon the administration of justice; and few unprejudiced men would hesitate as to where that strain would be most firmly borne."[82]

As it turned out, the jury acquitted Morris. Years later Dana credited Justice Curtis with conducting the trial with "more than passive impartiality," indeed, with "an affirmative determination that the trial should be had with absolute fairness." Curtis actually boosted Morris's chances at "a critical stage" by a comment on the evidence which, Dana believed, "in the measuring cast, secured the verdict of acquittal."[83] Although Dana did not identify the particular comments he had in mind, he may have been thinking of Curtis's jury charge. The justice's instructions made several points in Morris's favor. Regarding the rescue in the courthouse, did Morris tell Shadrach of the rescue plan, as the prosecution tried to suggest? The justice said that Morris, "as counsel, had the same rights and privileges as other counsel, and his conduct must be presumed right until proved to be wrong." What of Morris's purported statement outside the courtroom that it was a good "time" or "chance"? The jurors should take the view "most favorable to the prisoner," Curtis noted. As for the testimony placing Morris in the cab with Shadrach, Curtis seemed to gently cast doubt on the government's main witness for this point. The crime was "great," Curtis said, but he admonished the jurors "not to convict an innocent man."[84]

Curtis still sought to see the law obeyed. Shortly after Morris's trial ended, Curtis agreed to let the *Boston Advertiser* publish the grand jury charge he had delivered just a few weeks earlier.[85] It was an unmistakable warning of the severe consequences attending resistance to the Fugitive Slave Act.

IV

No other escaped slaves were recaptured in Boston until 1854, when a runaway named Anthony Burns was seized. His rendition was one of the most famous episodes in the history of the fugitive slave law.[86] Justice Curtis became involved when he issued another grand jury charge. This time the grand jurors, following the justice's lead, indicted Wendell Phillips and Theodore Parker for having some part, as tenuous as it was, in a failed rescue attempt.

After Burns was arrested, Commissioner Edward G. Loring granted a two-day postponement in his rendition proceedings. While abolitionist lawyers pursued various legal options, the Vigilance Committee contemplated other measures.[87] Phillips advised committee members to block all paths that could be used to remove Burns from Boston if Loring's decision was unfavorable. Phillips's strategy rested on the vague hope that the authorities would back down or that Burns would somehow be rescued with people milling about the streets. Some abolitionists in attendance were not satisfied with Phillips's proposal. On at least one item there was no dispute, however. The committee decided to hold a mass meeting in Faneuil Hall the night before Burns's hearing was scheduled to resume. Shortly before the rally started, an alternative to Phillips's plan took shape. Its ringleaders were Martin Stowell, who had taken part in a successful fugitive slave rescue in Syracuse, and Thomas Wentworth Higginson, a clergyman who had been involved in the abortive plan to have Thomas Sims jump from the third floor of the courthouse. Stowell suggested that during the meeting they attack the courthouse, where Burns was held. With a vanguard of ready participants waiting in Court Square, additional forces could be got from the audience once everyone was told an attack was underway.[88]

The rescue attempt was as poorly coordinated as it was bold. Stowell and Higginson had gathered what they needed to break into the courthouse—axes and a handful of men—but they were unable to communicate with Phillips before he addressed the densely packed audience. Unaware of their plan, Phillips fired up the crowd to act, but for the next day, not that evening. According to the *Liberator*'s account, Phillips opened with a simple demand: "I want that man set free in the streets of Boston. (Great cheering.)" There followed variations on what the next day would bring: whether "Virginia conquers Massachusetts. ('No.' 'Never.')"; whether "you adhere to the precedent of Thomas Sims ('No! No!')." Phillips directed everyone to keep Burns in sight the next day wherever "he stands in the streets of Boston." Parker followed with a specific appeal to reconvene at the courthouse at nine o'clock the next morning. While he made provocative statements ("sometimes peace is not the means"), the preacher countered cries from the audience for gunfire. Burns "won't go back," Parker assured them, "if we stand up there resolutely, and declare that this man shall not go out of the city of Boston, *without shooting a gun.*" By now, though, Faneuil Hall was in such a state that as suggestions surfaced from the crowd—move to the courthouse, get the slave catchers—Phillips rose again. Arguing against taking action that night, he told the crowd to "block every access and exit from the Court House" the next day. At that point, following the plan laid by Higginson and Stowell, a man shouted that a "mob of negroes is in Court Square, attempting to rescue Burns!" And the crowd rushed out of Faneuil Hall.[89]

As shots were fired and brickbats were thrown, several men used a large wooden beam as a battering ram against the locked western door of the courthouse. When they got the door barely open, Higginson and another person jumped through, only to be beaten back by the guards. The attack quickly broke off. When it was over, Burns remained in custody, and one of the deputy marshals was dead. The precise cause of his death was never established.

The short-term result was an impressive display of force by the authorities. The courthouse, surrounded by strong ropes, was put in the hands of federal troops with fixed bayonets. When the hearings resumed, over one hundred deputy marshals were stationed in the courtroom itself. Abolitionists still tried to figure how to rescue Burns, though nothing came of it. Crowds of several thousand gathered in Court Square during the weeklong proceedings, which ended in Commissioner Loring's decision to certify Burns's removal. A large military force took Burns to the Boston wharf at midday on June 2. Unlike Sims's predawn march, thousands lined the streets (estimates ranged to 50,000), surrounded by buildings draped in black.[90]

Burns's case contributed to a wholesale shift in mainstream public opinion in Massachusetts. His arrest coincided with Congress's passage of the Kansas-Nebraska Act, which abrogated the Missouri Compromise and opened more western territories to slavery. This legislation had a profound effect on northerners; Anthony Burns's case reinforced the view of an aggressive South. Perhaps there is no better indication of the change in attitude than the comment made by Amos A. Lawrence, scion of an immense fortune derived from cotton manufactures. "We went to bed one night old fashioned, conservative, Compromise Union Whigs," Lawrence said as Burns's proceedings drew to a close, and "waked up stark mad Abolitionists."[91]

Not Justice Curtis, however. Continuing his campaign against resistors, Curtis charged the grand jury on the federal crimes he considered applicable to recent events. Instead of treason, the justice outlined the elements of obstructing legal process. The maximum penalty was one year's imprisonment and a $300 fine. As Curtis described this statutory offense, it became clear that he had Parker and Phillips in mind. Parker later said that Curtis "could not have made the thing plainer" if "he had called us by our names."[92]

Curtis defined obstruction broadly to include "a multitude of persons" in a "public highway" preventing federal officers from executing legal process. It was unnecessary to show "active violence," Curtis said. Significantly, the justice extended criminal liability to persons who counseled others.[93] This included "language addressed to persons who immediately afterwards commit an offence, actually intended by the speaker to incite those addressed to commit it and adapted thus to incite them." Any doubt that Curtis considered Parker and Phillips liable was dispelled by his detailed explanation of the relationship between speech and act. It was irrelevant, according to the justice, whether the speaker's message was "departed from in respect to the time, or place, or precise mode or means of committing it."[94]

Curtis closed his charge by emphasizing what he believed was at stake. The justice built upon the Madisonian argument he had developed in his Faneuil Hall speech four years earlier. To demonstrate the danger of having the government under the sway of "local opinions" and "interests and passions," Curtis reminded the grand jury of southern opposition to federal tariff laws. It had been only two decades since South Carolina claimed the right to nullify federal law. With that in mind, Curtis stressed the need to enforce any "constitutionally enacted" law. To do otherwise was to submit to rule by "the strongest faction of the place and the hour." Curtis viewed "forcible resistance" to the 1850 act as a systematic effort to nullify this legislation, in effect turning the "power of the mob" into "one of the constituted authorities of the state." He added words of warning "that forcible and concerted resistance to any law is civil war, which can make no progress but through bloodshed."[95]

Curtis's gesture to the rule of law—his use of the familiar phrase "a government of laws not of men"—may appear a parody of legalism, given the severity of the 1850 act and the politics behind its enactment. The most forceful response to Curtis's charge came from William Lloyd Garrison. At an antislavery meeting in Framingham, Massachusetts, on the Fourth of July, the abolitionist leader set fire to the justice's grand jury charge, along with copies of the Fugitive Slave Act and Commissioner Loring's opinion. These were all "atrocities" committed in the name of the Constitution, Garrison said, as he prompted the audience to a chorus of amens. As he denounced the Constitution in the familiar abolitionist refrain as a "covenant with death" and "an agreement with hell," he burned it as well.[96]

The legal proceedings following Curtis's charge were anticlimactic. The federal grand jury indicted several men, including Parker, Phillips, Higginson, and Stowell. None of the cases was tried, however. Defense counsel moved to quash the indictments, and Curtis, sitting with Judge Sprague, granted the motion.

Curtis's reasons for doing so remain a mystery. His explanation of why the indictments should be quashed was strained. Even he admitted that his analysis was "technical." Curtis suggested that any indictment for obstructing legal process must state facts to show that the process (the warrant issued by Loring) was legal. The indictments failed to do that, the justice suggested, because they did not specify that Loring was among the federal commissioners empowered to issue warrants to recapture fugitive slaves (some commissioners had duties unrelated to the 1850 act). In a private meeting with the two judges, the prosecutor, Benjamin Hallett, sought new indictments, with the necessary details filled in. The judges explained that no indictment could cure the legal defect. Hallett gave up at that point rather than risk a damaging "decision establishing the invalidity of the legal process on the part of the Commissioner."[97]

Curtis's justification for quashing the indictments may be taken at face value, but there are reasons to think more was going on. Around the same time Curtis decided a circuit case in which he expressed a different view of what was required to quash an indictment concerning obstruction of the U.S. mail. More importantly, it is difficult to believe that he had not finally recognized that a trial afforded the defendants a platform to rail against the fugitive slave law. The abolitionists did in fact recognize the opportunity. "I am glad you have been indicted," Sumner wrote Parker, "for the sake of our cause." Of course, "you will defend yourself and answer the whilom speaker at Faneuil Hall face to face" (a reference to Curtis's speech in 1850, obviously still on the minds of abolitionists).[98]

V

Following the indictments of Parker and Phillips, Justice Curtis received more attention than he probably desired; his entire record on the fugitive slave law was seemingly up for review. The *New York Tribune* offered him unsolicited advice in an article headlined "FRIENDLY HINTS." The "public know how to appreciate legal subtilty and ingenuity," but having "had so many exhibitions of the ingenuity and adroitness of Mr. Curtis on the side of tyranny and injustice, they would like, for once at least, and just for a change if nothing else, to see him employ his abilities on behalf of justice and freedom." The *Liberator* questioned Curtis's objectivity: "In spite of his silk gown and his title of Judge," Curtis "is precisely neither more nor less the very same zealous partisan" who published a legal opinion supporting the "infamous" fugitive slave law. The most scathing attacks came from one of the defendants. Deprived of the opportunity to confront Justice Curtis directly in court, Parker published a little book he called *The Trial of Theodore Parker.* Curtis emerged as a central villain "most subtly active with all his force" in defending slavery; a "fugitive slave bill" judge who "began his career asking the Supreme Court of Massachusetts to restore Slavery to Lexington and Bunker Hill" (a reference to *Commonwealth v. Aves*) and served as counsel to "slave-hunters" (according to rumors, Parker said).[99]

64

If nothing else, such statements indicate the extent to which Curtis's contemporaries linked him with the fugitive slave issue. If his critics carried ad hominem arguments too far, there was an element of truth behind their charges. Curtis's arguments on and off the bench had shaped public opinion.

Uncharacteristically for Curtis, his legal analysis of the Fugitive Slave Act was superficial. Like his colleagues on the federal bench, the justice did not question the constitutionality of the 1850 act. He blithely resorted to the assumption that fugitive slave rendition was an extradition proceeding. As he was not about to pronounce the act's procedures frivolous, Curtis appeared indifferent to the rights of black persons claimed as runaways. In 1860 he belatedly conceded that the Fugitive Slave Act was too harsh and should be amended; at the same time he acknowledged southern demands for more efficient administration.[100]

Curtis put forward a stronger case when he met the antislavery arguments directly on moral grounds. He understood why people viewed the 1850 act as morally repugnant, but for Curtis the moral issue was not so one-sided. While abolitionists focused on the rights of the slave, Curtis perceived an overriding moral obligation to the law. He seemed to believe that fugitive slave rendition was not the issue to resolve the larger problem of slavery in the United States and that resistance to the 1850 act diminished the prospects for achieving an overall solution. Whatever the answer to the fugitive slave question, it had to be developed through the constitutional process in Curtis's view.

Yet Curtis's actions inadvertently confirmed the antislavery claim that slavery subverted the law and the Constitution. This was especially apparent in his grand jury charges on treason and speech. Less dubious was his opinion restricting the jury's authority to decide the law, although he implicitly conceded that the law diverged from the popular conception of justice. Missing from Curtis's various actions relating to the fugitive slave law was one of the defining characteristics of his constitutional jurisprudence: the creative use of legal process to develop solutions for controversial political problems, solutions that were at once responsive to the needs of government and solicitous of individual rights. While Curtis spent his energies mapping out a legal response to the opponents of the 1850 act, the truly creative outbursts in thought on this issue came from those operating outside the law who constructed philosophies of resistance.

3. FEDERAL-STATE CONFLICT IN A COMMERCIAL REPUBLIC

THE FEDERAL SYSTEM of government that emerged from the founding was a novel experiment in political thought. Antecedents, whether from ancient Greece or the more immediate example of the British Empire, did not supply the framers of the Constitution with a clear roadmap for allocating sovereign power between the states and the federal government. Before the Constitution was adopted, the former colonies, having come together for certain purposes, retained substantial interests in local autonomy and considered themselves separate sovereign states. The Constitution overlaid the states with a central government having powers over the same territory. The rationale for this, developed during the ratification debates, was that sovereignty resided in the people. This was a great innovation in political theory, but the practical operation of the federal system was left to be worked out later. The line dividing political authority between the states and the national government was not fixed. The nature of the federal-state relationship—the basic question of who had power over what—was still fresh when the Civil War generation confronted it, and it was, by any measure, at the heart of that conflict.

In a public address in 1852, Justice Curtis outlined his general views on this subject. Questions of "the last importance to the tranquillity and peace" of the nation "necessarily arose" when the federal "government was put in operation in the same territory and over the same people, having distinct State governments of their own," Curtis said. "Few men, whose attention has not been particularly directed to this subject, are aware of the number, the importance, or the difficulty of these questions." The justice did not enumerate the issues in this speech. Nor did he identify specific solutions, but he did say where he thought they could be found. It was the U.S. Supreme Court that had "the duty" of "restraining within their appropriate limits of power the state sovereignties." Curtis then revealed the key to his mind-set. "Questions which elsewhere could have been settled only by mere force" were "here to be brought to an arbitrament, according to the staid, settled and regular course of judicial procedure."[1]

Justice Curtis's approach to federal-state conflict, rooted in his Whig nationalism, is illustrated by his most important majority opinion, *Cooley v. Board of Wardens* (1852). Writing for the Court, Curtis sustained the constitutionality of state pilot laws, in this case a Pennsylvania statute that required ships using the port of Philadelphia to hire local pilots. The state legislature had authorized the port wardens to assess fees against shipowners who failed to do so, earmarking the funds to benefit needy pilots or their widows and children. Aaron Cooley, a merchant found liable to pay this fee, argued that this statute violated the commerce clause, which provides that Congress shall have power to "regulate Commerce with foreign Nations, and among the several States."[2]

This constitutional provision has been one of the most contentious in the Supreme Court's history, a classic example of power and policy turning on the interpretations given the Constitution's open-ended language. *Cooley* belongs in the category of cases involving the so-called dormant commerce clause. Although the Constitution's framers were acutely concerned with trade warfare between the states, the Constitution did not expressly delimit the scope of state powers over commerce. There was no genuine dispute that state laws in conflict with an act of Congress were invalid, but did the commerce clause preclude the states from regulating interstate commerce in the absence of controlling federal legislation, that is, when the power granted Congress was "in its dormant state"?[3] And did the Supreme Court have the authority to strike down state laws when Congress was silent?

Before *Cooley*, the justices abstractly considered these questions in terms of sovereign power. They quarreled in one case after another without making real progress, partly because whatever they decided had implications for slavery. Justice Curtis refocused the inquiry. He suggested that practical regulatory needs should guide the decision-making process, that the states had the power to regulate interstate commerce but not in every case, and that the Supreme Court had the authority under the commerce clause to nullify state laws when Congress had not acted. The opinion was a breakthrough. As Laurence Tribe suggested, in the attempt "to reconcile all that had gone before," *Cooley* "laid the groundwork for nearly all that has come since."[4]

Cooley is also a prime example of Curtis's constitutional principles and methods: his common-law pragmatism, his views of the Supreme Court and the judicial process, and his approach to constitutional interpretation. From language that by its terms only granted regulatory authority to Congress, the justice derived a judicial power and an implicit limitation on state actions. While the opinion bears the mark of Curtis's legal creativity, it also exposes the limitations of his constitutionalist approach. His interpretation was deceptively alluring, as the Supreme Court's later struggles over the commerce clause illustrate.

I

Economic growth was a hallmark of the antebellum period. The *Cooley* case arose at a critical juncture in that process. The nation's market economy had become truly continental following the war with Mexico and the admission of the state of California. The movement of goods and people over such a vast expanse was unprecedented. Old canals and turnpikes still operated; steamboats dotted the waterways; track laid for railroads more than tripled in the decade before the Civil War; the transcontinental railroad would be completed in 1869. With the emergence of industrial capitalism, questions concerning the regulation of interstate and foreign commerce demanded attention. Would the states hinder national economic development in favor of local concerns? Or would a continental market forge a national identity among Americans of disparate beliefs and interests? [5]

Cooley fit the pattern of commerce cases in the nineteenth century. As Congress was relatively inactive in economic regulation (certainly by later standards), the scope of its powers under the commerce clause was not put in question. Regulation was mainly left to the states, and issues arose concerning the constitutionality of state legislation that affected interstate commerce. Before *Cooley*, the Court's answers to this question revolved around two positions. On the one side, it was suggested that Congress's power over commerce was exclusive; the states had no authority to regulate interstate commerce when Congress did not act, and the Supreme Court was obliged to strike down state regulations that invaded this federal prerogative. On the other side, it was argued that the states had concurrent power over interstate commerce; state laws in this area were constitutional unless they conflicted directly with federal legislation, and the Court's authority to invalidate state laws was limited to determining whether Congress preempted the states. In either case, the scope of federal judicial power was a central issue.

Choosing between the doctrines of exclusive and concurrent power may appear to be an arcane enterprise, but to the best legal minds of the antebellum period it had undoubted significance. As Daniel Webster said, "No words embrace a wider field than *commercial regulation*" in "such an age as this," encompassing practically "all the business and intercourse of life." [6] The structure of the nation's economy was seen to depend upon which doctrine prevailed on the Court. Proponents of exclusive power like Webster and Justice Story envisioned a unified economic order, a regulatory system under national control. This stood in contrast with the Jacksonian thrust to decentralize, which found a congenial doctrine in concurrent power. This battle over legal doctrine was part of the broader debate over the Union. While nationalists favored the exclusive power doctrine, the concurrent power doctrine had become the legal theory of choice in defense of states' rights. In addition, important questions of public policy like temperance and immigration were at stake. And as the years progressed, slavery became an increasingly visible factor complicating commerce cases brought before the Supreme Court.

Notwithstanding Chief Justice John Marshall's nationalistic bent, the Court during his tenure (1801–1835) stopped short of converting the idea of exclusive power into an unequivocal constitutional ruling, though he came close to doing that. In *Gibbons v. Ogden* (1824), the Court invalidated a New York law which granted a monopoly for using steamboats on the state's waterways. In his opinion Marshall opened numerous avenues for the expansion of national authority, with commerce broadly defined to include "every species of commercial intercourse," Congress's commerce power extending to the interior of each state, and its power to regulate capable of being "exercised to its utmost extent" without judicial limitation. Marshall discussed the doctrine of exclusive power in favorable terms. He said that there was "great force" to the argument for exclusive power advanced by Webster, "and the Court is not satisfied that it has been refuted." However, the chief justice avoided a decision based on those grounds as he read the state statute to be in conflict with an act of Congress.[7] Some commentators believe that Marshall danced around the question of exclusive power because he felt it too controversial to settle at that time, the reaction in the slave states being one of his concerns.[8] In a separate opinion Justice William Johnson stated explicitly that the federal commerce power was exclusive and dismissed Marshall's statutory interpretation.[9]

Marshall appeared ready to build on *Gibbons*'s foundation in *Brown v. Maryland* (1827). There he invalidated a state law which had imposed a tax on the importation of goods from out of state. Two years later the chief justice gave an opinion in the case of *Willson v. Black Bird Creek Marsh Co.* (1829) which on its face may appear to be inconsistent with *Gibbons* and *Brown*. In *Willson* the Court sustained state legislation that authorized the construction of a dam on a small creek in the Delaware marshlands. Because the creek was navigable, there was a plausible claim that the state law obstructed interstate commerce. Writing for a unanimous Court, Marshall construed this statute as a legitimate application of the state's reserved powers to regulate the health and welfare of its inhabitants. He pointed to the health benefits derived from draining the marshland and the increased values in surrounding property that probably would result.[10] *Willson* can be synthesized with *Gibbons* and *Brown* to reflect the Marshall Court's basic stance: the states had power to regulate unless they threatened national interests (the creek in *Willson* was deemed insignificant to interstate commerce), but the Supreme Court was empowered to protect those interests when Congress was silent (following *Gibbons* and *Brown*).[11]

In fact, *Willson* reflected an important feature of the doctrine of exclusive power. Even its most zealous advocates recognized the authority of states to make laws concerning ferries, turnpikes, and roads or laws to inspect and quarantine goods if they endangered health. By the magic of labeling, laws like these were classified as something other than regulations of interstate commerce. Either they qualified as valid exercises of the states' so-called police power (regulatory authority to protect the public's health, safety, and welfare), or they were considered to involve "purely internal" commerce. Webster suggested that Congress had exclusive power over "the higher branches of commercial regulation."[12] In essence, the issue turned on the character attributed to the state law in question. Was the regulation commercial or police? Did it involve the higher branches of commerce, or was it a purely internal matter? The grounds for making these distinctions were not particularly well defined, and in the case of the police power, this mode of thinking created new difficulties for those who favored exclusive power. With the state's police power in question, the decisive point rested on what motivated the state legislature, whether the state law was designed to regulate commerce or to accomplish other purposes (health, safety, welfare). Such an open-ended inquiry could be used to promote states' rights as well as federal power. Indeed, during the Court's first term under Chief Justice Roger B. Taney, a determined opponent of the exclusive power doctrine, it endorsed an inflated conception of the states' police powers as "complete, unqualified, and exclusive."[13]

Until *Cooley* was decided fifteen years later, the justices debated the question of exclusive and concurrent power without reaching consensus. To observers it must have seemed as if every conceivable view gained an adherent on the bench. Story (and Webster too) engaged in a futile effort to portray *Gibbons* as having already decided this question in favor of exclusive power.[14] One justice used police power doctrine to circumscribe federal commerce power; another found a way to embrace broad state police powers while preserving exclusive national authority.

A justice from Georgia supported the exclusive power doctrine but asserted limits to national power whenever the interests of slave states were implicated; another southern justice with similar concerns remained unalterably opposed to the doctrine of exclusive power.[15]

The last was Chief Justice Taney, who issued perhaps the most forceful argument against exclusive power in a separate opinion in the *License Cases* (1847), in which the Court upheld various state laws regulating the sale of liquor. According to Taney the theory of exclusive power was derived from a wrongheaded construction of the commerce clause, an interpretive gloss put upon a "mere grant of power." He explained that the framers had anticipated that Congress would be occupied by "great concerns" while the states handled the "multitude" of minor commercial regulations that would be necessary. Taney skillfully showed that the doctrine of exclusive power was imprecise; for example, in the classification scheme—internal commerce and police—used to mark the boundaries of permissible state regulations. Specifically pointing to state pilot laws, Taney argued that it was not credible to separate pilotage from interstate and foreign commerce, yet these state regulations were acknowledged to be legitimate. It "will be difficult to show how this can be done," Taney asserted, "except upon the construction of the constitution which I am now maintaining." The chief justice also cited state health laws (recognized as valid police measures) that subjected shipments to inspection and placed goods in quarantine. These laws were also constitutional even though they were "unquestionably" commercial regulations that interfered with shipping and navigation, Taney said.[16]

In a significant passage Chief Justice Taney offered his version of state police powers. These were "the powers of government inherent in every sovereignty," he said, "the power to govern men and things within the limits of its dominion." In his view commercial regulations were as much a part of police powers as health laws. He was unwilling to have the constitutionality of this legislation depend upon a judicial inquiry into motive. What motivated the state legislature was irrelevant, according to Taney. "It is a question of power," he said in a simple statement which signaled what was at stake, and state power over interstate commerce was limited only when state laws conflicted with an act of Congress.[17] The chief justice was unable to get a majority to support his position, however.

All of this—the attention given to defining whether a state law was commercial or police, purely internal or among the higher branches—may look like a parlor game. Indeed, in 1841 Taney said that he regarded dormant commerce power as "an abstract question which the Court may never be called on to decide."[18] His suggestion appeared to have been offered more to influence his colleagues to leave the issue alone, thus leaving state laws in place, rather than to describe future events. It is clear that the participants in this debate, including Taney, regarded the issue of exclusive versus concurrent power as significant, particularly because of its connection with slavery.

That slavery was the subtext of the constitutional debate over commerce powers was indicated as early as *Gibbons v. Ogden*. Marshall there discussed state laws that prohibited the importation of slaves, as did the lawyers in their arguments.[19] The Taney Court was presented with the question of whether Congress had exclusive power over the interstate slave trade in *Groves v. Slaughter* (1841). This case concerned a provision of the Mississippi state constitution which banned the importation of slaves for sale in order to maintain the value of slaves held in the state. Writing for the Court, Justice Smith Thompson conveniently circumvented the issue of exclusive power (as implementing legislation was not in place during the time in question), but not without Justice John McLean venting antislavery views. He suggested that under the Constitution slaves were persons. This provoked a response from Taney "on account of the interest which a large portion of the Union feel in this matter." The chief justice insisted that the states had exclusive power over slavery, which "cannot be controlled by Congress, either by virtue of its power to regulate commerce, or by virtue of any other power conferred by the Constitution."[20]

Although the interstate slave trade was an obvious connection between commerce and slavery, southerners' concerns over the powers to regulate commerce were fueled by another seemingly tangential issue. Several slave states passed legislation that barred nonresident free blacks from entering. These laws, growing out of fears that free blacks threatened order in slave society, were an important part of the regulatory system of control in the South. Among the most controversial statutes of this kind were those enacted by southern coastal states which required that free black sailors be quarantined or jailed while their ships were in port. South Carolina's first law on this subject was especially harsh, putting free black seamen at risk to be sold as slaves if their jail costs were unpaid (this was later changed).[21]

From the time these seamen acts were passed in the 1820s, black sailors had powerful interests on their side contesting them. The British government took diplomatic and legal action, and Boston shipping concerns were behind appeals to Congress to intervene. The laws remained in effect, however. In 1823 Justice Johnson issued a circuit opinion in which he invoked the exclusive power doctrine to declare

South Carolina's law unconstitutional. The state ignored his decision, and the U.S. Supreme Court never reviewed the legislation. Chief Justice Marshall avoided the constitutional question when it was presented to him on circuit, as he was "not fond of butting against a wall in sport."[22]

The constitutionality of laws regulating the movement of free black persons was put into question, indirectly but unmistakably, in commerce cases involving the efforts of northern states to regulate immigration from Europe. In the *Passenger Cases* (1849), a bare majority of five justices invalidated laws adopted by Massachusetts and New York that assessed taxes against immigrants arriving by ship. Its potential significance in declaring a state law unconstitutional was diminished as the majority was unable to produce an agreed-upon rationale. All nine justices submitted opinions in this case. The state of the law was left in such confusion that the court reporter declined to provide his customary summary of the Court's opinion as there was, in his words, "no opinion of the court, as a court."[23]

One point was clear, however. Southerners perceived a serious threat to their section's interests. In his opinion Taney warned of "the most painful consequences" if the justices deprived states of the power to control the movement of free blacks. A Charleston newspaper reported that the Court swept away "all our laws made to prevent free colored persons—'citizens of Massachusetts,' or whatever abolition region—from entering our ports and cities. Thus it seems as if the Union is to be so administered as to strip the South of all power of self-protection." The same year the Court decided the *Passenger Cases*, a lawyer named Joel Tiffany published *A Treatise on the Unconstitutionality of American Slavery*. Supporting the exclusive power doctrine, he argued that Congress's authority over interstate commerce could be used, with other national powers, to abolish slavery.[24]

II

Three years later the *Cooley* case raised the question of the constitutionality of state pilot laws. "I expect my opinion will excite surprise," Curtis wrote George Ticknor on the eve of handing down the decision, "because it is adverse to the exclusive authority of Congress." The new justice noted that the Court had long struggled with this "much vexed" question of exclusive versus concurrent power. With some sense of accomplishment, he pointed out that he was able to garner a majority "on grounds perfectly satisfactory to myself."[25]

In sustaining Pennsylvania's law, Justice Curtis reconceptualized the problem at hand. Instead of arguing over power in the abstract (whether the commerce power was exclusive or concurrent), Curtis proposed looking at the "subjects" of that power, pilotage, for example. He observed that the power to regulate commerce "embraces a vast field" of "exceedingly various subjects, quite unlike in their nature." Justice Curtis divided these into two categories. In one he placed subjects "in their nature national," which he defined as those calling for a uniform system of regulation. The other category consisted of local subjects suited to diverse systems of regulation. Allocating authority between Congress and the states followed this classification. If the subject under review was national, then Congress's power was exclusive, and the Court was empowered to strike down state laws. On the other hand, if the subject was local, states were free to regulate until preempted by Congress. This formula became known as the doctrine of selective exclusiveness. Applying this new rule, Curtis found pilotage to be a local subject. Given "local peculiarities of the ports," he thought the states were best situated to regulate how pilots guided ships into harbor.[26]

Characterizing *Cooley* as a compromise has been a prevalent theme in commentary. It has been said, for example, that Curtis provided "the neutral ground for a compromise" as "neither localist nor nationalist could claim that the Court had wholly yielded to the other."[27] There is some truth to this. After all the doctrinal infighting, the *Cooley* formula was a hybrid of constitutional positions that had been considered incompatible. Curtis remained sensitive to the position of the states in the federal system, and he considered his opinion "adverse" to the exclusive power doctrine. The reaction of Curtis's colleagues seems to confirm that *Cooley* staked out the middle ground between extremes. His opinion drew fire from John McLean of Ohio and James Moore Wayne of Georgia, who dissented in favor of the exclusive power doctrine; Curtis called them "the most high-toned Federalists on the bench."[28] Peter V. Daniel, an uncompromising supporter of states' rights hailing from Virginia, concurred in the result but dissented from Curtis's reasoning. The four justices who signed onto Curtis's opinion reflected the regional diversity one would expect of a compromise solution: Robert Cooper Grier of Pennsylvania, John Catron of Tennessee, Samuel Nelson of New York, and Taney of Maryland.[29]

In a larger sense, though, Curtis's opinion was not a genuine compromise, especially if that is meant to imply neutrality between national power and states' rights. *Cooley* reflected Curtis's Whig nationalism, even though he projected his views with some subtlety. There was a difference between having the look of neutrality and what Curtis actually did, or more to the point, what he appears to have contemplated in this time of rising sectional tensions. By a politically astute orchestration of constitutional themes, Justice Curtis affirmed a role for the states without conceding national interests. The net effect was to enhance federal judicial power in a way that had eluded Story, Webster, and Marshall.

The nationalism of *Cooley* is evident, to begin with, when set against the competing views of federalism that predominated in the antebellum period. Two basic positions took root on the Supreme Court. One, exemplified by Chief Justice Taney's jurisprudence, supported states' rights, a position which scholars have since labeled dual federalism. The essential elements of this view were that the Constitution was a compact of the states; the nation and the states were equal sovereigns operating in mutually exclusive spheres with no overlapping powers; the existence of the states was by itself taken to limit national authority; the federal government's powers were strictly construed; and the Supreme Court's role was like that of an umpire keeping the national government and the states within proper bounds. In practice, dual federalism worked in favor of slavery.

The other doctrine, sometimes called constitutional nationalism, is often associated with Marshall, Webster, and Story. Like dual federalists, these jurists expressed concern about powers of the nation and states overlapping. Their motivation was different, though, stemming from a desire to block state encroachments on national interests. Constitutional nationalists conceived of the Constitution as a compact of the people rather than of the states. They favored a broad construction of the powers of the national government. Operating from these premises, the Marshall Court acted more like an agent of the national government than an umpire standing aloof.[30]

Dual federalism had been in ascendancy on the Supreme Court after Taney replaced Marshall in 1836. Outside the Court, there was another view of the federal system even more ominous for the prospects of national union, sometimes called the doctrine of state sovereignty. John C. Calhoun was one of its leading proponents. Like dual federalists, state sovereignty advocates considered the Constitution a compact among the states and strictly construed national powers. Calhoun and his followers went further: the federal government was the subordinate agent of the states, which had the authority to nullify federal laws, and the Supreme Court's judgments were not binding on the states. Not surprisingly, state sovereignty doctrine was not readily apparent in the justices' discourse. It never left antebellum political debates, though, as it ultimately furnished the grounds for secession.

Against that background, any ruling that concentrated power in the Supreme Court to declare state laws unconstitutional, as *Cooley* did, was not an even exchange between nationalism and states' rights. Expanding federal judicial power was *Cooley*'s outstanding feature. After years without definitive resolution, Justice Curtis put the Court in the position to be a nationalizing force based on the idea that the commerce clause by itself authorized the federal courts to strike down state actions. This was doubly significant in the antebellum period when Congress was not actively engaged in regulating the economy.

While *Cooley* did not hold that Congress had exclusive power over interstate commerce, Justice Curtis insulated national interests from state encroachments just as much as Marshall, Story, and Webster had hoped to do. Having a uniform system of regulation was at the heart of the concerns of exclusive power enthusiasts, a point that could be seen from the first commerce clause cases. Indeed, uniformity was a fundamental Whig and Federalist theme with roots stretching back to 1787, expressed by those like Alexander Hamilton, Marshall, and Webster who were most interested in forging a national market economy. Curtis's opinion was responsive to those concerns. He recognized that "one main object of the Constitution" was "to create a national control" over interstate and foreign commerce.[31] To that end the justice held that Congress had exclusive power whenever a "uniform system of regulation" was needed.

Moreover, the results portended by Curtis's opinion were no more tilted to the states than those sought by the leading advocates of exclusive power, and Curtis actually did a better job of preserving federal authority. Webster, Story, and Marshall believed that state pilot legislation was constitutional. They acceded to numerous state laws involving ferries, roads, turnpikes, health, inspection, and quarantine. Story and Marshall looked upon these state laws as regulations of police or internal commerce. Webster had floated the idea that even though these state laws affected interstate commerce, they should not be construed as commercial regulations under the meaning of the commerce clause; a "reasonable construction" of commerce was "necessary to the just power of the States, as to the authority of Congress."[32]

The vagueness surrounding these explanations was a looming problem. What they lacked was a unifying theory to account satisfactorily for results like the state pilot laws. No doubt there were ways to finesse the issue. Webster, for example, suggested that Congress had regulatory power over roads when they became matters of "great commercial concern." In his view the pilot laws were simply not commercial regulations. Marshall offered an alternative justification. The reason the state pilot laws were valid, Marshall said in *Gibbons*, was due to their geographic scope. Operating only "within the limits of some particular state," they were lawful regulations of police or internal commerce.[33]

Such explanations may have sufficed while Marshall was chief justice. Yet by failing to clarify how certain things like pilotage were subject to Congress's commerce power, exclusive power advocates left it open for dual federalists (with their view of mutually exclusive spheres) to deny Congress any power in those areas. In the *Passenger Cases*, for example, Taney not only justified power in the states to block immigrants from entering, he denied that Congress had any power over this. The states have this "exclusive right," he said, "free from the control of the general government." Logic of this kind was not easily cabined, as illustrated by Justice Daniel's separate opinion in *Cooley*. Applying a restrictive definition of commerce, he concluded that pilotage did not belong "essentially and regularly" within the power granted Congress under the commerce clause.[34]

In *Cooley*, Justice Curtis rebuffed Daniel's claim and any possible reading that pilotage was beyond Congress's reach. As if Curtis was frustrated with the untidiness left by his predecessors, his discussion took on an air of inevitability. There was no question in his mind that these were commercial regulations within the scope of the commerce clause, and he emphasized that this represented the view of a majority of the justices. Curtis's reasoning can be reduced to a straightforward syllogism. His major premise was that the power to regulate interstate and foreign commerce included the regulation of navigation. Curtis treated this point as "settled." The minor premise was that laws governing pilotage were regulations of navigation. This regulatory power extended to persons as well as the instruments of navigation, explained Curtis, citing federal legislation that covered officers and seamen.[35]

Justice Curtis also noted the potential "danger" that state pilot laws posed to the nation's commerce, with conflicting laws between neighboring states. This was not just a matter for speculation, Curtis emphasized. He pointed out that fifteen years before *Cooley*, Congress had been compelled to enact legislation to override state laws that had blocked the use of pilots licensed in other states. Pilotage was a subject which Curtis thought touched directly on "that equality of commercial rights, and that freedom from State interference, which those who formed the Constitution were so anxious to secure, and which the experience of more than half a century has taught us to value so highly."[36]

Curtis also validated a role for the states in regulating interstate commerce, as he recognized their authority over local subjects. This was an important new development, but it does not mean that Curtis was less nationalistic than those who had promoted the exclusive power doctrine. The key to reading *Cooley* on this point is to identify what the justice saw as the national interest at stake and how he sought to protect it. In essence, by reserving to Congress exclusive power over national subjects demanding uniform systems of regulation, Curtis found a way to permit the states to regulate interstate commerce without undermining national power.

Beyond that, Justice Curtis appears to have contemplated that state powers would be drawn into the service of the nation as a whole in developing a continental market, as his discussion of the state pilot laws suggests. Curtis's implicit assumption was that the free flow of interstate commerce depended upon a reliable transportation system. Safety was a central concern. Pilots, Curtis made clear, were necessary to ensure the safe transit of goods and people. Given temporary command of ships near port, pilots held a "most important and responsible place" in navigation, "charged with the safety of the vessel and cargo, and of the lives of those on board." The pilot laws, in turn, rested "upon the propriety of securing lives and property exposed to the perils of a dangerous navigation." Curtis was convinced that the states were better equipped then Congress to handle the finer points of pilot regulation. The reason can be found in the local character of the subject, a concept Curtis emphasized by repetition: the "local necessities of navigation," the "local peculiarities of the ports," "local knowledge and experience." [37]

In short, to acknowledge the states' responsibilities in matters of local competence was not by itself inconsistent with the primacy of national union. As Congress was not nearly so active as it would later become, there would have been a regulatory vacuum if states were barred from legislating in the area of interstate commerce. The absence of necessary regulation, Curtis's discussion suggests, would have hampered the nation's economic development.

The wonder is that Justice Curtis got a majority of the Court as it was then constituted to join an opinion whose salient points were that some part of the regulation of interstate commerce was an exclusive federal domain and that the Supreme Court had the power to nullify state laws in this area. It is reasonable to infer that Curtis recognized the difficulty in getting the Court to issue an authoritative ruling on his terms, given his colleagues' earlier statements. He understood that he needed the support of justices who had previously expressed views contrary to his own. The final vote was closer than it may at first appear. Of the eight justices participating, Wayne and McLean dissented and Daniel rejected Curtis's reasoning. That left only four others who joined Justice Curtis's opinion. They included Taney, whose support of the concurrent power doctrine was clear, as well as Grier, who had previously "leaned to" the exclusive power doctrine.[38] Each of the four votes was critical to Curtis. One more defection would have sapped his opinion of its authority, as he would not then have had a majority behind his reasoning.

The *Cooley* opinion bears the mark of judicial craftsmanship and diplomacy, prompting Catron to describe Curtis as a "first rate lawyer—exceedingly fair-minded." He "writes smoother than any man on the Bench," Catron said. In his discussion Curtis emphasized that the opinion was "confined" to the "precise questions before us" concerning pilotage. The justice avoided identifying any other subject as either national or local. Here was a new approach to a long-standing problem, yet the printed opinion totaled only ten pages.[39]

It looks like Curtis was purposefully concise, leaving unstated anything that would break up his majority. Judging from the compressed rendition of ideas from a wide range of authorities, he came to this case with a well-formed position on this constitutional problem. The justice appears to have been well versed in the intricacies of exclusive and concurrent power before his appointment (not surprising, given the importance attached to this issue). It is tempting to speculate that Curtis saw the *Cooley* case as an opportunity—and it was not clear when another would come along—in which he could in accordance with his own views uphold a state law regulating interstate commerce, gain support from the other justices on that basis, and put in place a nationalistic framework to guide future decisions.

The intriguing question is how Justice Curtis thought the *Cooley* doctrine should apply to issues relating to slavery, particularly powers assumed by slave states to control the movement of nonresident free blacks. Curtis never addressed this issue on the bench. Interestingly, though, as a private attorney in 1843, he signed a petition with other Bostonians requesting Congress to override the seamen acts of southern coastal states.[40]

III

In the course of justifying *Cooley*'s result, Curtis introduced a new way of thinking about the power to regulate interstate commerce. The significance of his approach went beyond the dormant commerce clause, as it marked one step in a series of advances in the conceptualization of federalism.

Before *Cooley*, the debate over that constitutional provision was conducted on an abstract plane focusing on sovereign power. Justice Curtis was engaged in a deliberate and undisguised effort to reorient the way in which the justices thought about this. "The diversities of opinion" on this issue, he said, arose "from the different views taken of the nature of this power." Was Congress's authority to regulate interstate and foreign commerce "absolutely and totally repugnant" or "compatible" with "the existence of similar power in the States"? That was the form of the question driving the debate, in Curtis's view, but he believed it was impossible to answer precisely because it compelled the justices to take an all-or-nothing position on problems that were more nuanced than that. "Either absolutely to affirm, or deny that the nature of this power requires exclusive legislation by Congress, is to lose sight of the nature of the subjects of this power, and to assert concerning all of them, what is really applicable but to a part." The justice redefined the issue. As the subjects in this "vast field" were "exceedingly various" and "quite unlike in their nature," he proposed moving the discussion beyond the nature of the commerce power to the "subjects" of that power.[41]

The logic is straightforward enough; Curtis's basic point may seem obvious in retrospect. Yet the whole opinion rested on the assumption that the power to regulate interstate commerce was divisible, a view that earlier jurists had resisted.

Those favoring the exclusive power doctrine were emphatic on this point. "Full power" to regulate interstate and foreign commerce, Justice Story said, "implies the whole power, and leaves no residuum; and a grant of the whole to one, is incompatible with a grant to another of a part." In *Gibbons*, Marshall explained that states cannot regulate interstate commerce because they would then be "exercising the very power that is granted to Congress." The operative concern was for avoiding points of conflict in a federal system in which "contests respecting power must arise," as Marshall put it. In an illuminating passage in *Gibbons*, the chief justice conceded that the states might adopt the "same measures" as Congress had, but he insisted that the source of power be kept distinct. The state, he said, "does not derive its authority from the particular power which has been granted" Congress but "from some other, which remains with the State."[42]

Concurrent power advocates did not share these concerns about the national government's authority, but they showed themselves to be of the same mind-set. While the concurrent power doctrine allowed the states to regulate interstate commerce until Congress enacted contrary legislation, its supporters did not perceive the commerce power to be divisible as Curtis did: partly exclusive and partly concurrent. Indeed, several justices on the Taney Court indicated that what they favored was actually not concurrent power at all but rather exclusive power in the states. The Taney Court's opening salvo in *New York v. Miln* (1837) heralded this view, when Justice Philip P. Barbour slipped in a statement that the states' police powers were "unqualified" and "exclusive." Chief Justice Taney's language in the *Passenger Cases* is revealing. Denying Congress any power to determine who should be allowed to reside in a state, Taney said that the "sovereignty which possesses the right must in its exercise be altogether independent of the other." Otherwise, there "would be a direct conflict of powers repugnant to each other, continually thwarting and defeating its exercise by either." [43]

In short, constitutional thinkers in the early nineteenth century tended to see "particular powers as unbreakable integers, like atoms," as Archibald Cox suggested in an arresting image.[44] This way of thinking— with its focus on abstractions over sovereignty, the skittishness about dividing power between Congress and the states; indeed, the inability to conceive of the possibility of doing that with interstate commerce— looks like the outgrowth of an older pattern of thought. For some time a cardinal assumption in Anglo-American political thought was that it was impossible to divide supreme political authority. This view persisted in America in spite of innovative thinking about federalism. In the 1760s some Americans ventured new ideas about dividing power between Parliament, in control of external matters like overseas trade and defense, and the colonial governments, responsible for internal affairs. The English countered with the conventional conception of indivisible sovereignty, and it was a common refrain on both sides of the Atlantic that two supreme powers in one state was a "political monster of an *imperium in imperio.*"[45] Even with the creation of a federal system of government under the Constitution, the power of this old assumption was still evident. The Anti-Federalists criticized the proposed Constitution for attempting to divide sovereignty. Rather than confute the assumption, the Federalists came up with an elegant theoretical solution. Sovereign authority was located in the people who delegated powers to the states and the national government.[46]

As for the practical side of dividing power in the federal system, the Federalists refrained from specifics in the drive to ratify the Constitution. Stating that the federal and state governments were "constituted with different powers and designed for different purposes," Madison seemed impressed by both the novelty of the federal arrangement and the problems it presented. He noted the pervasive difficulty the framers encountered "in delineating the boundary between the Federal and State jurisdictions." With the expectation of ongoing "controversies relating to the boundary between the two jurisdictions," Madison's basic suggestion was that the ultimate authority to resolve federal-state conflict should belong to some tribunal of the national government.[47]

In this context Curtis formulated the *Cooley* doctrine. Commentators have taken different views on whether his approach was original. Some have concluded that Curtis reiterated views expressed by Webster in *Gibbons* and Justice Woodbury later: that *Cooley* was the "exact doctrine" Webster had proposed; that Webster "first suggested the *Cooley* formula of partially concurrent power"; that Curtis had "no strikingly original ideas on the problem" and "drew liberally" from Woodbury as well as Webster; that the *Cooley* doctrine "was really the adoption of a rule first stated" by Woodbury. On the other hand, Archibald Cox thought the opinion represented "a major shift in style of legal analysis," and David P. Currie has described Curtis's reasoning as a "bolt out of the blue."[48]

The closest Webster came to *Cooley* was his explanation of the "true method of construction." He suggested that the Court consider "what parts" the grant of power to regulate commerce "is composed, and which of those, from the nature of the thing, ought to be considered exclusive." A "portion of the commercial power" was in his view "exclusive in Congress." The way Webster built on this idea, however, makes it clear that his conception of the commerce power was fundamentally different from that suggested by Curtis. While the justice explicitly divided the power to regulate interstate commerce between Congress and the states, Webster suggested that commerce must be given a "reasonable construction" and that what was left for the states to regulate should not be construed as "commerce, in the constitutional understanding of that term." He specifically stated that state pilot laws, along with health and quarantine laws, were not "to be called commercial regulations." Such state laws he considered either "internal legislation" or police regulations. These semantic differences were crucial for Webster. Allowing the states and Congress jointly to regulate interstate commerce would lead to "perpetual hostility," with "one sovereign power giving the rule, till another sovereign power should abrogate it."[49] In the final analysis, Webster was unable to conceive of dividing the power to regulate commerce as Curtis was.

As for Justice Woodbury, he did suggest in the *Passenger Cases* that "local matters" were the concern of the states and that so "far as reasons exist to make the exercise of the commercial power exclusive, as on matters of exterior, general, and uniform cognizance, the construction may be proper to render it exclusive, but no further, as the exclusiveness depends in this case wholly on the reasons, and not on any express prohibition, and hence cannot extend beyond the reasons themselves." Yet the most that can be said of Woodbury is that he stumbled onto the ideas Curtis developed without grasping their significance. To begin with, Woodbury specifically denied the main point that came out of *Cooley*. Woodbury said in a circuit opinion that "a mere naked power, unexercised and dormant in the general government, with no prohibition, express or implied, to the states, to act on the same matter, could not make the state legislation upon it nugatory or unconstitutional." Moreover, Woodbury did not really view the power to regulate interstate commerce as divisible. He suggested, like Webster, that laws for local purposes were simply not to be "considered, as laws 'to regulate commerce.'" Beyond that, Woodbury held a sharply limited view of the scope of Congress's authority. He thought, for example, that the state liquor laws presented in the *License Cases* did not concern interstate or foreign commerce because they did "not operate" until the goods had "entered the State and become component parts of its property." According to Woodbury, this was "internal commerce" which the state had "the exclusive power to regulate." Congress "can no more interfere in it than the States can interfere in the regulation of foreign commerce," Woodbury said.[50]

In short, while Webster and Woodbury made statements that may appear like *Cooley*, a close examination of their actions confirms that Curtis had indeed changed the equation. No doubt Justice Curtis had read their arguments. As he shared Webster's basic position that Congress had exclusive power when uniform regulation was required, it is not surprising to find similarities in their discussions. The underlying mind-set was different, however. It was something else to see, as Curtis did, that a power like that of regulating interstate commerce could be broken down into different parts.

As uneventful as this perception may appear, it represented an important development in nineteenth-century constitutional thought. With *Gibbons v. Ogden* the debate over the power of the states to regulate interstate and foreign commerce became a principal arena for working out the operation of the federal system. It seems too much to say that in this area *Cooley* represented an intellectual revolution, even such a revolution in miniature. The major innovations occurred earlier, at the Constitutional Convention and before that, with the American colonists in the 1760s. Yet by switching the focus from sovereign power to the subjects of power, like pilotage, Curtis brought practical considerations into the interpretation of the commerce clause. His frank acknowledgment that states regulated interstate commerce was refreshing. Curtis appreciated the superior capacity of state governments to understand local problems and address them in ways that the national government could not easily do. At the same time, the justice recognized that in some areas of regulation, state legislatures would lose sight of the national interest in a continental marketplace. Curtis put the Court in position to reserve these subjects for Congress to regulate. The master stroke behind *Cooley* lay in seeing the potential solution within the problem itself. Justice Curtis accepted federal-state tensions for what they did as he moved the debate beyond doctrinaire assertions about sovereignty.

IV

Underlying Justice Curtis's opinion—in some sense the key to his analysis—was his understanding of the role he thought the Supreme Court could play in resolving federal-state conflicts. That the Court had authority to invalidate some state laws under *Cooley* was clear. Curtis also suggested that the dormant commerce clause invested the Court with the power of judicial review over Congress as well. Once the justices declared a subject of interstate commerce "national," that was a constitutional determination Congress could not reverse. Congress could always step in to regulate subjects the Court deemed local under *Cooley*, but the justices had the final say to determine what subjects required uniform regulation, thus withdrawing them from the states' purview.[51]

This crucial point was contrary to the position Curtis's successors adopted. Unfortunately, Justice Curtis was not perfectly clear on this, perhaps because he had not made up his own mind. Most commentators have understood Curtis to mean that the Court had final authority over Congress.[52]

The issue arose as he discussed the relationship between a federal statute from 1789 and Pennsylvania's pilot law, passed fourteen years later. The act of Congress provided that pilots "shall continue to be regulated in conformity with the existing laws of the States" or "with such laws as the States may respectively hereafter enact for the purpose, until further legislative provision shall be made by Congress." Curtis thought that the Court "might" decide that Congress had adopted preexisting state laws, in effect giving them "the force" of federal legislation.[53]

The congressional declaration concerning state laws "hereafter" enacted called for a different analysis, in Curtis's view. "If the States were divested of the power to legislate on this subject by the grant of the commercial power to Congress, it is plain this act could not confer upon them power thus to legislate." Curtis restated the principle. "If Congress were now to pass a law adopting the existing State laws, if enacted without authority, and in violation of the Constitution, it would seem to us to be a new and questionable mode of legislation." Instead of ruling the 1789 act "inoperative" on this score, however, Curtis read the congressional statement as "an appropriate and important signification" of Congress's understanding that pilotage did not require uniform regulation.[54]

It is not clear how far Justice Curtis would have carried the idea of judicial supremacy implicit in these remarks. The logic of his sentences obscures their meaning. He repeatedly used if-then conditional statements with false antecedent clauses (he did not believe the states were divested of that power). A subsequent circuit opinion concerning legislation on debtors suggests Curtis's ambivalence. Citing *Cooley*, the justice reasserted that Congress could not delegate "its own legislative power" to the states; he also had "very serious doubts" whether national lawmakers could "adopt, prospectively, state legislation on any given subject." Yet he was inclined to uphold such a delegation of power if "positively required" by the statutory language and legislative intent.[55]

Curtis did not articulate exactly why he thought the Supreme Court could review federal legislation under the commerce clause. One point is clear, though. His position is not consistent with the view of the dormant commerce clause that came to predominate in the twentieth century. For some time the Court has regarded Congress as the ultimate authority in this field. The justices today do not declare acts of Congress unconstitutional based upon the dormant commerce clause. Congress can consent to state regulations of interstate commerce, even those invalidated by the Court.[56]

The reigning explanation today is that the Supreme Court has a role in this area when it supplements the political process without displacing it, on the assumption that legitimate out-of-state interests (including those of the whole nation) may be unrepresented in state legislatures and that it is too much to expect Congress by itself to oversee state actions affecting interstate commerce. The Court, then, is never justified in overriding congressional consent to these state laws. If the problem revolves around inadequate representation of national interests within the states, that is presumably solved when Congress addresses the issue. If the concern is that Congress may fail to detect state actions against the national market, there is no reason to block Congress from affirmatively allowing the states to regulate on some particular issue. Under the operative theory of the dormant commerce clause, the national legislature is not subordinate to the Court; indeed, it operates as a political check on the justices.[57]

Part of this theory was embedded in Curtis's analysis, as he acknowledged that state lawmakers promoted the commercial interests of their own states.[58] Yet he was unwilling to rely solely on Congress to protect national interests. What, then, was Curtis's theory of the Supreme Court's role? It seems as if he had no well-defined theory as such. Instead, his position derived from a collection of ideas he held about the Court, the judicial process, and economic regulation.

To begin with, Curtis came to the bench with a deep faith in the Court as an institution. This is illustrated by an effusive passage in his 1843 article on state debts, revealing not only for what Curtis said but also how he said it. Stretching to find a way to get disputes between foreign creditors and the states before the Supreme Court, Curtis described that body as "a tribunal known to the world as elevated far above all State biases and prejudices; whose members . . . listen to sovereign States, as they contest their claims to territory and jurisdiction; a tribunal which sits in judgment on the acts of the legislature of the nation, and decrees them to be valid or void; a tribunal which is our own ark of safety."[59]

One reason Justice Curtis perceived the Court in these terms was his conception of the decision-making process employed there, grounded, as he saw it, in common-law methods of reasoning. The judicial inquiry he proposed under the dormant commerce clause was in the classic common-law style. To be sure, Curtis stated the general principle without waiting for it to emerge from a series of cases; he set up the categories of national and local subjects. At the same time, the justice explicitly left for the future the question of what besides pilotage was national or local. This was to be decided case by case based upon pragmatic considerations presented by litigants in actual controversies. It was this practical spirit, evident throughout the *Cooley* opinion, that reflected the common-law mode of thought most of all. Look at the "nature of the subject on which that power was intended practically to operate"; that was Curtis's basic directive.[60]

Cooley was also a product of Curtis's understanding of the Court's role in forging an economic union. He believed that the federal system presented inherent obstacles to such a union, which depended in his view upon a uniform and stable body of law governing commercial activities. The corrective was to be found in the national judiciary, especially when Congress was inactive. This was standard Whig doctrine, and in several cases that had economic implications without calling for an interpretation of the commerce clause, Curtis carved out space for the federal courts to develop a coherent system of laws governing the nation's business.[61]

Following Justice Story's lead, Curtis used two methods to accomplish this. One was to enlarge the scope of jurisdiction over parties like corporations. The other was more subtle. It involved broadening the range of sources of law that federal courts could use to determine the applicable legal principles. The outstanding example of this strategy was Story's opinion in *Swift v. Tyson* (1842). This ruling enabled the federal courts to determine the principles of commercial law in cases between citizens of different states without being bound by the patchwork of state judicial decisions. (Over time, it became apparent that *Swift* let litigants shop for the state or federal forum that best served their interests, and the Court overruled *Swift* in *Erie Railroad Co. v. Tompkins* [1938]). Curtis endorsed *Swift* without reservation. Building on Story's doctrine, Justice Curtis made it clear that in cases of equity, which included claims for business fraud not covered by *Swift*, the federal judiciary was not bound to follow conflicting state rules.[62]

One area in which Curtis engaged in an ongoing effort to enhance federal judicial power over the nation's commerce was in the field of admiralty law. The Constitution is straightforward in extending federal power to "all Cases of admiralty and maritime jurisdiction."[63] Yet much remained open to interpretation. Did this authority extend to inland waterways? What were the appropriate sources of law?

In the 1850s, when steamboats were driving economic development in the heart of the country, Curtis applied the tort law of negligence to a steamboat accident in *Steamboat New World v. King* (1854). His opinion was one of a series of decisions extending admiralty jurisdiction inland. Curtis drew a predictable dissent from Justice Daniel, who considered the result a "mischievous interference" with the "internal and police powers of every community." This pattern was repeated in other admiralty cases, as a Curtis majority opinion provoked a sharp dissent from a southern colleague. In one case Curtis looked to the maritime code of prerevolutionary France to determine the governing rules. Justice John A. Campbell of Alabama complained that Curtis had introduced "a new principle into the American commercial system" that "adds to the jurisdiction of the Judiciary Department." In another case Curtis explicitly relied on the "ancient and general maritime law of the commercial world." This prompted Chief Justice Taney, considering the matter of "the highest importance," to take the unusual step of presenting his dissenting views from the bench for an hour.[64]

Expanding the Court's powers over commerce, as Curtis sought to do, was not without risk. *Cooley*, in particular, may appear to invite federal courts to engage in the sort of policy making best left to elected representatives, whether in Congress or the state legislatures. Justice Curtis arguably heightened the problem of judicial subjectivity by framing the issue at such a general level concerning the subjects of regulation. He offered minimal guidance on how judges were supposed to classify subjects as national or local. Prominent justices have not shared Curtis's confidence in the federal judiciary's capacity to oversee the regulation of interstate commerce. Nearly a century after *Cooley*, Justice Hugo L. Black suggested that "spasmodic and unrelated instances of litigation cannot afford an adequate basis for the creation of integrated national rules which alone can afford that full protection for interstate commerce intended by the Constitution."[65]

It appears that Justice Curtis was aware of the difficulties. While affirming the Court's power of judicial review in this area, he saw its authority tempered. There were the usual constraints associated with the common-law approach (one case at a time, adherence to precedent). In addition, Curtis applied a concept he called a "practical construction" of the Constitution, which served to circumscribe the judges' discretion. This meant that state and federal statutes reflected a legislative interpretation of the Constitution which judges were supposed to give substantial weight. Curtis did not invent this idea, but he used it on critical occasions: in the *Dred Scott* case and the Johnson impeachment trial, for example, where he cited *Cooley* as authority. In *Cooley*, Curtis noted the "practice of the States, and of the national government" under the federal statute of 1789 to reinforce his interpretation of the commerce clause.[66] One reason this interpretive device appealed to Curtis, it seems, was that it reflected his common-law ideology. Judges did not create legal rules in a vacuum, according to Curtis; they derived law from the customary practices of the people.

In any event, it is not clear that Curtis contemplated frequent use of judicial review under the dormant commerce clause. He recognized that the states had an important role in regulating commerce. Public safety in transportation was an ongoing concern of his. One year after *Cooley* he offered an unsolicited recommendation to Massachusetts governor John Henry Clifford, a close friend. "It has been my opinion for some time," Curtis wrote, that the state legislatures "have not done what they safely & usefully may to secure the public against such disasters, as have recently occurred on rail roads." Curtis argued for legislation extending criminal liability to "the highest officer" of railroad corporations.[67]

Moreover, Curtis never applied *Cooley* to invalidate a state law in his remaining years on the bench, despite some opportunities to do so. He voted with the majority to nullify a Virginia law chartering a bridge that obstructed steamboat traffic, but the Court's decision rested on public nuisance doctrine instead of the commerce clause.[68] Curtis signed onto an opinion written by Justice Daniel that upheld a Maine statute granting exclusive rights of steamboat navigation (in exchange for improvement of an impassable stretch of water). In *Smith v. Maryland* (1856), Justice Curtis backed off from using the commerce clause when the Maryland state legislature authorized the seizure of federally licensed boats that used prohibited devices to catch oysters.[69]

On the other hand, in a circuit opinion handed down the same year as *Cooley*, Curtis indicated that the regulation of liens on boats engaged in interstate commerce was "not a proper subject of state legislation." And when arguing before the Supreme Court in *Paul v. Virginia* (1869), Curtis embraced the view that a state law requiring out-of-state insurance companies to deposit bonds violated the commerce clause. He lost that case. The Court emphasized the "local transactions" of the insurance business. It was not until the mid-twentieth century that the justices reversed course, recognizing insurance as a "nationwide business" of "interstate character."[70]

Taken altogether, the role Justice Curtis envisioned for the Supreme Court on this important question of federalism was more involved than anything previously suggested. With *Cooley* in place, the Court was not there simply to determine whether state laws were regulations of interstate commerce, which was essentially the case with the exclusive power doctrine. Nor was the inquiry restricted to figuring out whether Congress preempted the state laws in question, as concurrent power advocates suggested. Curtis's doctrine of selective exclusiveness required a more discriminating approach. There was implicit in his opinion the sense that the states and Congress were engaged in a complex dance of power, that the Supreme Court should be a presence in that process, and that the justices must take a more discerning approach than they had exhibited to that point.

V

In holding that Congress had exclusive power over national subjects and that the Court was empowered to review state laws affecting interstate commerce, Justice Curtis confronted a fundamental question of constitutional interpretation. The Constitution has no express language mandating such a result. Curtis had touched upon one of the "great silences of the Constitution," to use the words of twentieth-century justice Robert H. Jackson. Curtis recognized the interpretive problem. As he noted, the "grant of commercial power to Congress does not contain any terms which expressly exclude the States from exercising an authority over its subject-matter."[71] To conclude that Congress had exclusive power to any extent would have to be justified, if at all, by implication.

How much latitude should the justices have to make judgments based upon their understanding of what the Constitution implies? This has been a perennial issue in American constitutional history, most recently involving the implied right of privacy. Whether the Constitution should be given a strict or a broad construction began with a feud within Washington's administration, as Hamilton and Jefferson argued over Congress's powers to charter a national bank. The scope of the national government's implied powers remained a central question throughout the nation's formative period. *Cooley* was part of this debate. The opinion was on all important points an exercise in implication, as Curtis concluded that Congress had exclusive power to some degree, that the states were denied power to some degree, and that the Supreme Court was charged with marking the line between.[72]

At the midpoint of the nineteenth century, the challenge to construing the commerce clause in this way had been laid down by Chief Justice Taney, and it appears that Curtis was mindful of his views. Arguing against the exclusive power doctrine in the *License Cases*, Taney said that the commerce clause operated as a "mere grant of power" to Congress. "The language," he noted, "certainly furnishes no warrant" to say Congress had exclusive power over interstate and foreign commerce. Nor did the Constitution explicitly preclude the states from regulating in that area. The case was different for other powers, Taney emphasized, citing several constitutional provisions that "in express terms" prohibited the states from exercising the same powers as Congress (for example, Article I says that "no State shall . . . coin Money").[73] From this, the chief justice reasoned that the Constitution's framers knew how to limit state powers when they wanted to do that. That they had not done so in the commerce clause was for Taney conclusive evidence of their understanding that the states were allowed to regulate in this area.

In the face of this, Justice Curtis portrayed the debate over commerce powers as having always involved, on both sides, an assessment of what was implied by the Constitution. He cleverly stitched together this passage, and it is difficult to believe that Taney completely agreed, even though the chief justice let it pass.

Justice Curtis's mode of interpretation can be traced to one of the essays Alexander Hamilton wrote in *The Federalist*. While explaining concurrent powers of taxation, Hamilton put forward a three-part test:

(1) whether the Constitution expressly stated that the power granted the federal government was exclusive, (2) whether the Constitution expressly prohibited the states from exercising the power in question, or (3) whether the power granted Congress was exclusive "by implication" because a similar power in the states was "absolutely and totally *contradictory* and *repugnant.*" This test was of course known to antebellum jurists. In *Gibbons v. Ogden,* Webster used a similar analysis, although he stated the third step differently, saying that some powers were exclusive in Congress by virtue of the "nature of the powers themselves." Marshall in a bankruptcy case likewise said that the nature of the power may deprive the states of authority, just as much as if this were expressly stated in the Constitution.[74]

In *Cooley,* Curtis suggested that the principle of interpretation was not in dispute; instead, the "diversities of opinion" on the commerce power grew out of "the different views taken of the nature of this power." The justice claimed that even concurrent power advocates assessed the nature of Congress's commerce power; only they concluded that it was "compatible" and not—bringing Hamilton's wording into play—"absolutely and totally repugnant" to the states having that authority. The picture that emerged from Curtis's opinion was that this wide-ranging interpretive exercise going beyond the express language of the Constitution was standard procedure. It started, according to Curtis, with "contemporary exposition of the Constitution" in *The Federalist* and continued with the judiciary's "most deliberate consideration"; here Curtis cited several Marshall Court opinions. The fact that all of these examples, like the power to tax, ended with a finding of concurrent powers was a possible problem with Curtis's argument. From his point of view, though, that was beside the point, as he was asserting that the absence of express language was not decisive, that such questions were open to judicial interpretation, and that the answer depended on construing the "nature of the power."[75]

Having trained the reader's sights on the nature of the power, Justice Curtis immediately altered the perspective. "When the nature of a power like this is spoken of," he said, "it must be intended to refer to the subjects of that power." This was the critical move in Curtis's analysis, dividing the subjects of the commerce power into two categories that he dubbed national and local. Interestingly, this binary classification has drawn objections in recent years, with Justice Antonin Scalia among the most prominent critics. In Scalia's view the *Cooley* formula has "no conceivable basis in the text of the Commerce Clause" because that constitutional provision by its terms treats its subject matter as "unitary."[76]

Why, then, did Curtis identify two categories of national and local subjects? On the face of it, *Cooley* rests on nothing more than the justice's assertion that some subjects require uniform regulation while others require diversity. Underlying this assertion was a more definite argument with unstated premises.

Curtis's national-local classification was based on an inference drawn from constitutional structure. By its nature such a structural method of reasoning goes beyond the language of the Constitution's text. It involves a more wide-ranging exercise in interpretation, with relationships (for example, between citizens and their elected representatives) deduced from basic structures that the Constitution put in place (like the federal system). Charles L. Black Jr., who was at the forefront among legal scholars analyzing this mode of interpretation, regarded the "economic structure of nationhood" as the most convincing justification for the dormant commerce clause. He attributed the Court's early difficulties to its undue focus on "textual construction and single-text implication." The doctrine, according to Black, did not make sense until the justices engaged in structural analysis. *Cooley*, he noted, "began to give this subject its modern shape."[77]

With that in mind, it is possible to reconstruct Curtis's thought process. By pitching the inquiry at the level of the subject of the commerce power, Curtis placed the emphasis on what type of regulatory system was needed, uniform or diverse. When he declared that some subjects "admit only of one uniform system," he had in effect grafted onto the commerce clause the Whig interest in uniformity, which the constitutional text makes explicit for other congressional powers. For example, Congress is authorized to establish "an uniform Rule of Naturalization" and "uniform Laws on the subject of Bankruptcies."[78] The question is why the uniformity principle was for Curtis implied in the commerce clause, where it was not expressly stated. His answer grew out of his understanding of the national market and the distinction between diverse and uniform regulation.

Despite its binary character, Curtis's analytic framework was really dedicated to one goal, to secure uniform systems of regulation when necessary. To be sure, Curtis understood the value of diverse regulatory systems. His discussion of pilotage attests to that. However, the unstated assumption in the opinion was that this interest in diversity can be left largely on its own, without the Court's intervention. *Cooley* allowed the states and Congress to work this out for themselves with the Court acquiescing in the result. The case was different for national subjects where "one uniform system" was needed. Curtis assumed, without saying so, that state legislatures left to their own devices had a natural tendency to produce different and conflicting rules. Hamilton made the same point graphically in *The Federalist* no. 32: "If each State had power to prescribe a DISTINCT RULE, there could not be a UNIFORM RULE." Thus there was a need to arrest any movement toward diverse regulation in those areas where uniformity was indispensable.[79]

The ruling in *Cooley* followed naturally for Curtis. To keep a uniform system of regulation intact, it was necessary in his view to operate wholesale and remove the entire area of regulation from the states. If subjects "imperatively" demanded "a single uniform rule" (Curtis's language), then Congress must have exclusive authority.[80] The critical developments in *Cooley*—that Congress has some exclusive power over interstate commerce and that the Court has a power of judicial review in this area—were a function of this perception.

While the *Cooley* opinion focused on the subjects of regulation, Curtis hinted that the national/local formula was the framework for decision making but not necessarily the end of the analysis. He indicated that state laws which discriminated against out-of-state interests might be held unconstitutional even if the subject was local. *Cooley* raised this question as the state pilot law did not require boats engaged in the Pennsylvania coal trade to hire local pilots. Justice Curtis was not bothered by this, but he did not relinquish the nondiscrimination principle. The statutory exemption reflected a "fair exercise of legislative discretion," Curtis said; the state lawmakers had reasonably concluded that these vessels did not need pilots. He considered this exception comparable to those granted smaller boats (because they were easy to maneuver) and those arriving from other ports on the Delaware River (whose captains were presumably familiar with navigating the port of Philadelphia).[81]

That Curtis contemplated more than simply classifying the subjects of regulation is shown by a legal opinion he issued in 1865. While in private practice then, Curtis was asked to evaluate a Maine law that prohibited its citizens from selling goods belonging to citizens from other states. This state statute ran afoul of the commerce clause in Curtis's judgment. Citing *Cooley*, he reiterated the idea that "when the subject in question is one which from its nature demands uniform regulation for the general benefit of the nation," Congress had exclusive power. In applying that principle, Curtis considered the discriminatory effect of this particular state law.[82]

In any event, the structural argument in *Cooley* was emblematic of Curtis's approach to constitutional interpretation generally, and it marks one point upon which he was headed toward a collision with Taney.

Although the chief justice went along here, his emphasis in the *License Cases* was substantially different, looking to the express language of the constitutional text in order to construe Congress's powers. Curtis's opinion in *Cooley* suggested a more supple process of interpretation. In locating an answer in political structure, Justice Curtis acted upon his view of the basic character of the Constitution. It was a "simple enumeration of the great powers and principles necessary to constitute the government" which did not explicitly provide the definitive answer to every problem that would arise.[83]

VI

The impact of Curtis's opinion was not immediate. Proceeding as if *Cooley* had never been decided, Justice McLean reasserted the exclusive power doctrine on circuit. Meanwhile, the Taney Court let pass opportunities to build on Curtis's analysis. The most striking example was a decision by Chief Justice Taney that a Charleston city ordinance specifying how ships in port should be lighted did not contravene the commerce clause. The case begged for a citation to *Cooley*, but Taney did not mention Curtis's opinion.[84]

It was not long after Taney's death in 1864 that the Court began to work with the ideas Curtis had suggested in *Cooley*. In one opinion after another, the justices referred to the "nature of the subject to be regulated," the need for commercial rules to be "uniform throughout the country," and the "National" character of a "class of legislation" that was "exclusively" in Congress's domain.[85] The "rule has been asserted with great clearness," said the Court in striking down a state tax on interstate cargo, that "whenever the subjects" are "in their nature national, or admit of one uniform system or plan of regulation," they require "exclusive legislation by Congress." The leading justices of the later nineteenth century specifically approved the *Cooley* doctrine. Writing for the Court in *Crandall v. Nevada* (1868), Samuel F. Miller described Curtis's opinion as probably the most "satisfactory solution" that had "ever been given" for this "vexed question," a statement later echoed by Stephen J. Field. When Joseph P. Bradley struck down a state law taxing a steamship company's gross receipts derived from interstate commerce, he reiterated "the rule established by *Cooley*" that "a matter of national importance, admitting of a uniform system or plan of regulation" is "exclusively subject to the legislation of Congress."[86]

In short, *Cooley* became the doctrinal engine for an unprecedented exercise of federal judicial power over the states. Using the commerce clause to nullify state laws—the action that had been bottled up for years—had become a regular event. Several factors contributed to this. The commerce question was no longer caught up in the sectional controversy over slavery, for one thing. For another, the justices were responding to changed economic conditions. Despite the rise of industrial capitalism on a national scale, Congress was not disposed to regulate. As state legislatures filled the regulatory vacuum, the justices had good reason to be concerned that state lawmakers were not always mindful of national interests. Several members of the Court were wary of governmental regulation of business in any event.

As state laws underwent greater scrutiny under the *Cooley* doctrine, the national/local formula degenerated as a tool for making reasoned judgments. The Court continued to recite Curtis's language, but its application of *Cooley* rested on assertions. What subjects were properly classified as national was as broad or as narrow as a majority of justices saw fit. More than once an opinion indicated that interstate transportation was by itself a national subject requiring uniform treatment. In the important case of *Wabash, St. Louis and Pacific Railway Co. v. Illinois* (1886), the Court denied the states power to regulate railroad rates for interstate cargo and passengers. The opinion closed with what was by then a familiar turn of phrase: "This species of regulation is one which must be, if established at all, of a general national character, and cannot be safely and wisely remitted to local rules and local regulations." This decision prompted Congress to establish the Interstate Commerce Commission in 1887, an exceptional case of federal regulation in the nineteenth century.[87]

In fact, the *Cooley* test became something of an empty vessel for various explanations of why a state law was unconstitutional. Charles W. McCurdy has suggested that it was "virtually useless" as "an adjudicatory mechanism." Instead of withdrawing an entire subject of regulation from the states, the justices often tied the *Cooley* formula to the effect of a particular state law (whether it discriminated against out-of-state goods, for example). Without forsaking *Cooley*, the Court by century's end had refocused the inquiry around the question whether a state law imposed a direct (and unconstitutional) or indirect burden on interstate commerce.[88]

Dissatisfaction with this method of reasoning, but not with the idea of judicial review in this area, stirred a move to reformulate the governing standards. At the head of this effort was Harlan Fiske Stone, supported by Oliver Wendell Holmes Jr. and Louis D. Brandeis. With palpable frustration that the direct/indirect burden test was "too mechanical, too uncertain in its application, and too remote from actualities," Stone launched the Court in a direction that, while new, was a throwback to Curtis's pragmatic style. Stone proposed "a consideration of all the facts and circumstances, such as the nature of the regulation, its function, the character of the business involved and the actual effect on the flow of commerce." He fit that into the *Cooley* dichotomy of whether the "regulation concerns interests peculiarly local and does not infringe the national interest in maintaining the freedom of commerce across state lines." Although Stone adjusted his position over time, *Cooley* remained in the background of his analysis. His definitive statement of the appropriate test appears in *Southern Pacific Co. v. Arizona* (1945), combining an analysis of the burden a state law placed on interstate commerce with a balancing test of the "relative weights of the state and national interests." Justice Curtis's century-old interpretation of the commerce clause was still evident as the Court struck down a state law limiting the length of trains as something to be regulated, if at all, by Congress in order to achieve the "national uniformity in the regulation" so "practically indispensable to the operation of an efficient and economical national railway system."[89]

A wider significance of the *Cooley* doctrine, and its variable use, can be observed as the Court addressed questions of racial segregation over the years. In the late nineteenth century, the justices struck down a Louisiana Reconstruction statute that prohibited racial discrimination in public transportation. The Supreme Court took a different view in the decade before *Brown v. Board of Education* (1954). *Morgan v. Virginia* (1946) declared unconstitutional a Virginia law which mandated segregated seating on buses. The rationale was based on the idea that "seating arrangements for the different races in interstate motor travel require a single, uniform rule to promote and protect national travel." Two years later the Court upheld a Michigan civil rights act that prohibited racial discrimination in public accommodations and conveyances. The justices were unable to perceive "what national interest or policy" in "securing uniformity in regulating commerce" was "adversely affected."[90]

One hundred and fifty years after *Cooley*, the dormant commerce clause has brought the federal courts to consider a wide range of policy questions, from the seemingly trivial (the color of margarine, for example) to the obviously consequential (environmental protection, highway safety, and food regulation).[91] The doctrine Justice Curtis laid down has evolved into a complex multipart analysis. Today the federal judiciary determines whether a state law discriminates against out-of-state interests or whether, by balancing local interests against the effect on interstate commerce, it places an undue burden on interstate commerce.[92] Although Justice Curtis's subject-by-subject mode of analysis proved difficult to apply, the national-local classification has never left the Supreme Court's lexicon.[93]

More enduring than *Cooley*'s specific formula were Curtis's basic propositions: first, that the Supreme Court could articulate the constitutional principles organizing national and state powers to regulate commerce; and second, that this would be done around some commonsensical understanding of how the federal system operates. As an authoritative decision recognizing the Court's power to nullify state laws affecting interstate commerce, *Cooley* ranks with the major cases of the Marshall Court in establishing the scope of federal judicial power. Few doctrines devised by a single justice have left such a lasting impression in American constitutional development. Without citing *Cooley*, Justice Holmes captured its significance. "I do not think the United States would come to an end if we lost our power to declare an Act of Congress void," said Holmes. "I do think the Union would be imperiled if we could not make that declaration as to the laws of the several States. For one in my place sees how often a local policy prevails with those who are not trained to national views and how often action is taken that embodies what the Commerce Clause was meant to end."[94]

No doubt such remarks appear exaggerated with the passage of time. Yet it is meaningful that, of all justices, Holmes—wounded three times in the Civil War—would link the Union's survival to this particular judicial power. His comments serve to recall the context in which Justice Curtis delivered the *Cooley* opinion. The doctrine of states' rights was more than idle philosophy. The country had only recently passed through the sectional controversy of 1850. While secession was averted, it had been threatened. Internal divisions on the Supreme Court over the commerce clause mirrored society's tensions.

Against that background Justice Curtis forged a consensus in *Cooley*. By formulating a solution congenial to the judicial mind, he rendered his Whig nationalism palatable to southern justices (notably Taney) who held different views on the nation-state relationship. Curtis redefined the constitutional issue, moving the Court past the question of sovereignty that had plagued the antebellum justices. The case was pivotal. In the space of a few years after the war, the justices were well on their way to supervising state regulation of interstate commerce (probably more than Curtis had contemplated). However untidy the dormant commerce clause may appear, the *Cooley* opinion itself embodied a new justice's faith in the Supreme Court as an institution and in the process of legal reasoning. With that, *Cooley* carried an implicit suggestion that federal-state conflicts, wherever they arose, were amenable to the constitutional process.

97

4. THE PROMISE OF DUE PROCESS

CURTIS'S FAITH IN the Supreme Court was still evident in his interpretation of the constitutional guarantee of due process. The language stating that no person shall be deprived of "life, liberty, or property, without due process of law" appears twice in the Constitution. The Fifth Amendment, adopted as part of the Bill of Rights in 1791, contains a due process clause applicable against the federal government. A comparable provision in the Fourteenth Amendment, ratified in 1868, covers state actions. By the end of the twentieth century, the due process guarantee had emerged as perhaps the single most important constitutional foundation for individual rights. Certainly it has been among the most versatile. Today the Supreme Court extends due process to rights ranging from free speech and privacy to fundamental protections for the accused.

When Benjamin Curtis was appointed to the bench, the Supreme Court had done nothing with the Fifth Amendment's due process clause. Indeed, the justices had not yet invoked any part of the Bill of Rights to declare legislation unconstitutional. It is true that due process received some attention outside the courts. Opposing sides in the public debate over slavery had pointed to this constitutional provision: abolitionists for its guarantee of liberty, proslavery advocates for its protection of property. Rhetorical points aside, neither group had much to show for this. Their interpretations of due process were not particularly well developed. In the words of Robert G. McCloskey, due process was "the vague and relatively feeble clause of the Anglo-American legal tradition" until the end of the nineteenth century.[1] Only then, according to conventional histories, did the Supreme Court transform due process into an effective basis of judicial review.

With the drama surrounding conservative judges striking down reform legislation from the Progressive Era to the New Deal, it is easy to overlook the quiet evolution in due process that occurred in the Civil War era. In that earlier time Justice Curtis was in the vanguard exploring the possibilities of this constitutional guarantee. He delivered the Supreme Court's first opinion interpreting the due process clause, in *Murray's Lessee v. Hoboken Land and Improvement Company* (1856). Not only did Curtis take the lead in speaking for the nation's highest tribunal on this subject, he stated unequivocally that due process was an appropriate ground for judicial review of legislation. This was not an incontestable point then. What Curtis said about due process is doubly significant by virtue of its timing. As Akhil Reed Amar has suggested, *Murray's Lessee* provided the "definitive statement" of the meaning of due process when the Fourteenth Amendment was being framed a decade later.[2]

Curtis's discussion in that case was brief and to the point. Yet when *Murray's Lessee* is placed alongside his other judicial opinions and legal arguments, it becomes clear that he viewed due process as a central juridical option to protect personal rights and that he was engaged in a conscious effort to lay the groundwork for its future use. The justice laid down several markers for its interpretation. Without suggesting that subsequent developments comported entirely with Curtis's views, it can be said that he anticipated the broad and multifaceted conception of due process to a surprising degree.

I

The significance of *Murray's Lessee* derives from Curtis's suggestions for interpreting the due process clause, not from his ruling on the peculiar facts presented. The case comprised one chapter of a major financial scandal of the antebellum period. Samuel Swartwout, a customs inspector for the Port of New York, had embezzled over one million dollars from the Treasury Department. He bought land in New Jersey with his ill-gotten gains. To recover the amount stolen, the Treasury Department used a nonjudicial remedy called a distress warrant to seize and sell this land. Congress in 1820 had authorized this process so that the Treasury Department could recover money from delinquent tax collectors without going to court. Parties claiming title through earlier purchases from Swartwout filed a federal lawsuit in which they argued that the statute was unconstitutional. For a unanimous Supreme Court, Justice Curtis held that the legislation did not violate the due process clause.

The starting point in Curtis's analysis was based upon drawing a connection between due process and a significant phrase from English legal history, the "law of the land." In chapter 39 of the Magna Carta, King John promised that he would not "proceed" against any free man "except by the lawful judgment of his peers and by the law of the land."[3] Writing in the 1600s, the eminent English judge Sir Edward Coke equated the "law of the land" with the words "due process of law" used in a statute Parliament adopted during King Edward III's reign.[4] Scholars have questioned Coke's conclusion, but his view was accepted by leading American jurists in the antebellum period, notably Kent, Story, and Webster. Justice Story, to take one example, suggested that the Fifth Amendment's due process clause should be read as an "enlargement" of the "law of the land."[5]

Curtis in *Murray's Lessee* said that the framers of the Fifth Amendment "undoubtedly intended" due process "to convey the same meaning" as the "law of the land." To clinch that point, the justice felt compelled to explain why the phrase "law of the land" did not appear in the Fifth Amendment. Before the Bill of Rights was adopted, American constitutions for the states and territories retained this language of Magna Carta. For instance, the Northwest Ordinance of 1787 provided that "no man shall be deprived of his liberty or property but by the judgment of his peers, or the law of the land." When James Madison proposed the Bill of Rights, he did not use the "law of the land" phrasing but rather the language of due process. Madison did not offer any explanation, and it remains unclear what he had in mind.[6] Possibly he got the idea of using "due process" from New York State's ratifying convention, which recommended an amendment to the federal Constitution that no person be deprived of "Privileges, Franchises, Life, Liberty, or Property but by due process of Law."[7]

This obscure record surrounding the origins of the due process clause did not stop Justice Curtis from speculating. He claimed that the terms "due process of law" were inserted in the Fifth Amendment to solve a problem in drafting. In Curtis's rendition, the framers of the Bill of Rights had two unsatisfactory alternatives. One was to copy Magna Carta's chapter 39 more fully: no person shall be deprived of life, liberty, or property but "by the judgment of his peers or the law of the land." This would have been "superfluous and inappropriate," Curtis said, because the Fifth Amendment then would have duplicated the right to jury trial provided in the Sixth and Seventh Amendments as well as Article III of the original Constitution. Curtis dismissed the second option: retain "law of the land" and omit "by the judgment of his peers." The justice did not elaborate, but he apparently thought the Fifth Amendment would then appear to dispense with the right to a jury in cases where that was not intended. At any rate, there was a ready-made solution in Curtis's view: substitute "due process of law" in accordance with Lord Coke's well-known commentary.[8] This reconstruction of the framing of the Fifth Amendment was conjecture, plausible perhaps, but conjecture nonetheless; and it is one measure of how deeply motivated Curtis was to develop due process that he passed off his supposition as clear beyond question.

By linking due process to Magna Carta, Curtis was not simply restating a prevalent definition. That connection accomplished some important things for him. The constitutional situation, as he saw it, was like writing on a blank slate. There was no precedent directly on point; no record of any discussion about due process from the framers of the Bill of Rights. As for the Constitution, Curtis said (with a plaintive air), it "does not even declare what principles are to be applied" to determine what is "due process of law."[9]

In that setting, it seems that Curtis meant to supply the due process clause with a meaningful historical foundation to aid in its interpretation. He gave more evidence of his thinking one year after *Murray's Lessee* when he said in the *Dred Scott* case that the due process guarantee was "borrowed" from Magna Carta and "brought to America by our ancestors, as part of their inherited liberties." With a nod to the Burkean philosophy he had discussed in his Deerfield speech several years earlier, Curtis had, before saying anything else, invested the due process clause with special meaning.[10] The justice set the stage to view the Fifth Amendment's due process clause as a recent chapter in a grand tradition of gradual development of constitutional rights, with its interpretation guided by the meanings accumulated over time. If the justices were called upon to settle difficult controversies under the rubric of due process, they had more to go on than abstract appeals to rights against which Curtis, like Burke, had inveighed.

The symbolic importance of Magna Carta's "law of the land" to Curtis is evident from a circuit opinion he issued three years before *Murray's Lessee*. In *Greene v. Briggs* (1852), Curtis considered a Rhode Island statute that established summary procedures to punish persons selling liquor without a license. This legislation empowered justices of the peace to declare a forfeiture of property (liquor) and impose punishment without a jury trial. The accused could get a trial only on appeal after paying a $200 bond. Expressing concern for those who could not afford this, Curtis decided that the legislation violated the state constitution's "law of the land" clause. The statute, he reasoned, deprived persons of liberty and property "not by the law of the land, but by an arbitrary and unconstitutional exertion of the legislative power."[11]

That Curtis considered the law of the land clause "important," as he said, is shown by some unusual steps he took before issuing his circuit opinion. Not only did he outline "its principles" to Chief Justice Taney, Curtis had the entire opinion read to two associate justices, Robert C. Grier and Samuel Nelson.[12] Such consultation appears to have been unique for Curtis, and with some understanding of his self-assurance, his actions look more like proselytizing than consulting.

Even more revealing were comments Curtis made about *Greene v. Briggs* in private correspondence. The decision came under fire from the temperance movement, whose members blamed the justice for a "great increase of drunkenness and rioting." [13] Horace Greeley's *New York Tribune* fueled the criticism, beginning with a New Year's Day headline, "JUDGE CURTIS ON RUMSELLING." Never "before did a Judge's fiat give such hearty and universal satisfaction to all who live in the Law's despite—to libertines, gamblers, tipplers, rowdies and brothel-keepers." Curtis "may defy those he has aggrieved and stricken," said the *Tribune*, "but how can he bear the laudations of those he has gratified?" The justice had an answer to that question. He pictured himself "restraining those who in the pursuit of an object deemed by them of great importance, have disregarded principles contained in Magna Charta" and "affirmed in every American Constitution which has been formed since 1776." Curtis added, perhaps with false modesty: "I have no doubt I may" and "shall make mistakes in my judicial opinions," but "I think I do *know* when I have got down to the primitive foundations whose situs will never be disturbed until our political fabric breaks up." [14]

II

Curtis could have said the same for *Murray's Lessee*. Having there connected due process to Magna Carta's "law of the land," Curtis then offered an idea that was as potentially far-reaching as it was briefly stated. The justice said the Fifth Amendment's due process clause was "a restraint on the legislative as well as on the executive and the judicial powers of the government, and cannot be so construed as to leave congress free to make any process 'due process of law,' by its mere will." Curtis treated this as self-evident. It was "manifest that it was not left to the legislative power to enact any process which might be devised." He did not provide any reason for this conclusion. Justice Curtis immediately went on to describe what principles should determine the constitutionality of Congress's actions. Such was the Supreme Court's first statement of its power of judicial review under the due process clause. For simply asserting such an important point, Curtis has been described as a self-appointed "lawgiver." [15]

While Curtis made his position seem so obvious that it required no proof, it was more open to question than he allowed. After bringing Magna Carta into the discussion, Curtis then ignored one lesson that might have been drawn from the Great Charter's history. The English did not treat the "law of the land" chapter as a constraint upon Parliament; rather, this language served to check the monarch's arbitrary actions by affording protections of the law to subjects of the realm. If a strict analogy to English experience held, the law of the land controlled executive power through the judicial process; it had nothing to do with legislative authority.[16] There was also a definitional hurdle for Curtis to overcome. Arguably, any statute was ipso facto the law of the land because whatever the legislature enacted was the law of the land.[17]

In addition, it is difficult to say that Americans before *Murray's Lessee* understood that the due process clause applied against Congress. The evidence is sparse and ambiguous. One statement noted by scholars was made by Alexander Hamilton in a debate before the New York Assembly in 1787. He said that the "words '*due process*' have a precise technical import, and are only applicable to the process and proceedings of the courts of justice; they can never be referred to an act of legislature." While this remark seems to rule out the use of due process against legislative enactments, scholars have drawn contrary conclusions about what Hamilton meant. Douglas Laycock has suggested that, in context, Hamilton was arguing that the proposed legislation would violate the state's due process clause.[18]

While Justice Curtis did not explain how he arrived at the conclusion that due process was "a restraint on the legislative," it appears that he carried over to the Fifth Amendment an emerging conception about the "law of the land" provisions of state constitutions. Tracing the progression of that line of thought suggests not only where Curtis got this idea but also why he considered it "manifest."

In the vanguard was Daniel Webster, arguing before the U.S. Supreme Court in *Dartmouth College v. Woodward* (1819). His discussion of the "law of the land" there was reputed to be the best-known commentary on that subject in the antebellum period.[19] He asked the justices to invalidate several acts of the New Hampshire legislature that, in essence, turned the private college into a public university subject to governmental control. To Webster's way of thinking, this was a classic case of the legislature transferring the private rights of one party to another; the trustees he represented had been denied rights they had under the original charter establishing Dartmouth. While the state constitutional provision of the "law of the land" was not technically before the U.S. Supreme Court, Webster discussed it anyway. He took it for granted that not everything passed in "the form of an enactment" should be "considered the law of the land." Otherwise, legislatures would be free to pass "acts directly transferring one man's estate to another, legislative judgments, decrees, and forfeitures, in all possible forms." His basic point was that there must be a judicial determination before the taking of life, liberty, or property. Applied to the case at hand, Webster argued that the trustees appointed under the terms of the original charter were deprived of rights without "due course and process of law," an idea Justice Story restated in his concurring opinion. "Each trustee has a vested right, and legal interest in his office," Story said, "and it cannot be devested but by due course of law."[20] In the end, the Court construed the legislative charter as a contract and held that the New Hampshire legislature had violated the federal Constitution's contracts clause (no state shall "pass any Law impairing the Obligation of Contracts").[21]

Between *Dartmouth College* and *Murray's Lessee*, several state judges interpreted the "law of the land" as a restraint on legislative power. The crucial line of development came by way of Chief Judge Thomas Ruffin, writing for the North Carolina supreme court in *Hoke v. Henderson* (1833). "Those terms 'law of the land' do not mean merely an act of the General Assembly," said Ruffin. "If they did, every restriction upon the legislative authority would be at once abrogated." Chancellor Kent set that interpretation before a national audience in his treatise *Commentaries on American Law*, where he noted Ruffin's opinion approvingly. In *Taylor v. Porter* (1843), Judge Greene C. Bronson of New York embraced the idea.[22] Ruffin and Bronson, along with other state judges, conveyed a sense of absolute certainty. It was inconceivable, they suggested, to exempt the legislature from the strictures of the law of the land clause, for in that case the legislative body could commit acts inconsistent with the basic character of American government, such as transferring property from one person to another without judicial determination. Curtis was familiar with this discussion. In *Greene v. Briggs* he not only cited Kent's *Commentaries, Hoke v. Henderson,* and *Taylor v. Porter,* Curtis also used phrasing similar to Ruffin's for the point in question. "Certainly," Curtis said, the law of the land "does not mean any act which the assembly may choose to pass. If it did, the legislative will could inflict a forfeiture of life, liberty, or property, without a trial."[23]

With this precedent on the "law of the land," it was a short step for Curtis to view the due process clause in the same light. Not surprisingly, *Murray's Lessee* had a similar turn of phrase mustered with equal conviction. It was "manifest," Curtis said, that the Fifth Amendment did not "leave congress free to make any process 'due process of law,' by its mere will." This statement may be viewed simply as a natural corollary to the precedent on the "law of the land." The larger context suggests Justice Curtis had something more in mind, however.

Curtis's statement on judicial review in *Murray's Lessee* may be viewed as part of a quest by various judges, as it has sometimes appeared, to identify a provision in the Constitution to serve as the foundation for unwritten higher law.[24] An early case familiar to antebellum jurists framed the issue. In *Calder v. Bull* (1798), Justice Samuel Chase indicated that inherent limits to legislative power could be found among the "vital principles in our free republican governments." He was unwilling to concede that legislation could be declared void only when "expressly restrained" by the Constitution. Surely, Chase argued, "a law that takes property from A. and gives it to B." was invalid even if no constitutional provision could be cited to proscribe such an act. Chase was taken then and later to refer to natural law, though that was not exactly what he said. In any event, Justice James Iredell felt compelled to reply that the "ideas of natural justice are regulated by no fixed standard." The Court should defer to elected representatives of the people, Iredell insisted, unless presented with a "clear and urgent case" of the legislature violating a written constitution.[25]

Chase's view—that unwritten principles of republican government by themselves limited legislative power—resonated with Marshall, Story, and Webster, among others. The particular example of a legislature stripping property from A for B can be found repeated throughout the antebellum period.[26] This strain of thought coalesced around what became known as the vested rights doctrine. The doctrine's basic idea, as its name implies, was that individuals had established rights that the government could not infringe. Property was of particular concern, though this could be broadly conceived to include personal liberty. The premise underlying the vested rights doctrine was that property was a foundation of civil society. It followed that the government exists to safeguard property and that such vested rights could not be left to the discretionary power of legislatures. As Webster put it to the Supreme Court in *Wilkinson v. Leland* (1829), "If at this period there is not a general restraint on legislatures, in favour of private rights, there is an end to private property." Story agreed that "government can scarcely be deemed to be free, where the rights of property are left solely dependent upon the will of a legislative body, without any restraint."[27]

Such bold assertions left unanswered the question of what were the appropriate grounds for the judiciary to protect property against legislative abuse. The Marshall Court, which championed the vested rights doctrine, flirted with declaring legislation unconstitutional based upon unwritten higher law. *Fletcher v. Peck* (1810) illustrates both the attractiveness of relying on unwritten norms and the evident uneasiness this caused. This case concerned a Georgia state statute that rescinded the state's earlier sale of huge tracts of land. The Court struck down this legislation. Marshall provided alternative reasons for the decision. He pointed to the "general principles which are common to our free institutions," echoing Chase's opinion in *Calder*. The chief justice also cited "particular provisions" of the Constitution, especially the prohibition against impairing the obligation of contracts.[28]

With that, the Marshall Court began to mold the contracts clause into a more comprehensive protection for vested rights than the Constitution's framers probably intended. This provision appears to have been drafted to stop the states from interfering with private contracts between individuals. Marshall and his colleagues extended the contracts clause to cover public contracts between state governments and individuals. These included corporate charters establishing banks or granting exclusive licenses to run bridges and canals. By protecting the rights of the earliest entrepreneurs, the Court's reconstruction of the contracts clause facilitated economic growth in the early national period. In terms of long-term constitutional developments, this marked the start of a sustained effort to locate a place in the Constitution to do the work of an unwritten higher law.[29]

By the time Curtis took his seat on the bench, the contracts clause had lost the status it had under Marshall's leadership. The Taney Court continued to apply this constitutional provision, but there was a perceptible shift in attitude. Less sympathetic to monopolies and vested rights, the Jacksonian Democrats on the Court employed a rule of strict construction. As stated in the *Charles River Bridge* case (1837), any ambiguity in a public charter would be interpreted against the private party in the state's favor. The federal courts would not consider such a license to be exclusive by implication.[30]

In his first term Justice Curtis tried to limit the scope of *Charles River Bridge* in a case involving a railway charter, but it was clear a majority of his colleagues did not share his views. The Virginia legislature had granted the Richmond, Fredericksburg, and Potomac Railroad Company the exclusive right to conduct rail traffic between Richmond and Fredericksburg for thirty years. Well within that period of time, the legislature permitted another railroad company to construct a line for a part of that same route. Mixing a dubious reading of the first charter with the strict rule of construction, the Supreme Court decided that there was no violation of the contracts clause. Curtis wrote a dissenting opinion arguing that the *Charles River Bridge* rule of construction was a last resort "never to be relied upon, but when all other rules of exposition failed." Only McLean and Wayne joined him.[31]

Curtis continued to press the contracts clause into service. He wrote for the Court in *Curran v. Arkansas* (1854), ruling that state legislation appropriating the property of a bank impaired contractual obligations to creditors. Overall, though, the Court in the 1850s did not apply the contracts clause as Curtis would have liked.[32] Moreover, the justices by mid-century were not so willing as before to rely on unwritten higher law, whether derived from nature or the essential principles of republican government. Against that background, *Murray's Lessee* made a timely contribution in the search for a versatile constitutional provision to serve as the basis for judicial review. Curtis's brief statement that the due process clause checked legislative power opened another avenue for the judiciary. It remains to be seen how much Curtis was willing to read into the due process clause: whether he saw it as an essential but limited protection or as an all-purpose vehicle for the protection of individual rights.

III

Having established that the due process clause limited legislative power, Justice Curtis turned to the question of its interpretation. He wanted it known that the Constitution's text offered little guidance: it "contains no description of those processes which it was intended to allow or forbid," nor did it "declare what principles are to be applied."[33]

Curtis proposed a two-part inquiry. The first may be called the constitutional test. "We must examine the constitution itself," the justice said, "to see whether this process be in conflict with any of its provisions." The second may be labeled the historical test. If the process in question was not prohibited by any particular constitutional provision, "we must look to those settled usages and modes of proceeding existing in the common and statute law of England, before the emigration of our ancestors, and which are shown not to have been unsuited to their civil and political condition by having been acted on by them after the settlement of this country."[34]

Commentators have dismissed Curtis's approach. The constitutional test has been considered "unnecessary" and "bizarre"; in fact, it is usually overlooked. His historical test has been read as a mechanical formula requiring little more than a survey of procedures in use when the Bill of Rights was adopted. This has led constitutional scholars to view Curtis's conception of due process as "fixed" in meaning, "highly implausible" and "narrow," or to conclude that he "laid fairly obvious limits on the capacity of the due process clause for growth." The implication is that

Curtis's historical focus limited the protection of individual rights, as if *Murray's Lessee* stuck Americans with antiquated practices from medieval England or, at best, the American founding.[35]

Curtis's opinion was not perfectly clear, but there appears to have been more to his thinking. To begin with, that procedures had been used in England was not decisive for Curtis; only those suited to American circumstances as shown by actual use were relevant. Whether Curtis meant to restrict due process to practices that existed in the founding period is debatable. His opinion is ambiguous on that point. On the one hand, as Curtis reviewed the history surrounding the distress warrant, he keyed his analysis to proceedings in existence before the Bill of Rights. On the other hand, his statement of the test—directed to proceedings employed after the country's settlement—specified no date as a bench-mark. If the justice considered the state of procedure in 1791 conclusive, he engaged in a bit of superfluous analysis himself when he examined the history of the distress warrant. He considered its use after the adoption of the Fifth Amendment to have "no inconsiderable weight."[36]

This still leaves the question of what exactly Curtis meant by his historical test. Perhaps the best explanation is that the justice was simply defining the Fifth Amendment's due process clause by the meanings due process had acquired over time, mainly in the common law. This was a conventional antebellum view. As Justice Story remarked in his *Commentaries*, the due process clause affirmed "the right of trial according to the process and proceedings of the common law." In his historical test Curtis referred directly to the settled usages and proceedings of the common law. The clue to what he had in mind came later in the opinion when he said that due process "generally implies and includes *actor* [plaintiff], *reus* [defendant], *judex* [judge], regular allegations, opportunity to answer, and a trial according to some settled course of judicial proceedings." This was the general rule, and history supplied a finite number of exceptions.[37]

It has been suggested that *Murray's Lessee*'s historical focus failed to guard against "new forms of oppression,"[38] but that is exactly what Curtis's historical test did. His opinion created a presumption that governmental actions deviating from traditional modes of proceeding were unconstitutional. The historical test was skewed to strike down new practices that did not accord with common-law process or well-established exceptions.[39] A more valid complaint about Curtis's opinion is that the historical test constitutionalized traditional practices, like the distress warrant, that perhaps should have been abandoned. Yet Curtis's exact wording suggested some flexibility. The Court, he said, should "look to" historical practices. Arguably he did not mean that the Court was bound to accept all procedures that were in place in the eighteenth century.

In any event, Curtis's suggested inquiry consisted of two parts, and his historical test must be read along with the constitutional test he proposed. While scholars have sometimes ignored the constitutional test, it was not gratuitous for Curtis. The language of *Murray's Lessee* was imperative on this point. The answer of what is due process, Justice Curtis said, "must be twofold." The Court "must examine the constitution itself, to see whether this process be in conflict with any of its provisions." In Curtis's initial statement of the tests, the constitutional one was the first to consider. If the Court found that the legislation violated another constitutional provision, that ended the inquiry and there was no need to examine historical practices. True, Curtis reversed the order when he applied these tests. Yet after reviewing the history surrounding the distress warrant, he did not sustain the legislation until he considered other constitutional provisions. To determine whether the claim should have been adjudicated in the federal courts, Curtis considered the scope of judicial power under Article III and Congress's implied powers under Article I.[40] Nothing would have prevented the Court from evaluating the distress warrant under the first and third articles without invoking due process. By bringing these other constitutional provisions into the analysis, Curtis indicated how broadly he viewed the Fifth Amendment's due process clause. Rather than a throwaway line, the constitutional test suggests that due process had a sort of superconstitutional status.

Today it is difficult to read Curtis's constitutional test without thinking of the doctrine of incorporation, a major theme in the interpretation of the Fourteenth Amendment's due process clause. Over several decades beginning in the late nineteenth century, the justices considered whether that provision incorporated the guarantees of the Bill of Rights against the states. *Barron v. Baltimore* (1833) had previously limited their application to the federal government. The Supreme Court never accepted total incorporation of the entire Bill of Rights, an idea associated primarily with Justice Black. The Court instead embarked on a process called selective incorporation, in the end applying practically all of the Bill of Rights against the states (the key exceptions being grand jury indictment and civil jury trial). Incorporation through due process underlies many leading cases including *Miranda v. Arizona* (1966) (privilege against self-incrimination) and *Gideon v. Wainwright* (1963) (right of counsel).[41]

Whether Curtis would have endorsed incorporation under the Fourteenth Amendment is a matter of speculation. His opinion, written in 1856, has nothing to do with the federal-state issues raised by the

Reconstruction Amendments. Even so, the justices in the initial stages of interpreting the Fourteenth Amendment's due process clause repeatedly referred to Curtis's two-part test. Even at the close of the nineteenth century, the Court was still able to say that what constituted due process was "perhaps as well stated by Mr. Justice Curtis" as "anywhere."[42] Yet while the Court noted Curtis's definition of due process, the justices actually thwarted early efforts to incorporate. The Court recited Curtis's definition of due process without making a concerted effort to apply the constitutional test. Moreover, a majority of the justices usually gave the historical test a more limited reading than *Murray's Lessee* warranted.

Hurtado v. California (1884) is a case in point. There the Supreme Court decided that the Fourteenth Amendment's due process clause did not require the states to secure a grand jury indictment in capital cases. Citing Justice Curtis's due process tests "as the foundation of a doctrine which has been reiterated by all the text-writers and State Courts," the defendant had argued that the grand jury was among the settled usages and modes of proceeding of the Anglo-American legal system and was therefore a required element of due process. The majority read *Murray's Lessee* differently. The "real syllabus" of Curtis's opinion, said the Court, was that a settled usage not otherwise prohibited "must be taken to be due process of law," but "it by no means follows that nothing else can be due process of law." Thus, new or different proceedings lacking the "sanction of settled usage" may nevertheless qualify as due process. The lone dissenter, Justice John Marshall Harlan, disagreed with this interpretation of *Murray's Lessee*. Pointing to Justice Curtis's "authoritative directions," Harlan applied the historical test to show that the grand jury was a required aspect of due process.[43]

In another case, *Twining v. New Jersey* (1908), the Court ruled that the Fourteenth Amendment's due process clause did not include the privilege against self-incrimination. The majority opinion noted that if Curtis's historical test were "taken literally, that alone might almost be decisive" in the defendant's favor. While the Court insisted it was not "repudiating" the "test proposed by Mr. Justice Curtis," the majority went on to apply a different standard. This right, according to the opinion, was not "a fundamental principle of liberty and justice" inherent "in the very idea of free government." Harlan dissented again.[44]

Notwithstanding this early record, the Supreme Court used Curtis's historical test in the famous Scottsboro cases. After several black men were convicted in a small town in Alabama of raping two white women, the Court concluded that the Fourteenth Amendment's due process clause required a fair trial, which may in turn require providing defendants with counsel. The Court, borrowing Curtis's language, relied on "settled usages and modes of proceeding under the common and statute law of England" not "unsuited to the civil and political conditions" in America.[45]

As the so-called incorporation debate continued into the twentieth century, Curtis's definition of due process faded from view as a specific reference. Interestingly, the leading alternatives reflected one aspect or another of Curtis's analysis. The constitutional test of *Murray's Lessee* can be viewed as an antecedent to Justice Black's efforts to limit judicial subjectivity by the wholesale incorporation of the Bill of Rights into the Fourteenth Amendment's due process clause. It is also possible to detect Curtis's style of thinking—recourse to common-law traditions—when the Court determines whether a procedure was fundamental in the common-law system, that is, "necessary to an Anglo-American regime of ordered liberty."[46]

IV

Curtis's suggestion that the due process clause checked legislative power was by itself significant. Combined with the interpretive principles that he outlined, the opinion opened up new possibilities for judicial review. On the other hand, the Court still had no precedent striking down legislation based on due process. *Murray's Lessee* upheld the statute in question, after all. For a better sense of how far Justice Curtis was willing to take the due process clause, it is useful to turn to his dissenting opinion in *Dred Scott* and private legal opinions he prepared in 1874. These place him at an early point of one of the most consequential developments in the history of judicial review: the rise of substantive due process.

Today, due process doctrine is divided into two areas. One is called procedural due process. This concerns how the government deprives persons of life, liberty, or property; whether, for example, there was proper notice and an opportunity to be heard. The other is substantive due process, by which courts review the content of legislation even when no procedural question is presented. Substantive interpretations of due process have been used to determine whether economic legislation was arbitrary and whether abortion regulations violated a fundamental right of privacy.[47]

In the standard historical reading, the Supreme Court's view of due process as a substantive constraint did not take hold until the late nineteenth century, with one critical exception.[48] That was the *Dred Scott* case (1857), where Chief Justice Taney relied on the Fifth Amendment's due process clause to invalidate the Missouri Compromise. He suggested that

Congress, by prohibiting slavery in some territories, deprived slave owners of their property without due process of law. No procedural issue was involved. Legal historians have also pointed to a series of cases in the state courts testing legislation against the vested rights doctrine. These decisions culminated in *Wynehamer v. People* (1856), where New York's highest court declared unconstitutional a statute that prohibited the sale of liquor. Without any question concerning the procedures employed, the court cited the state's due process clause to prohibit the destruction of property rights.[49] Commentators have also noted substantive interpretations of due process circulating outside the courts in the antebellum period. Abolitionists, for instance, focused on the word "liberty" in the Fifth Amendment's due process clause to show that slavery was prohibited in the federal territories.[50]

The adoption of the Fourteenth Amendment provided another outlet for using due process in a substantive vein, but the Supreme Court declined its first opportunity to do so. In the *Slaughterhouse Cases* (1873), a majority upheld a Louisiana state law that granted a monopoly for slaughtering cattle in New Orleans. Plaintiffs' counsel argued that this legislation violated due process because it deprived butchers of their "right to labor." Presumably with *Murray's Lessee* in mind, Justice Miller considered that interpretation inconsistent with any "construction of that provision that we have ever seen, or any that we deem admissible." The Court four years later intimated that the due process clause could be read in the manner Miller had flatly rejected. In the course of sustaining state regulations of grain elevators and storage charges, *Munn v. Illinois* (1877) noted that in "some circumstances" economic regulations might be considered a deprivation of private property without due process of law. The justices in 1890 found the right circumstances: a Minnesota state statute that insulated administrative rate making from judicial review. The "reasonableness" of fares charged by railroads was "eminently a question for judicial investigation, requiring due process of law for its determination," said the Court.[51]

By the turn of the century, the Supreme Court had tied the due process clause to a liberty of contract, a broadly defined "right of the citizen to be free in the enjoyment of all his faculties; to be free to use them in all lawful ways; to live and work where he will; to earn his livelihood by any lawful calling; to pursue any livelihood or avocation," and "to enter into all contracts" for those purposes. This concept, which had its roots in the Republican ideology of free labor from the Civil War period, was appropriated by a majority of the justices to strike down various regulatory reforms, notably efforts to protect workers.[52] The classic case of this era of economic substantive due process was *Lochner v. New York* (1905), which held that state legislation establishing maximum hours for bakery employees violated the Fourteenth Amendment's due process clause. Liberty of contract, and the laissez-faire capitalism it reflected, continued to influence judicial decision making through the Great Depression. Among its casualties were minimum-wage laws and legislation safeguarding the rights of employees to join labor unions.[53]

Curtis appeared at an incipient stage in these developments. According to the conventional view, *Murray's Lessee* represents the prevailing antebellum understanding of due process as "exclusively" procedural.[54] Yet the opinion has also been called the "true inception of substantive due process" on the Supreme Court in light of Curtis's statement about judicial review.[55] In fact, *Murray's Lessee* by itself does not shed much light on Curtis's position regarding substantive due process.

Curtis's actions in *Dred Scott*, which the next chapter examines, are suggestive. For the Court, Taney said that "an act of Congress which deprives a citizen of the United States of his liberty or property, merely because he came himself or brought his property into a particular Territory of the United States, and who had committed no offence against the laws, could hardly be dignified with the name of due process of law." It has been suggested that Curtis objected because of Taney's "amazing" use of due process as a substantive limit on legislation.[56] However, Curtis focused his disagreement on the special character of the property right in question, not on the substantive conception of due process. As slavery was "contrary to natural right," a creature of positive law, this "particular species of property" was outside the protection of the due process clause, according to Curtis. What the justice did not say is as important as what he said. He did not argue that the due process clause was exclusively directed to procedural issues. Curtis allowed that the due process clause protected natural rights in property (along with life and liberty). Given the way he framed the argument, the implication was that legislation like the Missouri Compromise that concerned ordinary property rights could be found to violate due process. This was not an explicit rejection of substantive due process.[57]

There is a risk in reading too much into Curtis's dissenting opinion on this point. Curtis neither endorsed nor opposed the idea of substantive due process as someone might today. Nor should it be expected that he could have done so. "Substantive due process" was not part of Curtis's legal vocabulary, but that does not mean that his view was strictly procedural. His conception of due process appears to have been more fluid with no sharply defined dichotomy between substantive and procedural due process in mind. It may be tempting to read the substantive/procedural classification into his jurisprudence, but this loses sight of the way due process was taking shape in the Civil War period.[58]

Further evidence of Curtis's views can be derived from his discussion of railroad regulations in 1874. That year the Chicago and Northwestern Railway Company requested Curtis to evaluate Wisconsin's Potter Act, which set maximum rates that railroads could charge for passengers and freight. Curtis also offered his legal opinion on a similar statute passed by the Iowa state legislature. He issued these opinions against the background of the Granger movement, collective action by farmers throughout the Midwest to secure legislative protection from the exploitative business practices of a number of railroads. The Grangers had substantial grounds for complaint. Railroads had charged exorbitant rates for short trips and compelled farmers to sell their crops at a discount to grain elevator companies, which were in turn owned by railroad corporations.[59]

In his two opinions Curtis put forward several ideas to analyze this legislation, but he did not specifically mention due process. This omission drew the attention of Charles Fairman, who concluded that Curtis had not "seen in the Fourteenth Amendment the substantive content later given to the Due Process Clause." Otherwise, Fairman said, Curtis "would hardly have failed" to offer that as a reason to consider the legislation unconstitutional.[60] There may have been other reasons why Curtis did not advise his clients to consider the due process clause, however. The *Slaughterhouse Cases* had given that provision a restrictive interpretation only one year earlier. Also, the Court had not made clear yet that the due process clause, which protected "any person," covered corporations.[61]

More telling than a specific reference to due process was the mindset Curtis displayed, as he had in place the basic elements of liberty of contract. "No department of government," Curtis asserted, "has power to make bargains for the people." He emphasized that to "fix and prescribe for the future, what prices shall be demanded either for commodities or for personal service" was "not within the field of legislation, under any American Constitution." While citing specific constitutional provisions (the Constitution's contracts clause and the Iowa state constitution's eminent domain clause), Curtis was willing to find rate-making legislation unconstitutional without relying on any written language from the Constitution. Calling to mind the well-worn injunction against governmental transfers of property from A to B, he recited what he described as an "admitted principle." Even "without any positive provision," it was beyond "the scope of Legislative power to take private property from one person and grant it to another." Significantly, Curtis assumed the judiciary's capacity to determine the reasonableness of railroad rates. He noted that common-law courts had done that for some time with common carriers in the business of transportation.[62]

It is an open question whether Curtis would have been more supple than the Supreme Court was in upholding a liberty of contract. His 1874 opinions mark out two alternate positions. The Potter Act, considered by some historians to be particularly radical legislation from the Granger era, prompted Curtis to take a more extreme view. Although the Court later upheld the Potter Act, Curtis argued that the Wisconsin state legislature had no authority to fix future rates. There was no middle ground for Curtis on this. Either the legislative power "does not exist at all, or it is unlimited."[63]

Curtis viewed the Iowa Railroad Act differently. He did not consider it patently unconstitutional; its validity depended on whether the rates were reasonable. This raised "practical" questions susceptible to judicial resolution, in Curtis's judgment. He outlined several areas of inquiry: whether the rates allowed the railroad to operate the line safely, to pay off debts to bondholders, and to compensate its stockholders. At the same time he recognized that "where the line should be fixed is at present an unsettled question, and I confess the difficulty of settling it is very great." Although it remains a matter for speculation as to how Curtis would have addressed the issues that arose in the early twentieth century, he offered a clue to his basic mode of thought. "I am aware that this is a new question in its form and circumstances," Curtis wrote. "It does not seem to me to be new in principle."[64]

V

Besides hinting at the substantive use of due process, Curtis associated this constitutional guarantee with the idea of equality. Arguing in a federal circuit case, *United States v. Union Pacific Railroad Co.* (1873), he said that the meaning of the Fifth Amendment's due process clause "ought to be extended, so far as its language will fairly admit, to accomplish that equality before the law" which is "the great fundamental principle of republican government."[65]

While this suggestion was significant, the litigation was noteworthy too. The case grew out of the Crédit Mobilier scandal that tainted President Grant's administration. Officers of the Union Pacific Railroad had bilked the corporation, stolen federal moneys and lands, and bribed U.S. senators and representatives. To provide a comprehensive remedy, Congress passed a bill authorizing the attorney general to bring all parties before a single circuit court.[66] As this legislation deviated from the normal rules of procedure, Curtis had an opening to raise the issue of equality under law.

There was precedent linking equality to the "law of the land" provisions of state constitutions. Antebellum jurists for some time had expressed concern over so-called partial legislation that treated individuals or particular groups differently than everyone else. Jacksonian Democrats cited the "law of the land" to challenge legislation granting special privileges and monopolies. Whigs found this constitutional language useful as well, paradoxically, to thwart legislative attempts to revoke special privileges that had been previously given. Daniel Webster invoked the "law of the land" in this way. "Every citizen shall hold his life, liberty, property, and immunities, under the protection of the general rules which govern society," he said in the *Dartmouth College* case. The logic behind this was that partial legislation was by definition not a "general law" and therefore could not be the "law of the land." The deeper concern was for protecting the minority. As the Tennessee Supreme Court explained, "If the law be general in its operation, affecting all alike, the minority are safe, because the majority, who make the law, are operated on by it equally with the others." This view of the "law of the land" was so firmly rooted in antebellum thought that Thomas Cooley considered the Fourteenth Amendment's equal protection clause redundant. The equal protection clause was made necessary, Cooley suggested, because states discriminated against freed slaves in violation of the "law of the land" provisions in state constitutions.[67]

Although the relationship between equality and the "law of the land" was fairly well established by the time Curtis participated in the *Union Pacific Railroad* case, he appears to have been the first to develop an extended argument about equality and the Fifth Amendment's due process clause.[68] Perhaps the most interesting part of his discussion is the way in which he overlaid a historical analysis with the theme of republicanism. He began by noting that in the late eighteenth century, "it was received universally as a fundamental principle of republican government that all citizens must stand equal before the laws of the land." According to Curtis, "one great" obstacle to the Constitution's ratification was "the apprehension that that great principle had not been sufficiently secured." It is "impossible," Curtis argued, to read the debates over ratification without concluding that the "friends of the Constitution" perceived this to be a major "difficulty." As Curtis related the story, the Federalists contended that the proposed Constitution adequately safeguarded equality under the law (through representation and provisions on jury trial, for example), but the public remained unconvinced. This led directly to the adoption of the Fifth Amendment's due process clause, a provision designed "beyond all doubt," Curtis suggested, "for the purpose of closing up every gap which had been left in the construction of the original constitution, whereby any inequality of citizens before the law could be created by the legislative power."[69]

Although Curtis implied that these "historical facts" were indisputable, this reconstruction of the founding was speculative.[70] It is possible to read the republican ideal of equality into the due process clause, but Curtis portrayed this as a more conscious production than the record suggests. The movement to add a bill of rights to the Constitution reflected wide-ranging concerns over the powers of the new central government. While Curtis attributed the adoption of the due process clause to specific concerns over equality, it is just as plausible to say that the Bill of Rights included this provision simply because it was considered a basic right in the Anglo-American legal tradition.

Curtis's questionable use of history suggests the depth of his commitment to the due process guarantee. He represented his clients, to be sure; but he appears to have been exploiting this case as an advocate for empowering this constitutional provision. The irony was that Curtis's claims about equality had no perceptible impact. Although the defendants in the *Union Pacific* case ultimately prevailed, the circuit court declined Curtis's invitation to use due process. On appeal before the Supreme Court, after Curtis's death, his cocounsel repeated his argument, but the Court's opinion made no mention of due process.[71]

At different points in the twentieth century, the Supreme Court located a principle of nondiscrimination in due process, but Curtis's analysis was lost from view. During the *Lochner* era the justices used due process to strike down what they considered to be class legislation (a perverse application of equality to labor relations given the uneven bargaining positions between employers and employees). The same day *Brown v. Board of Education* (1954) was decided, the Court invoked the Fifth Amendment's due process clause to combat racial segregation in public schools in the District of Columbia, where the Fourteenth Amendment's equal protection clause did not apply. Chief Justice Earl Warren suggested that due process embodied a principle of antidiscrimination as he viewed segregation as an "arbitrary deprivation" of liberty.[72]

VI

In the usual historical account, the due process clause was a largely unused, even "feeble," procedural protection for the better part of the nineteenth century.[73] Before 1850 the Supreme Court had paid little attention to this constitutional guarantee. No precedent defined its scope and meaning. There was no direct evidence of the intentions of those who adopted the Fifth Amendment. Nor did the Constitution "declare what principles are to be applied," as Justice Curtis pointed out.[74]

Against that background, Curtis did more than any other Supreme Court justice in the Civil War era to explore the meaning of this constitutional guarantee. The first justice to affirm that the due process clause provided the grounds for judicial review of legislation, he anticipated the expansive readings later given due process, even though subsequent developments evolved independently of his efforts. Curtis suggested that this provision incorporated other constitutional guarantees; a century later due process encompassed practically the whole Bill of Rights. Without clearly distinguishing between substantive and procedural due process, he recognized a liberty of contract two decades before the Supreme Court did. Curtis enthusiastically imported the principle of equality into the due process clause, a point the Court made when reviewing labor regulations and segregation practices. Curtis was, in short, at the forefront in the thinking about the idea of due process at an early stage in its development.

Far from holding to an "outworn 18th Century 'strait jacket'" view,[75] Curtis interpreted due process with some flexibility. His various discussions of due process exemplify his basic approach to constitutional interpretation. He proceeded step by step to define due process in the manner of the common law. It was important to him in shaping this legal concept for the future to place it within a long tradition, dating from Magna Carta. As it turned out, the logical progression of Justice Curtis's interpretations of due process, like his efforts to shape the Court's role in American government, was overtaken by *Dred Scott v. Sandford.*

5. THE *DRED SCOTT* CASE

THE *Dred Scott v. Sandford* decision of 1857 was one of the most notorious in the annals of the Supreme Court. Among a handful of critical events in the decade before the Civil War, this case raised two major issues concerning race and slavery. One involved the standing of blacks in the United States. A question arose over the citizenship of Dred Scott, who had been a slave and claimed his freedom in a lawsuit. Writing for the Court, Chief Justice Taney ruled that no black person, whether slave or free, could ever be a citizen of the United States. He said that blacks were not among the people of the United States. Asserting that at the nation's founding blacks had "no rights which the white man was bound to respect," Taney concluded that black persons could never claim any rights under the Constitution.[1] His discussion has left a lasting impression, although the Court's ruling on citizenship was overturned by the Fourteenth Amendment after the war.[2]

The other main issue in the case concerned the spread of slavery and particularly whether Congress had the authority to prohibit slavery in federal territories. It was widely believed at the time that slavery would die out if kept within the existing slave states. Thus the fate of slavery in America was seen to depend on the answer given this question, and the dispute over the territories had dominated national politics for several years. In these circumstances Taney declared the Missouri Compromise, which had excluded slavery from territories north of latitude 36° 30′ , unconstitutional. For the first time since *Marbury v. Madison* (1803), the Court had exercised the power of judicial review over an act of Congress. All federal territories were open to slavery, and Congress had no power to address this troublesome problem.[3]

Every justice filed an opinion in the *Dred Scott* case. Only McLean and Curtis dissented. In his opinion Justice Curtis argued that blacks were "in every sense part of the people of the United States." He pointed out that blacks were citizens with voting rights in at least five states when the Constitution was adopted. They had the power to vote on ratifying the Constitution, Curtis said, and on that basis he argued that it was "not true" that "the Constitution was made exclusively by the white race." Nor, he added, was it "made exclusively for the white race." On the territorial question Curtis challenged the legitimacy of Taney's ruling. This was "an exertion of judicial power" which "transcends the limits" of the Court's authority, Curtis charged.[4] He then explained why Congress had plenary power to regulate slavery in the territories, and, significantly, why slavery was not a property right protected by the Constitution.

Justice Curtis's opinion had a conspicuous effect on contemporary debate. While McLean also dissented, the antislavery press and the Republican Party turned mainly to Curtis's opinion for support. Lincoln, who carried Curtis's opinion as a reference when debating Senator Stephen A. Douglas, regarded the justice's evidence as conclusive proof that blacks were among the people of the United States. Justice Curtis "shows this with so much particularity as to leave no doubt of its truth," Lincoln said. Leading the attack on the Court, the *New York Tribune* used Curtis's opinion to whip up opposition. The young dissenter "ground up the very bones of the Chief-Justice's argument," according to the *Tribune*. Meanwhile, newspapers farther south advised Justice Curtis to "revise his opinion" in light of the "fulsome praise" coming from the "black-republican press."[5]

Curtis was on the right side in the judgment of history, but so too was McLean. Indeed, McLean advanced some conclusions that were more favorable to the antislavery movement. There was more to Curtis's dissent, however. While Taney's opinion looks like an easy target today, it was not obvious how to respond within the antebellum constitutional structure. In the course of refuting Taney's arguments, Curtis came up with his most artful reading of the Constitution. His dissenting opinion remains illuminating for the interpretive methods he used and for his views on judicial power. Despite its limitations, Curtis's argument on citizenship stands out even today. There was no more comprehensive statement from the antebellum Court showing why blacks were members of the American political community. Taken altogether, the justice offered an exacting demonstration of how to work through the problems posed by slavery within a legal framework.

I

In the 1830s Scott, a slave from the slave state of Missouri, accompanied his owner, John Emerson, to the free state of Illinois and the northern reaches of the Louisiana Purchase, free territory under the Missouri Compromise. Having returned to St. Louis, Scott sued for his freedom in the Missouri state courts on the grounds that he was emancipated after residing on free soil.[6] After several years of stop-and-start litigation,

Scott won a jury verdict. His victory was short-lived, however, as the Missouri Supreme Court reversed on appeal. Overruling precedent that favored Scott's position, the court declared that the state was not obliged to respect the laws of free jurisdictions prohibiting slavery.[7]

Dred Scott then brought his case to the U.S. circuit court. Emerson had died in 1843; his widow had nominally defended in the state courts. Her brother, John F. A. Sanford, was the defendant in the federal courts (his name was misspelled as Sandford in the record). The precise relationship between the two named parties in the federal case remains unclear. Sanford may have owned Scott by this time or served as his sister's agent. In any event, as Sanford had moved from St. Louis to New York, Scott sued under the diversity of citizenship clause of Article III of the Constitution, which extends federal court jurisdiction to cases "between Citizens of different States."[8]

Scott's initial filing therefore began with a critical allegation, that he was a citizen of Missouri. Sanford's response, called a plea in abatement, denied jurisdiction. Scott was not a citizen, it stated, "because he is a negro of African descent; his ancestors were of pure African blood, and were brought into this country and sold as negro slaves." U.S. District Judge Robert Wells ruled that Scott was a citizen, at least to establish diversity jurisdiction. Wells reasoned that residence and legal capacity to own property were sufficient indicia of citizenship for that purpose. Having taken jurisdiction of the case, Wells considered the ultimate question of Scott's citizenship differently (apparently with the Missouri Supreme Court's recent ruling in mind). He instructed the jury that "upon the facts in this case, the law is with the defendant," and Sanford prevailed.[9]

Scott's attorneys then brought the case to the U.S. Supreme Court. After hearing argument in February 1856, the justices divided as to whether the Court, at that point in the litigation, could properly entertain the jurisdictional issue raised by Sanford's plea in abatement. If not, they would have avoided the citizenship issue. Curtis agreed with Taney, Wayne, and Daniel that the Court could consider the plea in abatement. Four others (McLean, Campbell, Grier, and Catron) took the opposite view. The remaining justice, Nelson, was undecided but inclined to take the former position. The Court ordered reargument, directing the attorneys to address the question whether the justices could inquire into the plea in abatement and, assuming so, whether Dred Scott was a citizen entitled to file the lawsuit. However the justices resolved these questions, it appears that they did not plan to rule on Congress's authority over slavery in the territories. Although there had been moves in Congress to pass the territorial question to the Supreme Court, Curtis confided in George Ticknor that the "court will not decide the question of the Missouri Compromise line,—a majority of the judges being of the opinion that it is not necessary to do so."[10]

After the case was reargued the next term, Justice Nelson decided the plea in abatement was not reviewable, and he was assigned the task of writing the majority opinion. Nelson prepared a limited opinion saying that Scott's status was determined by state law as interpreted by the Missouri courts. He would have skirted the questions of black citizenship and congressional power over the territories. Though proslavery, Nelson's opinion would probably have avoided any controversy.[11]

It is obviously of some interest to know what transpired in the Supreme Court's internal deliberations leading to a vastly different outcome. At a conference held in February (about a month before the decision was announced), Wayne moved to reassign the Court's opinion to Taney, and a majority agreed. There are competing versions of the events leading to Wayne's motion. Catron privately informed President-elect James Buchanan that the dissenters had "forced up" the issue. Grier gave a similar account, though he focused on McLean's actions. What the dissenting justices hoped to gain by this remains unclear, but it is difficult to dismiss these remarks completely because Grier and Catron made them independently. Other snippets of information pointed to Taney and Wayne. Rumors had circulated as early as the first of the year that the Court would deliver a strong proslavery decision and that Taney was preparing a detailed opinion. A secondhand account supposedly based upon conversations with Curtis several years later suggested that Wayne was behind the enlarged decision.[12]

In this way a technical question of pleading brought the question of black citizenship before the Supreme Court. Although the Constitution refers to citizenship in several provisions, the framers left potentially explosive issues unanswered.[13] Who qualifies as a citizen of the United States? What rights are associated with citizenship? What is the relationship between national and state citizenship? None of these questions had to be addressed in *Dred Scott*. To be precise, the issue was whether Scott was a citizen of the state of Missouri. Like Judge Wells, the Supreme Court could have limited its inquiry to determine whether Scott was a citizen for the purpose of bringing a federal lawsuit under the diversity of citizenship clause. The Court had previously taken that approach in considering the citizenship of corporations.[14]

Neither Taney nor Curtis showed any reluctance in discussing citizenship in the broadest terms, however. They entered into a full-blown debate over race, equality, and the nature of the American political community. Both seemed eager to impress their views on the public, and each was affected by the other's interpretive choices, rhetorical strategies, and evidence. Curtis later said that he "shaped" his opinion in response to Taney. The chief justice was in turn reacting to Curtis. After the justices read their opinions from the bench, Taney added substantially to his opinion, "upwards of eighteen pages," by Curtis's estimate, in answer to Curtis's dissent.[15]

Their dispute over citizenship had much to do with the rights of free blacks. For some time southerners had expressed concern over what constructions might be placed upon the Constitution's privileges and immunities clause, which provided that "the Citizens of each State shall be entitled to all Privileges and Immunities of Citizens in the several States." Would free blacks from the North be entitled under this provision to enter slave states and claim the right to own property, to enter into contracts, to sue in court, or to travel without restriction? As a practical matter blacks were treated differently than whites throughout the North as well as the South, and most free states denied blacks the right to vote, a right closely associated with citizenship. More was at stake than the question of what rights free blacks actually possessed, however. Antebellum Americans understood citizenship in terms of equal standing under the law and belonging to the community. Citizenship connoted some measure of equality, and in the face of the more openly racist justifications for slavery espoused since the 1830s, considering some blacks as citizens called into question the treatment of any blacks as property.[16]

In this setting Taney held that no black person could become a citizen of the United States. He left no doubt as to what he meant by this. Blacks could not become members of the "political community formed and brought into existence by the Constitution," and they could never claim any rights of citizenship under the Constitution. His position is striking not only for projecting racism into the nation's fundamental law but also for trying to decide these questions for all time. To do that, Taney combined a skewed reading of history with a fixed and intentionalist mode of constitutional construction.[17]

At the start of his opinion, Taney focused on the opening words of the Constitution, "We the people of the United States." Construing this to be the equivalent of citizens, he asked whether the framers meant to include blacks among the "sovereign people." His answer was unequivocal: black persons could never be U.S. citizens because the framers did not consider them among the people of the United States. Racism at the founding was the central premise of the argument, and in the guise of deciphering the attitudes prevailing then, Taney issued a string of striking remarks. He said that when the Constitution was written, blacks were "considered as a subordinate and inferior class of beings, who had been subjugated by the dominant race." Surveying the "state of public opinion" in the eighteenth century, Taney thought it clear that Europeans regarded blacks "as beings of an inferior order, and altogether unfit to associate with the white race, either in social or political relations." Nowhere was this attitude "more firmly fixed" than in England and its colonies, Taney said. He cited colonial laws prohibiting intermarriage to prove that "a perpetual and impassable barrier was intended to be erected" between the races. Thus, with backhanded acknowledgments that the racist opinion of the eighteenth century was illiberal, Chief Justice Taney proceeded to interpolate his view of public opinion into the Constitution.[18]

The attitudes of whites toward blacks, as Taney reconstructed them, provided an insuperable tool to blunt any progressive language stemming from the Revolutionary period. The Declaration of Independence posed obvious problems for Taney. Conceding that the statement that all men are created equal "would seem to embrace the whole human family," he insisted that the authors of the Declaration "knew" that this language "would not in any part of the civilized world be supposed to embrace the negro race." Likewise, when the framers of the Constitution referred to the "people of the United States," Taney said, they needed no explicit reference to whites because the phrase was "so well understood" to exclude blacks.[19]

Appealing to contemporary racist views, Chief Justice Taney established the grounds of decision as if they permitted no accommodation between extremes. Don Fehrenbacher has described Taney's aim as removing the middle ground, with blacks having "equal rights with white men in *all* respects or in *none*." If blacks were citizens, Taney reasoned, "they would be entitled to all" privileges and immunities of citizenship; without that status, blacks could "claim none" of these rights. Following this strategy, Taney framed the issue in this way: "Can a negro, whose ancestors were imported into this country, and sold as slaves, become a member of the political community formed and brought into existence by the Constitution of the United States, and as such become entitled to all the rights, and privileges, and immunities, guarantied by that instrument to the citizen?" It was "obvious," Taney said, that blacks were "not even in the minds of the framers" when they drafted the privileges and immunities clause. It made no difference to Taney whether blacks were "emancipated or not." Free blacks "remained subject to" the authority of whites as much as slaves, in his view. Slave or free, blacks were the objects of "the deepest degradation," according to Taney.[20]

Taney also suggested that citizenship depended upon the opportunity to participate fully in the government. He cited several examples where states denied blacks that opportunity. Taney pointed to New Hampshire's all-white militia to show that blacks were not "permitted to share in one of the highest duties of the citizen" and were not considered "among its people." Only Maine, he said, allowed blacks to "participate equally with the whites in the exercise of civil and political rights." This argument presented difficulties that Taney ignored. He insisted that even if states granted blacks full voting rights, that would not make them eligible for U.S. citizenship. Taney also noted, without offering any clear explanation, that women and minors qualified for citizenship without voting rights.[21]

Chief Justice Taney's argument was essentially complete with a statement about how the Constitution should be interpreted. It "speaks not only in the same words, but with the same meaning and intent with which it spoke when it came from the hands of its framers." Even if public opinion toward blacks changed, the Court could not "give to the words of the Constitution a more liberal construction" than "they were intended to bear when the instrument was framed and adopted." This was, in short, a way of reading the Constitution which permitted no possibility of change through its interpretation. This mode of interpretation was not unique to Taney. Garrisonian abolitionists had a similar understanding that the Constitution was unalterably proslavery, only they sought to do away with the founding document.[22] Whatever deficiencies marred Taney's argument, he had struck a crucial point not easily dismissed: the incongruity of black citizenship under a charter which countenanced a race-based system of slavery.

Operating in the same historical arena, Justice Curtis put forward a radically different conception of American citizenship. He defined the issue before the Court as "whether any person of African descent, whose ancestors were sold as slaves in the United States, can be a citizen of the United States." His affirmative answer was based largely on a historical inquiry into who qualified for citizenship when the Constitution was adopted. Both the question and the answer responded directly to Taney's intentionalism. Curtis indicated some sensitivity to other approaches, but history was useful to him because of the evidence he was able to adduce.[23]

Before the Constitution was adopted, Curtis suggested, free blacks were recognized as citizens in five states: New Hampshire, Massachusetts, New York, New Jersey, and, perhaps surprisingly, North Carolina as well. Black persons who "had the other necessary qualifications possessed the franchise of electors, on equal terms with other citizens," Curtis said. To prove this point, he quoted extensively from the historical account given by Judge William Gaston for the North Carolina supreme court in 1844. According to Gaston, "all free persons" born within the colonies before the American Revolution, "whatever their color or complexion, were native-born British subjects." With the break from England, Gaston explained, "all free persons" including slaves "manumitted here" born "within the State are born citizens of the State." The North Carolina judge noted that his state's constitution granted voting rights to all freemen over the age of twenty-one who paid the appropriate tax. It was "a matter of universal notoriety" that "free persons, without regard to color, claimed and exercised the franchise" in North Carolina.[24]

No doubt Curtis considered it useful to point to the one slave state among the five he had identified. Turning to his home state, Curtis issued a pointed rebuke to Chief Justice Taney, who had referred to a Massachusetts antimiscegenation statute from 1786 to evidence the racist views of whites there. Such "an argument from speculative premises," Curtis said, "would be received with surprise by the people of that State, who know their own political history." Citing *Commonwealth v. Aves*, the case he had lost as a young lawyer, Curtis noted that the Massachusetts constitution adopted in 1780 recognized black persons as citizens and those meeting "the necessary qualifications" had voted over the years. Curtis then quoted from the state constitutions of New Hampshire, New York, and New Jersey to show that they made "no discrimination between free colored persons and others" in the right to vote.[25]

Curtis linked this historical record to the federal Constitution through Article II, which provides that the president must be "a natural born Citizen, or a Citizen of the United States, at the time of the Adoption of the Constitution." The justice interpreted this to mean that the Constitution "necessarily" referred "to citizenship under the Government which existed prior to and at the time of such adoption." Looking to the nature of the government under the Articles of Confederation, Curtis concluded that the "citizens of the several States were citizens of the United States under the Confederation." It followed for Curtis that blacks who were citizens in the five states were also U.S. citizens at the time of the adoption of the Constitution. According to the justice, they retained their standing as citizens unless the Constitution expressly divested them of their citizenship. "I can find nothing in the Constitution," he stated, "which, *proprio vigore*, deprives of their citizenship any class of persons who were citizens of the United States at the time of its adoption, or who should be native-born citizens of any State after its adoption."[26]

With that came the coup de grâce of Curtis's argument. Blacks in the five states mentioned had the "power to act" on ratifying the Constitution and "doubtless did act, by their suffrages, upon the question of its adoption." He said that it was "not true, in point of fact, that the Constitution was made exclusively by the white race." It would be "strange," the justice added, "if we were to find in that instrument anything which deprived of their citizenship any part of the people of the United States who are among those by whom it was established."[27]

If the argument seems obvious in retrospect, it appears that Justice Curtis was the first to piece together this evidence. Abolitionist Joel Tiffany had previously groped toward the conclusion that blacks were among the people of the United States, but his main reason for saying so was that the constitutional language was not qualified in any way. The significance of Curtis's analysis can be observed in how it was received in some quarters in the North. It was on this point that Lincoln found the dissenter's argument incontrovertible. Curtis showed that blacks were "part of the people who made" the Constitution "with so much particularity as to leave no doubt of its truth," Lincoln said. The *New York Tribune* suggested that Curtis had "placed his case" for black citizenship "upon immutable foundations." Curtis's argument "on this point" was "full, thorough, and unanswerable," said Timothy Farrar. In an exhaustive article in the *Monthly Law Reporter*, future Supreme Court justice Horace Gray and the *Reporter*'s editor John Lowell wrote that the only evidence needed to support the rights of blacks as citizens was "the proposition that they were part of the people of the United States when the Constitution was adopted." The justices of Maine's highest court used Curtis's evidence to confirm that blacks were citizens of their state.[28]

Curtis's historical account was not flawless. He overreached in his discussion of the Articles of Confederation, for example. The articles provided that "free inhabitants" had "all the privileges and immunities of free citizens in the several States." Curtis said that the delegates had explicitly rejected a proposal to amend this language so that it applied only to free white inhabitants. Though true, this was part of a wholesale rejection of all amendments, and it is not possible to draw any firm conclusion about the reasons for rejecting the addition of the term *white*.[29]

There were, moreover, significant limitations in Curtis's theory of citizenship. To begin with, he accepted the idea that the states determined the qualifications for U.S. citizenship. It was "left to each State to determine what free persons, born within its limits, shall be citizens of such State, and *thereby* be citizens of the United States." The justice thought it significant, if not conclusive, that the Constitution at several points referred to state rather than national citizenship. He noted that the privileges and immunities clause protected the rights of citizens as citizens of each state. Curtis also pointed out that the Constitution authorized the states to establish the qualifications for voters in federal elections.[30]

Curtis listed alternatives to his position but found each untenable. He noted that the text of the Constitution did not specify which native-born persons were U.S. citizens. He rejected the idea, which McLean had embraced, that all native-born free persons were automatically U.S. citizens.[31] The remaining possibility was that Congress could confer U.S. citizenship on native-born persons, but Curtis reasoned that this power was not implied as the authority to naturalize aliens was expressly granted.

Curtis's scheme led to some curious results. For one thing, a native-born person's claim to U.S. citizenship was conclusively determined by state of birth. For example, a black person born in Alabama in 1857 could not become a U.S. citizen after moving to Massachusetts (nor could a white person from Alabama who did not qualify for citizenship under that state's law). Then, too, following Curtis's approach, nothing in the federal Constitution prevented all of the states from disqualifying free blacks from citizenship. Left in the hands of the states, the prospects for blacks were dim in 1857, worse in some respects than at the founding. The slave states were not about to grant citizenship to blacks; neither were most free states. Of the five states that Curtis had cited, the justice acknowledged that New Jersey no longer permitted blacks to vote and New York imposed different voting qualifications for blacks than for whites. And, while he expressed concern about Congress having the authority to "create privileged classes" by determining the qualifications of citizenship, he seemed oblivious to the consequences of the states doing that.[32]

Another limiting factor in Curtis's theory had to do with the rights of black citizens. In his view the states determined what "civil rights shall be enjoyed by its citizens" as well as "whether all shall enjoy the same."[33] This applied to rights such as voting, holding office, conveying property, or transacting business. Under the privileges and immunities clause, each state also had substantial authority to determine what rights a citizen from another state could claim within its borders. Following the prevailing view of this constitutional provision, Curtis said that out-of-state citizens, "in common with the native-born citizens of that State, must have the qualifications prescribed by [state] law for enjoyment of such privileges."[34] Thus, if a state stipulated that only whites possessed a particular right, then citizens from other states had to be white to exercise that right in that state. Essentially, Justice Curtis viewed the privileges and immunities clause as a nondiscrimination provision which required that out-of-state citizens be treated the same as in-state citizens.

In short, Curtis deferred to the states to determine who qualified for citizenship and what rights citizens possess. Based on the limitations of his analysis, scholars have generally found his conception of citizenship wanting. Don Fehrenbacher described Curtis's position as "racially conservative and of limited scope," seemingly "enlightened" only in comparison with Taney's opinion. Robert Meister suggested that Curtis's interpretation of the privileges and immunities clause was "arguably less liberal" than Taney's. Earl M. Maltz said that Justice Curtis's views on citizenship "fell far short of advanced antislavery positions."[35]

When taken as a snapshot in 1857, Curtis's theory of citizenship was indeed limiting. States determined whether blacks were citizens, and free black citizens from one state were subject to the discriminatory practices of other states. However, Curtis's mode of analysis evinced a concern for establishing foundational principles, and when considered for the long term, the ideas he set forth were potentially far-reaching.

To begin with, Curtis said that "color was not a necessary qualification of citizenship" under the Constitution. From Article II's passing reference to a "natural born Citizen," he read the Constitution to accord with the English common-law doctrine of *jus soli* (citizenship derives from birthplace). He dismissed the alternative, *jus sanguinis* (citizenship by right of blood or descent). That by itself cut to the heart of the matter raised in Dred Scott's case as "African descent" did not disqualify blacks from U.S. citizenship. He bolstered that conclusion by citing actions taken by the federal government since the founding. The justice pointed out that treaties had granted citizenship to "large bodies of Mexican and North American Indians as well as free colored inhabitants of Louisiana."[36]

As Justice Curtis constructed a constitutional rule of citizenship from the history of the founding, he made a special point of insulating the question of whether blacks could qualify for citizenship from the actions taken by the states after the Constitution was adopted. The retrogressive changes made by North Carolina, New Jersey, and New York "can have no other effect upon the present inquiry, except to show, that before they were made, no such restrictions existed; and colored in common with white persons, were not only citizens of those States, but entitled to the elective franchise on the same qualifications as white persons."[37] In Curtis's view such changes were inconsequential to the overall principle he articulated. Whether blacks could qualify for U.S. citizenship was not subject to ongoing debate. In this way Curtis fashioned constitutional principle out of the laws of the most progressive states when the Constitution was adopted.

Moreover, one cannot discount the significance of a statement from a justice of the nation's highest court that blacks had actually participated in ratifying the Constitution. In saying this, Curtis was not only responding to Taney but to an entire mythology built around the idea of black inferiority. There was a widespread view of blacks as degraded, intellectually inferior, incapable of ruling themselves, let alone participating in the collective enterprise of government.[38] There was on the other hand a long tradition in political thought that the citizen had the necessary tools—reason and independence—to become an active participant in political activity of the highest order. With something like this conceptual opposition in the antebellum mind, it was inconceivable to many whites that blacks could be citizens sharing in the exercise of political power. This was particularly evident in the view of the American founding. As a justice of the Arkansas Supreme Court stated authoritatively, free blacks "certainly" were not "permitted to participate" in forming the Constitution. As Curtis noted, it "has been often asserted that the Constitution was made exclusively by and for the white race."[39] Thus, when Justice Curtis placed blacks at this extraordinary moment in American constitutional history—this novel exercise in republican government, with sovereignty exercised by the people in an unprecedented manner—he effectively repudiated the racist rationale for excluding blacks from political participation in the ordinary acts of government.

Curtis also questioned the conclusions Taney had drawn about the Declaration of Independence. The chief justice had said that the conduct of its authors "would have been utterly and flagrantly inconsistent with the principles they asserted" had they considered blacks among "all men . . . created equal." There was an edge to Curtis's response.

> My own opinion is, that a calm comparison of these assertions of universal abstract truths, and of their own individual opinions and acts, would not leave these men under any reproach of inconsistency; that the great truths they asserted on that solemn occasion, they were ready and anxious to make effectual, where a necessary regard to circumstances, which no statesman can disregard without producing more evil than good, would allow; and that it would not be just to them, nor true in itself, to allege

that they intended to say that the Creator of all men had endowed the white race, exclusively, with the great natural rights which the Declaration of Independence asserts. But this is not the place to vindicate their memory.

In a nutshell, Justice Curtis distanced the founding documents from Taney's reconstruction of the state of opinion on race in that period.[40]

As for the rights of black citizens, it is easy to dismiss Curtis's approach by today's standards, when a fair definition of citizenship incorporates some combination of legal, political, civil, economic, and social rights. However, it appears that Curtis was trying to secure the middle ground in response to Taney. If Curtis's conception of citizenship is subject to criticism for its apparent emptiness, it had the virtue of flexibility. In 1857 few whites subscribed to the view that blacks should have equal rights in all respects. Taney exploited that fact by suggesting that blacks, to be citizens, must possess all of the rights of citizenship. Justice Curtis countered with an open-ended test: citizenship under the Constitution did not depend "on the possession of any particular political or even of all civil rights; and any attempt so to define it must lead to error."[41] This kept the question of what rights a citizen had from limiting who qualified for citizenship.

The right to vote presented Curtis with a dilemma. On the one hand, voting rights were closely linked to citizenship; on the other hand, most states denied free blacks the vote. Had voting rights been the sine qua non of citizenship, many free blacks would have been disqualified from citizenship. When *Dred Scott* was decided, only a small minority of whites favored black suffrage. Even as the Civil War drew to a close, many congressmen were unwilling to go further than to grant the franchise to black soldiers.[42] The Fourteenth Amendment, ratified in 1868, accorded blacks equality in civil rights without mandating equality in voting rights. It was not until 1870 that the Fifteenth Amendment prohibited racial discrimination in voting rights. In *Dred Scott*, Curtis worked around this problem when he declared the right to vote "decisive evidence of citizenship" and one of its "chiefest attributes" but stated that he did not "think the enjoyment of the elective franchise essential to citizenship."[43]

In a more positive vein, the question remained as to what rights black citizens did possess. It appears that, for Curtis, the answer derived from the one right directly at issue in *Dred Scott*, that of bringing a lawsuit. Access to the federal courts opened a range of possibilities, although Justice Curtis did not spell them out. Under diversity jurisdiction, citizens of states could file lawsuits against citizens from other states provided the amount in controversy was greater than $500. That right by itself was potentially significant, for it provided the means for persons to protect their civil rights, which were understood then to include the rights to enter into contracts, to own property, to be a party in court, and generally to have the benefit of laws and legal proceedings. These were among the key rights protected by the Civil Rights Act of 1866. Moreover, having the ability to seek remedies in matters of private law in federal court could open opportunities for black citizens to participate in the market, one measure of freedom in this day.[44]

The federal courts also had jurisdiction over questions arising under the Constitution and the laws of the United States. Regarding the rights of citizenship, the most relevant constitutional provision was the privileges and immunities clause: "The Citizens of each State shall be entitled to all Privileges and Immunities of Citizens in the several States." When *Dred Scott* was decided, the meaning of this language was unsettled. In the federal courts the most extensive treatment of the rights it covered had been given in *Corfield v. Coryell* (1823). Writing on circuit, Justice Bushrod Washington denied that a right to gather oysters was protected under this provision, which he nevertheless construed broadly to protect "fundamental" rights. This included, in his opinion, "the enjoyment of life and liberty, with the right to acquire and possess property of every kind, and to pursue and obtain happiness and safety," along with the rights to travel, to bring lawsuits, and to own property.[45]

The privileges and immunities clause was not directly at issue in the *Dred Scott* case, but it was clearly on Taney's mind. The chief justice had raised the specter of free blacks claiming rights as citizens and roaming about the slave states with the "full liberty of speech in public and in private upon all subjects upon which its own citizens might speak; to hold public meetings upon political affairs, and to keep and carry arms wherever they went."[46] It was a parade of horribles from the southern perspective, pointed out to suggest that recognizing free blacks as citizens would undermine the system of slavery.

Sensitive to the incendiary nature of questions surrounding the privileges and immunities clause, Curtis, true to form, resorted to common-law methods to guide its interpretation. He discussed this provision in *Conner v. Elliott* (1856), decided while *Dred Scott* was pending before the Supreme Court. Writing for the Court, Justice Curtis noted that this "broad" language raised "matters of great delicacy and importance." He declined to offer a "merely abstract definition" which, he said, "could scarcely be correct" and "would certainly produce mischief." *Conner* was a puzzling little opinion. A widow living in Mississippi had asserted rights in property previously owned by her husband and located in the state of Louisiana, which refused to recognize her claim. Justice Curtis held that there was no violation of the privileges and immunities clause because the property rights did not "belong to citizenship" but rather derived from state contract law.[47]

The question which Curtis left unanswered, purposefully, was what rights "belong to citizenship." He repeated this phrase in *Dred Scott*, where he discussed this point with some care. Curtis allowed that the privileges and immunities clause did "not confer on the citizens of one State, in all other States, specific and enumerated privileges and immunities"; instead, the states determined the rights covered by this provision. The justice explained that if a state granted a right to its citizens "by reason of mere naked citizenship, then it may be claimed by every citizen of each State." If the state specified additional qualifications for its own citizens to possess a right, however, then out-of-state citizens would have to meet those qualifications as well. In short, the privileges and immunities clause prohibited discrimination against out-of-state citizens for the rights that the states associated with citizenship.[48]

As limited as this appears, it looks again like Curtis sought to articulate a middle ground against Taney's position. State law decided which rights came with citizenship, but that did not relieve the federal courts of responsibility for interpreting state law and, to that extent, defining and enforcing the rights of citizenship on a case-by-case basis. Curtis also gestured toward a broader view of the privileges and immunities clause when he recounted the controversy surrounding the admission of Missouri as a state in 1821. The proposed state constitution included a provision to prevent free blacks from entering and residing in Missouri. Congress admitted the state on the "fundamental condition" that its constitution never be construed to deprive any citizen "of any of the privileges and immunities to which such citizen is entitled under the Constitution of the United States."[49] The only conclusion Curtis drew from this episode was that Congress had construed the privileges and immunities clause to apply to free blacks. The implication, which Curtis left hanging, was that this constitutional provision did more than simply prohibit discrimination against out-of-state citizens. It was reasonable to infer from his discussion that the right to travel was secured by the privileges and immunities clause, whatever state law declared. This meant that the federal courts were not strictly bound by state laws in interpreting the rights of citizenship.[50]

In the final analysis, Curtis's interpretation of citizenship in *Dred Scott* represents an important example of his way of reading the Constitution. It was one thing to find, as antislavery proponents had, a statement of ideal principles in the Declaration of Independence.[51] It was another to locate an aspirational view in the Constitution. These two founding documents appeared to be at odds; the one proclaiming all men are created equal, the other containing several provisions conducive to slavery's continued existence. Curtis's discussion of citizenship in *Dred Scott* has some bearing on this. In response to Taney's argument that blacks, to be citizens, must have equal rights with whites in all respects, Curtis promoted an elastic definition of citizenship. Blacks who were denied the right to vote were not automatically disqualified from citizenship. Considered in the long term, the principles Curtis articulated were suggestive. Black persons were members of the American political community. At least some had the right to sue in court, and the federal judiciary had a role in enforcing their rights. He did not clarify exactly how progress toward racial equality should occur, but his discussion intimated that the law was not necessarily an obstacle but rather a framework for change.

II

In retrospect, the issue of black citizenship, embodying basic questions of race and equality, appears more consequential than that of slavery in the territories. Yet in the decade before the Civil War, the territorial question occupied center stage. It was, Curtis said in 1861, seen to be "not only the paramount, but almost the only, national question worthy of any consideration," of "such stupendous magnitude that the national existence must be staked on it." This issue became important partly due to the subjective beliefs in both North and South that the outcome of the struggle over the territories would decide the future of slavery in the United States. Stop the spread of slavery, Lincoln said, and "it *would* be in the course of ultimate extinction"; or as Charles Sumner put it, slavery would then die "as a poisoned rat dies of rage in its hole."[52] While the territorial question became a primary outlet for antislavery sentiment, some northerners opposed the extension of slavery not out of concern for the slave but rather to preserve opportunities for free white laborers in the West. Meanwhile, many southerners operated from the premise that their agricultural system, and their way of life, required continued expansion to survive.[53]

The problem of what to do about slavery in the territories had been around since the founding, but it was not always controversial. The Northwest Ordinance of 1787, adopted without rancor, disallowed slavery in territory north of the Ohio River; no similar prohibition was made for the area to the south. The battle that led to the Missouri Compromise focused more on the conditions for admitting Missouri as a state than on the disposition of slavery in the rest of the Louisiana Purchase. Again, there was little debate over the territorial solution, which in this case "forever" banned slavery north of the 36° 30' parallel.[54] With the acquisition of over one million square miles of new land between 1845 and 1853, tensions grew. Shortly after the start of the war with Mexico, Pennsylvania congressman David Wilmot introduced legislation to exclude slavery from any lands acquired from that nation. His proposal, called the Wilmot Proviso, never passed, but it had the effect of crystallizing sectional differences.[55]

In the election of 1848, the Free-Soil Party was formed. As its name implied, the party was committed above all else to halting the spread of slavery. Meanwhile, southerners embraced grandiose schemes for expanding slavery under the American flag, with Cuba, Baja California, and Nicaragua particular targets. Of the lands wrested from Mexico, the Compromise of 1850 admitted California as a free state and allowed slavery in the New Mexico and Utah territories. Passage of the Kansas-Nebraska Act four years later unleashed the country's passions surrounding the territorial issue. Applying the doctrine of popular sovereignty, Congress allowed the settlers to decide for themselves whether they wanted slavery in the Kansas and Nebraska territories, which comprised most of the Louisiana Purchase north of the 36° 30' parallel. This legislation led to a critical change in mainstream opinion in the North, the birth of the Republican Party, and skirmishing in so-called Bleeding Kansas.[56]

By the time of the presidential election in 1856, the various policies regarding slavery in the territories revolved around four mutually exclusive positions. With each, politics shaped the constitutional arguments, which were more dogmatic than reasoned. One view held that Congress must prohibit slavery in the territories. The Republican Party took this position in its platform on the theory that Congress had "sovereign powers" over the territories and that slavery violated the due process clause. Another was the doctrine of popular sovereignty, also called territorial sovereignty. A proponent of this view was Senator Stephen A. Douglas, a leading presidential contender in 1856 who issued a Senate committee report that year to explain why Congress had no legal authority to exclude slavery from the territories.[57] A third position was the proslavery doctrine, which held that Congress, as the states' agent for the territories (the common property of the states), had a constitutional obligation to protect the property rights of slave owners in federal territories. Senator John C. Calhoun had played an important part in shaping this view before he died in 1850.[58] Finally, there was the idea of dividing territory between slave and free, the solution embodied in the Missouri Compromise. Though not part of the Constitution itself, the Missouri Compromise was regarded by some as more than ordinary legislation—a "sacred" pact having quasi-constitutional status.[59]

That was the context in which Chief Justice Taney declared the Missouri Compromise restriction unconstitutional. This ruling was significant even though the Kansas-Nebraska Act had repealed the Missouri Compromise's prohibition against slavery three years earlier. The Kansas-Nebraska Act was based on the idea of popular sovereignty and had not covered the Minnesota Territory and northern territories extending to the Pacific Northwest.[60] Taney's decision opened all territories to slavery as a matter of constitutional principle.

The chief justice had a difficult position to establish in the law. That may account for the scholarly consensus that his discussion was "tortuous" and "labored."[61] To begin with, Taney denied that Congress had the power to ban slavery from the territories. It is difficult to imagine a more constrictive interpretation of the Constitution's text than the one Taney provided. Even though the territories clause stated that "Congress shall have Power to dispose of and make all needful Rules and Regulations respecting the Territory or other Property belonging to the United States," the chief justice insisted that there was "no express regulation in the Constitution defining the power which the General Government may exercise over the person or property of a citizen in a Territory." He said that the reference to "the Territory" applied only to land claimed by the national government at the founding while "other Property" referred to personal property. Based on this reading, whatever powers were granted did not pertain to the Louisiana Purchase, the area in dispute in *Dred Scott*. Taney also sought to narrow the meaning of the phrase "needful Rules and Regulations." He construed this phrase to refer to "particular specified" powers in contrast with broad "powers of sovereignty" (a jab at the Republican platform, whether intentional or not). In short, Taney concluded that the territories clause did not give Congress power to govern territories west of the Mississippi River.[62]

Having rendered the territories clause meaningless as a lasting source of authority, Taney closed off another avenue for Congress to prohibit slavery in the territories, that of implied powers. He conceded Congress's implied power to govern the territories, but this authority was limited by its purpose. Citing the Constitution's language that "new States may be admitted by the Congress into this Union," Taney suggested that Congress could govern the territories only to prepare them for statehood. He also incorporated the southern common property doctrine into his analysis. Congress served as "trustee" of the territories held for the "common and equal benefit" of the people, he said.[63]

The chief justice supplemented this argument with a revisionist history of the Northwest Ordinance, which had banned slavery in the Northwest Territory. This legislation presented Taney with a problem, as it suggested that Congress had the constitutional power to prohibit slavery in the territories. The chief justice essentially argued that the ordinance was not relevant. He exploited the fact that the Northwest Ordinance was originally enacted under the Articles of Confederation. Given the nature of the government then, Taney considered the action taken by the Confederation Congress to be a legitimate exercise of the collective powers of the states. Without offering any evidence, he suggested that members of the First Congress held the same view. They reenacted the ordinance, Taney suggested, only because they considered the issue "already determined." This assertion was not supported by the historical record. The First Congress acted because it was felt that the Confederation Congress lacked authority to enact the ordinance.[64]

Taney also said that the Missouri Compromise restriction infringed a slave owner's property rights that were protected by the Fifth Amendment's due process clause. Starting with the idea that U.S. citizens did not forfeit their constitutional rights in the territories, the chief justice identified several constitutional rights (such as free speech and the right to a jury trial) which he said were obviously protected in the territories. He called these "rights of person." Then he suggested that "rights of property" were "placed on the same ground by the fifth amendment" as "rights of person." With that, Taney concluded that an act of Congress "which deprives a citizen of the United States of his liberty or property, merely because he came himself or brought his property into a particular Territory of the United States, and who had committed no offence against the laws, could hardly be dignified with the name of due process of law."[65]

Taney's interpretation of due process was important in any event, but as he developed his argument, a significant point emerged regarding the constitutional protection of slavery and the right to own slaves. Within this segment of his opinion, Chief Justice Taney issued one of its most important statements; Lincoln called it the "essence" of the *Dred Scott* case. It seems to be supposed, Taney said, "that there is a difference between property in a slave and other property, and that different rules may be applied to it in expounding the Constitution." He then delivered a strongly worded statement that "the right of property in a slave is distinctly and expressly affirmed in the Constitution." According to the chief justice, one could point to a number of constitutional provisions to demonstrate this (the fugitive slave clause, for example). He also emphasized that "no word can be found in the Constitution" which affords slave property less protection than other forms of property. Thus Congress was powerless to designate any territory free. Not only that, Taney's language raised the possibility of slavery nationalized throughout the free states as well.[66]

Justice Curtis disputed his chief justice at every turn. Running through his discussion was a barely concealed sense of outrage at what Taney had done to the Court and the Constitution. Curtis began his discussion of the territorial question with a point of legal procedure, but what he said there had more of an immediate political impact than anything else in his seventy-page opinion. Curtis argued that once the Court had determined that jurisdiction was lacking, it had no authority to decide the territorial question. If Dred Scott was not a citizen, as Taney said, then Scott had no right to bring the lawsuit, and that was the end of the matter. The chief justice developed a clever response. He linked the territorial issue to the jurisdictional question. Noting that several justices questioned whether the citizenship issue was properly before the Court, Taney offered his ruling on the Missouri Compromise as an alternative rationale for the jurisdictional point. Because the Missouri Compromise was unconstitutional, Taney argued, Scott remained a slave, and he could not file this lawsuit for that reason.[67]

The arguments advanced by both jurists were more technical than this brief summary suggests.[68] While Justice Curtis elaborated upon the rules of pleading and appellate procedure, his discussion took on a larger dimension about the Supreme Court's role. "On so grave a subject as this," Curtis said, "such an exertion of judicial power transcends the limits of the authority of the court." He expanded on this view: "A great question of constitutional law, deeply affecting the peace and welfare of the country is not, in my opinion, a fit subject to be thus reached." The justice's tone turned provocative at one point. "I do not hold any opinion of this court, or any court, binding, when expressed on a question not legitimately before it."[69]

In the midst of the passionate national debate, these were weighty charges, and Curtis's challenge to the Court's authority laid the foundation for one of the most pervasive attacks on Taney's opinion. In his study *The Impending Crisis*, David M. Potter has noted the effect. As "the argument against the decision developed, it took the form, above all, of an elaboration of the statement in Justice Curtis's dissent." McLean raised a similar objection, but the challenge to the Court's authority "gained force," as Potter suggested, "from the assurance with which Curtis originally stated the point."[70] The *New York Tribune* declared the Court's decision, "as Mr. Justice Curtis substantially pronounced it, extra-judicial, and foreign to the case under review." According to the *Tribune*'s report, "Curtis created a very marked sensation among his colleagues by charging" them with "a violation of their own rules of judicial action." Thomas Hart Benton, the famed politician from Missouri, was so disturbed by the Court's ruling that he devoted his last days while dying of cancer to produce a monograph on the case. "I think, with Mr. Justice Curtis," Benton wrote, "that so grave an inquiry, going to the foundations of our government, ought not to be got hold of in that incidental, subaltern, and contingent way." It was the Republican Party that found this idea of judicial overreaching especially useful. After the decision was announced, the party's political opponents were quick to suggest that the Court's ruling effectively outlawed the "whole basis" of Republican doctrine. Curtis's argument provided the Republicans with a way to oppose the Court's ruling without flouting the law, and the view that Taney's position on the territories was unnecessary to the decision and not binding became, in the words of Don Fehrenbacher, the "Republican battle cry in the war upon the Dred Scott decision."[71]

Exactly how Justice Curtis assembled his substantive arguments on the territorial question reveals much about his approach to constitutional interpretation. It has been said that Curtis relied mostly on an originalist conception of the framers' intent.[72] Although Curtis alluded to the framers at several points, his interpretation was more intricate than that, combining arguments based on the constitutional text, history, and structure. Regarding the text, Curtis believed the territories clause granted Congress plenary power to govern the territories. Countering Taney's limited reading of "regulations," Curtis pointed to the "great system of municipal laws" enacted under the power "to regulate" interstate and foreign commerce. The dissenting justice also offered a different historical account. He cited *The Federalist* to show that the framers, in the belief that the Confederation lacked authority to enact the Northwest Ordinance, specifically included the territories clause to ensure that the new Congress had ample power to govern the territories.[73]

However, the driving force behind Curtis's argument was a structural analysis that went beyond the language of the Constitution. He said that even without an express grant of authority, it was possible to infer that Congress had power to govern the territories. As Curtis put it, "There is very strong reason to believe, before we examine the

Constitution itself," in "the necessity for a competent grant of power to hold, dispose of, and govern territory." Taney's position, Curtis added, was as "inconsistent with the nature and purposes of the instrument" as it was "with its language."[74]

As is often the case with this nontextual method of interpretation, Curtis's argument consisted of "deceptively simple logical moves." He began with a straightforward image of the nation. "We must take into consideration," Curtis said, the "great consideration, ever present to the minds" of the founding generation, that they were "making a frame of government" for the future with the expectation that the United States would become "a great and powerful nation." With that in mind, Curtis suggested that the framers invested the national government with the powers "to make war and to conclude treaties, and thus to acquire territory."[75]

He then deduced the structural relationship between Congress and the territories from the idea that one of the nation's essential character-istics was territorial expansion and, with that, the extension of republi-can government. As the territories required "social order," Congress was "granted the indispensably necessary power to institute temporary governments, and to legislate for the inhabitants of the territory." Cur-tis indicated that territorial governance could not be left to the settlers alone. He did not clarify exactly why that was the case, but the unspo-ken assumption behind his analysis was that for republican government to take root in territories acquired, the national legislature must be in charge of directing the government there.[76]

Curtis also exploited Taney's concession that Congress had implied powers over the territories. The dissenter's rejoinder came close to rid-icule: if the "necessity" of some power to govern the territory is "so great, that, in the absence of any express grant, it is strong enough to raise an implication of the existence of that power, it would seem to fol-low that it is also strong enough to afford material aid in construing an express grant of power respecting that territory." While Curtis dis-played a keen sense for exploiting the weaknesses in Taney's argument, a crucial problem remained. Even if Congress had the authority to gov-ern the territories, why did this include the power to prohibit slavery there? As Lincoln later pointed out, the Constitution did not expressly answer that question.[77] Indeed, a plausible argument could be drawn from this constitutional provision against Curtis. The territories clause authorized Congress to make "needful" rules and regulations. Arguably, this limited Congress's power over the territories. Why, in other words, was the Missouri Compromise restriction a needful law?

For Curtis the word "needful" marked the constitutional dividing line between legislative and judicial authority. In his view the question whether a law was needful was inherently legislative, with judicial scrutiny limited to determining whether the law violated an express constitutional prohibition. With that exception, it remained for Congress to judge the scope of its own powers. In Curtis's words, "Undoubtedly the question whether a particular rule or regulation be needful, must be finally determined by Congress itself. Whether a law be needful, is a legislative or political, not a judicial, question. Whatever Congress deems needful is so, under the grant of power." To rebut the idea that slavery "forms an exception" to legislative discretion, Curtis noted that the territories clause empowers Congress to make "all" needful rules, and "where the constitution has said *all* needful rules and regulations, I must find something more than theoretical reasoning to induce me to say it did not mean all."[78]

Curtis found confirmation for his interpretation in Congress's "practical construction, nearly contemporaneous with the adoption of the Constitution, and continued by repeated instances through a long series of years." Such a practical interpretation "may always influence, and in doubtful cases should determine, the judicial mind, on a question of the interpretation of the Constitution." Among a "long line of legislative and executive precedents," Curtis regarded the reenactment of the Northwest Ordinance as particularly influential, for it was "an assertion by the first Congress" of its power to prohibit slavery in the territories. Curtis pointed out that fourteen of the delegates to the Constitutional Convention, including James Madison, were members of that Congress.[79] The justice then recited over a dozen occasions when Congress exercised its power over slavery in the territories, either by banning or permitting the practice there.

All in all, Curtis's interpretation contained the basic ingredients of national power over slavery that southerners feared: broad legislative discretion in the Congress and limited judicial scrutiny. His reasoning was a logical follow-up to Chief Justice Marshall's opinion in *McCulloch v. Maryland* (1819), which had provoked extensive rebuttals from the South.[80] In fact, that case provides an instructive parallel to Curtis's structural reasoning.

McCulloch involved a tax that Maryland had imposed on notes issued by the national bank. One question raised was whether Congress had the power to incorporate the bank, as there was no express grant for that in the Constitution. Recognizing broad implied powers in Congress to adopt "appropriate" means to achieve "legitimate" ends, Marshall upheld its authority to charter the national bank. He pointed to the Constitution's necessary and proper clause, which authorizes Congress to "make all Laws which shall be necessary and proper for carrying into Execution" its enumerated powers. But constitutional structure was the rationale underlying Marshall's argument, as Charles Black has suggested. Marshall looked to the overall "nature" of the government to figure out its powers; he suggested that Congress would have discretion over the means chosen to implement its enumerated powers even in the absence of the necessary and proper clause. The chief justice also distinguished between the powers of Congress and the Court. The question of "degree" concerning the "necessity" of a law, Marshall stated, "is to be discussed in another place" (namely Congress). For courts "to inquire into the degree of its necessity, would be to pass the line which circumscribes the judicial department, and to tread on legislative ground." Marshall even alluded to the territories clause to support his interpretation.[81] With Marshall's structural approach and the way he divided legislative and judicial powers, it is difficult to believe Curtis did not have *McCulloch* in mind, though he did not cite that opinion.

At the conclusion of the argument on Congress's power over the territories, Curtis still had to contend with Taney's reference to the due process clause. Considering that, before *Dred Scott*, Curtis had done more than any other justice to foster the development of due process, it is ironic that Taney used this constitutional guarantee to justify his ruling on the Missouri Compromise. Justice Curtis pointed out the novelty in Taney's argument; strange, the dissenter thought, that "no one discovered" this constitutional violation until 1857. Curtis's basic strategy, along the lines taken by the Republican Party, was to focus on the character of the right at stake. The due process clause protected property, that was indisputable; but slavery was a "particular species of property" not protected by that constitutional provision. His argument rested on the *Somersett* doctrine that slavery could exist only where sanctioned by positive law. Slavery was "contrary to natural right," Curtis said, and slaves were "property only to the extent and under the conditions fixed" where "municipal laws on the subject of slavery exist." Where Congress prohibited slavery in the territories, there was no such law.[82]

It was in his discussion of due process that Taney had said that "the right of property in a slave" was "distinctly and expressly" protected by the Constitution.[83] Curtis's rebuttal is revealing. For years he had maintained that slavery contravened natural right. Yet in *Commonwealth v. Aves* and the fugitive slave debates, Curtis had objected to using principles of natural justice as a source for the law on slavery. In *Dred Scott*,

Curtis finally had an issue involving slavery where he was comfortable in applying natural right. The implication was that constitutional provisions like the fugitive slave clause did not spill over beyond their precise mandate (in that case the return of escaped slaves). Thus there was no constitutional protection for slavery merely as a property right, whether in the due process clause, the Bill of Rights, or anywhere else in the charter.

Along with the questions surrounding slavery in the territories, Curtis confronted a delicate conflict of laws problem. Even assuming that the Missouri Compromise was constitutional and that Scott had been a free man in federal territory, the question remained whether he was a slave under state law upon his return to St. Louis. According to Justice Curtis, the Missouri Compromise "absolutely" dissolved the master-slave relationship, but the Missouri Supreme Court had previously decided in *Scott v. Emerson* that Dred Scott reverted to slavery under state law. An earlier Taney opinion indicated that such a state court decision was controlling.[84] Abandoning his usually diplomatic approach to federal-state relations, Curtis argued that *Scott v. Emerson* was not binding on the U.S. Supreme Court. He distinguished the state court decision from the law of Missouri. As there was no applicable state statute, the justice reasoned that the governing law was the common law, which in turn incorporated the rules of international law. Curtis noted that the federal judiciary was not bound by state court determinations of the principles of universal jurisprudence. In addition, he pointed out that the *Emerson* opinion was contrary to the Missouri Supreme Court's own precedent. That court had justified its ruling based upon the political climate in the free states—the "dark and fell spirit in relation to slavery." Curtis suggested that it was not within "the province of any judicial tribunal" to refuse to recognize the law of other jurisdictions based upon such "political considerations."[85]

There was one additional fact which Curtis turned to his advantage. Dred Scott had married Harriet Robinson in the Wisconsin Territory. As a general rule, a slave could not enter into a legally enforceable marriage contract. Curtis construed Dr. Emerson's consent to the marriage as an act of emancipation. The justice further suggested that Missouri could not regard the Scotts as slaves without violating the constitutional requirement that no state impair the obligation of contracts.[86]

Taney's decision on the Missouri Compromise remains one of the most prominent examples of judicial overreaching in the Supreme Court's history. In the course of his discussion of the territorial issue, Curtis issued a forceful statement on the character of judicial interpretation and the relationship between law and politics.

Judicial tribunals, as such, cannot decide upon political considerations. Political reasons have not the requisite certainty to afford rules of juridical interpretation. They are different in different men. They are different in the same men at different
times. And when a strict interpretation of the Constitution, according to the fixed rules which govern the interpretation of
laws, is abandoned, and the theoretical opinions of individuals
are allowed to control its meaning, we have no longer a Constitution; we are under the government of individual men, who for
the time being have power to declare what the Constitution is,
according to their own views of what it ought to mean.

This passage seems straightforward enough—a resounding call to keep
politics out of the courts—and it has been noted by commentators over
the years.[87]

No doubt Curtis recognized differences between the judicial process and politics. Yet his conception of the judicial role was more complex than this statement standing alone suggests. It is important to bear
in mind that it served Curtis's rhetorical purpose to portray the Court's
decision as political.[88] More to the point, he offered these comments in
a specific context which colors their meaning. This discussion arose as
he interpreted the word "needful" in the territories clause. In construing that term, Curtis identified three positions circulating in the public
debate. First, there were those who favored excluding slavery from all
territories. They relied, according to Curtis, on the "moral evils of slavery," natural right, and the Declaration of Independence, along with republicanism. Second, others invoked the "right of self-government" to
justify territorial sovereignty. Third, slave owners claimed that barring
slavery from the territories violated their "equal right" to "go with their
property upon the public domain." In Curtis's view it was perfectly appropriate for Congress to examine these "general considerations," but
the Court had no concern with their "weight." That was the point to be
drawn from the language of the territories clause. These considerations
"may be justly entitled to guide or control the legislative judgment upon
what is a needful regulation."[89]

Curtis did not mean to exclude such general considerations from
constitutional analysis altogether. After all, within the space of a few
pages, he invoked natural right to interpret the due process clause. It
seems reasonable to infer that Curtis's remarks were meant as a comment on the specific constitutional provision in question. The territories clause allocated institutional responsibilities so that Congress had

complete discretion to decide what regulations were needful. Curtis believed that Taney had for "purely" political reasons created a "substantive" exception to this provision "not found in it." The consequences of this were magnified by the "complexity of the interests" involved.[90]

What, finally, did Curtis's opinion imply for the future of slavery in the territories? Some scholars have suggested that his position was "neither antislavery nor proslavery" but "neutral" on this issue.[91] On its face, Curtis's analysis was formally neutral: Congress could permit as well as prohibit slavery in the territories. Lawmakers had discretion to decide how to govern the territories; legislation regulating slavery in the territories raised political questions to be resolved by the electoral process, not by the Court. The justice did not embrace the Republican Party's view that the due process clause barred slavery from federal territory.

The charge of political gamesmanship cut in more than one direction, however. What was neutral in form was not neutral in effect. Curtis's interpretation of Congress's powers—legislative discretion mixed with minimal judicial scrutiny—raised an old bugaboo for southerners. He would have left the fate of slavery in the territories to the political process; in context, this was not a neutral act. The Kansas-Nebraska Act had spawned a grim determination throughout the North on the territorial question. The Republican Party was growing in strength. While southerners retained substantial power in Congress, the House of Representatives had selected a Republican as speaker in 1856.[92] Add to that Justice Curtis's contention that slavery was a unique form of property, lacking constitutional protection as a property right. This directly contradicted the proslavery position. Most telling perhaps was Curtis's challenge to the legitimacy of the Court's decision. It is inconceivable that he was oblivious to the effect that might have.

III

The *Dred Scott* case, the last on the docket for the 1856 term, was also Curtis's last with the Court. Curtis apparently discussed resigning after the decision was announced. His confidant Senator George E. Badger pleaded with the justice to avoid a "hasty decision." Curtis tendered his resignation to President Buchanan on September 1, 1857. A noteworthy episode in anyone's life, this was under the circumstances an extraordinary event in the Supreme Court's history.[93]

Curtis's resignation followed an unusual sequence of events set in motion after the justices read from their opinions on the bench. Curtis and McLean made copies of their opinions available to the press, and newspapers promptly published their dissents. According to Curtis's brother, Justice Curtis released his opinion on the assumption that all of the justices' opinions had been filed with the clerk of the Court and that the press could therefore obtain them as well. Yet Taney continued to work on his. When McLean heard that the chief justice was revising the opinion, he thought it "unusual, if not improper."[94]

When Curtis learned of this, he tried to obtain a copy of the new version from William T. Carroll, the clerk of the Court. Carroll wrote Curtis that the "Chief Justice had directed me not to furnish a copy of his opinion to any one without his permission before it is published in Howard's Reports." Taney had issued an order, signed by Wayne and Daniel, instructing the clerk to "give no copy of this opinion to *any one* until the Reporter has printed it."[95]

After receiving Carroll's note, Curtis repeated his request. "I can hardly suppose," the justice said, that the order was "intended to apply to and include a member of the court who has occasion to examine the opinion." The clerk reiterated that he was bound by Taney's directive. At this point Curtis wrote directly to the chief justice. "I can not suppose it was your intention to preclude me from having access to an opinion of the court," Curtis said, and "if it was not you will confer a favor upon me by directing the Clerk to comply with my request."[96]

In response, Taney noted that the order "applies to every individual member of this tribunal," but it is clear that his concern was to prevent Curtis from obtaining the opinion. He blamed his younger colleague for fueling the harsh criticism of the Court. Taney believed that newspapers had "greatly misunderstood and grossly misinterpreted" his opinion, which, he thought, "should be allowed to speak for itself and not be brought before the public garbled and mutilated."[97] Curtis's charge of judicial overreaching had rankled the chief justice. "You announced from the Bench," Taney wrote, "that you regarded the opinion as extrajudicial and not binding upon you or anyone else," and "I understand you" do not intend to use the opinion to discharge "your official duties."[98]

Curtis replied with a detailed explanation of his "official duty." He said: "I cannot doubt you will agree with me, a judge who dissents" on "questions of constitutional law which deeply affect the country, discharges an official duty when he lays before the country" his reasons. "That he may do so, it is necessary he should know, and know accurately, what the opinion of the majority is, and its grounds and reasons." Having structured his dissent to respond to the opinion Taney had read in conference, Curtis was determined to see "whether any alterations material to my dissent had been made" in the majority opinion. Curtis needled the chief justice for withholding the Court's opinion from public view. "I supposed that others would think as I did, that in our country it is impossible to keep from the public what passes in an open court of justice; especially in the Supreme Court, where the interests of the nation are discussed, and the people have the right to know what is done."[99]

Taney responded with a long letter, despite stating that he had "no desire to continue the unpleasant correspondence which you have been pleased to commence." The claim that he had "materially altered" the opinion had "no foundation in truth." There was, Taney said, "not one historical fact, nor one principle of constitutional law, or common law, or chancery law, or statute law, in the printed opinion, which was not distinctly announced and maintained from the Bench." Taney launched a counterattack. "I learned with great surprise that, immediately on your return to Boston, you had published" the dissenting opinion "in a political journal." Noting that Curtis's dissent was "widely circulated throughout the country," Taney declared this was "the first instance in the history of the Supreme Court" when the "assault" on that body was "commenced by the publication of the opinion of a dissenting Judge." The letter could hardly mask the chief justice's rancor. He would not hesitate to respond directly if "it is your pleasure to address letters to me charging me with breaches of official duty."[100]

Unable to let that pass, Curtis agreed that the correspondence had become "unpleasant." Yet he insisted on his rights. "I must be allowed to entertain my own opinions on all points connected with my office, and to express plainly, on proper occasions, my reasons for them." He cast doubt on Taney's characterization that only "proofs and authorities" had been added to the opinion. This may "embrace a wide field of examination and argument," Curtis pointed out. As for the charge that he had published his opinion for political purposes, Curtis felt it "impossible" to "carry on such a discussion without bitterness." It was "a sufficient reply for me to declare that I have no connection whatever with any political party and have no political or partisan purpose in view."[101]

By this time Taney had concluded that "every attempt" by Curtis "to justify what could not be justified can only plunge" him in "further difficulties." Meanwhile, Curtis vented his frustration in private notes, where he described Taney's action as "usurpation." When he read the printed opinion, Curtis estimated that Taney had added over eighteen pages. "No one can read them," Curtis noted, "without perceiving that they are *in reply* to my opinion." While the version Taney read from the bench was not preserved, two surviving later drafts contain several pages of the chief justice's handwritten additions responding to both dissenters.[102]

It may appear that these epistolary battles drove Curtis off the Court. It is difficult to imagine that Taney's actions played no part in Curtis's departure. Then again, in his biography of the justice, George Ticknor Curtis suggested that his brother left primarily for financial reasons. These were "controlling"; what happened in *Dred Scott* was "secondary," according to the memoir.[103]

It is true that Justice Curtis had been troubled by his finances and the difficulties of living apart from his family. He was unwilling to "subject them to a kind of vagrant life" in Washington's "boarding-houses." Dissatisfied with his annual salary of $6,000, he expressed particular concern about his ability to meet the "increased expenses of education" for his younger children.[104] Yet neither his salary nor his living conditions completely explain Curtis's resignation.

While the justice weighed financial pressures as he mulled over resignation, he had been unhappy with his salary for years. In fact, when he was appointed to the Court, Curtis complained to John Henry Clifford about sacrificing his earnings of $15,000 a year.[105] Moreover, there is nothing to indicate that Justice Curtis contemplated resignation in the months immediately preceding the Court's decision.

The evidence suggests that Curtis resigned on grounds of principle; if so, he was the only justice to do so in the Supreme Court's history. To be clear, Curtis took a stand not so much against slavery but rather against what the justices had done to the Court as an institution. "I cannot again feel that confidence in the court, and that willingness to co-operate with them," he confided in Ticknor. Some in the press suspected as much. On September 7 the *New York Tribune*'s correspondent openly doubted the "alleged" reason of "insufficiency of the salary." The "truth probably is that Mr. Curtis was disgusted with the scandalous perversion of law, and historic truth in the Dred Scott decision." The report added that "he saw that there was no possible chance of reforming the Federal judiciary by attempting to check its excesses."[106]

Shortly following Curtis's resignation, Senator Reverdy Johnson wrote Curtis that he believed that "many persons misunderstood" what motivated the justice to resign. The senator, a prominent Maryland politician friendly with Taney, sought to "put the matter on its true footing" by circulating editorials to correct "every misrepresentation." Curtis replied with a lawyer's sense of fine distinction. The insufficient salary was "the only cause justifying my resignation," but he still meant for the public to read his action as a commentary on the Court. "I had never authorized any one to *deny* that my regrets were diminished by the *state of the court*," Curtis said. Financial reasons provided a genteel explanation, as shown in a letter he wrote Millard Fillmore. "You will readily understand that this is a subject on which I cannot go into details, and I cannot without indelicacy even offer reasons." As Curtis's brother told the justice, "Undoubtedly, a serious lesson will be taught, which cannot fail to be felt by the country, by the resignation of a judge at your time of life, for the reasons which will govern you, and which, whether stated or not, will be apparent to the whole public." [107]

Even if principled, the merits of Curtis's resignation were debatable. It may be said that Curtis, in contrast with his fellow dissenter, was unwilling to persevere in trying circumstances. While considering resignation, Curtis communicated with McLean, who emphasized the service they could perform during the nation's "great crisis" by upholding "the great principles of the Constitution" even in dissent. Some northerners expressed deep disappointment in Curtis. "I may overrate the importance of his course," commented Robert C. Winthrop, but "I have never known a resignation" so like a "desertion." More charitably, Millard Fillmore urged Curtis to reconsider. There "is no man to whom the country looks with more hopeful confidence." Yet Curtis had concluded that he could exert "little beneficial influence" on the Supreme Court. [108]

IV

In the critical time remaining before the Civil War, *Dred Scott* brought Curtis into the "very front rank in resistance to the slave power." For the next four years after the Court's decision in *Dred Scott*, the *New York Tribune* sold a 25-cent pamphlet pairing the full opinions of Taney and Curtis against each other, with abstracts of the other justices' opinions. While there was no single northern view, Curtis, confronting Taney as he had, ended up defining a basic position for the free states on race as well as slavery. It was Curtis, rather than the Court, who "has made the law" on citizenship, said the *Tribune*. "He may be voted down by Legislatures, Courts, and Executives, but the argument will forever stand unimpeached." [109] Calling to mind Curtis's earlier defense of the Fugitive Slave Act, Charles Francis Adams thought it ironic that the justice would appear "to posterity as a champion of principles, for his opposition to which he obtained his seat on the bench." [110]

The *Dred Scott* case was a crisis not only in American politics but in constitutional thought as well. By combining extreme proslavery positions with a narrow mode of constitutional interpretation, Chief Justice Taney foreclosed any possibility of change short of formal amendment.

In dissenting, Justice Curtis not only identified flaws in Taney's analysis but also set before the nation an alternative view of how the Constitution operated. The key to reading Curtis is to understand his opinion as an expression of possibilities rather than an exact solution: the federal judiciary had a potentially expansive role in enforcing the civil rights of black Americans, Congress had plenary power to exclude slavery from the territories, slavery was not protected as a property right under the Constitution, and blacks were "in every sense" among the people of the United States.

6. THE PRESIDENT'S WAR POWERS

WHILE THE *Dred Scott* case represented a crisis in constitutionalism—
a pivotal episode involving what direction the Constitution should take
with respect to slavery—the Civil War presented Americans with their
first serious test of constitutional government during war. Difficult
questions arose; one that dogged the Lincoln administration concerned
the military arrests of civilians. Early on, the president suspended the
legal writ of habeas corpus, thus depriving prisoners of the right to be
brought before civil courts for a judicial determination of the lawfulness
of their detention. By the time the fighting ended, the army had arrested
perhaps as many as 18,000 citizens. Many were imprisoned for short
periods of time. Still, this was an extraordinary exercise of martial law,
with military tribunals empowered to try civilians and sentence them to
death.[1] Although Lincoln did not consider his actions a precedent for the
"indefinite peaceful future" that he believed lay ahead, the question of
civil liberties in wartime has reappeared, with the free speech cases from
World War I, the Japanese-American internment of World War II, and
national security issues during the Cold War and after September 11.[2]

At the start of the Civil War, Curtis supported President Lincoln.
There was only "one way to avert the peril," Curtis wrote a friend. "Sustain the established government, and especially the President, so long
and so far, and by all ways and means possible to a good citizen." By the
end of 1862, Curtis was bitterly disappointed in Lincoln's performance.
When it was suggested to Curtis that he visit the White House, he declined. "It would do no good, and would give me no pleasure," Curtis
told his wife. "I suppose he [Lincoln] would say the same. My hopes for
the Union and Constitution are *nowhere*." Curtis described Lincoln as
"shattered, dazed & utterly foolish." During the presidential campaign
of 1864, Curtis publicly supported General George B. McClellan for
president.[3]

The cause of Curtis's dissatisfaction can be traced precisely to two
presidential proclamations issued in September 1862. One imposed
martial law throughout the entire nation. The other was the Preliminary Emancipation Proclamation, in which Lincoln announced his intention to free all slaves held in rebel territory. In short order Curtis

published a pamphlet entitled *Executive Power* in which he challenged these "assertions of transcendent executive power." Privately he expressed doubt whether "any opposition to the President is now useful." While reluctant to enter "the arena," Curtis felt he had to try "to keep things from being turned over." There was, he noted, "a great and pressing danger to the country," which he underscored as the "*danger of the loss of ideas.*" As "I cannot help to subdue the enemy abroad,—I ought to do what I can to subdue the enemy at home."[4]

Despite Curtis's initial doubts, *Executive Power* had an immediate impact. Within three months of its publication, he reported that it had "produced a powerful impression upon the country." It was his understanding that Lincoln blamed him for provoking "hostile feeling" against the administration. Certainly Curtis's pamphlet had got the president's attention. When Charles P. Kirkland, a New York lawyer, responded to *Executive Power*, President Lincoln thanked him personally. "I have just received, and hastily read your published letter to the Hon. Benjamin R. Curtis," Lincoln said. "Under the circumstances I may not be the most competent judge, but it appears to me to be a paper of great ability, and for the country's sake, more than my own, I thank you for it."[5]

Executive Power is an important though somewhat neglected document in American constitutional history. Its significance derives partly from its timing. Curtis presented his views at a critical point during the war, before the Supreme Court spoke to the question of wartime civil liberties in *Ex parte Milligan* (1866). It is noteworthy that the author of this landmark decision, Justice David Davis, asked Curtis to defend the opinion against public criticism. Curtis's analysis in *Executive Power* is still seen to be "cogent," as Arthur M. Schlesinger Jr. has described it.[6]

While Lincoln did not respond directly to Curtis, it is possible to reconstruct a sophisticated exchange of views between these two seasoned lawyers. Each scored points in arguing over the scope of presidential powers, specifically in their interpretations of the commander in chief clause. Lincoln made a convincing case that military necessity was the driving force behind his authority. Curtis was insightful in his attempt to reconcile constitutional limitations with the need for swift executive action in crisis. He also sought to find a way to get Congress involved. Curtis was less of a constructive critic on the question of emancipation. His argument there rested on the idea that such an executive decree was not an appropriate vehicle for the far-reaching social change contemplated. On that issue, Lincoln appears to have promoted an organic constitutional theory more responsive to the extraordinary circumstances.

THE PRESIDENT'S WAR POWERS

I

Throughout American history the views of presidential war powers have revolved around two basic positions. One is based on a narrow reading of the commander in chief clause. Article II of the Constitution provides simply that the "President shall be Commander in Chief of the Army and Navy of the United States, and of the Militia of the several States, when called into the actual Service of the United States." This power has been interpreted to be "purely military," as Chief Justice Taney stated in *Fleming v. Page* (1850). This position finds support in Hamilton's statement in *The Federalist* that the commander in chief's authority was limited "to nothing more than the supreme command and direction of the military and naval forces, as first general and admiral." The basic purpose of the commander in chief clause, according to this view, was to ensure civilian control of the military, and the president did not acquire additional powers by virtue of being commander in chief.[7]

The alternative position ascribes to the president more expansive powers. According to this interpretation, the president has the duty to serve the public interest, and in certain conditions—whether styled as a national emergency or out of military necessity—the chief executive will be justified in violating the law, including the nation's most fundamental laws in the Constitution. This conception comported with a long-held theory of executive prerogative, stated by John Locke as the "power to act according to discretion for the publick good, without the prescription of the Law, and sometimes even against it." The underlying idea was that "a strict and rigid observation of the Laws may do harm"; thus, executive prerogative was justified when it served the "good of the people." Among American presidents, Franklin Delano Roosevelt was the modern incarnation of this doctrine. Thomas Jefferson was the earliest to lay claim to it, but Lincoln was perhaps its most eloquent spokesman.[8]

Lincoln stated his position neatly in a letter written to a Kentucky newspaper editor in 1864. "Was it possible to lose the nation," Lincoln asked, "and yet preserve the constitution?" The question as posed yields its own answer. Without the nation, there could be no Constitution. Lincoln drove the point home with a memorable metaphor. "By general law life *and* limb must be protected; yet often a limb must be amputated to save a life; but a life is never wisely given to save a limb." This clever analogy led to an inescapable conclusion, at least for Lincoln. "I felt that measures, otherwise unconstitutional, might become lawful, by becoming indispensable to the preservation of the constitution, through the preservation of the nation."[9] Lincoln believed that the law was not blind to circumstance, and with national survival at stake, the acceptable notions of what was lawful must be modified accordingly.

As for his powers as commander in chief, Lincoln saw himself invested "with the law of war, in time of war." Coupled with his oath of office to "preserve, protect and defend the Constitution of the United States," Lincoln's position "as commander-in-chief of the army and navy, in time of war," made him "suppose I have a right to take any measure which may best subdue the enemy." Lincoln evidently got that last phrase from an opinion in which Chief Justice Taney described the commander in chief's authority to employ armed forces "in the manner he may deem most effectual to harass and conquer and subdue the enemy." Taney meant this as a limitation on the president's powers. Lincoln used those same words to support a radically different interpretation.[10]

From the start of the war, Lincoln had taken extraordinary measures: blockading southern ports and using money without congressional authorization, for example.[11] He also authorized the army to arrest civilians. The constitutional validity of these arrests depended not only on the interpretation of the commander in chief clause but also on whether the president had the power to suspend habeas corpus. The Constitution does not identify whether Congress or the president has this power. It only states that "the Privilege of the Writ of Habeas Corpus shall not be suspended, unless when in Cases of Rebellion or Invasion the public Safety may require it." Since this provision appears in Article I (enumerating legislative powers) instead of Article II (discussing executive power), antebellum jurists assumed that only Congress had the authority to suspend the writ.[12]

Yet in 1861 President Lincoln suspended habeas corpus along any "military line" between New York and Washington. Maryland was within Chief Justice Taney's circuit, and an arrest there led to the first of his efforts to discredit the Lincoln administration. John Merryman was a state militia officer with clear secessionist sympathies; he had prepared men to fight against the North. On May 25 Union soldiers jailed him in Fort McHenry. When presented with a petition for habeas corpus the next day, Taney promptly issued the writ. Citing Lincoln's directive authorizing the suspension of habeas corpus, the army refused to comply but requested the chief justice to delay further proceedings until the president could be consulted. In no mood to let such an opportunity go to waste, Taney released an opinion declaring that Congress alone had the authority to suspend the writ of habeas corpus. He saw "no ground whatever for supposing that the president, in any emergency, or in any state of things, can authorize the suspension of the privileges of the writ of habeas corpus, or the arrest of a citizen, except in aid of the judicial power." Taney also denied that the executive could draw support from "the necessity of government, for self-defence in times of tumult and danger."[13]

Under the circumstances Taney's reading of executive power was severely limiting. It was unclear in the spring of 1861 whether Maryland could be kept in the Union. Soldiers from Massachusetts marching to Washington were assaulted in Baltimore, and four were killed; Marylanders had destroyed railroad bridges to cut Union supply lines. Besides that, Lincoln manifested an interest in discovering what legal precedent governed the actions he contemplated. Before suspending habeas corpus in Maryland, he asked the attorney general to furnish an opinion addressing the question whether martial law violated the Fifth Amendment's grand jury requirement. In May 1861 the president issued a directive to curb excesses: "Unless the *necessity* for these arbitrary arrests is *manifest*, and *urgent*, I prefer they should cease." More well known is Lincoln's plaintive question in his Fourth of July message to Congress. After noting that one-third of the states resisted the "whole of the laws," he then asked whether "all the laws, *but one*" (referring to the constitutional provision on habeas corpus), were "to go unexecuted, and the government itself go to pieces, lest that one be violated?" By this statement Lincoln meant to emphasize the reality of the situation; he denied that anyone had been unlawfully arrested.[14]

In the months immediately following the attack on Fort Sumter, another judge besides Taney might have approved a limited suspension of habeas corpus as a reasonable exercise of war powers. Republicans soon developed a theory of adequacy constitutionalism that marked out such an approach. Previously, the Constitution negated and limited the government's power; with adequacy constitutionalism, it supplied a positive source of authority. As Timothy Farrar explained in January 1862, "the adequacy of the Constitution to the exigencies of government and the preservation of the Union, has not hitherto been exhibited and proved in practice, nor fully asserted and insisted on by its friends, even in theory."[15] The question remained whether it was possible to empower the government to meet the crisis at hand without sacrificing limitations on the use of that power.

There was something to commend and criticize in the alternative positions taken by both Lincoln and Taney. *Merryman* has been considered a model of judicial resistance: the lone judge upholding civil liberties in the face of military power. Yet Taney gave no recognition to the apparent need for bold executive action, another example of his inelastic conception of the Constitution. Lincoln articulated a view more responsive to the emergency, as he tied the commander in chief's authority to executive prerogative. He failed to take notice, perhaps with a sense of his own self-restraint, of the risks of setting a dangerous precedent.

II

If Curtis questioned Lincoln's actions during the first year of the war, he kept those views to himself. The presidential proclamations of September 1862 provoked him to speak out. Unlike the president's previous orders which limited the area where habeas corpus was suspended, Lincoln now extended martial law throughout the entire nation. Specifically, the president ordered:

> that during the existing insurrection and as a necessary measure for suppressing the same, all Rebels and Insurgents, their aiders and abettors within the United States, and all persons discouraging volunteer enlistments, resisting militia drafts, or guilty of any disloyal practice, affording aid and comfort to Rebels against the authority of the United States, shall be subject to martial law and liable to trial and punishment by Courts Martial or Military Commission. . . . That the Writ of Habeas Corpus is suspended in respect to all persons arrested, or who are now, or hereafter during the rebellion shall be, imprisoned in any fort, camp, arsenal, military prison, or other place of confinement by any military authority or by the sentence of any Court Martial or Military Commission.[16]

The president began this proclamation with a finding that "disloyal persons are not adequately restrained by the ordinary processes of law from hindering" the militia draft. This was a reference to the events of the summer of 1862, when the federal government recruited volunteers and required states to fill quotas in their militias. Some states instituted drafts to satisfy this federal mandate. Militia drafts were resisted in scattered towns from Wisconsin to Pennsylvania, sometimes violently. Two recruitment officers were killed in Indiana. If that furnished good reason to impose martial law, the proclamation was not limited to stopping draft resistance. Lincoln made a more general statement that existing legal process was inadequate to prevent disloyal persons "from giving aid and comfort in various ways to the insurrection."[17]

This proclamation went too far, in Curtis's opinion. Equally troubling to Curtis was the theory behind it and the attitudes to the

Constitution and law it exposed. In the preface to his pamphlet, Curtis called attention to Lincoln's statement that the commander in chief "in time of war" has "a right to take any measure which may best subdue the enemy." Curtis expressed concern that with such thinking there was then no meaningful limit to the president's war powers. The basic problem with Lincoln's suggestion was that the president was the sole judge of what was required to subdue the enemy. As a result, Curtis believed, "every private and personal right of individual security against mere executive control, and every right reserved to the States or the people, rests merely upon executive discretion." Curtis emphasized that Lincoln's doctrine had enlarged the commander in chief clause so that it overrode all other constitutional limitations on executive power. If the president "has an *implied* constitutional right, as commander-in-chief" to "disregard any one positive prohibition of the Constitution, or to exercise any one power not delegated to the United States by the Constitution, because, in his judgment, he may thereby 'best subdue the enemy,' he has the same right, for the same reason, to disregard each and every provision of the Constitution, and to exercise all power, *needful, in his opinion,* to enable him 'best to subdue the enemy.'"[18]

At one point Curtis seemed to take the narrower view of the president as "general-in-chief," constrained by the limited purpose of placing the armed forces "in the hands of the chief civil magistrate."[19] As Curtis's argument unfolded, however, the scope of the power he was willing to concede the president was striking. The key for him was to combine power with constitutional limits. The way he did that distinguished his stance from the positions embraced by Taney and Lincoln.

In Curtis's view the Constitution gave the president "great and ample powers." He acknowledged that the president as commander in chief had implied powers. Like any other military commander, Curtis said, he "is lawfully empowered by the Constitution and laws of the United States to do whatever is necessary, and is sanctioned by the laws of war, to accomplish the lawful objects of his command." Curtis also embraced the idea that a wartime president must have "powers both over the persons and the property of citizens which do not exist in time of peace." Curtis even recognized executive prerogative: "In times of great public danger, unexpected perils, which the legislative power have failed to provide against, may imperatively demand instant and vigorous executive action, passing beyond the limits of the laws."[20]

To this point, Curtis's pamphlet may appear to reiterate Lincoln's position. The basic elements were present: implied power, necessity, and prerogative. There was a crucial though subtle difference in their views, however. For Curtis the source of executive power had to be found in the Constitution. The president has powers *"not in spite of the Constitution and laws of the United States, or in derogation from their authority, but in virtue thereof and in strict subordination thereto."* Curtis's reasoning, it appears, was that as the Constitution was the fountain of authority, it was also the source of limits. While he looked to necessity to determine the scope of the president's war powers, he considered this to be a constitutionally recognized value. There was no reason to go outside the Constitution to bring military necessity into play, and he denied that war could justify breaking the country's "fundamental laws."[21]

That was exactly what Curtis thought Lincoln did. The president appealed to national survival and the Union as sources for his authority. Curtis did not dispute these interests, but he did not bring them into the constitutional analysis like Lincoln had. The result to which Lincoln pointed was that the president's own understanding of military necessity guided his actions, and the limits to his power as commander in chief were to be found in personal discretion subject only to political checks.[22]

Against this line of thought, Curtis made several points. He indicated that the principle of separation of powers by itself furnished meaningful standards limiting executive authority. By ordering the military to arrest, try, and punish civilians for "any disloyal practice," Lincoln had undertaken functions reserved to the other branches of government. "It is a clear and undoubted prerogative of Congress alone," Curtis said, "to define all offences" and their punishments. The proclamation created new criminal offenses—like "any disloyal practice"—not "known to any law of the United States."[23]

Curtis also suggested that basic constitutional rights would be lost in implementing the proclamation; in fact, practically every part of the Bill of Rights dealing with criminal procedure. Instead of the Fifth Amendment's requirement for a grand jury indictment, Curtis noted that the army planned to use reports compiled by "some deputy provost marshal." The Sixth Amendment requires a public trial before a criminal jury; the administration had set up military commissions in place of that. The Eighth Amendment prohibits cruel and unusual punishment, but executive officials had complete discretion in sentencing.[24]

What worried Curtis most of all was that Lincoln's proclamation, operating for an "indefinite" period with "general rules of action, applicable to the entire country," had established a "system" of government revolving around the executive. His concern was not with President Lincoln or Secretary of War Edwin M. Stanton (so Curtis said) but rather over how their subordinates would put these powers into effect.

Curtis felt it was inevitable that these "great powers must be confided to persons actuated by party, or local or personal feelings or prejudices" or "a desire to commend their vigilance to their employers, and by a blundering and stupid zeal in their service."[25]

While Curtis accepted broad implied powers in the commander in chief, he thought it "obvious that this implied authority must find early limits somewhere." The difficulty facing Curtis, or anyone on this issue for that matter, was that the war power by its nature defies legal boundaries. Even Curtis defined martial law broadly as "the will of a military commander, operating without any restraint, save his judgment, upon the lives, upon the property, upon the entire social and individual condition of all over whom this law extends."[26] The problem then was how to subject the commander's will to legal limits. The analytical solution Curtis embraced was a legal standard to limit the power by the territory where it could be applied. The commander in chief's power extended only *"within the sphere of his actual operations in the field,"* he said.[27]

This was not a novel proposition. Harvard law professor Joel Parker had previously referred to martial law "within the scope of active military operations in carrying on the war."[28] As Curtis developed his argument, though, his sense of the Constitution's flexibility emerged, and he seemed to be searching for a middle ground between the positions taken by Taney and Lincoln.

The comparison with Lincoln is illuminating. Curtis expressed no doubt that imposing martial law throughout the whole country strained constitutional limits. "I do not yet perceive how it is that my neighbors and myself, residing remote from armies and their operations, and where all the laws of the land may be enforced by constitutional means, should be subjected to the possibility of military arrest and imprisonment, and trial before a military commission, and punishment at its discretion for offences unknown to the law." Lincoln had what might be described as a more functional approach. He drew on the language of the habeas corpus clause and suggested that military arrests could take place *"wherever the public safety"* requires. President Lincoln not only rejected a geographic requirement, he also admitted that some military arrests were "preventive," not "so much for what has been done, as for what probably would be done."[29]

While more restrictive than Lincoln, Curtis showed more flexibility than Taney had in *Merryman*. The rule suggested by Taney's opinion, later stated by the Supreme Court in *Ex parte Milligan*, was that civilians cannot be tried before military tribunals wherever civil courts remain open. It appears that Curtis would have accepted this open courts rule in most cases, but his approach was different. The situation in Maryland at the start of the war provides a case in point. Although the courts were still functioning in Maryland then, a good case could have been made justifying martial rule there: the risk of having the national capital surrounded by hostile states, the threat against military supply lines, the killing of Union soldiers. Arguably, Curtis would have considered his standard met so long as "particular actual military operations" were directly connected to an "existing and instant military emergency."[30] He did not limit the sphere of actual operations in the field to a well-defined battlefield with two opposing armies. Curtis allowed that military power over "the persons and property of citizens" extends control over anything "so near as to be actually reached by that force, in order to remove obstructions to its exercise." There was then some latitude in determining how far the field extended, which could include military operations "in their neighborhood."[31]

Wherever operations in the field extended, Curtis was willing to accept substantial military authority over civilians. He listed several actions that military commanders, or their commander in chief, could take affecting civilians. They could destroy supplies, move over private property, use property to transport or supply troops, and arrest suspected spies. Curtis recognized that military tribunals could be used to try persons charged with offenses against the articles of war.[32]

Applying some sort of legal standard was only one part of Curtis's argument. Equally important to Curtis, it seems, was to find some way to get the legislature and the judiciary involved. He suggested that President Lincoln had not given adequate consideration to using existing criminal offenses in established courts of law. Not only had Lincoln said that ordinary processes of law failed to stop disloyal persons from aiding the rebellion, he also considered the civil courts "inadequate" in this "gigantic case of Rebellion." Curtis pointed to the crime of treason as one possible solution. In truth, that probably would have accomplished little. This criminal offense, the only one defined in the Constitution, has always been difficult to prove. It requires the commission of overt acts for levying war against the United States or providing aid and comfort to its enemies. Evidence must consist of two witnesses to each act.[33]

At the same time that Curtis argued for greater consideration of existing laws, he recognized that there would be "exceptional cases" of "some instant emergency" to which the legislature could not respond in a timely manner. Where the need for immediate action put executive officials in a position so that they transgressed the "limits of the laws," Curtis offered a solution based upon English practice. In England officers who violated the rights of individuals during a state of martial law were accountable in courts of law. For example, soldiers who illegally detained a person were subject to criminal prosecutions or civil lawsuits for false imprisonment. Acting in good faith under orders from the king was not a valid defense. However, the British Parliament had adopted acts of indemnity that relieved executive officials of legal responsibility. These so-called indemnity acts operated as a retroactive sanction for executive actions.[34]

Although indemnity was a remedy waiting to be plucked from English history, Americans had not given it much attention in the first year of the war. Members of Congress were not unaware of this parliamentary practice. In 1861, for example, Senator John Sherman wrote that the executive ran the risk of having "a 'Bill of Impeachment,' or a 'Bill of Indemnity'" when compelled to act before Congress could. Yet lawmakers made no move to enact indemnity legislation. Some legal thinkers dismissed the English indemnity acts as irrelevant. In an influential pamphlet published in 1862, Horace Binney contrasted Parliament's "prepotent authority" to enact such legislation with Congress's more limited power under the American Constitution.[35]

With the debate revolving around the question of whether the president had the power to suspend habeas corpus, there was no agreed-upon solution, and the legitimacy of President Lincoln's actions remained in doubt. In his Fourth of July message in 1861, President Lincoln noted that the constitutional text was "silent" as to who had the power, and he hinted that Congress ought to settle the question.[36] The special legislative session of 1861 ended with Congress ratifying several actions taken by the president, like the blockade, but the habeas corpus question was left unresolved.[37] Congress came no closer to settling the issue the next year. The bone of contention was the scope of executive power. With each attempt to authorize the president to suspend habeas corpus, the question arose whether he had that power to begin with. No amount of ambiguity in proposed legislation on this subject could gain the votes necessary for passage because congressmen were concerned about what their recorded votes signified.[38]

In his pamphlet Curtis noted there had been "much discussion" over whether the Constitution vested Congress or the president with the power to suspend habeas corpus. Instead of Congress dithering over where the power resides, Curtis suggested that the legislators cut through to a practical solution. Granting that the president might have occasion to suspend habeas corpus in "exceptional" cases, the remedy was to admit the wrong and to indemnify executive officers. He said that "when the

Executive has assumed the high responsibility of such a necessary exercise of mere power, he may justly look for indemnity to that department of the government which alone has the rightful authority to grant it," that is, to Congress. Curtis emphasized that an indemnity "should be always sought and accorded *upon the clearest admission of legal wrong*, finding its excuse in the exceptional case which made that wrong absolutely necessary for the public safety." [39] Curtis did not expand on this idea, but there is at least one reason an indemnity act would appeal to him. Such legislation would enable Congress and the courts to counterbalance the president. The implication of Curtis's argument was that without indemnity legislation executive officers could be held liable for their actions.

Taken altogether, it appears that Curtis saw the proclamation as a sign that Lincoln was running away with his powers. Curtis sought some middle ground to constrain the president without undercutting his ability to conduct the war. To that end, he reminded his readers of the continuing importance of the principle of separation of powers, he alluded to the relevant provisions of the Bill of Rights, he suggested a flexible legal standard to determine the propriety of executive actions, and he pointed to the parliamentary act of indemnity as a model for Congress.

III

Had Curtis confined his discussion to the question of military arrests, his pamphlet might have left a more lasting impression as a statement on civil liberties. He joined that issue with emancipation, however, for the two questions were brought together in his mind as a constitutional problem of executive power. His argument about the president's authority to emancipate slaves was briefer but no less important in revealing his constitutionalism.

In the Preliminary Emancipation Proclamation issued in 1862, President Lincoln declared that all slaves in rebel states would be at the start of the next year "then, thenceforward, and forever free." He committed the Union army to "recognize and maintain" their freedom.[40] This proclamation marked a critical point in the struggle to end slavery. True, the president had applied the proclamation only to rebel territory. For loyal slave states Lincoln reiterated his call for a voluntary program of gradual compensated emancipation, which he contemplated lasting until 1900.[41] Some abolitionists could not conceal their disappointment.[42] Notwithstanding the president's measured approach, there was no turning back, and this too was recognized. Emerson perceptively called the Preliminary Emancipation Proclamation a "poetic act" of "great scope, working on a long future and on permanent interests." It cannot be "taken back," he said. "Done, it cannot be undone by a new administration."[43]

Curtis also regarded the proclamation as a "momentous proposal." Unlike Emerson, he hoped Lincoln would reconsider. Curtis's position contrasts with Lincoln's record as the Great Emancipator. As William R. Gillette has suggested, Curtis's opposition to emancipation cast "a pall over" his dissent in *Dred Scott*.[44] Lincoln appears more supple in his constitutional thinking than Curtis on this point, as the president gave the Constitution new meanings while the former justice still operated within an antebellum mind-set.

Lincoln and Curtis started from the same premises about the constitutional status of slavery. Both believed slavery violated natural rights, yet neither considered immediate abolition a viable alternative. These two lawyers had been willing to represent slave owners contesting the legal claims of slaves, Curtis in *Commonwealth v. Aves* and Lincoln fighting a freedom suit brought by slaves in Illinois.[45] In the 1850s each contested proslavery constitutionalism on the national stage. Curtis had his *Dred Scott* opinion; Lincoln developed more wide-ranging arguments on the stump. In some respects Curtis appeared more progressive on racial equality than Lincoln did before the Civil War. Without facing the pressures Lincoln had on the campaign trail, Curtis offered some elegant arguments on race and citizenship in *Dred Scott*. Meanwhile, Lincoln opposed granting blacks citizenship or the right to vote in Illinois. In his debates with Douglas, Lincoln maintained that "there is a physical difference between the white and black races which I believe will for ever forbid the two races living together on terms of social and political equality."[46]

As for federal authority to abolish slavery, both Lincoln and Curtis embraced the mainstream position that this was a matter for the states. In a speech delivered in Faneuil Hall in February 1861, Curtis said that every political party conceded that slavery "in any State is, and of right ought to be, wholly dependent on the will of the people of that State." The federal government had no "just right or claim whatsoever to interfere." In his first inaugural address, Lincoln expressed a similar view, though his tone was different. It was "implied constitutional law" that the federal government "shall never interfere with the domestic institutions of the States, including that of persons held to service."[47] With the secession crisis, Lincoln, like Curtis, was willing to accept a constitutional amendment expressly stating this.[48]

Even after issuing the Emancipation Proclamation, Lincoln held to this view, but with one important qualification. In his annual message to

Congress in December 1863, the president said that in "our political system, as a matter of civil administration, the general government had no lawful power to effect emancipation in any State." The next year Lincoln conceded that he was not ready to "declare a constitutional competency in Congress to abolish slavery in States." Yet, while there was no federal authority over slavery in the states "as a matter of civil administration," the war had changed the equation in the president's view. The national government had powers not available in peacetime, and in the summer of 1862, he had concluded that emancipation was a military necessity.[49] Lincoln wrote this into the Emancipation Proclamation: it was "warranted by the Constitution, upon military necessity." To Lincoln that was the only legally defensible approach. Though he also saw his proclamation as an "act of justice," it had "no constitutional or legal justification, except as a military measure."[50]

In fact, military necessity provided a plausible rationale for emancipation. As historian David Donald has suggested, slaves had become the "backbone of the Confederate labor force," performing a wide array of jobs necessary to maintain and supply the rebel army, from munitions production to medical care.[51] By proclaiming their freedom, President Lincoln officially deprived the Confederacy of this manpower resource. He also set the stage for the Union army to employ freed slaves as soldiers.

Curtis challenged this doctrine of military necessity. He contended that this proclamation was not an appropriate action for the commander in chief to take. How, he asked, had the people of the United States "conferred *on him* the rightful power *to determine for them* this question." Lincoln had in effect prescribed "future rules of action touching the persons and property of citizens." This had nothing to do with "military relations," in Curtis's view, but rather with "domestic relations" between "master and servant." He also applied the Union position that secession was null: the southern states remained within the Union, and their laws were still valid. It followed for Curtis that the president had abrogated "valid" state laws on slavery.[52]

Curtis also asked his readers to consider the "practical consequences" of Lincoln's action. Without explicitly disputing the end sought, Curtis questioned the means selected. Wondering what "scenes of bloodshed, and worse than bloodshed," might occur, he suggested that such an executive decision imposed by force could produce serious problems. The implication was that the president had not really considered what the abrupt overturning of the South's social structure meant for the entire country. Curtis expanded the argument in the second edition of his pamphlet. "To set free about four millions of slaves, at an early fixed day, with absolutely no preparation for *their* future, and with no preparation for *our* future, in their relations with us, and to do this by force, must be admitted to be a matter of vast concern not only to them and to their masters, but to the whole continent on which they must live." Curtis highlighted the contrast between the magnitude of the president's action, which affected the whole nation, and the nature of this executive decision rendered by one person. If the "social condition" of millions of people "has, in the providence of God, been allowed to depend upon the executive decree of one man," Curtis said, "it will be the most stupendous fact which the history of the race has exhibited."[53]

Besides that, Curtis indicated that there was a legal framework in place to emancipate slaves. He alluded to the second confiscation act that Congress had adopted two months before Lincoln issued the Preliminary Emancipation Proclamation. This legislation established procedures for finding slave owners guilty of treason or lesser crimes of inciting, aiding, or engaging in rebellion. The penalty included the emancipation of their slaves. This act also provided that all slaves who escaped from rebel slaveholders to Union lines would be "forever free."[54] With this statute in place, Curtis suggested, the president's action had a perverse result. It only freed the slaves owned by loyal southerners in states of rebellion.[55]

The question, though, was whether the confiscation act was workable. Historians have suggested that this confusing law would have proved ineffective had it not been superseded by the Emancipation Proclamation.[56] One problem concerned obtaining jurisdiction over traitors. To remedy that, Congress authorized the use of proceedings so that legal action could be taken against the defendant's property in his absence. Yet this was uncomfortable reading to northerners because it classified slaves as property. Abolitionists worried that the task of freeing slaves would get bogged down in litigation to determine each slave owner's loyalty. They questioned such a piecemeal approach.[57]

Curtis did not discuss the statute in detail. It is easy to imagine that he would find the law appealing for exactly the reasons that abolitionists considered it objectionable. This legislation invested the federal courts with the power to determine case by case each slave owner's criminal liability; a finding of guilt was a necessary precondition for the forfeiture of slaves; all in all, legal process mattered. In addition, Curtis could have pointed to substantial progress on the legislative front. In the few months before Lincoln issued the Preliminary Emancipation Proclamation, Congress had banned slavery from the territories and the District of Columbia, abrogated the Fugitive Slave Act, and favorably considered various emancipation measures besides the confiscation act. Just one year earlier, the adoption of these measures would have been unthinkable.

Curtis's underlying motives for opposing Lincoln's proclamation remain unclear. It is possible that Curtis acted solely based upon constitutional concerns over presidential power. He did suggest that if the Constitution needed amendment, the people would "amend it themselves." On the other hand, Curtis may have exploited the legal problems surrounding the proclamation to turn the country against Lincoln's policy.[58] Curtis did not concede that emancipation was a worthy goal. Nowhere did he credit the president for exercising moral leadership. Curtis recognized that the Emancipation Proclamation changed the character of the war, but he seemed blind to the stake that free blacks as well as slaves had in the outcome. He said, "I do not yet see that it depends upon his executive decree whether a servile war shall be invoked to help twenty millions of the white race to assert the rightful authority of the Constitution and laws of their country, over those who refuse to obey them."[59]

IV

Whatever questions hang over Curtis's arguments on emancipation, *Executive Power* contributed to the debate over the president's powers during the Civil War. One of Curtis's goals—bringing Congress into the process—was soon realized. As Carl B. Swisher has suggested, the "Curtis thesis" found "its way repeatedly into Congressional debates."[60] When Congress convened two months after *Executive Power* was published, Democratic senator Lazarus W. Powell of Kentucky quoted extensive excerpts from the "very elaborate and able article."[61] Some lawmakers seemed to rely on Curtis's arguments without identifying the former justice as their source.[62]

The concept of indemnity was taken up by Representative Thaddeus Stevens. At the start of the legislative session in December 1862, the Republican leader submitted a bill "to indemnify the President and other persons for suspending the privilege of the writ of habeas corpus, and acts done in pursuance thereof." Stevens did not mention Curtis, and it remains unclear where the congressman got the idea for his bill. In any event, Stevens departed from Curtis's proposal in at least one important respect. Following parliamentary practice, Curtis had suggested that the admission of illegality was critical: an indemnity should be given "*upon the clearest admission of legal wrong.*" Representative Stevens, by contrast, said, "I have not confessed the illegality" of the executive acts.[63] The legislation adopted in March 1863, called the Habeas Corpus Act or the Indemnity Act, erected a sweeping legal defense for executive officials. It authorized the president to suspend habeas corpus "during the present rebellion . . . whenever, in his judgment, the public safety may require it." One section provided that "any order of the President, or under his authority, made at any time during the existence of the present rebellion, shall be a defence in all courts" for "any search, seizure, arrest, or imprisonment."[64] For the remainder of the war, the Indemnity Act mostly put to rest the squabbling over whether President Lincoln had authority to suspend habeas corpus, although the constitutional validity of military trials of civilians remained an open question.

The impact of Curtis's *Executive Power* on the public debate was evident in the response it generated, for example, in Charles P. Kirkland's *A Letter to the Hon. Benjamin R. Curtis*, Charles Mayo Ellis's *The Power of the Commander-in-Chief . . . As Shown from B. R. Curtis*, and Grosvenor P. Lowrey's *The Commander-in-Chief . . . and an Answer to Ex-Judge Curtis' Pamphlet*. Curtis's influence was itself a common theme among pamphleteers. Lowrey went so far as to suggest that "it entered no man's mind to question" the Emancipation Proclamation "upon legal ground, until Ex-Judge Curtis" laid "that issue before the public." That was undoubtedly an overstatement. Kirkland was probably closer to the truth when he suggested that Curtis had been injudicious in bringing his authority to bear at the most "inopportune moment." Kirkland thought Curtis had lost sight of the reality of events. "Mark the existing state of things," Kirkland scolded; the southerners "totally condemn and repudiate" the Constitution. "It is difficult to imagine under what hallucination you were laboring when you gave utterance to those sentiments." Mixed with harsh rhetoric were compelling counterarguments. Ellis contested Curtis's test restricting the commander in chief's power to the sphere of military operations in the field. Pointing to the character of the Civil War, Ellis conveyed a more realistic view. "Unhappily the field of this dire war is the whole Union," and the "sphere of his actual operations in the field is not only Bull Run or Antietam, but Washington, Baltimore, New Orleans, St. Louis, Boston."[65]

Judges were more receptive to Curtis's arguments. Before the Indemnity Act was passed, the Wisconsin Supreme Court considered the legality of the military detention of over one hundred draft resisters. While rejecting some of Curtis's views, particularly on emancipation, the justices embraced his reasoning on military arrests. "I have read the argument of Judge CURTIS," said one, "and so far as it relates to this power to declare martial law, it is presented with great force and clearness, and seems to me unanswerable."[66]

There was no such direct citation of *Executive Power* by the U.S. Supreme Court, but there is reason to view Curtis's pamphlet as a background influence behind *Ex parte Milligan*. This case concerned Lambdin P. Milligan, a resident of Indiana who was linked to plans to launch a military strike against the North. Arrested by the Union army in 1864, Milligan was tried by a military commission and sentenced to death. He filed a petition for habeas corpus with the U.S. circuit court in Indiana, which sent his case to the Supreme Court. In an opinion joined by four other justices, Justice David Davis held that the military trial was illegal, and he converted the open courts rule into the law of the land. In the course of his opinion, Davis made several statements that resonated with Curtis's arguments, although they could have been made without the benefit of Curtis's pamphlet. "No doctrine" involved "more pernicious consequences," Davis said, than that any constitutional provision "can be suspended during any of the great exigencies of government." The "theory of necessity" on which such a doctrine "is based is false," he continued. The government under the Constitution "has all the powers granted to it, which are necessary to preserve its existence." Noting that Congress had prescribed criminal penalties covering Milligan's activities, Davis suggested that the case should have been brought before the federal courts in Indiana from the start. Although the justice held that martial rule cannot be imposed where civil courts remain open, he also considered martial rule permissible in "the theatre of active military operations, where war really prevails."[67]

The influence that *Executive Power* had on Justice Davis is indicated mostly by private correspondence he had with Curtis. In his opinion Justice Davis went beyond the question of executive power and suggested that Congress could not have authorized military trials where civil courts were operating. Published in December 1866, a critical point in Reconstruction, the *Milligan* opinion was widely criticized by Republicans concerned about the Union army's power to reconstruct the South. Davis's discussion had prompted Chief Justice Salmon P. Chase to write a concurring opinion, joined by three of his associates, which disputed Davis's reading of congressional power.[68] Congressional Republicans read Davis's opinion as a signal that the Supreme Court might try to undermine their Reconstruction program. Justice Davis was surprised to find his opinion susceptible to such a broad reading. There was "not a word said in the opinion about reconstruction," he noted, and "the power is conceded in insurrectionary States."[69]

For a public defense of *Milligan*, Justice Davis turned to Curtis. Initially, Curtis informed Davis that there would be "no difficulty in showing that your opinion did not go beyond the case." The task evolved in Curtis's mind. In "sitting down before this subject," Curtis subsequently explained to Davis, "I have found that it was so large & so important that I could do no proper justice to it, without more time." Later, Curtis contemplated a much broader essay. "I do not think an elaborate defense of your opinion either necessary or expedient," Curtis wrote Davis. "It must stand by its own strength and *that* is sufficient." Instead, Curtis contemplated "a *clear* & *solid* statement of the part which the judiciary has in the govt of the U.S. not only from the express provisions of the constitution but from the very nature of the government & the necessities of our condition, in all times, both bad and good." Citing ill health and the press of business, Curtis never completed the work.[70]

Had Curtis done so, he might have left an even clearer record of his conception of judicial power in times of war. *Ex parte Milligan* raises the question of whether it is realistic to expect the Supreme Court to be able to restrain wartime presidents. While some have hailed *Milligan* as a landmark for civil liberties, others believe that this case exposes the ineffectiveness of judicial power in confronting a wartime president. The Court rendered its decision after the war was over, after all. The operative rule has been whatever presidents do in practice. During World War II the Supreme Court itself sidestepped *Milligan's* strictures in approving FDR's use of a military commission to try Nazi saboteurs captured on American soil.[71]

While praising Justice Davis for his "*great decision*," Curtis was under no illusion about the difficulties judges face, standing alone, in restraining the commander in chief. He perceived that the public provided the ultimate check on the president. "The Supreme Court must rely on the *final* judgment of the people to support its decision," and "I hope & yet believe that final judgment will be right."[72]

V

Whatever common ground Curtis and Lincoln shared, their differences over executive power reveal much about their understanding of American constitutionalism. It has been said that Lincoln showed himself to be a "pragmatic constitutionalist" during the war, and it may be argued that his September 1862 proclamations were simply decisive actions putting adequacy constitutionalism into effect. Meanwhile, Curtis has been criticized for failing to appreciate the depth of the crisis. William Gillette considered him "oblivious to the desperate war emergency and obtuse to the uses of expediency in public action."[73]

From Curtis's perspective, it was the president and his supporters who had panicked. He saw the September proclamations as one more example of "the tendency to lawlessness" sweeping the country. Curtis drew attention to a comment about the Preliminary Emancipation Proclamation which appeared in the newspapers: "Nobody pretends that this act is constitutional, and nobody cares whether it is or not." For Curtis, this statement, even if melodramatic, was a direct corollary to Lincoln's misguided justification that the commander in chief had a right to take any measure which might best subdue the enemy. Lincoln had lost his constitutional compass, Curtis believed. He expressed horror with the result. To Justice Davis he confided, "Mr. Stanton is, of course, ready to swear to the law under which he has caused people to be hanged; for if there is *no* such law *what has he done!!*"[74]

Curtis had no doubt that "the times are most critical." Nor did he discount the need to fully press the war to its conclusion. This "just and necessary" war "must be prosecuted with the whole force of this government," he said. Yet the crisis did not relieve the government of its obligation to act within constitutional boundaries. Curtis cleverly framed his arguments to suggest that this war had a special character which made that obligation paramount. The Union's central aim, he said, was to compel southerners to submit to the U.S. Constitution as "the supreme law of the land." Curtis then asked "with what sense of right can we subdue them by arms to obey the Constitution as the supreme law of *their* part of the land, if we have ceased to obey it, or failed to preserve it, as the supreme law of *our* part of the land."[75] Any executive action contrary to the Constitution was, in the broadest sense, self-defeating.

Pamphleteers responded by emphasizing that rebels—"in arms against the Constitution," as one put it—had no constitutional rights.[76] Curtis addressed this point in the second edition of *Executive Power.* "None are so degraded, even by crime, as to be too low" for protection under the law. It was, in Curtis's opinion, one thing to try rebels for treason with whatever protections the Constitution afforded, another to say they relinquished every right. The real point for Curtis was that everyone's rights depended upon adhering to constitutional principle. As he put it, "The inquiry which I have invited is not what are *their* rights, but what are *our* rights."[77]

Furthermore, Curtis believed that the president's course of action needlessly sacrificed principle, and he proceeded to identify alternative constitutional means. On the question of martial law, Curtis promoted a flexible legal standard to enable the commander in chief to respond swiftly to unanticipated dangers within the sphere of actual military operations. He thought that Congress should be involved, and to that end he broached the idea of indemnity. Curtis also argued that Lincoln had not given adequate consideration to applying existing laws like treason, though Curtis's pamphlet ignored the practical difficulties in doing that. On emancipation, Curtis was less detailed in suggesting solutions, but he did point to the confiscation act as an acceptable approach.

As Lincoln and Curtis considered the implications for the future, each advanced arguments with merit. Lincoln believed that his actions should not be considered a precedent. He could not envision a repetition of civil war, and with a lawyer's penchant for distinction, he considered his proclamation on martial rule sui generis. Curtis suggested that no matter what the circumstances, the chief executive could not shed constitutional constraints. Skeptical of the broad powers Lincoln claimed, Curtis expressed concern for the principle involved. It was not, he said, "this or that particular application of power which is to be considered" but "following out the principle" that the president asserted. "A wise people does not trust its condition and rights to the happy accident of favorable times or good hands."[78]

Curtis closed his pamphlet with an explicit call to the public to engage in constitutional argument. The courts were not in his view the sole or even the principal check on wartime presidents. "The sober second thought of the people has yet a controlling power," said Curtis. "Let this gigantic shadow, which has been evoked out of the powers of the commander-in-chief, once be placed before the people, so that they can see clearly its proportions and its mien, and it will dissolve and disappear like the morning cloud before the rising sun." More eloquent perhaps was his simple cadence: "Let the people but be right, and no President can long be wrong."[79]

In January 1867, when Justice Davis first solicited Curtis to defend *Milligan*, the Boston lawyer postponed this project because he felt it was impossible then "to attract the attention of the people to a calm & dispassionate statement of the office of the Su. Ct. in our govt & to what the Court has done." Ten days earlier, the House of Representatives had instructed its judiciary committee to report on whether President Andrew Johnson had committed any impeachable offenses. The challenge to constitutional government was no longer coming from the presidency, Curtis thought. "At present, the question is whether Congress can destroy the Executive power," and that issue, he believed, "must assume some more definite shape."[80]

7. THE JOHNSON IMPEACHMENT TRIAL

AFTER THE HOUSE OF Representatives voted on February 24, 1868, to impeach Andrew Johnson, the president met with his cabinet to select counsel to represent him in the trial before the Senate. The "first name suggested," Attorney General Henry Stanbery later disclosed, "was that of Judge Curtis, and no sooner suggested than accepted in full Cabinet, and emphatically by the President himself." Johnson eventually added four more lawyers to his defense team. The most prominent besides Curtis were William M. Evarts, a conservative Republican from New York, and Stanbery, who resigned from the cabinet to avoid any charge of impropriety. Johnson also retained two Democrats: William Groesbeck of Ohio and Thomas A. R. Nelson from Tennessee. For a brief period before the trial, Curtis was the only attorney preparing the defense. Stanbery was still occupied with his work as attorney general, and the other lawyers were not yet on the scene. Alone in his room in Willard's Hotel in Washington, Curtis drafted the president's answer to the charges. By his own account, he felt the weight of "this portentous business" on his shoulders.[1]

As the trial date approached, most observers believed that the president had no chance. He "will be convicted without doubt," said House Speaker Schuyler Colfax. Radical Republicans wasted no time planning for a new administration. Benjamin F. Wade, the Senate's president pro tempore, next in line to succeed Johnson, put together a cabinet as the trial got underway. Johnson's supporters in turn feared the worst. Secretary of the Navy Gideon Welles recorded the cabinet's judgment: conviction was "a foregone conclusion." Bookmakers in Washington agreed; President Johnson, it was said, "sells very low."[2]

The trial began with the case against Johnson laid out by the impeachment managers, the House members acting as prosecutors. The seven managers included leading Republicans: radical Thaddeus Stevens; John A. Bingham, a moderate congressman who was among the most influential architects of Reconstruction; George S. Boutwell, who guided the Fifteenth Amendment through floor debate in the House; and the colorful Benjamin F. Butler, who, as a Union army general in 1861, was at the forefront of the drive toward emancipation when he declared

172

runaway slaves free as contraband of war. The other managers were John A. Logan, Thomas Williams, and James F. Wilson. Butler delivered their opening argument, and for the next several days, they called their witnesses.

Under the circumstances, the opening for the defense promised to be a critical moment in the trial. According to news accounts, the public's demand for tickets that day was "unprecedented," and the galleries above the Senate floor overflowed with spectators. "Every seat, indeed, every foot of space where man or woman could stand was occupied." When the managers concluded presenting their evidence, Chief Justice Salmon P. Chase, the presiding judge, addressed Johnson's lawyers. "Gentlemen of counsel for the President, you will proceed with the defence."[3] The New York Tribune captured this precise moment. "The galleries were instantly hushed into attentive silence, and all eyes were turned toward the table to the right of the Chief-Justice, around which the President's counsel sat. It was easy to tell who was about to speak, from the books of law and general literature and sheets of manuscript notes in front of Judge Curtis."[4]

Curtis argued for several hours over two days. He began by emphasizing the judicial character of the proceedings, where "party spirit" and "political schemes" had no place. Then he launched into a point-by-point attack on the articles of impeachment. Although various factors led to Johnson's acquittal, contemporary accounts indicate that Curtis's opening marked the turning point in the president's fortunes. "Some of the points made by Judge Curtis are regarded as unanswerable," the New York Herald reported, "and even fatal to the whole prosecution."[5] With one exception, all cabinet members who had previously thought conviction inevitable now believed Johnson would prevail.[6] When the trial was over, the Senate by a vote of thirty-five to nineteen fell one vote short of the two-thirds required for conviction. Seven Republicans broke ranks with their party and joined twelve Democrats to acquit. One, William Pitt Fessenden, said simply, "Judge Curtis gave us the law, and we followed it."[7]

For its dramatic setting, historic importance, and most of all, as an exemplar of argumentation, Curtis's opening statement ought to be ranked among the great speeches of American legal history. It is striking how much opponents as well as allies considered his argument effective. In the brief episodic history of presidential impeachment, Curtis's opening constitutes a major statement of the law on this subject. On the constitutional standard of high crimes and misdemeanors, he sought to raise the bar for removing the president from office, contrary to what the framers probably intended. Curtis also explained how he thought this first-ever trial of the president should be conducted. He insisted that the Senate should follow customary judicial procedures, that legal reasoning should be the basis for decision, and that even such a politically charged trial must operate within a legal framework. On these points Curtis appears to have influenced a number of senators. In the course of defending Johnson, Curtis also analyzed several constitutional questions of some importance. He supported the president's plenary authority to remove executive officials, a question that came before the Supreme Court years later. Curtis described a role for the chief executive along with the Supreme Court in evaluating the constitutionality of legislation. Against charges that Johnson undermined Congress's authority through campaign speeches, Curtis defended the right of free political expression, one of the few occasions in the nineteenth century where the First Amendment was invoked in a major legal argument. Depending on the view one takes of the consequences that would have followed a conviction, Curtis may be credited with playing some part in preserving the constitutional balance of power between the legislative and executive branches of government.

I

The impeachment of Andrew Johnson grew out of the political struggle between Congress and the president over Reconstruction. In late 1863 Lincoln had ushered in a period of presidential Reconstruction with his so-called 10 Percent Plan, announcing that he was willing to recognize state governments in the South once 10 percent of the number of voters in 1860 swore loyalty to the Union and embraced emancipation.[8] The next year Lincoln pocket-vetoed the Wade-Davis bill, which would have required loyalty oaths from 50 percent of the state's voters and guaranteed equality under the law to freed slaves. The president's plan reflected his wartime interest in quickly assembling state governments in order to end the fighting. If his first term was any indication, he would have adapted his views to circumstances, and in any event, he would have found ways to accommodate congressmen on postwar Reconstruction without sacrificing his fundamental objectives. Even so, tensions had become apparent between Lincoln and the radical wing of his party.[9]

Following Lincoln's assassination, some Radical Republicans who later became leading advocates of impeachment had high hopes for the new chief executive. "Johnson, we have faith in you," declared Senator Wade. "By the Gods, there will be no trouble now in running the government."[10] Given some of Johnson's previous statements, such optimism was not unfounded. As the war drew to a close, Johnson said that treason "must be made odious, and traitors must be punished and im-poverished." He publicly likened himself to Moses, prepared to fulfill biblical promise for slaves in their journey toward freedom.[11] Sumner, who three years later considered impeachment "one of the last great battles with slavery," pronounced the newly installed president "the sincere friend of the negro" and "ready to act for him decisively."[12]

Early on in Johnson's administration, however, it became clear that the president was unwilling to promote the Radicals' agenda, particularly regarding the rights of blacks. President Johnson required the former Confederate states to ratify the Thirteenth Amendment, but he refused to take stronger measures. A critical turn of events involved the southern Black Codes and northern reaction to them. These laws were enacted by state legislatures Johnson had recognized. At first glance, these codes might have appeared to be constructive measures. They enumerated var-ious rights of freed slaves, including the rights to enter into contracts, hold property, and bring lawsuits. On closer scrutiny, though, the Black Codes reasserted the antebellum theme of racial subordination. The more vicious were in effect slave codes without the formal recognition of slavery. Some Black Codes declared wages forfeit when workers left their jobs before their contracts ended. Other laws defined vague crimes that were selectively enforced against freed slaves, such as vagrancy. Penalties included involuntary servitude and whipping. To many north-erners the Black Codes represented an effort to void the Thirteenth Amendment. The forced repeal of the most repressive provisions failed to assuage northerners' concerns, particularly in light of numerous re-ports of violent acts committed against blacks in the South.[13]

To protect former slaves, congressional Republicans led by Senator Lyman Trumbull, a moderate from Illinois, put forward two bills in early 1866. One renewed the Freedmen's Bureau, established by Con-gress near the end of the war. This temporary agency was created to aid southern blacks in the transition from slavery to freedom, whether by providing immediate economic relief or beginning long-term projects of education. Trumbull's idea was to enhance the bureau's enforcement powers to combat discrimination. The other piece of legislation, the civil rights bill, explicitly defined the rights of national citizenship to in-clude the rights to file lawsuits, enter into contracts, hold property, and more generally to possess "full and equal benefit of all laws and pro-ceedings for the security of person and property."[14] Johnson not only vetoed both bills; his uncompromising veto messages convinced moder-ate Republicans that it was futile to depend upon the president to safe-guard the rights of freed slaves.[15]

Though unable to override the veto of Trumbull's bureau bill, Congress passed the civil rights bill over Johnson's opposition and a few months later enacted veto-proof Freedmen's Bureau legislation. In the same session Republican lawmakers had been working toward a constitutional solution, a fourteenth amendment. It was designed to confirm federal authority to protect individuals from state action. Reversing *Dred Scott*, the amendment defined all native-born persons as U.S. citizens and prohibited states from infringing on the rights of citizenship. This amendment also guaranteed all persons equal protection of the law. Republican legislators also forced southern whites to make a choice: either grant freed slaves the right to vote or forfeit the number of representatives that would have been allocated based upon the state's black population. Ratification was set as a condition for having representatives admitted to Congress. Citing procedural irregularities, Johnson opposed the proposed amendment.[16]

While many Republicans had been willing to work with Johnson when he became president, his relations with Congress were strained to the breaking point within a year. By 1867 Republicans in Congress had gained the upper hand in developing a comprehensive program for Reconstruction. Putting the southern states under the Union army's control, the Reconstruction Acts authorized the troops to protect all persons, use military tribunals, register voters, and supervise elections. Congress also mandated black suffrage in the southern states.[17] Johnson had become consigned to play the part of obstructionist. Instead of creating a workable alliance with moderates, the president had alienated congressmen in the middle whom he needed to sustain his policies. More than once, his vetoes and provocative messages startled centrist Republicans. A less stubborn president might have avoided the repeated drives to impeachment that ended in near conviction.[18]

There was talk of impeaching Johnson a few months after he took office.[19] The first sustained effort began in January 1867, when Representative James M. Ashley sponsored an impeachment resolution. He accused President Johnson of usurpation of power and corruption, among other things. The House referred the matter to its judiciary committee, which investigated a wide range of charges, including sensational claims that Johnson conspired in Lincoln's assassination. The committee recommended impeachment, but most congressmen entertained doubts over the vague and unsupported allegations. The House by a decisive margin (108 to 57) declined to bring the president to trial.[20]

Although this result can be attributed to various causes—for example, several lawmakers worried about the Radicals' financial policies—what restrained many representatives was their interpretation of the Constitution. The impeachments clause provides that the president "shall be removed from Office on Impeachment for, and Conviction of, Treason, Bribery, or other high Crimes and Misdemeanors."[21] Legislators debated whether this constitutional standard was met. Some said the president could be impeached only for indictable crimes, offenses previously defined in the criminal law. While Radicals could cite impressive authority to the contrary (Story, for example), many congressmen remained uncertain, and Johnson survived the impeachment scare.[22]

As the absence of an indictable crime was a principal obstacle to impeachment, it is ironic that within three months of this vote, the president supplied his opponents with the legal hook they needed. For some time Johnson had wanted to replace Secretary of War Edwin M. Stanton. This was complicated by the Tenure of Office Act adopted by Congress in March 1867. Republicans drafted this legislation to prevent Johnson from using his powers of patronage to gain support for his Reconstruction policies. The act prohibited the president from removing executive officers appointed with the Senate's approval without first securing that body's consent. Any violation was declared to be a "high misdemeanor."[23] Whether this legislation applied to cabinet secretaries was debatable. Nevertheless, in accordance with the act, Johnson twice suspended Stanton when Congress was out of session and unsuccessfully sought the Senate's approval later. On February 21, 1868, President Johnson, making no effort to comply with the Tenure of Office Act, directed that Stanton be removed. The president named General Lorenzo B. Thomas interim secretary of war.

Stanton informed Republican legislators, who advised him to hold on. Sumner sent him a brief note: "Stick." The secretary barricaded himself in his office while rumors circulated that Johnson would resort to military force. The *New York Tribune* declared the president's "usurpation" a coup d'état. Radicals could now make a prima facie case of an impeachable criminal offense, and three days after Johnson issued his order, the House voted 126 to 47 to impeach him. No Republican voted against the impeachment resolution.[24]

The House of Representatives adopted eleven articles of impeachment. Most charged Johnson with statutory violations for his actions on February 21. The Tenure of Office Act provided the principal ground of attack. The House also cited a conspiracy statute in alleging that Johnson secretly plotted with General Thomas to prevent Stanton from holding office. In addition, the president was accused of overriding an appropriations measure by directing Major General William H. Emory to circumvent the chain of command established by Congress.[25] Several articles charged Johnson with exceeding his constitutional authority as president. Article X, the so-called Butler article, named for the impeachment manager who drafted it, said that Johnson had tried in campaign speeches to "set aside the rightful authority and powers of Congress." The catchall Article XI, sponsored by Thaddeus Stevens, reiterated many of the charges and added that President Johnson had wrongfully denied the legislature's power to propose constitutional amendments.[26]

II

Perhaps the most fundamental issue in Johnson's trial, in terms of presidential impeachment itself, concerned the law and politics of impeachment, or, in the words of Manager Butler, the "nature of the proceedings" and the "character and powers" of the Senate. Arguing that senators were "bound by no law," the impeachment managers suggested that "political considerations" were legitimate grounds for decision. Senator Sumner concisely stated the Radicals' view: the trial was "political in character— before a political body—and with a political judgment, being expulsion from office and nothing more." The president's counsel, by contrast, stressed that there must be a legal basis to convict. Curtis opened the defense by characterizing the Senate's role "in its judicial capacity as a court of impeachment" where "party spirit, political schemes, foregone conclusions, outrageous biases can have no fit operation."[27]

This issue of law versus politics first arose during preliminary skirmishing over procedural matters. When defense counsel requested forty days to file an answer to the articles of impeachment, the managers opposed any extension. They argued that Senate rules required the president to file his answer that day. Curtis, offering a legal interpretation of these rules, pointed out that "similar rules existing in courts of justice" distinguished between the dates for appearance and answer. Butler responded, "Let us not belittle ourselves with the analogies of the common-law courts, or the equity courts, or the criminal courts." This trial, Butler argued, should proceed "under the rules and forms prescribed by" the Constitution, and "all the likeness to a common and ordinary trial of any cause, civil or criminal," should "cease at once."[28] In the end, the Senate gave the president's counsel an additional ten days.

The exchange between Butler and Curtis was itself significant. It foreshadowed their opening arguments, both in style and substance. No two lawyers in the impeachment trial personified the issue of law versus politics any better. Curtis was a lawyer's lawyer recognized for his abilities in the fine art of legal reasoning. Butler was a rough-and-tumble politician. Straightforward to the point of being tactless, he was known for his outbursts in floor debate.[29]

In his opening Butler suggested that each senator had the duty "to sit upon the trial as he would upon any other matter." If the Senate was a court, then "many if not all the analogies" of court procedures "must obtain," Butler reasoned. Yet in his view normal judicial procedures did not apply. He noted that senators could not be challenged for bias, judicial precedent was not binding, and the evidentiary standard was less than the reasonable doubt required in criminal cases. Butler also argued that no language in the Constitution could be cited to show that the Senate had the "attributes of a judicial Court." Better to look upon the Senate as a "constitutional tribunal"; its precedent was the "law and custom of parliamentary bodies." He told the senators directly, "You are bound by no law, either statute or common, which may limit your constitutional prerogative." Butler continued with a flourish: "You are a law unto yourselves, bound only by the natural principles of equity and justice" and a sense of the public good.[30]

Butler was flamboyant, to be sure, but that did not mean his argument had no logical basis. It was not frivolous to contend that presidential impeachment involved political considerations not present in ordinary judicial proceedings. With the exception of a general statement of what constituted impeachable offenses, the framers left the decision to remove the president in the hands of the senators. That it was left to the discretion of the Senate to determine how to proceed, Butler might well have added, was attributable to the framers' conception of the members of that body, wise, virtuous, and equipped to determine what was in the public interest in an inherently difficult task. Whatever the framers had in mind, notable antebellum legal authorities bolstered Butler's position. Justice Story had stated that the "very habits growing out of judicial employments; the rigid manner, in which the discretion of judges is limited, and fenced in on all sides, in order to protect persons accused of crimes by rules and precedents; and the adherence to technical principles" were "ill adapted to the trial of political offences in the broad course of impeachments."[31]

Curtis keyed his opening argument to exploit Butler's rhetoric. Certainly, Curtis declared, the Constitution had not "clothed every one of you with imperial power" to say "I am a law unto myself, by which law I shall govern this case." He rejected Butler's suggestion that because the Senate was a legislative body it could not also perform a judicial function in impeachment. As for the framers, Curtis noted that *The Federalist* no. 64 described the Senate's "judicial character as a court for the trial of impeachments." He then cited several constitutional provisions to illustrate this point: the chief justice presided; the result was acquittal or conviction; in case of conviction, there was a judgment of removal from office. In short, the Constitution required a trial, and Curtis reminded senators of their oath to do "impartial justice according to the Constitution and the laws."[32]

Curtis understood the politics surrounding the impeachment trial. At the time of his opening, Curtis sized up the situation. He estimated that there were twenty-two to twenty-five senators "with a fixed determination" to convict, and he doubted they could be "shaken." Curtis thought that twelve to fifteen of "the dominant party had not abandoned all sense of right." What "will become of them I know not, but the *result* is with them."[33]

Of the eleven articles of impeachment, none presented the issue of law and politics so clearly as the Butler article. According to Curtis, this article fell "within that category which the honorable manager announced here at an early period of the trial; articles which require no law to support" it.[34] Because the Butler article was not based upon existing criminal law, it invited discussion about the interpretation of the impeachments clause. What constitutes an impeachable offense, and what exactly are high crimes and misdemeanors? This question has appeared in one form or another in the impeachment inquiries concerning Presidents Johnson, Nixon, and Clinton. Through the years there have been two basic positions. Under a narrow reading of the impeachments clause, Congress can impeach the president only for indictable crimes. In the broader view high crimes and misdemeanors can include activities not previously defined as criminal offenses. Most students of presidential impeachment have favored the latter position based upon their understanding of the purpose of impeachment. It is a mechanism to check serious abuses of power, so the argument goes, which may be thwarted if an indictable crime is required. It is too difficult, according to this school of thought, to draft the criminal code to anticipate precisely how the nation's leaders might subvert the government.[35]

The framers did not provide a definitive answer to the question of what are high crimes and misdemeanors. The relevant discussion at the Constitutional Convention began with consideration of language limiting impeachment to treason and bribery. George Mason expressed concern that this left out "great and dangerous offences" that "subvert the Constitution." He proposed adding the word "maladministration." Madison felt that "maladministration" was so "vague" that it would reduce the president to serving at the "pleasure of the Senate." Mason then offered to substitute "high crimes & misdemeanors against the State" in place of "maladministration." Presumably Mason believed this addressed his concern over great subversive offenses. In any event, his proposal was accepted without further debate, although "against the State" was later deleted.[36]

That the framers held the broader view of "high crimes and misdemeanors" is suggested by at least two points. First, they were familiar with English history in which that phrase was not restricted to indictable crimes under the common law. Second, in *The Federalist* Hamilton described impeachable offenses as "POLITICAL, as they relate chiefly to injuries done immediately to the society itself."[37]

The Butler article charged Johnson with ridiculing Congress in "hatred, contempt, and reproach" with the intent to "set aside" its "rightful authority and powers." The president did this in "intemperate, inflammatory, and scandalous harangues," in which he issued "loud threats and bitter menaces" against Congress and the laws of the United States. Butler placed in the article extracts of speeches that Johnson delivered during the 1866 campaign. The most startling was his counterattack on leading Radicals. "I have been called Judas Iscariot," Johnson had said. "If I have played the Judas, who has been my Christ that I have played the Judas with? Was it Thad. Stevens? Was it Wendell Phillips? Was it Charles Sumner? These are the men that stop and compare themselves with the Saviour; and everybody that differs with them in opinion, and to try to stay and arrest their diabolical and nefarious policy, is to be denounced as a Judas."[38]

The Butler article was contrived, yet when Curtis turned his attention to it, he had "much to say." The reason Curtis discussed this article at length was not, it seems, because he feared its success but rather because it served his strategic purpose. Butler had defined high crimes and misdemeanors broadly to include acts "subversive of some fundamental or essential principle of government, or highly prejudicial to the public interest" without necessarily "violating a positive law." This presented Curtis with an opportunity to address the governing standard for presidential impeachment. Embracing the indictable offenses test, Curtis defined high crimes and misdemeanors as "*high* criminal offences against the United States, made so by some law of the United States existing when the acts complained of were done."[39]

As Philip B. Kurland has suggested, while we "ordinarily welcome and pay heed" to Curtis's views, the advocate's proposed definition was colored by the fact that it served his client's interests. Even so, Curtis offered some convincing reasons for the position he had taken. His basic idea revolved around fairness to the person accused. He stressed the Constitution's "direct prohibitions" against bills of attainder and ex post facto laws; it was fundamentally wrong to target specific individuals and penalize them for actions that were not previously proscribed. The English Parliament had made "law for the facts they find," an abuse, Curtis thought, that the managers sought to replicate. Each senator is, "to use the phrase of the honorable managers, 'a law unto himself,' and according to his discretion," he "frames a law to meet the case."[40]

Although Curtis endorsed the indictable crimes standard, his conception of what that implied was more open-ended than might be thought. He indicated that impeachable offenses could be defined at common law as well as by statute. When Curtis directed attention to Butler's statement that the Senate was bound by no law, the manager interrupted, "Will you state where it was I said it was bound by no law?" Stanbery responded, "A law unto itself." Butler then restated his position: "'No common or statute law' was my language." Curtis's response was based on his conception that common law and statute comprehended the "field." As he put it, "When you get out of that field you are in a limbo, a vacuum, so far as law is concerned." Curtis added that the applicable law could be "written or unwritten, express or implied."[41] This suggested interesting possibilities for impeachment, but as Curtis was not engaged in a theoretical discussion, he did not elaborate.

There were plausible responses to the position Curtis advanced. The governing law could be considered to be what the Constitution prescribed, and the charter vested Congress with the authority to define high crimes and misdemeanors. Statute and common law could be considered useful but not necessarily binding precedent. Notice to the accused was a basic tenet of the criminal law, but presidential impeachment was distinguishable in purpose (to protect the state) and in effect (to remove the president from office). At some points Curtis's logic was subject to question. He noted that Article III of the Constitution provides that the "trial of all Crimes, except in Cases of Impeachment, shall be by Jury." From that, Curtis inferred that the impeachment proceeding is "the trial of a crime." This inference is debatable. Just because some crimes may be impeachable does not mean that all impeachable offenses are crimes.[42]

Curtis was on stronger ground when he parsed the impeachments clause. The Constitution provides for impeachment in cases of treason, bribery, and other high crimes and misdemeanors. Curtis emphasized that crimes and misdemeanors must be extraordinary to be impeachable. To interpret the meaning of "high Crimes and Misdemeanors," he applied the legal maxim *noscitur a sociis*, a rule of interpretation that the meaning of a word is known by its accompanying words. Curtis suggested that other crimes and misdemeanors must be "so high that they belong in this company with treason and bribery." The fundamental point, Curtis reasoned, was that a president may be impeached only for "offences which strike at the existence" of the government.[43]

His conclusion was clear: the charges based upon President Johnson's campaign speeches were not "high" crimes. Curtis's treatment of Article X illustrates his rhetorical style. He ridiculed the claim that Johnson's speeches undermined congressional authority. One of the president's statements which the House found objectionable was directed against Stevens and Sumner. "Well, who are the grand jury in this case?" Curtis asked. "One of the parties spoken against. And who are the triers? The other party spoken against. One would think there was some incongruity in this." Curtis poked fun at Butler's expense. As the trial progressed, it became clear that Butler was given to harangues himself. Curtis remarked, "The honorable House of Representatives sends its managers to take notice of what? That the House of Representatives has erected itself into a school of manners, selecting from its ranks those gentlemen whom it deems most competent by precept and example to teach decorum of speech." According to news accounts, this comment "created a little merriment throughout the Chamber."[44]

Curtis closed his discussion of the Butler article on a more serious note—a plea for free political speech. He asked what rule of law the senators would consult to judge the president's speeches. Butler had said in his opening that words can be dangerous but noted that the article did "not raise the question of freedom of speech, but of propriety and decency of speech and conduct in a high officer." Curtis turned this concession to his advantage. "The only rule I have heard," he said, "is that you may require the speaker to speak properly." Pointing to the excesses of European history, Curtis said: "That is the same freedom of speech, senators, in consequence of which thousands of men went to the scaffold under the Tudors and the Stuarts. That is the same freedom of speech which caused thousands of heads of men and of women to roll from the guillotine in France. . . . Is that the freedom of speech intended to be secured by our Constitution?" With that question hanging in the Senate chamber, Curtis closed his discussion of the Butler article.[45]

III

Although the Butler article was significant for highlighting the question of what are high crimes and misdemeanors, the trial centered around President Johnson's dismissal of Secretary of War Stanton and the Tenure of Office Act. Some Radicals considered the attention given Stanton's removal a mistake. Representative Ashley considered that "one of the smallest" of Johnson's crimes, but congressmen favoring broader charges were unable to prevail upon more conservative members of the drafting committee who insisted on indictable offenses. Radicals pushed through the Butler and Stevens articles on the House floor.[46]

By concentrating on Stanton's dismissal and the Tenure of Office Act, the House set the field of battle on grounds favorable to the president's counsel. The articles invited debate over statutory construction and constitutional interpretation. This put a premium on lawyerly tools of trade in which Curtis excelled.

His argument at trial consisted of three main parts. He began with a close examination of the Tenure of Office Act, which, he claimed, did not protect Stanton. Turning to the Constitution, Curtis said that the president had the authority to remove officers in the executive branch, including cabinet secretaries, without congressional approval. Lastly, Curtis argued that the president was not obliged to implement legislation, like the Tenure of Office Act, which he reasonably believed to be an unconstitutional invasion of executive authority. Curtis cast Johnson's actions as an effort to preserve presidential power against legislative encroachments.

The conclusions to which Curtis pointed were neither entirely new nor irrebuttable. Although the president and his supporters had advanced similar arguments, Curtis's opening was distinguished by its legal craftsmanship. Curtis elided the difficulties in defending the president. With clever emphasis and subtle development, he displayed a precise sense of the minimal and least offensive positions required to prevail. Practically every line of Curtis's argument extended upon his basic theme that law should govern the impeachment trial. His message was that his way of reading the statute and the Constitution was the lawyerly approach which must be adopted by the senators sitting as judges.

Curtis's skill and advocacy were on display in his construction of the Tenure of Office Act. It is evident from Curtis's speech that he saw the managers' reliance on this legislation as a fundamental weakness in their case. He did not disguise his eagerness to uncover every detail concerning the statute. This was "dry work," Curtis conceded, while proceeding at such "considerable length" that he felt compelled to apologize for "trying" the senators' "patience." Curtis stressed that the case against the president depended almost entirely on the Tenure of Office Act, which "enters deeply" into eight articles and "materially touches" two others.[47]

Whatever advantage he perceived in focusing on this statute, Curtis's task was complicated by the fact that senators participating in the impeachment trial had voted on the Tenure of Office Act the previous year. Presumably, they needed no instruction on what they had intended. Butler seized on this point in his opening: "I shall not argue to the Senate, composed mostly of those who passed the bill, what their wishes and intentions were." Confident that most senators shared their views of the act, the managers were content to leave the issue in their hands. The managers could draw comfort from the facts surrounding the act's passage. The Senate had overridden Johnson's veto of this legislation 35 to 11, the two-thirds supermajority required to convict the president. All Republicans had voted against the veto.[48]

In these circumstances, Curtis deftly suggested that the controlling issue was not what senators intended. Evidence of Congress's intent was relevant, but to senators disposed to read the act according to their own recollections, Curtis suggested that the real question at trial was how a judge would interpret this statute. In other words, senators were bound to review the statute as judges would. Personal views on what was intended were beside the point. The argument coincided with Curtis's basic theme that law, not politics, provided the guiding principles for decision.

Curtis proceeded to put forward a "judicial interpretation" of the Tenure of Office Act. Starting with the statutory language, he argued that the legislation by its terms did not cover Secretary Stanton. Under the act "every person holding any civil office" who had been appointed with the advice and consent of the Senate "shall be entitled to hold such office" until the Senate approves a successor, "except as herein otherwise provided." The following proviso became the center of debate. This qualifying clause stated that cabinet secretaries "shall hold their offices... for and during the term of the President by whom they may have been appointed," subject "to removal by and with the advice and consent of the Senate."[49]

Curtis explained how he thought a judge would apply this proviso to Stanton's case. Focusing on the phrase "the term of the President," Curtis argued that, as used in the singular, "the term" could only be taken to refer to Lincoln's first term, when the secretary was appointed. Curtis said that "an expounder of this law judicially" had no authority to add the phrase "and any other term" for which the president "may afterward be elected." If the statute's words did not accurately reflect what some senators meant, they were nevertheless stuck at trial with the language as written. Congress was free to amend the act in the course of its ordinary legislative process, but the Senate was not in that position during the impeachment trial.[50]

This straightforward reading invited the objection of being hyper-technical—a "quibble," Sumner later remarked.[51] In any event, Curtis did not dwell on this argument. Whether he considered his construction of the word "term" decisive, his opening salvo demonstrated the precision with which he thought a judge would examine this legislation.

Curtis turned his attention to the broader phrase, "for and during the term of the President by whom they [cabinet secretaries] may have been appointed." Even if the proviso covered a president's second term in office, the question was whether Lincoln's term ended when he was assassinated. The managers took the position that Johnson was serving out Lincoln's term; Curtis argued to the contrary. Using the idea of "conditional limitation" (and leaving no doubt as to its roots in legal doctrine), Curtis said that a "'conditional limitation,' as the lawyers call it, is imposed" on the president's term of office. The Constitution did not recognize an absolute term of four years, he contended. Article II of the Constitution specified events (removal, resignation, death, incapacity) that, Curtis argued, conditionally limit the chief executive's term in office. In Curtis's view death ended Lincoln's term, and even if the Tenure of Office Act covered Stanton, his protected tenure ended in 1865.[52]

Curtis's interpretation on this point was open to question. While the Constitution states that the vice president assumes the "powers and duties" of the presidency, it does not clarify whether the vice president acquires his own term.[53] Curtis did not rest his argument on the statute's language, however. He found support for his position in what he considered to be the proviso's purpose, and he used the Constitution to validate his reading of that purpose. There was a constitutional reason, according to Curtis, for treating cabinet secretaries differently from other executive officers. The Constitution provides that the president "may require the Opinion in writing of the principal Officer in each of the executive Departments upon any subject relating to the Duties of their respective Offices."[54] As cabinet secretaries advise the president on matters concerning the administration generally as well as departmental issues, they serve as the president's "immediate confidential assistants"— "the hands and the voice of the President." Given these constitutionally prescribed duties, Curtis concluded that Congress could not have meant "to compel" the president "to continue in office a Secretary not appointed by himself."[55]

Having examined the statute's language and purpose, Curtis then found confirmation for his position in its legislative history. He focused on what he considered the key point in deciphering Congress's intent: the statements made by the ranking members of the conference committee that had drafted the proviso. Before that committee met, the House bill had treated cabinet secretaries like other executive officials, but the Senate had rejected this version. Curtis noted Representative Robert C. Schenck's explanation that with the proviso cabinet members' terms "expire with the term of service of the President who appoints them, and one month after, in case of death." Evidence Curtis produced from the Senate was even more compelling. When the bill was considered there, a senator expressed concern that the legislation would keep Stanton in office. Senator John Sherman of the conference committee responded, "We do not legislate in order to keep in the Secretary of War."[56]

Curtis admitted that some legislators might have a "different view" of the proviso. Whatever their interpretation, Curtis felt that they must agree that reasonable people could differ over the act's meaning. "I think they will in all candor admit that there is a question of construction" of "what the meaning of this law was" and "whether it was applicable in Mr. Stanton's case." With that, Curtis stressed the element of intent in the articles, the allegations that Johnson "wilfully misconstrued" the act. The president's advocate asked whether the Senate was prepared to conclude that Johnson "must" have engaged in "a wilful misconstruction— so wilful, so wrong, that it can justly and properly, and for the purpose of this prosecution, effectively be termed a high misdemeanor." Given the legislative history he recited, Curtis asked the Senate, "How is it possible for this body to convict the President of the United States of a high misdemeanor for construing a law as those who made it construed it at the time when it was made?"[57]

As Curtis laid out the steps he thought a judge would take in construing the Tenure of Office Act, his argument amounted to a series of directives to the senators: read the statutory language precisely, apply the legal principle of conditional limitation, interpret the statute to accord with constitutional practice, and consider the legislative history fairly. Putting the finishing touch on his statutory analysis, Curtis argued that it was not Johnson but Stanton who had violated the law. Secretary Stanton, Curtis explained, did not hold office under the Tenure of Office Act but rather under a 1789 statute establishing the Department of War. That legislation expressly stated that the department's head served "at the pleasure" of the president. Reiterating his central theme, Curtis suggested that the law was again on the president's side. When Johnson dismissed Stanton, the secretary "was bound by law to obey that order" and "quit the place instead of being sustained by law in resisting that order."[58]

That left the constitutional question concerning the president's power to remove executive officers. Evidently confident that most senators agreed that Johnson violated the Constitution by dismissing Stanton, the managers acknowledged the high stakes of this issue. Butler conceded that eight articles of impeachment depended upon their constitutional position. If the managers were mistaken in this, he said, Johnson "ought to go quit and free" on those articles. Butler could not conceive of that possibility, however. Laying claim to the basic principles of free government, Butler considered the power to remove executive officers "at will" a "more than kingly prerogative." He wondered whether the office of the presidency *"ought, in fact, to exist as a part of the constitutional government of a free people"* if the president possessed that power under the Constitution.[59]

Notwithstanding Butler's high-flown rhetoric, the scope of the president's removal power was debatable, and the Supreme Court wrestled with this issue in a number of cases in the twentieth century.[60] The Constitution specifies the manner of appointment for executive officers: the president "shall nominate and, by and with the Advice and Consent of the Senate, shall appoint . . . Officers of the United States." Except for cases of impeachment, the text of the Constitution says nothing about removal. In *The Federalist*, Hamilton wrote that the Senate's consent "would be necessary to displace as well as to appoint" officers in the executive branch. The First Congress took the contrary position in 1789. Legislation establishing the Departments of War, Treasury, and Foreign Affairs recognized the president's authority to remove these department heads without Senate approval. The vote was close. The Senate's roll call ended in a tie twice, and Vice President John Adams as president of the Senate decided the issue.[61]

The prevailing view among antebellum jurists like Kent and Story was double-edged. They disagreed with the "decision of 1789," as it was known, as a matter of constitutional interpretation. Yet they recognized the First Congress's action as a legislative construction of the Constitution which was subsequently confirmed by continuing practice. Even then, the scope of the president's removal power remained in question. Webster suggested that Congress could "reverse" the decision of 1789. In 1833 the Senate censured President Jackson for removing the treasury secretary (the censure was later stricken from the legislative record).[62] Six years later the Supreme Court stated the general rule somewhat vaguely: the power of removal was "incident to the power of appointment." This was understood to mean that executive officials appointed with the Senate's consent could not be removed by the president acting alone.[63]

In the Johnson trial the lawyers on both sides apparently believed that the decision of 1789 was critical. Butler sought in his opening to undermine the First Congress's authority. As the margin of victory was exceptionally close, Butler asked why the issue was not "more authoritatively" decided when Congress enacted the Tenure of Office Act by clear majorities in both chambers.[64]

Curtis had a ready answer. In another appeal to trump momentary political considerations, he described a rule of interpretation which, he emphasized, had long standing in the Anglo-American legal tradition. A "contemporary exposition of a law" made by "competent" authority has "very great weight." For the rationale behind the rule, Curtis invoked a statement made by Sir Edward Coke that "the sages who lived about the time" a law was adopted "were best able to judge of the intention" of those who made the law. Coke's language was "quaint," but Curtis thought the sentiment reflected an integral part of every sophisticated legal system. This "long settled" principle existed in "all civilized countries," Curtis asserted; "certainly in every system of law that I have any acquaintance with."[65]

Applying this interpretive principle, Curtis reviewed three theories of the removal power considered by the First Congress. One held that the president and Senate shared this power, so that the president could remove executive officers only after obtaining the Senate's consent. According to the second theory, Congress was empowered to determine the manner of removing executive officers (the legislature could authorize the president to act alone). Curtis believed that the Tenure of Office Act rested on this theory, which, he said, received little support in the First Congress. It was promoted by "comparatively few persons" and "rejected by the ablest minds that had this subject under consideration in 1789." Under the third theory, adopted by the First Congress, the Constitution authorized the president to remove executive officers without the Senate's consent.[66]

Alluding to the First Congress's unique position on questions of constitutional interpretation, Curtis suggested that its debate over the removal power was conducted with "surpassing ability and knowledge of the frame and necessities of our government." He pointed out that James Madison seconded the motion to clarify that the removal power was "solely" the president's, a fact which Curtis related by quoting from John Marshall's approving account. Curtis recited Marshall's conclusion that the decision of 1789 "has ever been considered as a full expression of the sense of the legislature on this important part of the American Constitution."[67]

The debate in 1789 was more complicated than Curtis let on. The House of Representatives was more evenly divided, and Madison's position more nuanced, than the president's lawyer indicated.[68] Perhaps sensing the need for something more, Curtis bolstered his position with another rule of interpretation—a personal favorite of his—"practical construction." Again, he found an appropriate legal maxim in Coke: "Practice is the best interpreter of law." The American judiciary had embraced this principle in "very numerous cases," Curtis said, citing his own *Cooley* opinion. The idea of practical construction was not merely to take legislative and executive actions into account but to give "long-continued" practice "decisive weight." In other words, practical construction settled the meaning of open-ended constitutional language. It is "now a fixed and settled rule," he stated, "which I think no lawyer will undertake to controvert, that the effect of such a construction is not merely to give weight to an argument, but to fix an interpretation."[69]

The problem with Curtis's line of argument was that actual practice was less clear than he might have liked. The usual course of action was for the president to notify the Senate of a removal while submitting a nomination requiring approval (A. B. nominated, in place of C. D.). While Curtis at one point asserted that "every President and every Congress participated in and acted under the construction given in 1789," he elsewhere admitted that cases of removal without accompanying nominations were infrequent.[70] The managers cited counterexamples. In 1863, for instance, Congress explicitly declared that the president and Senate shared the power to remove the comptroller of the currency. As the trial progressed, this issue turned into a battle over documentary evidence, with each side producing lists and tables of past removals.[71]

Whatever the difficulties in his position, Curtis had set the stage for senators to resolve the issue at trial in the president's favor. As he had done with his interpretation of the Tenure of Office Act, Curtis argued that there was at least reasonable doubt over this constitutional question. He did not insist that other positions on the removal power were "unfounded." Instead, he suggested that "no fair and candid mind can deny that it is capable of being doubted." On those grounds Curtis invited senators to acquit. The constitutional theory underlying the Tenure of Office Act "may be the truth, after all; but it is not a truth which shines with such clear and certain light that a man is guilty of a crime because he does not see it."[72]

Curtis did not rest his constitutional argument on the removal power, as he also articulated a "broader view" of the president's constitutional authority. He suggested that in a limited set of circumstances, the chief executive could rightfully refuse to implement legislation which he considered unconstitutional. It was a risky argument to make in the political context, given senators' concerns over the Reconstruction Acts.

The question was by itself significant. Did the president, as the head of a coordinate branch of the government, have coequal authority with Congress to interpret the Constitution? Jefferson and Jackson had previously affirmed their power to do that. According to this line of thought, the fundamental check on the president was political. At one point in the impeachment trial, Curtis's colleague Thomas Nelson stated this position: so long as the president acted in good faith, his judgment was only reviewable by the people in presidential elections.[73]

Curtis approached this question more cautiously. "I am not intending" to "occupy any extreme ground." He denied that the president could "erect himself into a judicial court and decide that the law is unconstitutional." Curtis insisted that the chief executive could refuse to enforce legislation only in limited circumstances. Curtis identified two preconditions: first, that Congress "cut off a power confided" in him "by the people, through the Constitution," and second, that only the president could bring the issue before the judiciary. By this, Curtis meant to exclude legislation affecting either third parties who could protect their own interests in court or the general public interest, when the people could defend themselves "at the polls."[74]

With judicial review in a well-defined set of cases the desired result, Curtis neatly converted resistance to law into civic virtue. He fit Johnson's refusal to abide by the Tenure of Office Act into a general rule applicable to all citizens. A citizen, Curtis reasoned, may have a "high and patriotic duty" to test legislation in court. To enable the courts to determine the constitutionality of legislation, it was sometimes necessary to disregard "those laws which have been passed through" the "forms of legislation."[75]

According to Curtis, this principle applied to the president as well as ordinary citizens. Curtis found an additional justification in the president's case. The chief executive was the "trustee for the people of powers confided to him for their protection, for their security, for their benefit."[76] As such, President Johnson was obliged to defend his office against congressional encroachment. As Johnson thought the Tenure of Office Act invaded the powers of the presidency, it was his duty to bring that legislation before the courts. Curtis also suggested that by doing so the president fulfilled his oath to preserve the Constitution. In this way Johnson's advocate turned on its head the argument that the president had defied the people's will by resisting this statute. Legislation contrary to the Constitution did not reflect the will of the people; thus, popular sovereignty was on Johnson's side.

Curtis concluded his discussion of this "broader view" with an argument that caught the attention of several senators. In a style reminiscent of John Marshall's opinion in *Marbury*, Curtis offered arresting hypotheticals. Suppose a statute prohibited the president from making a treaty with England, or legislation deprived the president of the powers as commander in chief. Surely in these cases, Curtis argued, the president was not bound to follow such legislation. These were "plain cases" of powers expressly granted in the Constitution, and he saw no logical reason to distinguish from them the president's implied powers, such as removing a cabinet secretary.[77]

Even with these qualifications, Curtis's argument was chancy. He left the impression that the military reconstruction acts differed materially from the Tenure of Office Act, but it was hard to keep the subtle distinctions in mind. Curtis's cocounsel failed to follow through on the intricacies of his argument. Indeed, his own example of legislation involving the commander in chief's powers opened the door for Johnson to defy congressional Reconstruction.[78] Besides, the prospect of testing the Reconstruction Acts before the Supreme Court provided little comfort to Republicans on Capitol Hill. They worried that the justices were prepared to declare their legislation unconstitutional. While the impeachment trial was under way, a case, *Ex parte McCardle*, was pending before the Court which threatened Congress's Reconstruction program.[79] The reaction in Congress was revealing. One proposed bill would have required a two-thirds majority of justices to invalidate any legislation; another defined Reconstruction as political and beyond the Court's jurisdiction. Three days before the impeachment trial began, Congress repealed the statute that gave the Court jurisdiction to hear McCardle's appeal. The Court dismissed the case for lack of jurisdiction a few months later.[80]

Curtis's "broader view" was open to criticism on other grounds as well. For lawmakers who had watched Johnson comply with the Tenure of Office Act over the past year, it was difficult to believe that the president sought to test the statute in court. On this point Curtis used legal doctrine to override bad facts. "All of us who have read law-books know that there is in the common law a doctrine called rules of estoppel," prohibiting a party from asserting facts contrary to actions previously taken. Then, Curtis browbeat senators with the idea that the rule obviously did not apply. "Did anybody ever hear," Curtis asked, "that a man was convicted of crime by reason of an estoppel under any system of law that ever prevailed in any civilized State?"[81]

Curtis went on to cover every article point by point, but the essential aspects of his argument had been made. He ended his speech, it appears, to match Butler's conclusion. Both lawyers nicely combined eloquent appeals of what was at stake with meaningful extensions of their positions. Butler portrayed the trial as a fateful episode in the advance of liberty, with the meaning of the Civil War and the end of slavery at stake. The "future political welfare and liberties of all men hang trembling on the decision of the hour." Curtis, in turn, broadened his insistence on law over politics into a claim for justice. "It must be apparent to every one," he said, "that this is and will be the most conspicuous instance which ever has been or can ever be expected to be found of American justice or American injustice." Intimating that no good could come out of an unjust result, Curtis warned that in the divine order of things, injustice was "certain to return to plague its inventors."[82]

IV

After opening for the president, Curtis wrote that he had "no means of judging" whether his argument had "much permanent and useful effect." An early twentieth-century commentator thought otherwise: "At the close of his masterly dissection of the eleven articles Curtis might safely have rested his case." That was in fact the position Curtis advocated to his colleagues shortly after delivering his speech. According to Secretary of the Navy Gideon Welles, who attended the lawyers' strategy sessions, Curtis along with Evarts "thought the President had a perfectly good case as it stands, without farther testimony." Curtis "feared every new witness," Welles noted, as the other side was "fishing for evidence." Stanbery wanted to introduce one other witness at least, General William T. Sherman.[83]

As it turned out, the general's testimony highlighted the difficulties the president's lawyers faced. In February 1868 President Johnson had asked Sherman to serve as secretary of war in place of Stanton. Stanbery asked General Sherman a key question at the trial. Did Johnson indicate that he sought to test the Tenure of Office Act in court? The managers objected to this question, put in various forms by Stanbery. Chief Justice Chase would have admitted the evidence, but a majority of the senators overruled him (following the procedures of the impeachment trial). Stanbery was unable to get this evidence before the Senate until Democratic senator Reverdy Johnson submitted a question to determine whether Sherman understood the president's purpose. By one vote (26–25), the legislators allowed an answer. After all that, General Sherman at first testified that the president "did not state to me then that his purpose was to bring it to the courts directly" and that Johnson thought "a case could not be made up." Stanbery immediately tried to have the general clarify his remarks. The managers objected to further questioning. "If I heard aright," Bingham said, the testimony "utterly disappointed and confounded the counsel for the accused." When Sherman was allowed to respond, he said that it "was the constitutionality of that bill" that the president "seemed desirous of having tested and which, he said, if it could be brought before the Supreme Court properly, would not stand half an hour."[84]

The trial ended with four lawyers for each side giving closing arguments. Neither Curtis nor Butler participated. After opening, Curtis had predicted that the case would be "effectively and actually settled *before*" final arguments. In keeping with his original plan, he left for Boston without hearing them.[85]

The outcome remained in doubt until the senators voted on May 16, although it looked like President Johnson would prevail.[86] It was clear that the margin of decision would be close. The Senate had fifty-four members. Thirty-six would have to vote to convict in order for Johnson to be removed from office. The president could count on the twelve Democrats; he needed at least seven votes from the forty-two Republicans.[87] Proponents of impeachment arranged for the first vote to be taken on Article XI, the Stevens article, which they considered most likely to prevail. The roll call began with the chief justice polling each senator: "How say you? Is the respondent, Andrew Johnson, President of the United States, guilty or not guilty of a high misdemeanor, as charged in this article?" Thirty-five voted guilty. Seven Republicans voted to acquit; others would have done so if necessary.[88] The Senate postponed further consideration for ten days. After the senators rejected two additional articles by the same vote, the trial came to a close.[89]

Historians can point to several factors leading to Johnson's acquittal. The president's counsel derived some advantage from the inherent weakness of the impeachment articles and the excesses of the managers' presentation.[90] Issues outside of the proceedings were significant. Some Republicans were concerned about putting Senator Wade into the White House, given his progressive views on the rights of women and labor.[91] As for the future of Reconstruction policy, Evarts had assured key senators that Johnson would not oppose congressional Reconstruction any longer. Besides, the crisis atmosphere of February 1868 had faded. The next presidential election was only six months off. Indeed, while the Senate's vote on impeachment extended over several days, the Republican Party held its convention and nominated Ulysses S. Grant to run for president.[92]

Historians have also credited Evarts, Stanbery, and Groesbeck for their contributions to the president's legal defense.[93] To actual participants and close observers, though, Curtis's speech was pivotal. With the odds prevailing against the president before the defense opened, Curtis was seen to have arrested the momentum to convict Johnson. His "lucid and powerful address," the *Nation* reported, was the "first coherent presentation that had ever been made of the President's case." More than one contemporary suggested that Curtis's opening argument struck the death knell of impeachment. Echoing the *New York Herald*'s characterization—Curtis's analysis was "fatal to the whole prosecution"—Manager Boutwell considered Curtis's interpretation of the proviso "fatal" to the case against Johnson. Even efforts to discredit Curtis's argument demonstrate its effectiveness. When "the best has been said for the President," *Harper's Weekly* declared, "how unsatisfactory it is!" "It was known" that Curtis "would say the best that could be said for his client; that he would subject the letter of the law to the most trying ordeal of possible interpretation; and that he would ingeniously shift the lights and shadows upon the facts of the case to favor his own view, in the manner of all great advocates." Butler regarded the defense team's closing arguments superfluous. After Curtis "had presented the case of his client," Butler said, "in my judgment nothing *more* was said" in the president's behalf, although "much *else* was said" by his other counsel.[94]

The closing arguments provide further evidence of the impact Curtis had at the trial. His cocounsel, as might be expected, followed his lead. "I shall not repeat," Nelson said, "what I esteem to be the unanswerable argument of Judge Curtis" on Stanton's removal. Even more illuminating are the managers' responses. Trying to take the luster off Curtis's argument, Bingham described "the learned gentleman from Massachusetts" as "too self-poised." The impeachment managers struggled to work around Curtis's rules of interpretation. "I am not here," said Thomas Williams, "to question the doctrine which has been so strongly urged, upon the authority of Lord Coke, that contemporaneous exposition is entitled to great weight in law."[95] Bingham misstated Curtis's broader view of presidential power, purposefully it appears, in an effort to diminish its effect.[96] Meanwhile, Boutwell and Stevens scrambled to rebut Curtis's interpretation of the Tenure of Office Act.[97]

Senators had the opportunity to file written opinions explaining their votes. Those voting to acquit relied on Curtis's arguments while some supporting impeachment were preoccupied with his opening in one way or another. Curtis's gambit on reading "term" in the singular caught the favor of several lawmakers.[98] Significantly, Senator Timothy Otis Howe voted to convict, but he could not bring himself to do so on any article based on the act because he interpreted "term" as Curtis had. Democrat Charles R. Buckalew thought that the president's position on refusing to enforce legislation had been "grossly misrepresented," although it had been stated "by Judge Curtis, in his opening for the defence, with a clearness and completeness which leave nothing to be desired, and remove all excuse for a misconception or complaint." On the other side of the aisle, Sumner was bothered by Curtis's hypotheticals of plainly unconstitutional legislation. "Ingenuity seeks to perplex the question by putting impossible cases," Sumner said. These few examples cannot fully capture the extent to which Curtis set the grounds of debate.[99]

The key to assessing Curtis's part in the trial, however, rests with the seven Republicans who voted to acquit. Despite Senator Fessenden's statement that "Judge Curtis gave us the law, and we followed it,"[100] these lawmakers were motivated to some degree by extralegal considerations.[101] Senator Edmund G. Ross apparently was influenced by his desire to secure patronage positions for friends in his home state of Kansas.[102] Peter G. Van Winkle, senator from West Virginia, worried about the nation's financial situation.[103]

Of the seven voting to acquit, all but Ross filed written opinions. Granted that their public statements may imperfectly reveal their actual decision-making process, these opinions show that at a minimum they relied on Curtis's argument to justify their votes and to shield themselves from public and party pressure. The senators restated the authorities Curtis had quoted, followed his logic, and applied his legal concepts and interpretive rules. Five of these six statements reiterated Curtis's explanation of the Tenure of Office Act. Trumbull echoed Curtis's question: "I could never consent to convict the Chief Magistrate" for "a misconstruction of what must be admitted to be a doubtful statute, and particularly when the misconstruction was the same put upon it by the authors of the law at the time of its passage." Fessenden closely followed the opening argument's interpretation of the proviso. Senator Joseph S. Fowler repeated Curtis's description of a "conditional limitation." Putting a "judicial interpretation" on the Tenure of Office Act, Senator James W. Grimes relied on Curtis's explanation of the act's legislative history. The senators turned to Curtis's opening for other points as well. Like Curtis, John B. Henderson used plain cases in his argument on the president's removal power. Fowler restated the view of practical construction that Curtis gave to the president's removal power.[104]

Curtis's overriding theme of law over politics and the judicial character of the impeachment trial found its way into practically all of the statements issued by the acquitting Republicans. Referring to the "character of the tribunal," Fowler noted that the chief justice presided over the Senate, "organized as a court of impeachment." Both Fowler and Fessenden recited their oath to render impartial justice. Senator Trumbull said that "party considerations" should have no bearing on the decision, a view shared by Grimes. "However widely . . . I may and do differ with the President," Senator Grimes said, "I am acting in a judicial capacity."[105]

Beyond Johnson's trial, Curtis's opening argument was a significant statement on the law of presidential impeachment. Before that trial it was open to maintain that impeachment was fundamentally political. Curtis forcefully contested that view. He argued that the proceedings were judicial in nature, the Senate acted as a court, the trial must be conducted according to legal procedures, and law rather than politics should determine each senator's vote. Presidential impeachments undoubtedly arise out of highly charged political circumstances. Yet since 1868 the managers' position on law and legal procedure has faded from view.[106]

Whether the country would have been better served if Johnson had been convicted is open to debate. Michael Les Benedict has argued that President Johnson thwarted the law and that Congress was justified in trying to remove him from office. Other commentators as diverse as William H. Rehnquist and Arthur M. Schlesinger Jr. have suggested that a conviction could have introduced a basic structural shift in the American system of government. If Johnson had been removed from office, so the argument runs, his trial might have served as a precedent rendering presidential impeachment the equivalent of a parliamentary vote of no confidence. The acquittal therefore signified that presidential impeachment was not an appropriate remedy to settle policy differences.[107] On this view, Curtis's argument was perhaps his greatest contribution to American constitutional law. Certainly Curtis thought the future of constitutional government was at stake. "If this prosecution fails there is hope," Curtis wrote Evarts before the outcome was clear. "There is time & opportunity to make a stand & the great fortress of constitutional govt will not have been occupied by hostile men. God grant the result."[108]

CONCLUSION

ALTHOUGH JOHNSON's impeachment was an important episode in the power struggle over Reconstruction, the Senate trial barely touched upon the underlying questions of policy. What conditions should be set before restoring southern states into the Union? How should former Confederates be treated? What if anything should be done for freed slaves beyond emancipation? And, after all that had transpired, what exactly was the position of black persons in American political society?

These issues, involving the social fabric of a large section of the country, were not simply constitutional in nature. Yet many northerners felt the need to outline the answers in the Constitution. The Thirteenth Amendment, adopted in December 1865, converted wartime emancipation into official constitutional doctrine. Six months later Congress submitted the Fourteenth Amendment to the states for ratification. In answer to several pressing questions, this amendment disqualified a significant number of leading southerners from holding office, nullified the Confederacy's debt, and denied former slave owners compensation for freed slaves. Congress also tried to induce the South to grant black males voting rights by reducing the number of congressmen for states that failed to do so. More enduring were the Fourteenth Amendment's provisions recognizing black Americans as citizens and validating federal authority to protect individuals against states that denied them due process or equal protection of the law.

The adoption of the Fourteenth Amendment was the critical moment in the constitutional transformation of the Civil War era. With the fighting over, the issues that had long divided the nation were ripe for constitutional resolution. The question naturally arises as to where Curtis stood, given not only his reputation in matters of constitutional law but also the specific positions he had taken in the past, especially in the *Dred Scott* case. The setting had changed, to be sure, but Curtis's analysis of the qualifications and rights of citizenship in some sense anticipated the Fourteenth Amendment's major theme.

Against that background, what is most striking about Curtis during Reconstruction is the extent to which he withdrew from public debate. There is no record of Curtis discussing the Fourteenth Amendment's language on citizenship, equal protection, and due process. His reticence was by itself revealing, an outgrowth of his view of the constitutional transformation in progress. He understood that his constitutionalist approach did not fit the spirit of the times. As he told Justice Davis in early 1867, it was clear that "we are in the midst of" a "revolution." Curtis seemed to sense that his capacity to impress his views on the public was limited by circumstance. "Events move fast in such a revolution," he said, and "a wise man will watch their course and succession without undue eagerness to interpose when his action would prove useless— perhaps worse than useless." [1]

Curtis's retreat from public life was not due to lack of opportunity. After the impeachment trial President Johnson asked him to serve as attorney general. Curtis declined. Possibly he did not relish having his name put before the Senate, which had already turned down the president's renomination of Stanbery. It appears that Curtis had more in mind, though, as shown by his insistent explanation. There "is *no* public office which I shall ever be induced to accept willingly," and "I shall never accept one save from such imperative commands of duty as I can not resist." Even an enviable position on the Supreme Court could not entice him. When Chief Justice Salmon P. Chase died in 1873, leading members of the bar favored Curtis to fill the vacancy. "I do not want the office of Chief Justice," the Boston lawyer wrote Reverdy Johnson, "and shall be better pleased to have it offered to another than to myself." [2]

Despite his reluctance to interpose, Curtis's views on Reconstruction can be pieced together from various statements he made. What emerges above all else is Curtis's opposition to the Radical Republicans in Congress. His most detailed analysis appeared in a letter written in the summer of 1866 that was published in newspapers around the country. Curtis prepared this letter at the request of Orville Hickman Browning, who had solicited prominent individuals to support the National Union Convention. Held in Philadelphia before the congressional elections, this political gathering drew on a powerful legacy of wartime unity, for the convention that had nominated Lincoln and Johnson in 1864 bore the same name. In the planning stages moderates wrestled with conservatives for control of this postwar National Union movement. By the time the convention was over, it had taken a decidedly conservative turn as part of Johnson's attempt to form a third political party committed to his Reconstruction program. Most Republicans steered clear of it. The most notable exception was Seward, who hoped to advance his own political agenda by redefining the Republican Party. [3]

Before the convention began Curtis had misgivings about its prospects. "Neither you nor I have much confidence in 'conventions,'" he wrote Ticknor, "but, in the present state of our country, I have hope from all *honest* expressions of popular feeling, and I do not despair that this may be such an expression." Curtis told his son that he had written the letter with "much reluctance," a point he made abundantly clear to Browning. "Let me say, in entire sincerity, that though I have written this letter to you at your request, *I* have no wish that it should be published." Emphasizing that he would be "better pleased not to be heard from than to make myself conspicuous in any way," Curtis went on to explain that he had written the letter out of a sense of "public duty," however "distasteful its dictates." As for the upcoming convention, Curtis warned Browning that the "whole affair" would be "useless" and "worse than useless" if the "old Democratic Party men are prominent" or if the meeting reasserted "any such principles as wrecked" the Democratic convention of 1864 that had nominated General George McClellan.[4]

While wary of old Democrats, Curtis was thoroughly disenchanted with the Republican-controlled Congress. "They have proved wholly unequal to their great task," he confided in Ticknor.[5] Without criticizing particular actions Congress had taken the previous session (like the Civil Rights Act or the Fourteenth Amendment), Curtis's letter was in effect a legal brief for President Johnson's position on Reconstruction. Curtis responded to various constitutional theories of Reconstruction that Republicans had advanced to justify continuing federal authority over the South. Each of these theories was designed to get around the Republican Party's premise of "an indestructible Union, composed of indestructible states."[6] Thaddeus Stevens, for example, promoted the idea that the southern states were conquered provinces that could be governed as territories. Sumner argued that the states had destroyed themselves by state suicide. Other Republicans suggested less dramatically that southerners had forfeited the right to govern themselves. Still others believed that the former Confederate states remained in the grasp of war, subject to the national government's war powers. Some grounded federal authority in the Constitution's guarantee clause, which provides that the "United States shall guarantee to every State in this Union a Republican Form of Government." Constitutional specialists might detect meaningful differences among these positions, but all drove to the same conclusion. The former rebel states were not automatically in the Union, and the federal government had unprecedented powers over the South.[7]

In his letter Curtis indicated why he considered that result mistaken. Mixing assertion with argument, he struck at the different theories in turn. It was obvious to him that the United States cannot "destroy a State, or acquire its territory by conquest." Nor, he added, can "the people of a State" destroy their state. Curtis distinguished the states themselves from the "usurping and unlawful" state governments of the Confederacy, which the United States rightfully destroyed "by force." Turning on its head the argument based upon the guarantee clause, Curtis interpreted this constitutional provision to require republican state governments "so organized as to be *in this Union*." It needed "no enabling act of Congress." Whether the South was in the grasp of war was a "military and executive question" for the president to decide. Disclaiming any "partiality for Executive power," Curtis embraced the Lincolnian position that combined the powers of commander in chief with his authority as "chief executive officer, whose constitutional duty it is to see that the laws are faithfully executed." Curtis seemed to take particular delight in challenging what was probably his easiest target, the conquered provinces idea. "The title of a conqueror," which Curtis made clear was one of "absolute control over the persons and property" of the people, was "necessarily inconsistent with a republican government, which can be formed only by the people themselves, to express and execute their will." Underlying Curtis's entire argument was his understanding of the "nature of our Government." He made his conclusion appear to be the self-evident corollary of the principles of American constitutionalism.[8]

Curtis also echoed Lincoln's "malice towards none" theme, though his letter hardly equaled the fallen president's great second inaugural address. A "magnanimous clemency," Curtis wrote, "can reach and subdue what laws and bayonets cannot control" (an interesting acknowledgment of law's limits). The work of Reconstruction was obviously difficult, he suggested; the "long and bloody civil war" had created "deep and formidable" passions that were easily exploited. Curtis closed with a plea to overcome "party spirit" and "self interest."[9]

If the constitutional logic was sound, Curtis's argument was nevertheless vulnerable to the charge that he ignored what had transpired since Appomattox, particularly the degree of southern intransigence and the mistreatment of freed slaves throughout the South. There were Republicans—moderates and conservatives—who shared Curtis's views on one point or another. Many northerners considered the conquered provinces idea extreme. Sumner's state suicide theory was also disfavored. Some Republicans were uncomfortable with relying on the guarantee clause because it appeared to sanction permanent national authority over the states. Yet few congressional Republicans were willing to relinquish national power in the South as readily as Curtis was.[10]

It remains an open question as to how far Curtis affirmatively supported Johnson's conservative policies. When Curtis declined to take the post of attorney general, he told the president that he was "not in the least degree influenced" by anything "which I apprehend in the future policy or measures of your administration." This statement may reflect Curtis's unqualified support of presidential Reconstruction. Then again, it may evince Curtis's understanding that Johnson had committed himself during the impeachment trial to moderate his policies in the future. To Ticknor, Curtis offered a double-edged assessment of the president. "He is a man of few ideas, but they are right and true"; he is "honest, right-minded, and narrow-minded; he has no tact, and even lacks discretion and forecast."[11]

Whatever Curtis thought of Johnson, the former justice was motivated by his desire to see a constitutional counterweight to a runaway legislature. After Grant was elected in 1868, Curtis expressed concern over the movement toward a "centralized parliamentary government." If Grant "appreciates his position," Curtis wrote Ticknor, "he also knows that the legislative power, having, with the acquiescence of the country, conquered one President, and subdued the Supreme Court," will not "subside into that coequal position assigned to them by the Constitution without a desperate struggle."[12]

Curtis's views on Reconstruction can also be gleaned from legal arguments he made before the U.S. Supreme Court. It is risky to assume that the positions he advocated there always coincided with his personal beliefs. Yet as one of the elite members of the Court's bar after the war, Curtis argued in over forty appeals in eight years. Some had implications for Reconstruction policy. They afforded him the opportunity to build on the themes he had set forth in his letter to the National Union Convention.

One such case was *Virginia v. West Virginia* (1871), in which Curtis, without directly challenging congressional Reconstruction, reiterated his position that the national government cannot destroy the states and that any legislation having that effect was unconstitutional.[13] This lawsuit grew out of the wartime formation of the new state of West Virginia, formerly a part of the Commonwealth of Virginia. Curtis represented the old state in its attempt to reclaim two counties. In the end, the Court resolved a complex set of questions in West Virginia's favor. One important point concerned the constitutionality of the First Reconstruction Act of 1867, which was conceivably in issue since it declared that no legal state government existed in Virginia. Curtis did not press the Court to invalidate the statute. "Certainly this Court will go no further in this direction than it shall find to be absolutely necessary." If the justices concluded that the act destroyed the state of Virginia, however, Curtis offered a different view. In that case, he said, "I respectfully insist and submit to this Court that Congress exceeded its power." Rather than demanding that the Court strike down Reconstruction legislation, it looks like Curtis tried to put Radical Republicans in the position of moderating their views in court to save the statute.[14]

In *McVeigh v. United States* (1871), Curtis presented a favorite theme of his: the need to adhere to the fundamental requirements of legal process no matter who was involved, in this instance a southerner said to be a rebel. This case brought into question proceedings under the confiscation act adopted by Congress in 1862. After the government submitted a claim for the forfeiture of William McVeigh's home in Alexandria, Virginia, his attorney filed an answer in his behalf. Refusing to entertain any defense, the federal district judge dismissed the answer and declared the defendant in default. The judge reasoned that the answer disclosed that McVeigh was a rebel and a resident behind enemy lines. In oral argument before the Supreme Court, Curtis noted that Congress had not intended the confiscation act to be a "sweeping" condemnation "against all rebels." The legislation had instead specified particular offenses for which the penalty was forfeiture of property. Responding to the government's broad contention that enemies have no standing in court, Curtis pointed out that the common law allowed alien enemies to be heard in some circumstances, that the defendant was an American citizen, and that the statutory scheme contemplated a hearing. A unanimous Court agreed. To deny a hearing "would be a blot upon our jurisprudence and civilization," the Court said.[15]

Even though Curtis had concerns over the rise of "centralized parliamentary government," he supported broad congressional powers in one of the most significant cases during Reconstruction, the *Legal Tender Cases*. To finance the war the Union government had issued over $400 million in paper money which Congress declared to be legal tender. Creditors who had to accept these so-called greenbacks in payment of debts brought suit. Curtis had a prominent role in the appeals before the Supreme Court. Although the framers of the Constitution had frowned upon the use of paper money, he argued that Congress had implied powers to put greenback dollars in circulation. The Court rejected Curtis's position in *Hepburn v. Griswold* (1870) but reversed course one year later.[16]

As for Curtis's views on freed slaves and the rights of black persons, the best glimpse into his innermost thoughts during Reconstruction appears in his private correspondence. As the impeachment trial drew to a close in May 1868, he made a brief comment in a letter to William Evarts. The Fourteenth Amendment, close to ratification, was evidently on Curtis's mind. He referred to its second section, which conditioned full political representation in the southern states on black suffrage. Curtis was willing to see that happen so long as white southerners consented. The actual words he used were far more revealing. "The people have a fair chance—Southern niggers can not govern them without their consent—if they give that consent I am submissive—but I stipulate for a chance to disagree."[17]

Today that statement would be unquestionably racist. This language was derogatory in Curtis's time as well.[18] Putting aside the offensive labeling, Curtis's suggestion that the "people have a fair chance" was significant, contrary to the inclusive concept of political community he had articulated in *Dred Scott*.

Such a remark is bound to tarnish Curtis's legacy. It says something of the times that whatever else he accomplished, his career is inevitably linked with slavery and race. Curtis was in the first rank of the legal profession. Few rivaled his technical expertise in so many areas of practice. Yet his years on the bench were punctuated by controversy over slavery, beginning with a fugitive slave rescue trial and ending with *Dred Scott*.

This reference to black Americans renews the question of what to make of Curtis's overall record on slavery. Certainly he was no crusading abolitionist. Nor did he exhibit the progression of thought on race relations that others like Lincoln, Trumbull, and Bingham did. While they reshaped the nation's fundamental law during the war and Reconstruction, Curtis kept his distance. Whether in public or private, he displayed little sensitivity to the human face of the tragedy.

It may also be suggested that Curtis's foremost achievement, his dissenting opinion in *Dred Scott*, did not reflect any egalitarian impulse, that the eloquence he displayed there sprang from his frustration with Chief Justice Taney's extremism, and that the dissenting arguments were of little consequence in improving the lot of free blacks before the war or freed slaves afterwards. Indeed, Curtis's analysis was so finely drawn—reserving authority in the states to determine the qualifications of citizenship—that opponents of the civil rights bill in 1866 were able to cite his dissent in legislative debates.[19]

Yet Curtis's opinion in some sense foreshadowed the great transformation of the Constitution from a charter that protected slavery to one which guaranteed racial equality. In the course of disproving Taney's racist claims, Curtis gave constitutional standing to the principle that black persons were "people of the United States." Though not associated with the antislavery movement, the justice was the first to bring attention to evidence from the founding period that blacks had voted on the Constitution's ratification. Northerners considered Curtis especially persuasive on this point. As Lincoln said, the justice left "no doubt of its truth." Some recognized Curtis's opinion for anticipating the Reconstruction doctrine of equal citizenship. Benjamin Butler, one of the most committed Radical Republicans, credited Curtis with having "opened and developed an idea as to the rights of citizens, which has since been embalmed in constitutional law." Even John A. Campbell, one of the southern justices who had joined the majority in *Dred Scott,* conceded in 1874 that Curtis had shown "a broader appreciation" than his colleagues of "the true principles of our government" on this question. Campbell added that "the contrary opinion of the court has been without any considerable weight or influence" on "account of the overwhelming force" with which Curtis "made the reason and justice" of his position felt.[20]

The same could have been said of the effect that Curtis's dissenting arguments had on the Court's entire opinion. No doubt the *Dred Scott* decision would rank among the worst ever delivered by the Supreme Court if Curtis had not dissented. Yet his seventy pages of closely reasoned arguments, along with the specific charge that the Court's decision on the territories was illegitimate, fueled the immediate rejection of the decision in the North. Chief Justice Taney was right on one point at least. The "assault" on the Supreme Court was "commenced by the publication" of Curtis's dissent, "carrying with it the weight and influence of a judicial opinion delivered from the bench in the presence and hearing of the court." And that "assault" left a lasting impression. Justice Benjamin N. Cardozo later hailed Curtis's opinion as one of the "great dissents" in American judicial history, a classic example of a justice who "speaks to the future."[21]

Considering Curtis's role in constitutional history more broadly, with slavery a critical issue but not the only one in which he was involved, the justice emerges as a transitional figure in the development of judicial review on the Supreme Court. Curtis was heir to the Federalist-Whig tradition of Marshall, Story, and Webster. As profound as their influence has turned out to be, it was unclear at the midpoint of the nineteenth century how far the Court would build upon their early achievements. *Marbury v. Madison* implied a broader power over Congress than the justices had exercised to that point. Aside from isolated dicta, the judiciary had done little to review the president's actions. The Supreme Court had not yet applied the Bill of Rights to strike down legislation, and the grounds for nullifying state laws were unsettled. The contracts clause, a favorite of the Marshall Court, had lost its luster. That was more than could be said of the commerce clause, the object of such divided opinion that it could hardly be considered a source of judicial power.

In that setting Justice Curtis latched onto the constitutional concepts—the dormant commerce clause and due process—that became twin pillars of judicial power for decades. His opinion in *Cooley* represents a pivotal point in the interpretation of the commerce clause. Curtis sought to transform an old-fashioned debate over sovereign power into a pragmatic inquiry into regulatory policy. In doing so, he recast the constitutional nationalism of Marshall, Story, and Webster into a form congenial to later justices. Curtis made it seem natural to review state laws based on the commerce clause. Whatever problems arose later in applying his national/local formula, the *Cooley* principle of federal judicial review remained in place.

With his prescient inquiry into due process, Justice Curtis was at the cutting edge of a dramatic change in constitutional thought. Of course he could not have foreseen the adoption of the Fourteenth Amendment when he wrote his opinion in *Murray's Lessee*. Nor did that decision have the precedential impact that *Cooley* had. Still, in the long line of constitutional developments, Curtis was again at a crossroads. Earlier judges derived amorphous limits on legislative power from the vested rights doctrine and unwritten higher law. Curtis was the first justice to say explicitly that the due process clause provided the grounds to declare legislation unconstitutional. His thinking prefigured the broad interpretations on incorporation, liberty of contract, and equality under law, although much of what transpired later evolved independently of his efforts.

It would be a mistake to focus exclusively on Curtis's actions on the bench in assessing his contributions to constitutional law. His pamphlet *Executive Power* deserves to be considered alongside the Supreme Court's major opinions on the question of civil liberties in wartime. Partly this was due to timing. The Civil War was in many ways the first modern "total war," and Curtis entered the debate precisely at the moment when the president subjected civilians everywhere to martial law. Beyond that, Curtis brought a broader perspective to the discussion that had previously centered around the suspension of habeas corpus. His analysis of the commander in chief's authority, Congress's indispensable role in wartime, and constitutional limits in crisis still reads well after two world wars, the Cold War, and the war on terrorism.[22]

Perhaps most striking about *Executive Power* was that for all that Curtis had invested in the judiciary, he sought to foster a public debate over the constitutionality of the president's actions. These were "subjects in which the people have vast concern," he wrote. "It is their right, it is their duty, to themselves and to their posterity, to examine and to consider and to decide upon them."[23] Implicit in this public appeal was an important assumption of limits to judicial power. The remedy was to bring the people and Congress into the equation.

Curtis's defense in the impeachment trial was a fitting capstone to his constitutional career. It is ironic that the former justice, having withdrawn from public affairs during Reconstruction, would play such a prominent role in one of its most dramatic moments. Probably anyone who opened for the impeached president in the first such trial would have earned a place in history. Curtis made the most of the opportunity. Although he did not secure the acquittal by himself, his argument marked a major turning point in the trial. Perhaps his most enduring contribution growing out of these proceedings concerned the character of presidential impeachment and, with that, the independence of the presidency. It was not implausible to contend, as the impeachment managers had, that congressmen had substantial discretion to weigh policy and politics in these decisions. Curtis disputed that idea throughout his argument. The consensus is that high crimes and misdemeanors are not limited to indictable criminal offenses as he had argued, but Congress since then has not sought to remove the president from office without legal foundation.

Through all of this, Curtis was involved in an ongoing debate over the meaning of American constitutionalism. Government under the Constitution was still a novel experiment. The Civil War generation was not far removed from the founding; *Dred Scott* was decided seventy years after the Constitution was adopted. In the crucible of the most serious and wide-ranging constitutional crisis in the nation's history, a number of basic questions concerning the Constitution came to the fore. How exactly did this written charter—such a concise statement of the basic principles for the organization of a political society—work, especially in times of crisis? How did law limit power? How was power controlled without disabling its necessary exercise? Was it possible to resolve political conflict, even at its most passionate, through the constitutional process rather than by force? What was the meaning of liberty in a republic that tolerated slavery? What were the prospects for adapting the Constitution to new thinking and changed circumstances? What was the judiciary's role in all this? And what was the place of the Constitution in American life?

Curtis addressed each of these questions. Although the idea of constitutionalism was broad enough to permit people of disparate views to claim its mantle, he effectively positioned himself as a leading spokesman for the Constitution. At its most basic level, Justice Curtis kept in view of the public the idea of limited government constrained by the rule of law. Few others in American history have had similar opportunities to challenge in succession the highest court, the president, and the Congress for abusing power. In the *Dred Scott* case, Curtis castigated his colleagues for "an exertion of judicial power" which "transcends the limits of the authority of the court." He criticized President Lincoln for asserting "transcendent executive power." Arguing against the impeachment managers' claim that each legislator was "a law unto himself," Curtis invoked James Madison: the "legislature, no less than the executive, is under limitations of power."[24] Each of these incidents was revealing not simply for Curtis's assertion that others had overstepped their authority but for his explanation of why that was the case and his artful interpretations on the questions presented.

Notwithstanding the continuities in constitutional interpretation from the founding to the present, the context in which Curtis operated had a particular character. The framers had skirted some difficult questions, and with rising tensions it might easily have seemed to antebellum Americans that the more divisive the issue, the more sparing was the Constitution's text. In retrospect, the style of constitutional interpretation prevailing then looks like a freewheeling exercise. Legal precedent was often unavailing or nonexistent. Judges displayed a willingness to go beyond the language of the Constitution. Natural law was an acceptable source for constitutional doctrine; so too were the fundamental principles of republican government. Some legislation was considered unconstitutional even if it did not violate any particular provision of the Constitution (laws transferring property from A to B, for example).

In this setting supporters and opponents alike recognized Curtis for his interpretive abilities. To fill the gaps left by the framers, Curtis relied mainly on a common-law approach. Yet he was not "living from hand to mouth" from one case to the next with little idea of where he was heading, as the English common law has been portrayed.[25] He was more like a chess player thinking several moves ahead. Paradoxically the constraints of professional craft, as he understood them, enabled him to range widely in his interpretations of the Constitution.

One of his main concerns was the direction of constitutional change. In this period when the Constitution was radically transmuted, Curtis sought to mark out a path for gradual progress. The common law furnished him with a model for adapting the Constitution to changing social and economic conditions. The justice was not committed to traditional order simply for its own sake, though it had its appeal for him. He seemed to believe that incremental growth in the law could produce enduring, and ultimately dramatic, departures from the existing state of affairs. For Curtis there was a logic to constitutional transformation, and the demands for reform could be met without sacrificing continuity. His approach was decidedly at odds with the revolutionary temper of the times.

It was clear to Curtis that the judiciary had a key role in making constitutionalism work. Curtis had a broad conception of judicial power, but he saw the Supreme Court in a complex relationship with the Congress, the president, the states, and the people. Not every justice shared his view of judicial power and its limits. Perhaps it was a failing in Curtis to expect more of his colleagues. When their limitations struck home in *Dred Scott*, he saw no alternative to resigning. As he said, he could not "co-operate with them" any longer.[26]

Curtis sometimes acted with a touch of arrogance as if his approach was the only one that was constitutional. Perhaps it was the boldness with which he justified his positions that led Henry Adams to call him the "last of the strong jurists in Marshall's school," a reference to the great chief justice. This remark is suggestive not only as a description of Curtis but also as a comment upon the passing of an age in constitutional development. Although the Supreme Court's powers have grown considerably over the years, justices then had unique opportunities to shape American constitutionalism. It is difficult to imagine anyone seizing that opportunity any better than Marshall had.

Curtis had his opportunities as well. In comparison with Marshall's tenure during the early years of the Republic, the whole constitutional system was unraveling by the time Curtis came to the bench. The fate of constitutional government seemed to be at stake, not just in the United States but for any nation "so conceived," as Lincoln put it. At times despondent with "the blackest clouds lowering around our national life," Curtis nevertheless retained a Pauline faith in the Constitution. Right or wrong, he persisted during this time of civil war in his efforts to show how he thought reason, deliberation, and law guided Americans in their public affairs.[27]

NOTES

ABBREVIATIONS

CWAL   *The Collected Works of Abraham Lincoln*, ed. Roy P. Basler (New Brunswick, N.J., 1953–55)
CG   *Congressional Globe*
DLC   Library of Congress, Manuscript Division, Washington, D.C.
MHS   Massachusetts Historical Society, Boston
Memoir [George Ticknor Curtis], *A Memoir of Benjamin Robbins Curtis, LL.D., with Some of His Professional and Miscellaneous Writings*, ed. Benjamin R. Curtis (Boston, 1879)

INTRODUCTION

1. For divergent views, see Roger L. Ransom, "Fact and Counterfact: The 'Second American Revolution' Revisited," *Civil War History* 45 (1999): 28–60; Herman Belz, *Abraham Lincoln, Constitutionalism, and Equal Rights in the Civil War Era* (New York, 1998), 1–15; James M. McPherson, *Abraham Lincoln and the Second American Revolution* (New York, 1991), 3–22; Charles A. Beard and Mary R. Beard, *The Rise of American Civilization* 2 (New York, 1933): 52–121.
2. Ticknor to George Ticknor Curtis, 30 July 1869, *Life, Letters, and Journals of George Ticknor* 2 (Boston, 1876): 485.
3. On constitutional change in the Civil War and Reconstruction, see Bruce Ackerman, *We the People: Transformations* (Cambridge, Mass., 1998), 99–254; Michael W. McConnell, "The Fourteenth Amendment: A Second American Revolution or the Logical Culmination of the Tradition?" *Loyola of Los Angeles Law Review* 25 (1992): 1159–76; Harold M. Hyman, *A More Perfect Union: The Impact of the Civil War and Reconstruction on the Constitution* (New York, 1973); Michael Les Benedict, "Preserving the Constitution: The Conservative Basis of Radical Reconstruction," *Journal of American History* 61 (1974): 65–90.
4. On constitutional change generally, see Bruce Ackerman, *We the People: Foundations* (Cambridge, Mass., 1991); "Symposium: Moments of Change: Transformation in American Constitutionalism," *Yale Law Journal* 108 (1999): 1917–2349.
5. James M. McPherson, *For Cause and Comrades: Why Men Fought in the Civil War* (New York, 1997), 93–94.
6. *CWAL* 4:267. The significance of constitutional interpretation is also evident in Jefferson Davis's inaugural address. He said that the "Constitution formed by our fathers is that of these Confederate States, in their exposition of it, and in the judicial construction it has received, we have a light which reveals its true meaning." *The Papers of Jefferson Davis*, ed. Lynda Lasswell Crist and Mary Seaton Dix, 7 (Baton Rouge, La., 1992): 49–50.

7. *Life and Times of Frederick Douglass* (1881; reprint, Secaucus, N.J., 1983), 267.

8. Scott v. Sandford, 60 U.S. (19 How.) 393 (1857).

9. *Liberator*, 7 July 1854 (reporting on William Lloyd Garrison's speech denouncing the Constitution); [Wendell Phillips], *The Constitution a Pro-Slavery Compact* (1844; reprint, New York, 1969); *The Frederick Douglass Papers*, ser. 1, *Speeches, Debates, and Interviews*, ed. John W. Blassingame, 3 (New Haven, 1985): 340-66.

10. William M. Wiecek, *The Sources of Antislavery Constitutionalism in America, 1760-1848* (Ithaca, N.Y., 1977), 249-75; Eric Foner, *Free Soil, Free Labor, Free Men: The Ideology of the Republican Party before the Civil War* (New York, 1995), 73-102. On antislavery constitutional thought, see Robert M. Cover, "The Supreme Court, 1982 Term—Foreword: *Nomos* and Narrative," *Harvard Law Review* 97 (1983): 35-44; Robert M. Cover, *Justice Accused: Antislavery and the Judicial Process* (New Haven, 1975), 149-58; William E. Nelson, "The Impact of the Antislavery Movement upon Styles of Judicial Reasoning in Nineteenth Century America," *Harvard Law Review* 87 (1974): 538-47; Jacobus tenBroek, *Equal under Law* (New York, 1965).

11. *CWAL* 4:169, 7:23. For a sampling of interpretations of Lincoln, see Garry Wills, *Lincoln at Gettysburg: The Words that Remade America* (New York, 1992), 90-147; Harry V. Jaffa, *Crisis of the House Divided: An Interpretation of the Issues in the Lincoln-Douglas Debates* (New York, 1959), 308-29; Belz, *Lincoln*, 86-90. On higher lawmaking during Reconstruction, see Ackerman, *Transformations*, 99-252.

12. Philip Bobbitt, *Constitutional Fate: Theory of the Constitution* (New York, 1982), 151; Henry Steele Commager and Richard B. Morris, editors' introduction to Harold M. Hyman and William M. Wiecek, *Equal Justice under Law: Constitutional Development, 1835-1875* (New York, 1982), xiii.

13. Later judges and scholars have ranked Curtis highly. William D. Pederson and Norman W. Provizer, eds., *Great Justices of the U.S. Supreme Court: Ratings and Case Studies* (New York, 1994), 24-28; Albert P. Blaustein and Roy M. Mersky, "Rating Supreme Court Justices," *American Bar Association Journal* 58 (1972): 1185; Stuart S. Nagel, "Characteristics of Supreme Court Greatness," *American Bar Association Journal* 56 (1970): 957; John P. Frank, *Marble Palace: The Supreme Court in American Life* (New York, 1958), 43; Felix Frankfurter, "The Supreme Court in the Mirror of Justices," *University of Pennsylvania Law Review* 105 (1957): 783; Richard H. Leach, "Benjamin R. Curtis: Case Study of a Supreme Court Justice" (Ph.D. diss, Princeton University, 1951).

14. See chap. 1 below.

15. *Memoir* 1:115-16; *Proceedings of the Constitutional Meeting at Faneuil Hall, November 26th, 1850* (Boston, 1850); [Benjamin R. Curtis], *Address to the People of Massachusetts* [Boston, 1851].

16. Theodore Parker, *The Trial of Theodore Parker . . .* (1855; reprint, New York, 1970), 167; *Twentieth Annual Report Presented to the Massachusetts Anti-Slavery Society . . .* (1852; reprint, Westport, Conn., 1970), 22; *Liberator*, 17, 24 Oct. 1851.

17. Cooley v. Board of Wardens, 53 U.S. (12 How.) 299 (1852); Murray's Lessee v. Hoboken Land and Improvement Co., 59 U.S. (18 How.) 272 (1856).

18. 60 U.S. at 582 (Curtis, J., dissenting); *CWAL* 2:403.

19. *Memoir* 1:262.

20. B. R. Curtis, *Executive Power* (Boston, 1862).

21. Records of the Harvard College Class of 1829, p. 197, HUD 229.714, Harvard University Archives, Cambridge, Mass.; *Memoir* 1:417.

22. "Address of Justice Miller," *Western Jurist* 13 (1879): 245; *New York Tribune*, 9 Apr. 1855.

23. Curtis, *Executive Power*, 29.

24. *A Memorial of Daniel Webster, from the City of Boston* (Boston, 1853), 115, 116. On applying the common law to constitutional questions, see Harry H. Wellington, *Interpreting the Constitution: The Supreme Court and the Process of Adjudication* (New Haven, 1990); David A. Strauss, "Common Law Constitutional Interpretation," *Chicago Law Review* 63 (1996): 877–935.

25. *Memorial of Daniel Webster*, 117.

26. Conner v. Elliott, 59 U.S. (18 How.) 591, 593 (1856).

27. *Memorial of Daniel Webster*, 116; 60 U.S. at 426. On antebellum understandings of the framers' intent, see Howard Gillman, "The Collapse of Constitutional Originalism and the Rise of the Notion of the 'Living Constitution' in the Course of American State-Building," *Studies in American Political Development* 11 (1997): 203–13; Morton J. Horwitz, "The Supreme Court, 1992 Term—Foreword: The Constitution of Change: Legal Fundamentality without Fundamentalism," *Harvard Law Review* 107 (1993): 49–51.

28. Marbury v. Madison, 5 U.S. (1 Cranch) 137 (1803). For recent interpretations on the development of judicial review, see Larry D. Kramer, "The Supreme Court, 2000 Term—Foreword: We the Court," *Harvard Law Review* 115 (2001): 4–169; Barry Friedman, "The History of the Countermajoritarian Difficulty, Part One: The Road to Judicial Supremacy," *New York University Law Review* 73 (1998): 333–433; Mark A. Graber, "The Problematic Establishment of Judicial Review," in *The Supreme Court in American Politics: New Institutionalist Interpretations*, ed. Howard Gillman and Cornell Clayton (Lawrence, Kans., 1999), 28–42.

29. 5 U.S. at 177; Jefferson to William Charles Jarvis, 28 Sept. 1820, *The Works of Thomas Jefferson*, ed. Paul Leicester Ford (New York, 1904–5), 12:162; James D. Richardson, ed., *A Compilation of the Messages and Papers of the Presidents, 1789–1897* (Washington, D.C., 1896–99), 2:582; *CWAL* 3:255, 4:268. See generally Walter F. Murphy, "Who Shall Interpret? The Quest for the Ultimate Constitutional Interpreter," *Review of Politics* 48 (1986): 401–23.

30. *Memorial of Daniel Webster*, 116.

1. IN THE WHIG TRADITION

1. On the Whig Party, see Michael F. Holt, *The Rise and Fall of the American Whig Party: Jacksonian Politics and the Onset of the Civil War* (New York, 1999). Standard accounts of the Jacksonian era include Arthur M. Schlesinger Jr., *The Age of Jackson* (Boston, 1953), and Marvin Meyers, *The Jacksonian Persuasion: Politics and Belief* (Stanford, Calif., 1957).

2. Daniel Walker Howe, *The Political Culture of the American Whigs* (Chicago, 1979). See also Glyndon G. Van Deusen, "Some Aspects of Whig Thought and Theory in the Jacksonian Period," *American Historical Review* 63 (1958): 305–22.

3. Marshall Foletta, *Coming to Terms with Democracy: Federalist Intellectuals and the Shaping of an American Culture* (Charlottesville, Va., 2001); Linda K. Kerber, *Federalists in Dissent: Imagery and Ideology in Jeffersonian America* (Ithaca, N.Y., 1970).

4. On the split between the Cotton and Conscience factions, see Kinley J. Brauer, *Cotton versus Conscience: Massachusetts Whig Politics and Southwestern Expansion, 1843–1848* (Lexington, Ky., 1967); Thomas H. O'Connor, *Lords of the Loom: The Cotton Whigs and the Coming of the Civil War* (New York, 1968), 65; Frank Otto Gatell, "'Conscience and Judgment'; The Bolt of the Massachusetts Conscience Whigs," *Historian* 21 (1958): 18–45.

5. *Memoir* 1:1–6; Greenwood v. Curtis, 6 Mass. (5 Tyng) 358, 359 (1810). On this family history, see Albert J. Von Frank, *The Trials of Anthony Burns: Freedom and Slavery in Emerson's Boston* (Cambridge, Mass., 1998), 299.

6. David B. Tyack, *George Ticknor and the Boston Brahmins* (Cambridge, Mass., 1967), 1, 39–40, 47–51, 87, 183.

7. *Journals of George Ticknor* 2:402.

8. *Memoir* 1:17.

9. *The Poetical Works of Oliver Wendell Holmes* (Boston, 1880), 213. For a listing of Curtis's classmates, consult the *Harvard University Quinquennial Catalogue of the Officers and Graduates, 1636–1925* (Cambridge, Mass., 1925), 203–4.

10. Joseph Story, "Value and Importance of Legal Studies," in *The Miscellaneous Writings of Joseph Story . . .* , ed. William W. Story (Boston, 1852), 503–48; R. Kent Newmyer, "Harvard Law School, New England Legal Culture, and the Antebellum Origins of American Jurisprudence," *Journal of American History* 74 (1987): 818–19; R. Kent Newmyer, *Supreme Court Justice Joseph Story: Statesman of the Old Republic* (Chapel Hill, N.C., 1985), 240–48; Arthur E. Sutherland, *The Law at Harvard: A History of Ideas and Men, 1817–1967* (Cambridge, Mass., 1967), 85.

11. Curtis to George W. Phillips, 11 Feb. 1832, *Memoir* 1:55.

12. Ibid., 48, 58.

13. Curtis to Ticknor, 22 Sept. 1833, ibid., 63.

14. William Gillette, "Benjamin R. Curtis," in *The Justices of the United States Supreme Court, 1789–1969: Their Lives and Major Opinions*, ed. Leon Friedman and Fred L. Israel, 2 (New York, 1969): 897; Morton Horwitz, *The Transformation of American Law, 1780–1860* (New York, 1992), 137; James M. McPherson, *Battle Cry of Freedom: The Civil War Era* (New York, 1988), 14, 19, 26; William E. Nelson, *Americanization of the Common Law: The Impact of Legal Change on Massachusetts Society, 1760–1830* (Cambridge, Mass., 1975), 133–36; Kermit L. Hall, *The Magic Mirror: Law in American History* (New York, 1989), 92; Howe, *American Whigs*, 104–5.

15. Curtis to Lemuel Shaw, 21 July 1848, Lemuel Shaw Papers, MHS; *Argument of B. R. Curtis, Esq., of Boston, in the Case . . . for an Infringement of the Letters Patent of Samuel F. B. Morse, for the Electro Magnetic Telegraph . . .* (Portland, 1850); Smith v. Downing, 22 F. Cas. 511 (C.C.D. Mass. 1850) (No. 13,036); Charles Warren, *A History of the American Bar* (New York, 1966), 457–58.

16. Smith v. Hurd, 53 Mass. (12 Met.) 371 (1847); Cary v. Daniels, 49 Mass. (8 Met.) 466, 473 (1844); Commonwealth v. Alger, 61 Mass. (7 Cush.) 53 (1851). See also

Hall, *Magic Mirror*, 116; Horwitz, *Transformation of American Law*, 41-43; Leonard W. Levy, *The Law of the Commonwealth and Chief Justice Shaw* (New York, 1957), 247-54.

17. Curtis to Ticknor, 3 Nov. 1843, Curtis Papers, DLC; [Benjamin R. Curtis], "Debts of the States," *North American Review* 58 (1844): 109-57.

18. Curtis to Ticknor, 22 Oct. 1837, *Memoir* 1:78. Chief Justice Shaw asked Curtis, among all Boston's attorneys, to administer a trust for his daughter and her husband, Herman Melville. Shaw to Curtis, 2 Aug. 1847, Curtis Papers, DLC; Hershel Parker, *Herman Melville: A Biography*, vol. 1, *1819-1851* (Baltimore, 1996), 542.

19. Records of the Harvard Alumni Association, Constitution [1841?], HUD 3137.1141, and Records of the Harvard College Class of 1829, Class Book, p. 300, HUD 229.714, Harvard University Archives.

20. Records of the Harvard Corporation, 8:292, 294, UAI.V.30, ibid.; Curtis to Ticknor, 9 Jan. 1846, Curtis Papers, DLC. While serving on the corporation, Curtis participated in the law school's affairs. When the university encountered difficulty finding a suitable replacement for Justice Story after he died, Curtis considered taking the post himself. Curtis to Ticknor, 5 May 1846, ibid. He also proposed changes to the curriculum to better prepare students for professional activity. Curtis to Shaw, 21 July 1848, Shaw Papers, MHS.

21. Class Book of 1829, 299, Harvard University Archives; Robert Rich, "'A Wilderness of Whigs': The Wealthy Men of Boston," *Journal of Social History* 4 (1971): 273; Jacob Bigelow, *A History of the Cemetery of Mount Auburn* (Boston, 1860), 34. See also Stanley French, "The Cemetery as Cultural Institution: The Establishment of Mount Auburn and the 'Rural Cemetery' Movement," in *Death in America*, ed. David E. Stannard (Philadelphia, 1975), 69-91; Ronald Story, *The Forging of an Aristocracy: Harvard and the Boston Upper Class, 1800-1870* (Middletown, Conn., 1980).

22. *The Massachusetts State Record and Year Book of General Information, 1849*, ed. Nahum Capen, 3 (Boston, 1849): 46; "The Law's Delay in Massachusetts," *Law Reporter* 10 (1847): 145-46; Curtis to Briggs, 3 May 1849, Grenville H. Norcross Autograph Collection, MHS; Curtis to Briggs, 9 July 1849, Washburn Autograph Collection, ibid.; Massachusetts House of Representatives, *Report of the Commissioners Appointed to Revise and Reform the Proceedings in the Courts of Justice in This Commonwealth* (1851), 11; *Boston Advertiser*, 18, 22 Dec. 1851.

23. *The Rich Men of Massachusetts . . .*, 2d ed., enl. (Boston, 1852), 22; *Memoir* 1:183.

24. Benjamin R. Curtis, *An Address Delivered at the Centennial Celebration of the Birth Day of Washington at Deerfield . . .* (Greenfield, Mass., 1832), 3.

25. Howe, *American Whigs*, 236. Interpretations of Burke's thought that have been particularly helpful include J. G. A. Pocock, *Politics, Language, and Time: Essays on Political Thought and History* (1971; reprint, Chicago, 1989), 202-32, and James Boyd White, *When Words Lose Their Meaning: Constitutions and Reconstitutions of Language, Character, and Community* (Chicago, 1984), 192-230.

26. *Address Delivered at the Centennial Celebration*, 22, 21, 22; *The Writings and Speeches of Edmund Burke*, ed. Paul Langford, vol. 8, *The French Revolution, 1790-1794*, ed. L. G. Mitchell (Oxford, 1989), 109.

27. *Address Delivered at the Centennial Celebration,* 17, 20.
28. Ibid., 20; *Writings and Speeches of Edmund Burke* 8:112, 111; *Address Delivered at the Centennial Celebration,* 20.
29. *Address Delivered at the Centennial Celebration,* 19, 17, 20.
30. See Pocock, *Politics, Language, and Time,* 202–8.
31. *Writings and Speeches of Edmund Burke* 8:82–83. For Burke, this was "constitutional policy, working after the pattern of nature," that "we receive, we hold, we transmit our government and our privileges, in the same manner in which we enjoy and transmit our property and our lives." Ibid., 84.
32. Curtis said: "The first Magna Charta extorted from John, was but a confirmation of a more ancient one of Henry I.; and this too was in affirmance of the ancient standing laws of the land. . . . In the famous Law of the 3d Charles I., the Parliament say to the king, '*we have inherited this freedom,*' and the same idea is expressed in all the laws which since that period have been framed for the preservation of their liberties." *Address Delivered at the Centennial Celebration,* 6–7.
33. Ibid., 21–22.
34. This feeling of inheritance, Curtis added, served as a "constant check upon a wild and careless spirit of innovation." *Address Delivered at the Centennial Celebration,* 22. Burke had also criticized a narrow "spirit of innovation," by which people fail to look to the past as well as the future. *Writings and Speeches of Edmund Burke* 8:83.
35. *Address Delivered at the Centennial Celebration,* 13, 10.
36. Ibid., 16, 9, 22.
37. *The Writings and Speeches of Daniel Webster* (Boston, 1903), 11:220; Sparks quoted in J. V. Matthews, "'Whig History': The New England Whigs and a Usable Past," *New England Quarterly* 51 (1978): 202. See also Jean V. Matthews, *Rufus Choate: The Law and Civic Virtue* (Philadelphia, 1980), 99; Tyack, *Ticknor,* 199–201; Howe, *American Whigs,* 70–71.
38. *The Collected Works of Ralph Waldo Emerson,* vol. 3, *Essays: Second Series* (Cambridge, Mass., 1983), 126; George M. Fredrickson, *The Inner Civil War: Northern Intellectuals and the Crisis of the Union* (New York, 1965), 9, 11, 22; Stanley M. Elkins, *Slavery: A Problem in American Institutional and Intellectual Life,* 3d ed., rev. (Chicago, 1976), 150–51. Cf. Anne C. Rose, *Transcendentalism as a Social Movement, 1830–1850* (New Haven, 1981), 217; Ronald G. Walters, *The Antislavery Appeal: American Abolitionism after 1830* (Baltimore, 1976), 6, 9.
39. *The Collected Works of Ralph Waldo Emerson,* vol. 2, *Essays: First Series* (Cambridge, Mass., 1979), 30.
40. Ibid., 3:122, 2:29; *The Writings of Henry David Thoreau* 2 (Boston, 1906): 190; Phillips quoted in Elkins, *Slavery,* 175.
41. *Journals of Ralph Waldo Emerson,* ed. Edward Waldo Emerson and Waldo Emerson Forbes, 2 (Boston, 1909): 448; *Address Delivered at the Centennial Celebration,* 22, 4–5.
42. For the common-law mind-set in the antebellum period, see Perry Miller, *The Life of the Mind in America: From the Revolution to the Civil War* (New York, 1965), 99–265.

43. Elizabeth Gaspar Brown, *British Statutes in American Law, 1776–1836* (Ann Arbor, Mich., 1964), 23–26; Hall, *Magic Mirror,* 79; Gerard W. Gawalt, *The Promise of Power: The Emergence of the Legal Profession in Massachusetts, 1760–1840* (Westport, Conn., 1979), 63–64, 105.

44. *Memoirs, Speeches, and Writings of Robert Rantoul Jr.,* ed. Luther Hamilton (Boston, 1854), 279; Frederick Robinson, *A Letter to the Hon. Rufus Choate, Containing a Brief Exposure of Law Craft and Some of the Encroachments of the Bar upon the Rights and Liberties of the People* (n.p., 1832), 10; Robinson quoted in Charles M. Cook, *The American Codification Movement: A Study of Antebellum Legal Reform* (Westport, Conn., 1981), 160.

45. For a useful analysis, see Robert W. Gordon, review of *The American Codification Movement: A Study of Antebellum Legal Reform* by Charles M. Cook, *Vanderbilt Law Review* 36 (1983): 431–58.

46. "Codification of the Common Law," in *Writings of Joseph Story,* 718; see also Joseph Story, "Law, Legislation, and Codes," in James McClellan, *Joseph Story and the American Constitution: A Study in Political and Legal Thought* (Norman, Okla., 1971), 350–72; Newmyer, *Joseph Story,* 272–81.

47. Quoted in Cook, *Codification Movement,* 174.

48. Curtis to Ticknor, 21 Feb. 1836, *Memoir* 1:75.

49. "Codification of the Common Law," in *Writings of Joseph Story,* 717; Kent quoted in Cook, *Codification Movement,* 114.

50. *Writings of Robert Rantoul Jr.,* 278, 282; Timothy Walker, "Codification," in *The Golden Age of American Law,* ed. Charles M. Haar (New York, 1965), 257.

51. *Writings of Joseph Story,* 405, 505; G. Edward White, *The Marshall Court and Cultural Change, 1815–35* (New York, 1988), 128; Lawrence M. Friedman, *A History of American Law,* 2nd ed. (New York, 1985), 17–25; Karl N. Llewellyn, *The Common Law Tradition: Deciding Appeals* (Boston, 1960), 36.

52. Daniel J. Boorstin, *The Mysterious Science of the Law: An Essay on Blackstone's Commentaries . . .* (1941; reprint, with a foreword by Daniel J. Boorstin, Chicago, 1996), 11–30; William P. LaPiana, *Logic and Experience: The Origin of Modern American Legal Education* (New York, 1994), 29–38.

53. Story, "Law, Legislation, and Codes," in McClellan, *Joseph Story,* 359; *Memoir* 1:292.

54. *Writings of Robert Rantoul Jr.,* 279, 280.

55. Massachusetts House of Representatives, *Report of the Commissioners Appointed to Revise and Reform the Proceedings in the Courts of Justice in This Commonwealth,* no. 17 (1851), 11. On custom and common law, see A. W. B. Simpson, "The Common Law and Legal Theory," in *Oxford Essays in Jurisprudence,* 2d ser., ed. A. W. B. Simpson (Oxford, 1973), 91–94; Arthur R. Hogue, *Origins of the Common Law* (Bloomington, Ind., 1966), 179–88.

56. William Blackstone, *Commentaries on the Laws of England,* 9th ed. (1783; reprint, New York, 1978), 4:442.

57. Florida v. Georgia, 58 U.S. (17 How.) 478, 504 (1855) (Curtis, J., dissenting); The Larch, 14 F. Cas. 1139, 1141 (C.C.D. Me. 1855) (No. 8,085); Salmon Falls Manufacturing Co. v. The Tangier, 21 F. Cas. 259, 260 (C.C.D. Mass. 1857)

(No. 12,265); Oliver v. Mutual Commercial Marine Insurance Co., 18 F. Cas. 664, 671 (C.C.D. Mass. 1855) (No. 10,498).

58. Antonin Scalia, *A Matter of Interpretation: Federal Courts and the Law* (Princeton, N.J., 1997), 3–4.

59. Cooley v. Board of Wardens, 53 U.S. (12 How.) 299, 320 (1852).

60. John Davies, *Les Reports* . . . (London, 1674), quoted in J. G. A. Pocock, *The Ancient Constitution and the Feudal Law: A Study of English Historical Thought in the Seventeenth Century* . . . (1957; reprint, with a retrospect, New York, 1987), 33.

61. Quoted in Miller, *Life of the Mind in America*, 234; *Writings of Robert Rantoul Jr.*, 280.

62. On Whig views of natural aristocracy, see Howe, *American Whigs*, 31; Matthews, *Rufus Choate*, 181; John Ashworth, *'Agrarians' and 'Aristocrats': Party Political Ideology in the United States, 1837–1846* (Cambridge, 1987), 33. There were Whig judges serving on the lower federal courts who believed in the "natural right of educated, well-born, and wealthier men to be leaders of society." Christian G. Fritz, *Federal Justice in California: The Court of Ogden Hoffman, 1851–1891* (Lincoln, Nebr., 1991), 3.

63. Compare Justice Story's reference to lawyers as a "professional intelligentsia," Chancellor Kent's conception of lawyers as "guardians," and John Marshall's understanding of the lawyers' role in self-government. Newmyer, "New England Legal Culture," 168; Robert A. Ferguson, *Law and Letters in American Culture* (Cambridge, Mass., 1984), 25; R. Kent Newmyer, *John Marshall and the Heroic Age of the Supreme Court* (Baton Rouge, La., 2001), 72–102. For Alexis de Tocqueville's views on lawyers, see Robert W. Gordon, "The Independence of Lawyers," *Boston University Law Review* 68 (1988): 14. On the rise of the legal profession, see Samuel Haber, *The Quest for Authority and Honor in the American Professions, 1750–1900* (Chicago, 1991).

64. "Debts of the States," 109–57.

65. Curtis to Ticknor, 14 May 1837, *Memoir* 1:76; "Debts of the States," 121.

66. Carl B. Swisher, *The Taney Period, 1836–1864* (New York, 1974), 128–31.

67. "State Credit," *United States Magazine and Democratic Review* 10 (1842): 3–16.

68. Ward to Joshua Bates, 14 Nov. 1843, 12 Jan. 1844, Bates to Ward, 3 Feb. 1844, Thomas Wren Ward Papers, MHS; Ralph W. Hidy, *The House of Baring in American Trade and Finance: English Merchant Bankers at Work, 1763–1861* (Cambridge, Mass., 1949), 313–17.

69. "Debts of the States," 150, 116, 142, 144, 146, 145, 146.

70. Ibid., 133.

71. Joyce Oldham Appleby, *Economic Thought and Ideology in Seventeenth-Century England* (Princeton, N.J., 1978), 25; "Debts of the States," 150.

72. "Debts of the States," 128.

73. Ibid., 129, 128, 114.

74. Ibid., 116.

75. Compare Home Building and Loan Association v. Blaisdell, 290 U.S. 398 (1934) (upheld Minnesota state law which authorized state courts to temporarily extend the time for repayment of mortgages).

76. "Debts of the States," 115, 116.

77. Ibid., 156.
78. U.S. Constitution, art. 3, sec. 2; amend. 11; "Debts of the States," 155; Monaco v. Mississippi, 292 U.S. 313 (1934).
79. Story to Curtis, 2 Jan. 1844, Curtis Papers, DLC.
80. Parker, *The Trial,* 167–68; Levy, *Chief Justice Shaw,* 66; Cover, *Justice Accused,* 176.
81. Commonwealth v. Aves, 35 Mass. (18 Pick.) 193 (1836).
82. It was generally understood that the common law conformed to the law of nature. This raised some perplexing questions because slavery was recognized at common law. See generally Boorstin, *Mysterious Science of the Law,* 59–61; Erwin N. Griswold, *Law and Lawyers in the United States: The Common Law under Stress* (Cambridge, Mass., 1965), 104–7.
83. Blackstone, *Commentaries* 1:423.
84. Bailyn, *Ideological Origins of the American Revolution,* 237; Donald L. Robinson, *Slavery in the Structure of American Politics, 1765–1820* (New York, 1971), 73–78.
85. *William Lloyd Garrison, 1805–1879, The Story of His Life Told by His Children* (New York, 1885), 1:410; *Writings of Joseph Story,* 136.
86. *Blackstone's Commentaries: With Notes of Reference . . . ,* ed. St. George Tucker, 2 (1803; reprint, Union, N.J., 1996): note H, 54, 55; Rankin v. Lydia, 9 Ky. (2 A. K. Marsh.) 467, 470 (1820); Thomas R. Dew, *Review of the Debate in the Virginia Legislature of 1831 and 1832* (1832; reprint, Westport, Conn., 1970), 87, 103; McDuffie quoted in George M. Fredrickson, *The Black Image in the White Mind: The Debate on Afro-American Character and Destiny, 1817–1914* (New York, 1971), 46; *The Works of John C. Calhoun,* ed. Richard K. Crallé (New York, 1851–56), 2:631, 630. See generally David Donald, "The Proslavery Argument Reconsidered," *Journal of Southern History* 37 (1971): 3–18.
87. *Report of the Arguments of Counsel, and of the Opinion of the Court, in the Case of Commonwealth vs. Aves . . .* (Boston, 1836), 11; *Constitutional Meeting,* 17.
88. Cover, *Justice Accused,* 35.
89. Somersett v. Stewart, Lofft 1, 98 Eng. Rep. 499, reprinted in 20 *Howell's State Trials* 1, 79, 82 (K.B. 1772); William M. Wiecek, "*Somerset:* Lord Mansfield and the Legitimacy of Slavery in the Anglo-American World," *Chicago Law Review* 42 (1974): 106–7.
90. [John A. Campbell], "Slavery in the United States," *Southern Quarterly Review* 12 (1847): 96; *Annual Report of the Boston Female Anti-Slavery Society; Being a Concise History of the Cases of the Slave Child, Med . . .* (Boston, 1836), 66–67. The case is analyzed in Paul Finkelman, *An Imperfect Union: Slavery, Federalism, and Comity* (Chapel Hill, N.C., 1981), 101–25; Levy, *Chief Justice Shaw,* 62–68.
91. Francis Newton Thorpe, ed. and comp., *The Federal and State Constitutions . . .* (Washington, D.C., 1909), 3:1889; John D. Cushing, "The Cushing Court and the Abolition of Slavery in Massachusetts: More Notes on the 'Quock Walker Case,'" *American Journal of Legal History* 5 (1961): 133; Wiecek, *Antislavery Constitutionalism,* 47–48; Joseph Story, *Commentaries on the Conflict of Laws . . .* (Boston, 1834), 92.
92. Blackstone, *Commentaries* 1:424; Wiecek, *Antislavery Constitutionalism,* 35; Story, *Conflict of Laws,* 93.

93. Story, *Conflict of Laws*, 7, 33, 34, 95.

94. *Report of the Boston Female Anti-Slavery Society*, 66; Child to E. Carpenter, 4 Sept. 1836, *Letters of Lydia Maria Child . . .* (Boston, 1883), 20.

95. *Arguments of Counsel*, 7, 5, 8.

96. Ibid., 26.

97. Ibid., 11. See generally Alfred L. Brophy, "John Quincy Adams: Harriet Beecher Stowe's Interpretation of the 'Slavery of Politics' in *Dred: A Tale of the Great Dismal Swamp*," *Oklahoma City Law Review* 25 (2000): 69–70.

98. The Antelope, 23 U.S. (10 Wheat.) 66, 121, 114, 116 (1825).

99. United States v. La Jeune Eugenie, 26 F. Cas. 832, 846 (C.C.D. Mass. 1822) (No. 15,551).

100. *Arguments of Counsel*, 11.

101. Ibid., 16.

102. Ibid., 12, 10, 15.

103. Ibid., 9, 8.

104. *Writings and Speeches of Daniel Webster* 2:163; *Works of John C. Calhoun* 6:107.

105. *Arguments of Counsel*, 10.

106. 35 Mass. at 193, 210, 217, 218, 220–21.

107. *Liberator*, 24 Sept. 1836; Finkelman, *Imperfect Union*, 114; *Augusta Sentinel*, quoted in the *Liberator*, 15 Oct. 1836.

108. *Garrison* 1:492–516; Curtis to George and Anna Ticknor, 23 Aug. 1835, *Memoir* 1:72.

109. Curtis to Webster, [Oct. 1851], copy, Curtis Papers, DLC; *Twentieth Annual Report Presented to the Massachusetts Anti-Slavery Society*, 22; *Liberator*, 17, 24 Oct. 1851.

110. *The Papers of Daniel Webster*, ser. 4, *Speeches and Formal Writings*, ed. Charles M. Wiltse (Hanover, N.H., 1974–89), 1:294; Sumner quoted in David Donald, *Charles Sumner and the Coming of the Civil War* (New York, 1960), 147.

111. Brauer, *Cotton versus Conscience*, 30–245; O'Connor, *Lords of the Loom*, 58–76; Donald, *Sumner and the Coming of the Civil War*, 130–59; Samuel Shapiro, *Richard Henry Dana, Jr., 1815–1882* (East Lansing, Mich., 1961), 29–44; Maurice G. Baxter, *One and Inseparable: Daniel Webster and the Union* (Cambridge, Mass., 1984), 399.

112. Quoted in McPherson, *Battle Cry of Freedom*, 63–64.

113. David M. Potter, *The Impending Crisis, 1848–1861*, completed and ed. by Don E. Fehrenbacher (New York, 1976), 86, 122–24; Holman Hamilton, *Prologue to Conflict: The Crisis and Compromise of 1850* (Lexington, Ky., 1964), 69; Allan Nevins, *Ordeal of the Union* 1 (New York, 1947): 250, 261.

114. *Papers of Daniel Webster*, ser. 4, *Speeches* 2:515–51.

115. *Boston Atlas*, 11 Mar. 1850; Winthrop to Everett, 17 Mar. 1850, Edward Everett Papers, MHS; *Liberator*, 29 Mar. 1850; *The Poetical Works of John Greenleaf Whittier*, ed. W. Garrett Horder (London, 1910), 204.

116. Everett to Robert C. Winthrop, 8 May 1850, Edward Everett Papers, MHS. Along with several hundred so-called Webster Whigs, Curtis signed a public letter that expressed "entire concurrence in the sentiments" of the Seventh of

March speech. Everett, for one, refused to sign it. Everett to Robert C. Winthrop, 10 Apr. 1850, ibid. Never had "an event half so painful occurred in Boston as the letter," Emerson thought. *Boston Advertiser*, 3 Apr. 1850; *Boston Courier*, 3 Apr. 1850; *The Journals and Miscellaneous Notebooks of Ralph Waldo Emerson*, ed. A. W. Plumstead and William H. Gilman, 11 (Cambridge, Mass., 1975): 249.

117. *Memoir* 1:116. A slightly different version of Curtis's remarks appeared in the *Boston Advertiser*, 30 Apr. 1850.

118. Donald, *Sumner and the Coming of the Civil War*, 98−182.

119. Curtis to Webster, 23 Feb. 1851, Curtis Papers, DLC; Donald, *Sumner and the Coming of the Civil War*, 186−202.

120. Everett to Curtis, 1 May 1851, Everett to Webster, 1 May 1851, Edward Everett Papers, MHS; Samuel Hooper to Franklin Haven, 4 May [1851], Daniel Webster Papers, bMS AM 322 (308), Houghton Library, Harvard University, Cambridge, Mass.

121. *Address to the People of Massachusetts*, 8, 14.

122. Everett to Clay, 3 Dec. 1851, Edward Everett Papers, MHS.

123. Fillmore to Webster, 10 Sept. 1851, Daniel Webster Papers, DLC; Webster to Fillmore, 10 Sept. 1851, *Papers of Daniel Webster*, ser. 1, *Correspondence* 7:272−73; see also Fillmore to Webster, 12 Sept. 1851, Daniel Webster Papers, DLC.

124. Webster to Curtis, 24 Dec. 1851, Curtis Papers, DLC; Curtis to Fillmore, 7 Oct. 1851, *Memoir* 1:156.

2. THE FUGITIVE SLAVE CONTROVERSY

1. U.S. Constitution, art. 4, sec. 2; *Stats. at Large of USA* 1 (1848): 302−5; *Stats. at Large of USA* 9 (1862): 462−65; Potter, *Impending Crisis*, 121.

2. *Boston Advertiser*, 24 Sept. 1850.

3. Parker, *Trial*, 168; *New York Tribune*, 9 Apr. 1855.

4. *New York Tribune*, 9 Apr. 1855.

5. Charge to Grand Jury—Neutrality Laws and Treason, 30 F. Cas. 1024 (C.C.D. Mass. 1851) (No. 18,269); Charge to Grand Jury, 30 F. Cas. 983 (C.C.D. Mass. 1854) (No. 18,250); United States v. Morris, 26 F. Cas. 1323 (C.C.D. Mass. 1851) (No. 15,815).

6. U.S. Constitution, art. 4, sec. 2; *Stats. at Large of USA* 1 (1848): 302−5; Thomas D. Morris, *Free Men All: The Personal Liberty Laws of the North, 1780−1861* (Baltimore, 1974), 42−58.

7. Prigg v. Pennsylvania, 41 U.S. (16 Pet.) 539, 615, 618−20, 576−78, 625 (1842).

8. Ibid., 625, 622 (Story, J.); 658−73 (McLean, J., dissenting). Story later portrayed Prigg as a "triumph of freedom." *Life and Letters of Joseph Story . . .*, ed. William W. Story, 2 (Boston, 1851): 392. However, Justice Story's concern was for federal power rather than the plight of fugitive slaves. Shortly after the opinion was handed down, he proposed legislation to enhance federal enforcement. McClellan, *Joseph Story*, 262.

9. Jones v. Van Zandt, 46 U.S. (5 How.) 215, 229 (1847). Cf. S. P. Chase, *Reclamation of Fugitives from Service: An Argument for the Defendant . . . in the Case of Wharton Jones vs. John Vanzandt* (1847; reprint, Freeport, N.Y., 1971), 71, 73.

10. "The Latimer Case," *Law Reporter* 5 (1843): 481–98; Newmyer, *Joseph Story*, 376; Levy, *Chief Justice Shaw*, 78–82.

11. Wiecek, *Antislavery Constitutionalism*, 237.

12. *Liberator*, 11, 4 Nov. 1842; Irving H. Bartlett, *Wendell Phillips: Brahmin Radical* (Boston, 1961), 118.

13. Massachusetts House of Representatives, Report No. 41 (1843), in *Fugitive Slaves and American Courts: The Pamphlet Literature*, 2d ser., vol. 1, ed. Paul Finkelman (New York, 1988), 177; *Liberator*, 3 Feb. 1843; Stanley W. Campbell, *The Slave Catchers: Enforcement of the Fugitive Slave Law, 1850–1860* (Chapel Hill, N.C., 1970), 14; see Paul Finkelman, "*Prigg v. Pennsylvania* and Northern State Courts: Anti-Slavery Use of a Pro-Slavery Decision," *Civil War History* 25 (1979): 5–35.

14. Everett reported that the bill was "highly offensive." Everett to Abbott Lawrence, 2 Apr. 1850, Edward Everett Papers, MHS.

15. *Stats. at Large of USA* 9 (1862): 462–65.

16. See Allen Johnson, "The Constitutionality of the Fugitive Slave Acts," *Yale Law Journal* 31 (1921): 161–82.

17. *Liberator*, 4, 11, 18 Oct. 1850; *Boston Advertiser*, 23 Oct. 1850.

18. *Liberator*, 1 Nov. 1850; *Boston Atlas*, 29 Oct. 1850; Gary Collison, *Shadrach Minkins: From Fugitive Slave to Citizen* (Cambridge, Mass., 1997), 98.

19. *Boston Atlas*, 26 Oct. 1850; Parker, *Trial*, 163. On the Crafts, see Collison, *Shadrach Minkins*, 91–100; James Oliver Horton and Lois E. Horton, *Black Bostonians: Family Life and Community Struggle in the Antebellum North* (New York, 1979), 103–4; Lawrence Lader, *The Bold Brahmins: New England's War against Slavery, 1831–1863* (Westport, Conn., 1961), 139–43.

20. Parker, *Trial*, 163.

21. B. R. Curtis, Opinion of 9 Nov. 1850, in *Boston Advertiser*, 19 Nov. 1850, and *Boston Courier*, 16 Nov. 1850; Webster to Fillmore, 15 Nov. 1850, *Papers of Daniel Webster*, ser. 1, *Correspondence* 7:180.

22. Dana told Devens that the marshal could not use force as this was a civil action, and abolitionists threatened to haul Devens into court. Shapiro, *Richard Henry Dana*, 58.

23. A state judge in New York reportedly refused to be named a commissioner because he doubted that Congress had the constitutional authority to pass such legislation. *Boston Advertiser*, 28 Oct. 1850.

24. Opinion of 9 Nov. 1850, in *Boston Advertiser*, 19 Nov. 1850.

25. *Papers of Daniel Webster*, ser. 1, *Correspondence* 7:85–95; *Boston Atlas*, 30 May 1850; opinion of 9 Nov. 1850, in *Boston Advertiser*, 19 Nov. 1850.

26. *Liberator*, 1 Nov. 1850. Another opponent of the 1850 act explained that fugitive slave proceedings were "wholly unlike" extradition because the person seized was "not sent home to be tried for his freedom" but rather "delivered over to his master, to be as fully and as finally a slave as any other slave, and with no other right to claim his liberty than any other slave has." *Boston Atlas*, 29 Oct. 1850.

27. *CG*, 31st Cong., 1st sess., 1850, 22, pt. 2, app.:1611.

28. See, for example, Hudgins v. Wrights, 11 Va. (1 Hen. & M.) 134, 137 (1806); see generally Morris, *Free Men All*, 2–3.

29. Chase, *Reclamation of Fugitives*, 91; *Slavery Letters and Speeches by Horace Mann* (1851; reprint, New York, 1969), 311; *CG*, 31st Cong., 1st sess., 1850, 22, pt. 2, app.: 1063.
30. Commonwealth v. Griffith, 19 Mass. (2 Pick.) 11, 18 (1823).
31. Opinion of 9 Nov. 1850, in *Boston Advertiser*, 19 Nov. 1850; *Liberator*, 6 Dec. 1850.
32. *Speeches by Horace Mann*, 307; *Boston Advertiser*, 23 Oct. 1850.
33. *Memoir* 1:122; Cover, *Justice Accused*, 195, 197.
34. Nevins, *Ordeal of the Union* 1:347.
35. Webster to Fillmore, 5 Nov. 1850, *Papers of Daniel Webster*, ser. 1, *Correspondence* 7:178; George T. Curtis to George G. Smith, 18 Nov. 1850, Miscellaneous Manuscripts, MHS. The other two speakers were Benjamin F. Hallett and S. D. Bradford.
36. *Boston Advertiser*, 23 Oct. 1850; Theodore Parker, *The Function and Place of Conscience, in Relation to the Laws of Men; a Sermon for the Times . . .* (Boston, 1850).
37. Senator William F. Seward used the phrase "a higher law than the Constitution" in a major speech. *CG*, 31st Cong., 1st sess., 1850, 22, app.: 265; see also Ferenc M. Szasz, "Antebellum Appeals to the 'Higher Law,' 1830–1860," *Essex Institute Historical Collections* 110 (1974): 46.
38. *Constitutional Meeting*, 11.
39. 41 U.S. at 611.
40. *Constitutional Meeting*, 14; Paul Finkelman, "Story Telling on the Supreme Court: *Prigg v. Pennsylvania* and Justice Joseph Story's Judicial Nationalism," *Supreme Court Review*, 1994: 259–63; John Phillip Reid, "Lessons of Lumpkin: A Review of Recent Literature on Law, Comity, and the Impending Crisis," *William and Mary Law Review* 23 (1982): 581–83.
41. *Constitutional Meeting*, 17, 16.
42. *The Federalist* no. 10; see also no. 27. Among numerous commentaries, see particularly Wood, *Creation of the American Republic*, 504–18; Cass R. Sunstein, *The Partial Constitution* (Cambridge, Mass., 1993), 20–23; Richard K. Matthews, *If Men Were Angels: James Madison and the Heartless Empire of Reason* (Lawrence, Kans., 1995), 84–85.
43. *Constitutional Meeting*, 7.
44. Ibid., 16, 14.
45. *Journals and Miscellaneous Notebooks of Emerson* 11:350; see also Charles Sumner in *CG*, 32d Cong., 1st sess., 1852, 21, pt. 2:1113.
46. *Constitutional Meeting*, 7.
47. Parker, *Function and Place of Conscience*, 26, 32–33.
48. *Constitutional Meeting*, 9; *Boston Atlas*, 27 Nov. 1850; Parker, *Trial*, 166.
49. *Constitutional Meeting*, 9, 7.
50. Ibid., 9; Cover, *Justice Accused*, 232.
51. Samuel Willard, *The Grand Issue: An Ethico-Political Tract* (Boston, 1851), 4.
52. See James Oliver Horton and Lois E. Horton, "A Federal Assault: African Americans and the Impact of the Fugitive Slave Law of 1850," *Chicago-Kent Law Review* 68 (1993): 1193; John Aldrich Christie, "Thoreau on Civil Resistance," *Emerson Society Quarterly* 54 (1969): 5–12; William A. Herr, "Thoreau: A Civil Disobedient?" *Ethics* 85 (1974): 87–91; John Demos, "The Antislavery

Movement and the Problem of Violent 'Means,'" *New England Quarterly* 37 (1964): 501-26.

53. *Constitutional Meeting*, 6-7; Curtis to Clifford, 28 Nov. 1850, John H. Clifford Papers, MHS.

54. *Boston Advertiser*, 26 Nov. 1850; *Boston Atlas*, 23 Nov. 1850; Georgia Platform quoted in Potter, *Impending Crisis*, 126, 128.

55. *Constitutional Meeting*, 17-18, 12, 13.

56. *Boston Advertiser*, 27, 28 Nov. 1850; *Boston Atlas*, 28 Nov. 1850; *Liberator*, 6, 20 Dec. 1850.

57. Collison, *Shadrach Minkins*, 110-33; Levy, *Chief Justice Shaw*, 87-91; *Boston Advertiser*, 17 Feb. 1851; *Report of the Proceedings at the Examination of Charles G. Davis, Esq., on a Charge of Aiding and Abetting in the Rescue of a Fugitive Slave* (Boston, 1851).

58. *Boston Advertiser*, 19 Feb. 1851; Levy, *Chief Justice Shaw*, 89; *CG*, 31st Cong., 2d sess., 1851, 22, app: 321.

59. *Messages and Papers of the Presidents* 5:110; *Boston Atlas*, 28, 25 Feb. 1851; Curtis to Webster, 23 Feb. 1851, Curtis Papers, DLC.

60. *Boston Courier*, 2 Apr. 1851; Webster to Fillmore, 9 Apr. 1851, *Papers of Daniel Webster*, ser. 1, *Correspondence* 7:230.

61. Theodore Parker, "The Boston Kidnapping: A Discourse to Commemorate the Rendition of Thomas Sims . . . ," in *Additional Speeches, Addresses, and Occasional Sermons* . . . (Boston, 1855), 1:68-69; *Boston Courier*, 5 Apr. 1851; Thomas Wentworth Higginson, *Cheerful Yesterdays* (Boston, 1901), 146.

62. *Boston Courier*, 5 Apr. 1851. Phillips advocated nonviolent resistance except when blacks defended themselves against capture. Bartlett, *Wendell Phillips*, 156.

63. *Trial of Thomas Sims* . . . (Boston, 1851); "The Case of Thomas Sims," *Monthly Law Reporter* 14 (1851): 1-16; Thomas Sims's Case, 61 Mass. (7 Cush.) 285 (1851); Levy, *Chief Justice Shaw*, 91-104; Vincent Y. Bowditch, *Life and Correspondence of Henry Ingersoll Bowditch* 1 (Boston, 1902): 215-29.

64. U.S. Constitution, art. 3, sec. 3; *Boston Atlas*, 25 Feb. 1851; 30 F. Cas. at 1024, 1025, 1026.

65. Charles Francis Adams, *Richard Henry Dana: A Biography*, 3d ed., 1 (Boston, 1891): 208. Cf. Justice Story's Charge to Grand Jury—Treason, 30 F. Cas. 1046 (C.C.D. R.I. 1842) (No. 18,275) and U.S. District Judge John K. Kane's Charge to Grand Jury—Treason, 30 F. Cas. 1047 (C.C.E.D. Pa. 1851) (No. 18,276). Kane's charge grew out of the so-called Christiana riot, a skirmish in Christiana, Pennsylvania, between blacks and Marylanders searching for escaped slaves. The fight left a slave owner dead and several others wounded. Following Kane's charge, a grand jury indicted Castner Hanway, a Quaker, for refusing to help capture the runaways. Supreme Court Justice Robert C. Grier presided over the trial. Striking a different tone than Curtis and Kane had, Grier warned against the "dangerous precedent" set if treason extended "by construction to doubtful cases." He also said that the defendant's actions did not rise to "the dignity of treason or a levying of war." The jury acquitted Hanway. United States v. Hanway, 26 F. Cas. 105 (C.C.E.D. Pa. 1851) (No. 15,299); Paul Finkelman,

"The Treason Trial of Castner Hanway," in *American Political Trials*, ed. Michael R. Belknap (Westport, Conn., 1981), 79–100.

66. 30 F. Cas. at 1026.

67. Benjamin R. Curtis, "Notes of Cases before the Circuit Court," 1:235, Harvard Law School MS 2066; *Liberator*, 18 Oct. 1850; *Boston Courier*, 17, 27 Feb. 1851; Pauline E. Hopkins, "Famous Men of the Negro Race: Robert Morris," *Colored American Magazine* 3 (1901): 337–42; Horton and Horton, *Black Bostonians*, 55–57.

68. Parker, *Function and Place of Conscience*, 32–33; Lysander Spooner, *A Defence for Fugitive Slaves . . .* (Boston, 1850), 27–43; 26 F. Cas. at 1323. In the previous spring Judge Peleg Sprague had conducted the trials of two other men charged with helping Shadrach escape. In both cases the jurors divided and failed to reach a verdict. Morris's case came before Sprague at this time. After jury selection the prosecutor produced evidence that one of the jurors who belonged to the Vigilance Committee was biased. Sprague removed him. The prosecutor sought to postpone the trial to another term; the defense pressed to go forward without delay. It looks like all parties realized that no conviction would be forthcoming that term. The judge declared that Morris's case raised difficult and significant questions of law and transferred the case to the U.S. circuit court. *Boston Courier*, 7, 18–20 June, 8 July 1851.

69. "Notes of Cases," 1:159–279, Harvard Law School MS 2066.

70. Ibid., 236, 207, 232, 202, 243–45, 254.

71. Ibid., 221, 230. Examples of the testimony of other witnesses can be found at pp. 260, 266.

72. Ibid., 180, 184, 238.

73. It is not clear whether Curtis or Sprague interjected, though it appears that the district judge had taken a secondary role. 26 F. Cas. at 1331; "Notes of Cases," 1:273–77, Harvard Law School MS 2066.

74. "Notes of Cases," 1:277, Harvard Law School MS 2066.

75. Thomas Andrew Green, *Verdict according to Conscience: Perspectives on the English Criminal Trial Jury, 1200–1800* (Chicago, 1985); Albert W. Alschuler and Andrew G. Deiss, "A Brief History of the Criminal Jury in the United States," *University of Chicago Law Review* 61 (1994): 867–928; "The Changing Role of the Jury in the Nineteenth Century," *Yale Law Journal* 74 (1964): 170–92; Mark DeWolfe Howe, "Juries as Judges of Criminal Law," *Harvard Law Review* 52 (1939): 582–616.

76. United States v. Battiste, 24 F. Cas. 1042, 1043 (C.C.D. Mass. 1835) (No. 14,545); Sparf and Hansen v. United States, 156 U.S. 51, 78, 76 (1895).

77. 26 F. Cas. at 1332; Commonwealth v. Porter, 51 Mass. (10 Met.) 263 (1845). Cf. Stettinius v. United States, 22 F. Cas. 1322, 1327 (C.C.D.C. 1839) (No. 13,387) (jury has no right to decide law) with United States v. Hodges, 26 F. Cas. 332, 334 (C.C.D. Md. 1815) (No. 15,374) (jurors have a right in all criminal cases to decide on the law). As Curtis noted, there was not "an entire uniformity of opinion" on this subject. 26 F. Cas. at 1332.

78. U.S. Constitution, art. 3, sec. 2; 26 F. Cas. at 1332.

79. U.S. Constitution, art. 6, sec. 2; 26 F. Cas. at 1332. The principle of uniformity underlay Whig constitutional thought; it was especially evident in Justice Story's jurisprudence. See, for example, Martin v. Hunter's Lessee, 14 U.S. (1 Wheat.) 304 (1816) (U.S. Supreme Court had ultimate authority to review state court judgments on federal questions).

80. 26 F. Cas. at 1332; *The Federalist* no. 80.

81. 26 F. Cas. at 1336.

82. Ibid. Elsewhere, Justice Curtis expressed concern over civil juries undermining uniformity in the enforcement of federal revenue laws, but he regarded the jury's authority to determine when federal tariffs applied to imports a necessary "evil." Wilkinson v. Greely, 29 F. Cas. 1257, 1259 (C.C.D. Mass. 1851) (No. 17,671). See also Wilkinson v. Greely, 29 F. Cas. 1259, 1263 (C.C.D. Mass. 1853) (No. 17,672) (reliance on expert witness testimony would increase "uncertainty" and make the revenue laws "variable, unequal, and consequently unjust").

83. Dana did not specify which rescue case he was discussing, but other statements of his indicate that the case was tried in the fall of 1851 and that date could only refer to Morris's trial. *Proceedings of the Bench and Bar of the Circuit Court of the United States, District of Massachusetts, upon the Decease of Hon. Benjamin Robbins Curtis, September and October, 1974* (Boston, 1875), 31.

84. The effort to prosecute others for rescuing Shadrach failed. District Attorney Lunt brought to trial Elizur Wright, the white abolitionist editor of the *Boston Commonwealth* and a member of the Vigilance Committee. With Dana handling the defense, Wright was acquitted. Dana believed that Curtis had "taken pains to aid the prisoner" and that the justice's jury charge was "a model of impartiality." Adams, *Richard Henry Dana* 1:221, 222.

85. *Boston Advertiser*, 1 Dec. 1851.

86. Von Frank's *Trials of Anthony Burns* thoroughly explores the events surrounding the Burns rendition. Also useful is Jane H. Pease and William H. Pease, *The Fugitive Slave Law and Anthony Burns: A Problem in Law Enforcement* (Philadelphia, 1975).

87. On the legal proceedings, see "The Case of Anthony Burns," *Monthly Law Reporter* 17 (1854): 181–210; *Boston Slave Riot, and Trial of Anthony Burns* (Boston, 1854), 5–84.

88. Von Frank, *Burns*, 12, 32–36; Higginson, *Cheerful Yesterdays*, 148–51.

89. *Liberator*, 2 June 1854; *Boston Slave Riot*, 7–12.

90. "Case of Anthony Burns," 203–10; McPherson, *Battle Cry of Freedom*, 119–20.

91. Amos A. Lawrence to Giles Richards, 1 June 1854, quoted in Pease and Pease, *Fugitive Slave Law*, 43.

92. 30 F. Cas. at 983; Parker, *Additional Speeches* 2:281.

93. 30 F. Cas. at 984. Cf. 30 F. Cas. at 1026.

94. 30 F. Cas. at 985.

95. Ibid.

96. *Liberator*, 7 July 1854.

97. United States v. Stowell, 27 F. Cas. 1350, 1353, 1352 (C.C.D. Mass. 1855) (No. 16,409); Hallett to Franklin Pierce, 9 June 1855, quoted in Campbell, *Slave Catchers*, 132.

98. United States v. Pond, 27 F. Cas. 590, 591 (C.C.D. Mass. 1855) (No. 16,067); Sumner to Parker, 12 Dec. 1854, Theodore Parker Papers, MHS.

99. *New York Tribune*, 9 Apr. 1855; *Liberator*, 9 Feb. 1855; Parker, *Trial*, 218, 181, 167.

100. *Memoir* 1:345.

3. FEDERAL-STATE CONFLICT IN A COMMERCIAL REPUBLIC

1. *Memorial of Daniel Webster*, 116, 117.

2. Cooley v. Board of Wardens, 53 U.S. (12 How.) 299 (1852); U.S. Constitution, art. 1, sec. 8.

3. Willson v. Black Bird Creek Marsh Co., 27 U.S. (2 Pet.) 245, 252 (1829).

4. Laurence H. Tribe, *American Constitutional Law*, 3d ed., 1 (New York, 2000), 1047.

5. George Rogers Taylor, *The Transportation Revolution, 1815–1860* (New York, 1951), 15–175; Robert V. Remini, ed., *The Age of Jackson* (Columbia, S.C., 1972), 189–96.

6. Gibbons v. Ogden, 22 U.S. (9 Wheat.) 1, 9–10 (1824) (Webster).

7. Ibid., 193, 196, 211–21.

8. Maurice G. Baxter, *The Steamboat Monopoly Case:* Gibbons v. Ogden, *1824* (New York, 1972), 56–60; Charles Warren, *The Supreme Court in United States History*, rev. ed. (Boston, 1947), 1:622–28.

9. 22 U.S. at 222–39 (Johnson, J.).

10. Brown v. Maryland, 25 U.S. (12 Wheat.) 419, 445–49 (1827); 27 U.S. at 251.

11. In *Willson*, Marshall ignored the federal statute that he had used in *Gibbons*, although it was arguably more relevant to the Delaware case. For further analysis of commerce powers by the Marshall Court, see White, *Marshall Court and Cultural Change*, 567–85; Felix Frankfurter, *The Commerce Clause under Marshall, Taney, and Waite* (Chicago, 1964), 11–45.

12. Joseph Story, *Commentaries on the Constitution . . .* (1833; reprint, New York, 1970), 2:515; 22 U.S. at 18–19, 14 (Webster).

13. New York v. Miln, 36 U.S. (11 Pet.) 102, 139 (1837). Compare Webster's description of Congress's commerce power as "complete, entire, and uniform." Gibbons, 22 U.S. at 14 (Webster).

14. 36 U.S. at 158 (Story, J., dissenting); Groves v. Slaughter, 40 U.S. (15 Pet.) 449, 494 (1841) (Webster).

15. 36 U.S. at 130–43 (Barbour, J.); License Cases, 46 U.S. (5 How.) 504, 588, 592 (1847) (McLean, J.); Passenger Cases, 48 U.S. (7 How.) 283, 426 (1849) (Wayne, J.); ibid., 464–94 (Taney, C.J.).

16. 46 U.S. at 579, 580, 581.

17. Ibid., 583.

18. 40 U.S. at 510.

19. 22 U.S. at 20, 107–9, 206–7.

20. 40 U.S. at 506 (McLean, J.); ibid., 509, 508 (Taney, C.J.).

21. John Codman Hurd, *The Law of Freedom and Bondage in the United States* 2 (1862; reprint, New York, 1968): 77–78, 86, 97, 161.

22. Swisher, *Taney Period,* 378–82; Philip M. Hamer, "Great Britain, the United States, and the Negro Seamen Acts, 1822–1848," *Journal of Southern History* 1 (1935): 3–28; Elkison v. Deliesseline, 8 F. Cas. 493 (C.C.D. S.C. 1823) (No. 4,366); Marshall quoted in Warren, *Supreme Court in United States History* 1:626.
23. 48 U.S. at 283.
24. Ibid., 474 (Taney, C.J.); *Charleston Mercury,* 14 Feb. 1849, quoted in Swisher, *Taney Period,* 393; Joel Tiffany, *A Treatise on the Unconstitutionality of American Slavery: Together with the Powers and Duties of the Federal Government, in Relation to That Subject* (1849; reprint, Miami, Fla., 1969), 133–36.
25. Curtis to Ticknor, 29 Feb. 1852, Curtis Papers, DLC.
26. 53 U.S. at 319.
27. R. Kent Newmyer, *The Supreme Court under Marshall and Taney* (New York, 1968), 106; Robert G. McCloskey, *The American Supreme Court,* 2d ed., rev. and enl. Sanford Levinson (Chicago, 1994), 58; see also Frankfurter, *Commerce Clause,* 57; John B. Sholley, "The Negative Implications of the Commerce Clause," *University of Chicago Law Review* 3 (1936): 576.
28. Curtis to Ticknor, 29 Feb. 1852, Curtis Papers, DLC.
29. 53 U.S. at 321–25 (McLean, J., dissenting); ibid., 325–26 (Daniel, J.). Justice John McKinley did not participate in *Cooley.* For further discussion of the justices on the Taney Court, see Timothy S. Huebner, *The Taney Court: Justices, Rulings, and Legacy* (Santa Barbara, Calif., 2003), 31–114.
30. Useful summaries can be found in Michael Les Benedict, "Abraham Lincoln and Federalism," *Journal of the Abraham Lincoln Association* 10 (1988): 4–19; Edward S. Corwin, "The Passing of Dual Federalism," in *Corwin on the Constitution: On Liberty against Government,* ed. Richard Loss (Ithaca, N.Y., 1981–88), 3:240–58; see also Raoul Berger, *Federalism: The Founders' Design* (Norman, Okla., 1987), 48–76.
31. 53 U.S. at 317.
32. Story, *Commentaries on the Constitution* 2:515; 22 U.S. at 203; ibid., 19, 20 (Webster).
33. 22 U.S. at 20, 18, 208.
34. 48 U.S. at 467 (Taney, C.J.); 53 U.S. at 325 (Daniel, J.).
35. 53 U.S. at 315, 316.
36. Ibid., 317; An Act concerning Pilots, *Stats. at Large of USA* 5 (1860): 153–54.
37. 53 U.S. at 316, 312, 319, 320.
38. John Catron to James Buchanan, 3 Mar. 1852, James Buchanan Papers, Historical Society of Pennsylvania.
39. Ibid.; 53 U.S. at 320.
40. House Committee on Commerce, *Free Colored Seamen—Majority and Minority Reports,* 27th Cong., 3d sess., 1843, Rept. 80, 7–9.
41. 53 U.S. at 318, 319.
42. 36 U.S. at 158 (Story, J., dissenting); 22 U.S. at 199, 205, 204. In the context of analyzing *Cooley,* with its breakdown of the commerce power into subjects, Story's complete statement is potentially confusing. Justice Story used the phrase "full power to regulate a particular subject"; by "subject," Story meant

interstate and foreign commerce. Chief Justice Marshall considered the taxing power concurrent because the states and Congress were "taking small portions from a perpetually accumulating mass, susceptible of almost infinite division." There was no direct clash of sovereign powers in his view. 22 U.S. at 199; see also *The Federalist* no. 32.

43. 36 U.S. at 139; 48 U.S. at 466, 467.

44. Archibald Cox, *The Court and the Constitution* (Boston, 1987), 89.

45. *The Federalist* no. 15.

46. Bailyn, *Ideological Origins of the American Revolution*, 209–11, 358; Wood, *Creation of the American Republic*, 349–53, 530–32; Garry Wills, *Explaining America: The Federalist* (Garden City, N.Y., 1981), 162–75; Andrew C. McLaughlin, *The Foundations of American Constitutionalism* (New York, 1932), 144–45; Akhil Reed Amar, "Of Sovereignty and Federalism," *Yale Law Journal* 96 (1987): 1430–51; *The Federalist* nos. 20, 46.

47. *The Federalist* nos. 46, 37, 39.

48. John P. Frank, *Justice Daniel Dissenting: A Biography of Peter V. Daniel, 1784–1860* (Cambridge, Mass., 1964), 197; Baxter, *Daniel Webster and the Supreme Court*, 225; Newmyer, *Supreme Court under Marshall and Taney*, 106; Warren, *Supreme Court in United States History* 2:238; Cox, *Court and the Constitution*, 91; David P. Currie, *The Constitution in the Supreme Court: The First Hundred Years, 1789–1888* (Chicago, 1985), 231.

49. 22 U.S. at 10, 18, 14, 19, 24–25.

50. 48 U.S. at 559, 546 (Woodbury, J., dissenting); United States v. New Bedford Bridge, 27 F. Cas. 91, 99 (C.C.D. Mass. 1847) (No. 15,867); 46 U.S. at 625 (Woodbury, J.).

51. 53 U.S. at 318, 321.

52. Tribe, *American Constitutional Law* 1:1242; Gerald Gunther and Kathleen M. Sullivan, *Constitutional Law*, 14th ed. (New York, 2001), 323; William Cohen, "Congressional Power to Validate Unconstitutional State Laws: A Forgotten Solution to an Old Enigma," *Stanford Law Review* 35 (1983): 395. For an alternative reading, see Noel T. Dowling, "Interstate Commerce and State Power," *Virginia Law Review* 27 (1940): 21.

53. Act of Aug. 7, 1789, *Stats. at Large of USA* 1 (1848): 54; 53 U.S. at 317.

54. 53 U.S. at 318, 319, 321, 320.

55. In re Freeman, 9 F. Cas. 751, 752 (C.C.D. Mass. 1855) (No. 5,083). Cf. 22 U.S. at 208, and 46 U.S. at 580.

56. Prudential Insurance Co. v. Benjamin, 328 U.S. 408, 423–26 (1946); Southern Pacific Co. v. Arizona, 325 U.S. 761, 769 (1945); In re Rahrer, 140 U.S. 545, 562 (1891); Leisy v. Hardin, 135 U.S. 100, 124 (1890).

57. 325 U.S. at 767–68; Tribe, *American Constitutional Law* 1:1049–59; Gunther and Sullivan, *Constitutional Law*, 323–28; Daniel A. Farber, "State Regulation and the Dormant Commerce Clause," *Constitutional Commentary* 3 (1986): 395–414; Cohen, "Congressional Power to Validate Unconstitutional State Laws," 387–422; Mark Tushnet, "Rethinking the Dormant Commerce Clause," *Wisconsin Law Review*, 1979: 125–65.

58. Dowling viewed *Southern Pacific* as a "clear echo" of *Cooley*. Noel T. Dowling, "Interstate Commerce and State Power—Revised Version," *Columbia Law Review* 47 (1947): 551.

59. Curtis, "Debts of the States," 156.

60. 53 U.S. at 320.

61. See Richard B. Collins, "Economic Union as a Constitutional Value," *New York University Law Review* 63 (1988): 43–129.

62. Lafayette Insurance Co. v. French, 59 U.S. (18 How.) 404 (1856); Swift v. Tyson, 41 U.S. (16 Pet.) 1 (1842); Erie Railroad Co. v. Tompkins, 304 U.S. 64 (1938); Gloucester Insurance Co. v. Younger, 10 F. Cas. 495 (C.C.D. Mass. 1855) (No. 5,487); Russell v. Southard, 53 U.S. (12 How.) 139 (1851); Neves v. Scott, 54 U.S. (13 How.) 268 (1852). For analysis of Swift in historical context, see Tony Freyer, *Harmony and Dissonance: The Swift and Erie Cases in American Federalism* (New York, 1981); Tony Allan Freyer, *Forums of Order: The Federal Courts and Business in American History* (Greenwood, Conn., 1979).

63. U.S. Constitution, art. 3, sec. 2.

64. Steamboat New World v. King, 57 U.S. (16 How.) 469 (1854); E. I. Dupont de Nemours & Co. v. Vance, 60 U.S. (19 How.) 162, 181 (1857) (Campbell, J., dissenting); Thomas v. Osborn, 60 U.S. (19 How.) 22, 38 (Taney, C.J., dissenting); Swisher, *Taney Court*, 447.

65. McCarroll v. Dixie Greyhound Lines, 309 U.S. 176, 189 (1940) (Black, J., dissenting).

66. New Jersey Steam Navigation Co. v. Merchants' Bank of Boston, 47 U.S. (6 How.) 344, 389 (1848); Scott v. Sandford, 60 U.S. (19 How.) 393, 617 (1857); *Trial of Andrew Johnson* . . . (Washington, D.C., 1868), 1 : 389–91; 53 U.S. at 320.

67. Curtis to Clifford, 8 May 1853, John Henry Clifford Papers, MHS.

68. Pennsylvania v. Wheeling and Belmont Bridge Co., 54 U.S. (13 How.) 518 (1852). A few years later Curtis went along when the Court deferred to Congress's approval of the bridge. Pennsylvania v. Wheeling and Belmont Bridge Co., 59 U.S. (18 How.) 421 (1856).

69. Veazie v. Moor, 55 U.S.(14 How.) 567 (1853); Smith v. Maryland, 59 U.S. (18 How.) 71 (1856).

70. Smith v. Eastern Railroad, 22 F. Cas. 526, 528 (C.C.D. Mass. 1852) (No. 13,039); Paul v. Virginia, 75 U.S. (8 Wall.) 168, 170–74, 183 (1869); United States v. South-Eastern Underwriters Association, 322 U.S. 533, 547 (1944). Congress then passed the McCarran Act of 1945, which permitted the states to continue to regulate insurance.

71. Hood & Sons v. Du Mond, 336 U.S. 525, 535 (1949); 53 U.S. at 318.

72. Archibald Cox characterized what Curtis did as an "invention built upon the bare words of the Framers." Cox, *Court and the Constitution*, 91.

73. 46 U.S. at 579 (Taney, C.J.); U.S. Constitution, art. 1, sec. 10.

74. *The Federalist* no. 32; 22 U.S. at 10 (Webster); Sturges v. Crowninshield, 17 U.S. (4 Wheat.) 122, 193 (1819).

75. 53 U.S. at 319, 318.

76. Ibid., 319; Tyler Pipe Industries v. Washington State Department of Revenue, 483 U.S. 232, 262 (1987) (Scalia, J., concurring in part and dissenting in part);

see also Currie, *Constitution in the Supreme Court*, 232; Martin H. Redish and Shane V. Nugent, "The Dormant Commerce Clause and the Constitutional Balance of Federalism," *Duke Law Journal*, 1987, no. 4:582.

77. Charles L. Black Jr., *Structure and Relationship in Constitutional Law* (Baton Rouge, La., 1969), 21, 20. For further discussion of structural argument, see Bobbit, *Constitutional Fate*, 74; Vince Blasi, "Creativity and Legitimacy in Constitutional Law," *Yale Law Journal* 80 (1970): 176–84; Epstein, "Proper Scope of the Commerce Power," 1409; Martin H. Redish, *The Constitution as Political Structure* (New York, 1995), 85–86.

78. 53 U.S. at 319; U.S. Constitution, art. 1, sec. 8.

79. *The Federalist* no. 32.

80. 53 U.S. at 319.

81. Ibid., 313.

82. *Memoir of Curtis* 1:303. He also tied the constitutional analysis to the privileges and immunities clause. U.S. Constitution, art. 4, sec. 2.

83. *Memorial of Daniel Webster*, 475.

84. Rogers v. Cincinnati, 20 F. Cas. 1111 (C.C.D. Ohio 1852) (No. 12,008); Cushing v. Owners of the John Fraser, 62 U.S. (21 How.) 184 (1859).

85. Gilman v. Philadelphia, 70 U.S. (3 Wall.) 713, 727 (1866); Ex parte McNiel, 80 U.S. (13 Wall.) 236, 240 (1872); Hinson v. Lott, 75 U.S. (8 Wall.) 148, 152 (1869).

86. Case of the State Freight Tax, 82 U.S. (15 Wall.) 232, 279–80 (1873); Crandall v. Nevada, 73 U.S. (6 Wall.) 35, 42 (1868); County of Mobile v. Kimball, 102 U.S. 691, 701 (1880); Philadelphia and Southern Steamship Co. v. Pennsylvania, 122 U.S. 326, 339 (1887).

87. 82 U.S. at 280; 122 U.S. at 339; Welton v. Missouri, 91 U.S. 275, 280 (1876); Wabash, St. Louis and Pacific Railway Co. v. Illinois, 118 U.S. 557, 577 (1886).

88. Charles W. McCurdy, "American Law and the Marketing Structure of the Large Corporation, 1875–1890," *Journal of Economic History* 38 (1978): 636; 91 U.S. at 280–81; Smith v. Alabama, 124 U.S. 465 (1888).

89. Di Santo v. Pennsylvania, 273 U.S. 34, 44 (1927) (Stone, J., dissenting); 325 U.S. at 770, 771.

90. Hall v. DeCuir, 95 U.S. 485 (1878); Morgan v. Virginia, 328 U.S. 373, 386 (1946); Bob-Lo Excursion Co. v. Michigan, 333 U.S. 28, 40 (1948).

91. Collins v. New Hampshire, 171 U.S. 30 (1898); Maine v. Taylor, 477 U.S. 131 (1986); Bibb v. Navajo Freight Lines, 359 U.S. 520 (1959); Reid v. Colorado, 187 U.S. 137 (1902).

92. Philadelphia v. New Jersey, 437 U.S. 617 (1978); Hunt v. Washington State Apple Advertising Commission, 432 U.S. 333 (1977); Pike v. Bruce Church, 397 U.S. 137, 142 (1970); Gunther and Sullivan, *Constitutional Law*, 268; Tribe, *American Constitutional Law* 1:1048–49.

93. Recent decisions limiting Congress's commerce powers have invoked a "distinction between what is truly national and what is truly local." United States v. Lopez, 514 U.S. 549, 567–68 (1995). For further discussion, see Tribe, *American Constitutional Law* 1:1050.

94. Oliver Wendell Holmes, *Collected Legal Papers* (New York, 1920), 295–96.

4. THE PROMISE OF DUE PROCESS

1. McCloskey, *American Supreme Court*, 124.
2. Murray's Lessee v. Hoboken Land and Improvement Co., 59 U.S. (18 How.) 272 (1856); Akhil Reed Amar, *The Bill of Rights: Creation and Reconstruction* (New Haven, 1998), 173.
3. In full, chap. 39 stated: "No free man shall be taken, imprisoned, disseised, outlawed, banished, or in any way destroyed, nor will We proceed against or prosecute him, except by the lawful judgment of his peers and by the law of the land." A. E. Dick Howard, *Magna Carta: Text and Commentary* (Charlottesville, Va., 1964), 43. For another version, see Carl Stephenson and Frederick George Marcham, ed. and trans., *Sources of English Constitutional History: A Selection of Documents from 600 A.D. to the Present* (New York, 1937), 121. See generally A. E. Dick Howard, *The Road from Runnymede: Magna Carta and Constitutionalism in America* (Charlottesville, Va., 1968).
4. Sir Edward Coke, *The Second Part of the Institutes of the Lawes of England* (1642; reprint, New York, 1979), 50. The phrase "due process of law" appeared in a statute providing "That no man of what Estate or Condition that he be, shall be put out of land or Tenement, nor taken, nor imprisoned, nor disinherited, nor put to death, without being brought in answer by due process of law." 28 Ed. III, ca. 3 (1354).
5. Raoul Berger, "'Law of the Land' Reconsidered," *Northwestern University Law Review* 74 (1979): 2; Edward S. Corwin, "The Doctrine of Due Process of Law before the Civil War," pt. 1, *Harvard Law Review* 24 (1911): 368; James Kent, *Commentaries on American Law*, 5th ed. (New York, 1844), 2:12; Story, *Commentaries on the Constitution* 3:661; Dartmouth College v. Woodward, 17 U.S. (4 Wheat.) 518, 581 (1819) (Webster).
6. 59 U.S. at 276; Neil H. Cogan, ed., *The Complete Bill of Rights: The Drafts, Debates, Sources, and Origins* (New York, 1997), 356; *Annals of Congress*, 1st Cong., 1st sess., 434.
7. Cogan, *Complete Bill of Rights*, 348.
8. 59 U.S. at 276.
9. Ibid.
10. Scott v. Sandford, 60 U.S. (19 How.) 393, 626 (1857) (Curtis, J., dissenting); *Address Delivered at the Centennial Celebration*, 6–7.
11. Greene v. Briggs, 10 F. Cas. 1135, 1140 (C.C.D. R.I. 1852) (No. 5,764).
12. Ibid.; Curtis to Ticknor, 14 Jan. 1853, Curtis Papers, DLC.
13. *New York Tribune*, 17 Mar. 1853; see also ibid., 11 Feb. 1853.
14. Ibid., 1, 8 Jan. 1853; Curtis to Ticknor, 14 Jan. 1853, Curtis Papers, DLC. Curtis said that the criticism revealed "the position which the judiciary hold in the country, that in the same year I have been accused of trenching on the right of trial by jury, & of extending it too far." Curtis to Clifford, 17 Jan. 1853, John H. Clifford Papers, MHS. The Rhode Island legislature adopted a new statute, but the state's supreme court declared it unconstitutional. State v. Snow, 3 R.I. 64 (1854). Justice Curtis agreed with its judgment. Greene v. James, 10 F. Cas. 1151, 1152 (C.C.D. R.I. 1854) (No. 5,766); see also *New York Tribune*, 26 Feb. 1853.

Eventually the state supreme court upheld temperance measures against constitutional attack. State v. Keeran, 5 R.I. 497 (1858); State v. Paul, 5 R.I. 185 (1858).

15. 59 U.S. at 276; Currie, *Constitution in the Supreme Court*, 279.

16. Berger, "'Law of the Land' Reconsidered," 4.

17. Dartmouth College v. Woodward, 1 N.H. 111, 130 (1817), rev'd, 17 U.S. (4 Wheat.) 518 (1819); Mayo v. Wilson, 1 N.H. 53, 57 (1817). This point was also made by counsel, but rejected by the court, in Trustees of the University of North Carolina v. Foy, 5 N.C. (1 Mur.) 58, 87–88 (1805). See Berger, "'Law of the Land' Reconsidered," 23.

18. *The Papers of Alexander Hamilton*, ed. Harold C. Syrett and Jacob E. Cooke, 4 (New York, 1962): 35; Douglas Laycock, "Due Process and Separation of Powers: The Effort to Make the Due Process Clauses Nonjusticiable," *Texas Law Review* 60 (1982): 890–92. Cf. Frank H. Easterbrook, "Substance and Due Process," *Supreme Court Review*, 1982: 98–99 (Hamilton's conception of due process was restricted to judicial proceedings).

19. 17 U.S. at 518; Thomas M. Cooley, *A Treatise on the Constitutional Limitations Which Rest upon the Legislative Power of the States of the American Union*, 8th ed. (Boston, 1927), 2:736.

20. 17 U.S. at 581, 581–82 (Webster); ibid., 705 (Story, J.).

21. U.S. Constitution, art. 1, sec. 10.

22. Hoke v. Henderson, 15 N.C. (4 Dev.) 1, 12 (1834); Kent, *Commentaries on American Law* 2:12; Taylor v. Porter, 4 Hill 140, 145–46 (N.Y. 1843). For further details, see Corwin, "Due Process of Law before the Civil War," pts. 1 and 2, 367–85, 460–79.

23. 10 F. Cas. at 1140.

24. Thomas C. Grey, "Do We Have an Unwritten Constitution?" *Stanford Law Review* 27 (1975): 716; Edward S. Corwin, "The 'Higher Law' Background of American Constitutional Law," pts. 1 and 2, *Harvard Law Review* 42:2 (1928): 149–85, 42:3 (1929): 365–409.

25. Calder v. Bull, 3 U.S. (3 Dall.) 386, 388, 399 (1798). On Chase's position, see John Hart Ely, "Foreword: On Using Fundamental Values," *Harvard Law Review* 92 (1978): 26–27.

26. Wilkinson v. Leland, 27 U.S. (2 Pet.) 627, 647 (1829) (Webster); 4 Hill at 145. On the A-to-B line of thought, see John V. Orth, *Due Process of Law: A Brief History* (Lawrence, Kans., 2003).

27. 27 U.S. at 646, 657.

28. Marshall also noted the ex post facto clause, even though *Calder v. Bull* had limited that provision to criminal matters. Fletcher v. Peck, 10 U.S. (6 Cranch) 87, 139 (1810).

29. Leonard W. Levy, *Original Intent and the Framers' Constitution* (New York, 1988), 124–36; Benjamin Fletcher Wright Jr., *The Contract Clause of the Constitution* (Cambridge, Mass., 1938), 4–16, 27–61.

30. Charles River Bridge v. Warren Bridge, 36 U.S. (11 Pet.) 420 (1837).

31. Richmond, Fredericksburg, and Potomac Railroad Co. v. Louisa Railroad Co. 54 U.S (13 How.) 71, 86 (1852) (Curtis, J., dissenting).

32. Curran v. Arkansas, 56 U.S. (15 How.) 304 (1854); Piqua Branch of the State Bank of Ohio v. Knoop, 57 U.S. (16 How.) 369 (1854); Ohio Life Insurance and Trust Co. v. DeBolt, 57 U.S. (16 How.) 416 (1854). Curtis continued to find opportunities to apply the contracts clause after he left the Court. Chief Justice Chase appointed him to arbitrate rights granted by the New York legislature to lay telegraphic cable from New York to France. Curtis concluded that New York State could not revoke that right without violating the contracts clause. *Memoir* 1 : 313.

33. 59 U.S. at 276.

34. Ibid., 277.

35. John Hart Ely, *Democracy and Distrust: A Theory of Judicial Review* (Cambridge, Mass., 1980), 194; Sanford H. Kadish, "Methodology and Criteria in Due Process Adjudication—A Survey and Criticism," *Yale Law Journal* 66 (1957): 322; Grey, "Do We Have an Unwritten Constitution?" 710; Howard, *Road from Runnymede*, 351; Donald A. Dripps, "The Constitutional Status of the Reasonable Doubt Rule," *California Law Review* 75 (1987): 1681; Corwin, "Due Process of Law before the Civil War," pt. 2, 476; Hannis Taylor, *Due Process of Law and the Equal Protection of the Laws . . .* (Chicago, 1917), 202.

36. 59 U.S. at 280.

37. Ibid.; Story, *Commentaries on the Constitution* 3 : 661. Judge Ruffin had described the law of the land clause in similar terms, providing for "the course, mode and usages of the common law as derived from our forefathers." 15 N.C. at 13; see also Westervelt v. Gregg, 12 N.Y. 202, 209 (1855) (Edwards, J.).

38. Dripps, "Reasonable Doubt Rule," 1681.

39. For another view on Curtis's test, see Rodney L. Mott, *Due Process of Law . . .* (Indianapolis, 1926), 241–45.

40. Ibid., 277, 280, 285.

41. Barron v. Baltimore, 32 U.S. (7 Pet.) 243 (1833); Adamson v. California, 332 U.S. 46, 68–123 (1947) (Black, J., dissenting); Palko v. Connecticut, 302 U.S. 319, 325 (1937); Miranda v. Arizona, 384 U.S. 436 (1966); Gideon v. Wainwright, 372 U.S. 335 (1963).

42. Holden v. Hardy, 169 U.S. 366, 390 (1898).

43. *Landmark Briefs and Arguments of the Supreme Court of the United States: Constitutional Law*, ed. Philip B. Kurland and Gerhard Casper, 8 (Arlington, Va., 1975): 425–26; Hurtado v. California, 110 U.S. 516, 528, 542 (1884).

44. Twining v. New Jersey, 211 U.S. 78, 102, 106 (1908). See also Maxwell v. Dow, 176 U.S. 581 (1900) (upholding state trial by jury of eight persons).

45. Powell v. Alabama, 287 U.S. 45, 65 (1932).

46. Duncan v. Louisiana, 391 U.S. 141, 150 (1968).

47. For example, Lochner v. New York, 198 U.S. 45 (1905); Roe v. Wade, 410 U.S. 113 (1973). For analysis of the interpretive questions, see John Harrison, "Substantive Due Process and the Constitutional Text," *Virginia Law Review* 83 (1997): 493–558.

48. Cf., for example, Robert E. Riggs, "Substantive Due Process in 1791," *Wisconsin Law Review*, 1990, no. 4:941–1005.

49. 60 U.S. at 450; Wynehamer v. People, 13 N.Y. 378 (1856). For a sampling of commentary, see Ely, *Democracy and Distrust*, 14–18; Wallace Mendelson,

"A Missing Link in the Evolution of Due Process," *Vanderbilt Law Review* 10 (1956): 125–37; Corwin, "Due Process of Law before the Civil War," pts. 1 and 2, 367–85, 460–79.

50. Wiecek, *Antislavery Constitutionalism*, 190, 255, 265; tenBroeck, *Equal under Law*, 119–22; Howard Jay Graham, "Procedure to Substance—Extra-Judicial Rise of Due Process, 1830–1860," *California Law Review* 40 (1952): 483–500.

51. Slaughterhouse Cases, 83 U.S. (16 Wall.) 36, 56, 81 (1873); Munn v. Illinois, 94 U.S. 113, 125 (1877); Chicago, Milwaukee and St. Paul Railway Co. v. Minnesota, 134 U.S. 418, 458 (1890).

52. Allgeyer v. Louisiana, 165 U.S. 578, 589 (1897); Foner, *Free Soil*, ix–xxxix, 11–39. Liberty of contract was given further impetus by Justice Field's judicial opinions and Thomas Cooley's *Constitutional Limitations*.

53. 198 U.S. 45 (1905); Adair v. United States, 208 U.S. 161 (1908); Coppage v. Kansas, 236 U.S. 1 (1915); Adkins v. Children's Hospital, 261 U.S. 525 (1923); Morehead v. New York ex rel. Tipaldo, 298 U.S. 587 (1936). See also Howard Gillman, *The Constitution Besieged: The Rise and Demise of Lochner Era Police Powers Jurisprudence* (Durham, N.C., 1993).

54. Charles A. Miller, "The Forest of Due Process of Law: The American Constitutional Tradition," in *Due Process*, ed. J. Roland Pennock and John W. Chapman (New York, 1977), 13, 15; Leach, "Benjamin R. Curtis," 356.

55. Hyman and Wiecek, *Equal Justice under Law*, 187, 188; see also William M. Wiecek, *Liberty under Law: The Supreme Court in American Life* (Baltimore, 1988), 70. Thomas C. Mackey detected an "ambiguous hint" of substantive doctrine in Curtis's opinion. *The Oxford Companion to the Supreme Court of the United States*, s.v. "Murray's Lessee v. Hoboken Land & Improvement Co."

56. 60 U.S. at 450; Edward S. Corwin, "The Dred Scott Case in Light of Contemporary Legal Doctrines," in *Corwin on the Constitution* 2:307; see also Miller, "Forest of Due Process of Law," 15. Taney had made a similar statement about the due process clause in a patent case, *Bloomer v. McQuewan*, 55 U.S. (14 How.) 539, 553 (1853).

57. 60 U.S. at 624–25 (Curtis, J., dissenting).

58. The next time the Supreme Court construed due process substantively was in *Hepburn v. Griswold* (1870), one of the *Legal Tender Cases*. In a decision overruled one year later, the *Hepburn* Court invalidated wartime statutes that had made paper money an acceptable payment for debts. As this legislation had the effect of diminishing the value of creditors' preexisting contracts, the Court construed it as a taking of property without due process. Hepburn v. Griswold, 75 U.S. 603, 624 (1870). Curtis happened to be one of the lawyers who appeared before the Supreme Court arguing in support of the Legal Tender Acts. He pressed the point that these statutes were within Congress's implied powers. He kept clear of the due process clause, even though opposing counsel had alluded to this provision. Brief for the Complainant, Willard v. Tayloe; Clarkson N. Potter, Argument, 41, Hepburn v. Griswold, File Copies of Briefs, U.S. Supreme Court, vol. 1, Dec. Term 1868. Henry Adams, who observed the oral argument, reported that Curtis seemed "to dread and shun" any question going beyond that

of implied powers. [Henry Adams], "The Argument in the Legal Tender Cases," *Nation,* 17 Dec. 1868.

59. Curtis, Opinion: Wisconsin Railroad Act—"Potter Law," 10 Apr. 1874, Opinion: Iowa Railroad Act, 30 June 1874, Opinions of Benjamin R. Curtis, 3:444–51, 452–58, Harvard Law School MS 2065; excerpts from Curtis's opinion on the Potter Act reprinted in "The Wisconsin Railroad Acts," *American Law Review* 9 (1875): 50–73. See also George H. Miller, *Railroads and the Granger Laws* (Madison, Wis., 1971); Robert S. Hunt, *Law and Locomotives: The Impact of the Railroad on Wisconsin Law in the Nineteenth Century* (Madison, Wis., 1958); Charles Fairman, "The So-called Granger Cases, Lord Hale, and Justice Bradley," *Stanford Law Review* 5 (1953): 607.

60. Charles Fairman, *Mr. Justice Miller and the Supreme Court, 1862–1890* (Cambridge, Mass., 1939), 199.

61. See Santa Clara County v. Southern Pacific Railroad Co., 118 U.S. 394, 396 (1886).

62. Opinions of Benjamin R. Curtis, 3:446, 452, Harvard Law School MS 2065.

63. Friedman, *American Law,* 392; Peik v. Chicago and North-western Railway Co., 94 U.S. 164 (1877); Opinions of Benjamin R. Curtis, 3:450, Harvard Law School MS 2065.

64. Opinions of Benjamin R. Curtis, 3:453, 458, Harvard Law School MS 2065. As it turned out, determining reasonableness raised a more complex set of legal and economic questions than Curtis anticipated, as shown by the Supreme Court's subsequent attempts, eventually abandoned, to review public utility rates. Smyth v. Ames, 169 U.S. 466 (1890); Federal Power Commission v. Hope Natural Gas Co., 320 U.S. 591 (1944).

65. Argument in United States v. Union Pacific Railroad Co., in *Memoir* 2:431.

66. Charles Fairman, *Reconstruction and Reunion, 1864–88,* pt. 2 (New York, 1987), 598–602.

67. Wally's Heirs v. Kennedy, 10 Tenn. (2 Yer.) 554, 555 (1831); 17 U.S. at 581; Bank of the State v. Cooper, 10 Tenn. (2 Yer.) 599, 606 (1831); Cooley, *Constitutional Limitations* 2:845. See also Gillman, *Constitution Besieged,* 49–60; Michael Les Benedict, "Laissez-Faire and Liberty: A Re-Evaluation of the Meaning and Origins of Laissez-Faire Constitutionalism," *Law and History Review* 85 (1985): 314; Howard, *Road from Runnymede,* 307–15; David M. Gold, *The Shaping of Nineteenth-Century Law: John Appleton and Responsible Individualism* (Westport, Conn., 1990), 137–53.

68. The New York courts had previously applied the idea of equality under law through that state's due process guarantee. 12 N.Y. at 212.

69. *Memoir* 2:426, 427.

70. Ibid., 427.

71. United States v. Union Pacific Railroad Co., 28 F. Cas. 333, 335 (C.C.D. Conn. 1873) (No. 16,598); United States v. Union Pacific Railroad Co., 98 U.S. 569, 589–91 (1878).

72. Bolling v. Sharpe, 347 U.S. 497, 499–500 (1954).

73. McCloskey, *American Supreme Court,* 124.

74. 59 U.S. at 276.

75. Adamson v. California, 332 U.S. 46, 68 (1947) (Black, J., dissenting). Justice Black was not referring to Curtis's position.

5. THE *DRED SCOTT* CASE

1. Scott v. Sandford, 60 U.S. (19 How.) 393, 400, 407 (1857). Whether Taney's views actually commanded a majority has been called into question. In their contemporary review of the case, Horace Gray and John Lowell wrote that Taney "speaks only for himself and Mr. Justice Wayne, and that each of the other justices defines his own position." [Horace Gray and John Lowell], "The Case of Dred Scott," *Monthly Law Reporter* 20 (1857): 67. On the other hand, Don Fehrenbacher, the leading authority on the case, concluded that "none of the major rulings in Taney's opinion can be pushed aside as unauthoritative." Don E. Fehrenbacher, *The Dred Scott Case: Its Significance in American Law and Politics* (New York, 1978), 333.
2. "All persons born or naturalized in the United States and subject to the jurisdiction thereof, are citizens of the United States and of the State wherein they reside." U.S. Constitution, amend. 14, sec. 1.
3. Marbury v. Madison, 5 U.S. (1 Cranch) 137 (1803).
4. 60 U.S. at 582, 589 (Curtis, J., dissenting).
5. *Memoir* 1:354; *CWAL* 2:403; *New York Tribune,* 10 Mar. 1857; *Washington Union,* 17 Mar. 1857.
6. Along with some other slave states, Missouri expressly permitted freedom suits by slaves. Act of 27 Jan. 1835, *Missouri Revised Statutes* 284–86 (3d ed. 1841).
7. Scott v. Emerson, 15 Mo. 576, 583–87 (1852). On the background of these proceedings, see Walter Ehrlich, *They Have No Rights: Dred Scott's Struggle for Freedom* (Westport, Conn., 1979); Vincent C. Hopkins, *Dred Scott's Case* (New York, 1951); Swisher, *Taney Period,* 599–623; Lea VanderVelde and Sandhya Subramanian, "Mrs. Dred Scott," *Yale Law Journal* 106 (1997): 1050–90.
8. Fehrenbacher, *Dred Scott Case,* 256, 270–76; U.S. Constitution, art. 3, sec. 2.
9. Scott v. Sandford, Transcripts of Records, U.S. Supreme Court, Dec. Term 1856, 1:3, 5–6; John D. Lawson, ed., *American State Trials* 13 (reprint, Wilmington, Del., 1972): 252; Fehrenbacher, *Dred Scott Case,* 279.
10. Campbell to Samuel Tyler, 24 Nov. 1870, in Samuel Tyler, *Memoir of Roger Brooke Taney, LL.D., Chief Justice of the Supreme Court of the United States,* 2d ed., rev. and enl. (Baltimore, 1876), 382–84; Nelson to Tyler, 13 May 1871, *Memoir of Roger Brooke Taney,* 385; 87 U.S. (20 Wall.) x–xi (1875); Supreme Court Minutes, 12 May 1856, RG 267, National Archives; Fehrenbacher, *Dred Scott Case,* 148–51, 169–71, 176; Curtis to Ticknor, 8 Apr. 1856, *Memoir* 1:180.
11. Nelson to Tyler, 13 May 1871, *Memoir of Roger Brooke Taney,* 385.
12. Campbell to Tyler, 24 Nov. 1870, ibid., 382–84; Catron to Buchanan, 19 Feb. 1857, in Philip Auchampaugh, "James Buchanan, the Court, and the *Dred Scott* Case," *Tennessee Historical Magazine* 9 (1926): 236; Grier to Buchanan, 23 Feb. 1857, James Buchanan Papers, Historical Society of Pennsylvania; Paul Finkelman, "What Did the *Dred Scott* Case Really Decide?" *Reviews in American*

History 7 (1979): 373–74; Fehrenbacher, *Dred Scott Case*, 305–11; Clement Hugh Hill to George Ticknor Curtis, 5 Aug. 1878, *Memoir* 1:234–35.

13. For example, U.S. Constitution, art. 4, sec. 2 (privileges and immunities), and art. 2, sec. 1 (qualifications for president).

14. Louisville, Cincinnati, and Charleston Rail-road Co. v. Letson, 43 U.S. 497 (1844) (corporations are citizens for diversity jurisdiction); Bank of Augusta v. Earle, 38 U.S. 519 (1839) (corporations are not citizens under the privileges and immunities clause).

15. Curtis to Taney, 13 May 1857, *Memoir* 1:219; handwritten note by Curtis, "Some observations on the above correspondence," Curtis Papers, DLC.

16. U.S. Constitution, art. 4, sec. 2. For various interpretations of citizenship in the antebellum period, see Rogers M. Smith, *Civic Ideals: Conflicting Visions of Citizenship in U.S. History* (New Haven, 1997), 165–271; Anne Norton, *Alternative Americas: A Reading of Antebellum Political Culture* (Chicago, 1986), 232–34; Kenneth L. Karst, *Belonging to America: Equal Citizenship and the Constitution* (New Haven, 1989), 34–35, 45–49; James H. Kettner, *The Development of American Citizenship, 1608–1870* (Chapel Hill, N.C., 1978), 287–333.

17. 60 U.S. at 403. For a contrarian account, see Mark A. Graber, "Desperately Ducking Slavery: *Dred Scott* and Contemporary Constitutional Theory," *Constitutional Commentary* 14 (1997): 294–302.

18. 60 U.S. at 404, 404–5, 407, 409.

19. Ibid., 410, 411.

20. Fehrenbacher, *Dred Scott Case*, 355; 60 U.S. at 423, 404, 403, 411–12, 405, 409. A year after the decision, Taney issued a supplementary opinion which made clear his position that blacks whose ancestors were not slaves were excluded as much as those descended from slaves. "Supplement to the *Dred Scott* Opinion," in Tyler, *Memoir of Roger Brooke Taney*, 579.

21. 60 U.S. at 422.

22. Ibid., 426; Wiecek, *Antislavery Constitutionalism*, 228–48.

23. 60 U.S. at 572.

24. Ibid., 573.

25. Ibid., 574. These state constitutions are reprinted in Thorpe, *Federal and State Constitutions* 3:1888–1923 (Massachusetts), 4:2451–73 (New Hampshire), 5:2594–98 (New Jersey), 2623–38 (New York).

26. U.S. Constitution, art. 2, sec. 1; 60 U.S. at 572, 576.

27. 60 U.S. at 576, 582.

28. Tiffany, *Unconstitutionality of American Slavery*, 88–94; *CWAL* 2:403; *New York Tribune*, 10 Mar. 1857; [Timothy Farrar], "The *Dred Scott* Case," *North American Review* 85 (1857): 404; [Gray and Lowell], "Case of Dred Scott," 73; see also [W. A. Learned], "Negro Citizenship," *New Englander* 15 (1857): 484; "Opinions of the Justices of the Supreme Judicial Court, on Question Propounded by the Senate, March 26, 1857," 44 Me. 505, 510–14, 545, 559 (1857).

29. 60 U.S. at 575; Fehrenbacher, *Dred Scott Case*, 66.

30. 60 U.S. at 577–82.

31. Ibid., 531 (McLean, J., dissenting).

32. Ibid., 573–74, 577.

33. Ibid., 583.
34. Livingston v. Van Ingen, 9 Johns. Repts. 507 (N.Y. 1812); 60 U.S. at 584.
35. Fehrenbacher, *Dred Scott Case*, 407; Robert Meister, "The Logic and Legacy of *Dred Scott:* Marshall, Taney, and the Sublimation of Republican Thought," *Studies in American Political Development* 3 (1989): 238; Earl M. Maltz, "The Unlikely Hero of *Dred Scott:* Benjamin Robbins Curtis and the Constitutional Law of Slavery," *Cardozo Law Review* 17 (1996): 2009; see also Wayne D. Moore, *Constitutional Rights and Powers of the People* (Princeton, N.J., 1996), 25; Smith, *Civic Ideals*, 271.
36. U.S. Constitution, art. 2, sec. 1; Scott v. Sandford, Transcripts of Records, U.S. Supreme Court, Dec. Term 1856, 1:5; 60 U.S. at 587. See also McLean's discussion, ibid., 533.
37. 60 U.S. at 574.
38. Cobb, *Law of Negro Slavery*, 27–37; Eric Foner, "The Meaning of Freedom in the Age of Emancipation," *Journal of American History* 81 (1994): 447.
39. Pendleton v. State, 6 Ark. 509, 512 (1844); 60 U.S. at 582.
40. 60 U.S. at 410, 574–75.
41. Ibid., 583.
42. Herman Belz, *Reconstructing the Union: Theory and Policy during the Civil War* (Ithaca, N.Y., 1969), 296.
43. 60 U.S. at 581.
44. *Stats. at Large of USA* 1 (1845): 78; Civil Rights Act of 1866, ibid., 14 (1868): 27; Hyman and Wiecek, *Equal Justice under Law*, 395–96; Foner, "Meaning of Freedom," 446.
45. Corfield v. Coryell, 6 F. Cas. 546, 551 (C.C.E.D. Pa. 1823) (No. 3,230). Interestingly, while Justice Washington in *Corfield* had decided that the right to gather oysters was not protected by the privileges and immunities clause, Justice Curtis left that question open in *Smith v. Maryland*, 59 U.S. (18 How.) 71, 75 (1855).
46. 60 U.S. at 417.
47. Conner v. Elliott, 59 U.S. (18 How.) 591, 593 (1856).
48. 60 U.S. at 584.
49. Ibid., 588.
50. The petition Curtis signed in 1843, discussed in chap. 3, may be useful to consider. This petition solicited Congress to take action against the black seamen acts of southern states, specifically requesting that Congress "render effectual in their behalf the privileges of citizenship secured by the constitution." This phrasing is ambiguous on the issue of citizenship. It is possible to interpret its reference to the privileges of Boston shipowners rather than free black sailors. House Committee on Commerce, *Free Colored Seamen—Majority and Minority Reports*, 27th Cong., 3d sess., 1843, Rept. 80, 7–9.
51. *CWAL* 2:406.
52. *Memoir* 1:343; *CWAL* 3:18; Sumner quoted in David Herbert Donald, *Liberty and Union* (Boston, 1978), 58.
53. Foner, *Free Soil*, 116, 311–12; Donald, *Liberty and Union*, 57–58.
54. Act of March 6, 1820, *Stats. at Large of USA* 3 (1861): 548. For accounts of the congressional debates, see Fehrenbacher, *Dred Scott Case*, 101–15; Glover

Moore, *The Missouri Controversy, 1819–1821* (Lexington, Ky., 1953), 99–118.

55. Potter, *Impending Crisis*, 20–23.

56. McPherson, *Battle Cry of Freedom*, 103–16; Act of May 30, 1854, *Stats. at Large of USA* 10 (1855): 283; Nevins, *Ordeal of the Union* 2:408–11, 434–37, 471–86.

57. Kirk H. Porter and Donald Bruce Johnson, comps., *National Party Platforms, 1840–1956* (Urbana, Ill., 1956), 27; Fehrenbacher, *Dred Scott Case*, 195–96.

58. *CG*, 29th Cong., 2d sess., 1847, 17:455; Arthur Bestor, "State Sovereignty and Slavery: A Reinterpretation of Proslavery Constitutional Doctrine, 1846–1860," *Journal of the Illinois State Historical Society* 54 (1961): 147–72.

59. Donald, *Liberty and Union*, 61; McPherson, *Battle Cry of Freedom*, 124. On the policies regarding the territories, see Arthur Bestor, "The American Civil War as a Constitutional Crisis," in *American Law and the Constitutional Order*, ed. Lawrence M. Friedman and Harry N. Scheiber, enl. ed. (Cambridge, Mass., 1988), 219–34; Robert R. Russell, "Constitutional Doctrines with Regard to Slavery in Territories," *Journal of Southern History* 32 (1966): 466–86.

60. Fehrenbacher, *Dred Scott Case*, 185–86.

61. Hyman and Wiecek, *Equal Justice under Law*, 184; McPherson, *Battle Cry of Freedom*, 175.

62. U.S. Constitution, art. 4, sec. 3; 60 U.S. at 447, 436–37, 440.

63. U.S. Constitution, art. 4, sec. 3; 60 U.S. at 448.

64. 60 U.S. at 434, 439.

65. Ibid., 450.

66. *CWAL* 3:230; 60 U.S. at 451, 452.

67. 60 U.S. at 588–90, 427–30.

68. Curtis argued that the Court must stick to the points raised by the plea in abatement. Taney insisted that it was proper to examine the record, namely Dred Scott's bill of exceptions (a post-trial statement listing objections to the trial judge's rulings), in which Scott admitted that he had been a slave but claimed freedom by residence on free soil. Ibid., 589–90, 427. These arguments are examined in Corwin, "*Dred Scott* Decision," in *Corwin on the Constitution* 2:302; Fehrenbacher, *Dred Scott Case*, 365–66.

69. 60 U.S. at 589, 590.

70. Potter, *Impending Crisis*, 281; 60 U.S. at 549–50. The *New York Tribune*, 11 Mar. 1857, reported that Curtis was "more pointed and emphatic on this point."

71. *New York Tribune*, 10 Mar. 1857; [Thomas Hart Benton], *Historical and Legal Examination of . . . the* Dred Scott *Case* (New York, 1857), 8; *New Orleans Picayune*, 20 Mar. 1857; Fehrenbacher, *Dred Scott Case*, 439. See, for example, Senator Seward's remarks at *CG*, 35th Cong., 1st sess., 1858, 27, pt. 1:941.

72. Keith E. Whittington, "The Road Not Taken: *Dred Scott*, Judicial Authority, and Political Questions," *Journal of Politics* 63 (2001): 387; Robert H. Bork, *The Tempting of America: The Political Seduction of the Law* (New York, 1990), 33.

73. 60 U.S. at 614, 608.

74. Ibid., 608, 613.

75. Bobbit, *Constitutional Fate*, 74; 60 U.S. at 611.
76. 60 U.S. at 615, 610, 606–7.
77. Ibid., 610; *CWAL* 4:267.
78. 60 U.S. at 614–15.
79. Ibid., 617.
80. McCulloch v. Maryland, 17 U.S. (4 Wheat.) 316 (1819); R. Kent Newmyer, "John Marshall and the Southern Constitutional Tradition," in *An Uncertain Tradition: Constitutionalism and the History of the South*, ed. Kermit L. Hall and James W. Ely Jr. (Athens, Ga., 1988), 105–24; Gerald Gunther, ed., *John Marshall's Defense of* McCulloch v. Maryland (Stanford, Calif., 1969).
81. 17 U.S. at 421, 405, 419, 423, 422; U.S. Constitution, art. 1, sec. 8. In *Dred Scott*, Justice McLean and Scott's counsel noted *McCulloch* in passing. 60 U.S. at 542, argument of Montgomery Blair for Plaintiff in Error, File Copies of Briefs, U.S. Supreme Court, vol. 1, Dec. Term 1856, 31.
82. 60 U.S. at 627, 624, 625; Wiecek, *Antislavery Constitutionalism*, 219.
83. 60 U.S. at 451.
84. Ibid., 591; Scott v. Emerson, 15 Mo. at 584–86; Strader v. Graham, 51 U.S. (10 How.) 82 (1850).
85. 60 U.S. at 594.
86. Ibid., 599–601.
87. Ibid., 620–21; Bork, *Tempting of America*, 33; Currie, *Constitution in the Supreme Court*, 273; Whittington, "Road Not Taken," 384.
88. 60 U.S. at 621.
89. Ibid., 620.
90. Ibid., 624, 620.
91. Maltz, "Unlikely Hero of *Dred Scott*," 2006; Kenneth M. Stampp, "Comment on Earl Maltz," *Cardozo Law Review* 17 (1996): 2019.
92. McPherson, *Battle Cry of Freedom*, 144.
93. Badger to Curtis, 8 March 1857, Curtis Papers, DLC; Curtis to Buchanan, 1 Sept. 1857, *Memoir* 1:249–50. See generally David N. Atkinson, *Leaving the Bench: Supreme Court Justices at the End* (Lawrence, Kans., 1999).
94. *Memoir* 1:211; McLean to Montgomery Blair, 30 Mar. 1857, Blair Family Papers, DLC.
95. Carroll to Curtis, 6 Apr. 1857 (copy), Taney to Carroll, 6 Apr. 1857 (copy), Curtis Papers, DLC.
96. Handwritten notes by Curtis, 9 and 18 Apr. 1857, ibid.
97. Taney to Curtis, 28 Apr. 1857, to Carroll, 6 Apr. 1857 (copy), ibid.
98. Taney to Curtis, 28 Apr. 1857, ibid.
99. Curtis to Taney, 13 May 1857, *Memoir* 1:218, 219, 220.
100. Taney to Curtis, 11 June 1857, Curtis Papers, DLC.
101. Curtis to Taney, 16 June 1857, ibid.
102. Taney to David M. Perine, 16 June 1857, Perine Family Papers, 1783–1941, MS 645, H. Furlong Baldwin Library, Maryland Historical Society, Baltimore; handwritten note by Curtis, "Some observations on the above correspondence," Curtis Papers, DLC; Supreme Court Records, Opinions in Appellate Cases, box 52, RG 267, National Archives.

103. See Richard H. Leach, "Justice Curtis and the *Dred Scott* Case," *Essex Institute Historical Collections* 94 (1958): 55; Fehrenbacher, *Dred Scott Case*, 318; *Memoir* 1:243, 244. Some historians have accepted this explanation. For example, Warren, *Supreme Court in United States History* 2:320. F. H. Hodder suggested that Curtis wrote his opinion to curry favor in Boston before returning to practice law there. F. H. Hodder, "Some Phases of the *Dred Scott* Case," *Mississippi Valley Historical Review* 16 (1929): 14–15.

104. Curtis to Ticknor, 3 July 1857, *Memoir* 1:247.

105. Curtis to Clifford, 3 Oct. 1851, John H. Clifford Papers, MHS.

106. Curtis to Ticknor, 3 July 1857, *Memoir* 1:247; *New York Tribune*, 7 Sept. 1857.

107. Johnson to Curtis, 22 Sept. 1857, note by Curtis on letter to Johnson, n.d., Curtis to Fillmore, 1 Sept. 1857, George Ticknor Curtis to Curtis, 3 July 1857, *Memoir* 1:261, 262, 251, 245. Curtis confided the real reasons motivating his resignation to Clifford, who did not record their discussion. John Henry Clifford to Robert C. Winthrop, 28 Sept. 1857, Winthrop Family Papers, MHS.

108. McLean to Curtis, 30 July 1857, Curtis to George Ticknor, 3 July 1857, *Memoir* 1:259, 247; Winthrop to John Henry Clifford, 21 Sept. 1857, Winthrop Family Papers, MHS; Fillmore to Curtis, 4 Sept. 1857, Curtis Papers, DLC.

109. Eliab Parker Mackintire to William Salter, 14 Mar. 1857, *Letters of Eliab Parker Mackintire . . .*, ed. Philip Dillon Jordan (New York, 1936), 112; *New York Tribune*, 10 Mar. 1857.

110. Adams to Charles Sumner, 7 Apr. 1857, Charles Sumner Papers, MS Am 1 (31), Houghton Library, Harvard University.

6. THE PRESIDENT'S WAR POWERS

1. On the number of people arrested, see Hyman and Wiecek, *Equal Justice under Law*, 233; Mark E. Neely Jr., *The Fate of Liberty: Abraham Lincoln and Civil Liberties* (New York, 1991), 233–35; Mark E. Neely Jr., "The Lincoln Administration and Arbitrary Arrests: A Reconsideration," *Papers of the Abraham Lincoln Association* 5 (1983): 8.

2. *CWAL* 6:267. For general histories, consult William H. Rehnquist, *All the Laws but One: Civil Liberties in Wartime* (New York, 1998); Clinton Rossiter, *The Supreme Court and the Commander in Chief*, exp. ed. with additional text by Richard P. Longaker (Ithaca, N.Y., 1976).

3. Curtis to William W. Greenough, n.d., to Maria Malleville Allen Curtis, 26 Dec. 1862, *Memoir* 1:347, 353; Curtis to Greenough, 1 Jan. 1863, Curtis Papers, DLC; *Boston Advertiser*, 17 Sept. 1864.

4. *CWAL* 5:433–37; Curtis, *Executive Power*, 9; Curtis to Maria Malleville Allen Curtis, 6 Oct. 1862, *Memoir* 1:351.

5. *Memoir* 1:354; *CWAL* 5:544; Charles P. Kirkland, *A Letter to the Hon. Benjamin R. Curtis . . . in Review of His Recently Published Pamphlet on the "Emancipation Proclamation" of the President* (New York, 1862).

6. Ex parte Milligan, 71 U.S. 2 (1866); Arthur M. Schlesinger Jr., "War and the Constitution: Abraham Lincoln and Franklin D. Roosevelt," in *Lincoln, the War*

President: The Gettysburg Lectures, ed. Gabor S. Boritt (New York, 1992), 159; Gillette, "Curtis," 906.

7. U.S. Constitution, art. 2, sec. 2; Fleming v. Page, 50 U.S. (9 How.) 603, 614 (1850); *The Federalist* no. 69. Hamilton suggested that the war powers of the national government as a whole were practically unlimited to do whatever was necessary to meet the need. *The Federalist* no. 23.

8. John Locke, *Two Treatises of Government*, ed. Peter Laslett, 2d ed. (Cambridge, 1960), 393; Jefferson to John B. Colvin, 20 Sept. 1810, *Works of Thomas Jefferson* 11:146-50.

9. *CWAL* 7:281.

10. U.S. Constitution, art. 2, sec. 2; *CWAL* 5:421; 50 U.S. at 614.

11. *CWAL* 4:338-39, 346-47; Philip Shaw Paludan, *The Presidency of Abraham Lincoln* (Lawrence, Kans., 1994), 71.

12. U.S. Constitution, art. 1, sec. 9; Story, *Commentaries on the Constitution* 3:209.

13. *CWAL* 4:347, 419; Ex parte Merryman, 17 F. Cas. 144, 149 (C.C.D. Md. 1861) (No. 9,487).

14. Neely, *Fate of Liberty*, 4; *CWAL* 4:372, 430.

15. [Timothy Farrar], "Adequacy of the Constitution," *New Englander* 78 (1862): 52; see also Hyman, *More Perfect Union*, 124-40.

16. *CWAL* 5:437.

17. McPherson, *Battle Cry of Freedom*, 492-93; *CWAL* 5:437.

18. Curtis, *Executive Power*, v, 19, 17.

19. Ibid., 19, 29, 24.

20. Ibid., 24, 13.

21. Ibid., 24, 29.

22. On Lincoln's "nonlegalistic" conception of the Constitution, see Herman Belz, "Lincoln and the Constitution: The Dictatorship Question Reconsidered," *Congress and the Presidency* 15 (1988): 159.

23. Curtis, *Executive Power*, 17, 18.

24. Ibid., 18.

25. Ibid., 13, 30.

26. Ibid., 24, 23. Compare Curtis's jury instruction in a circuit case concerning the liability of a military officer who had arrested a civilian in the Dorr Rebellion, when there were two competing state governments in Rhode Island. Curtis stated, "The existence of martial law does not authorize general military license, or place the lives, liberty, or property of the citizens of the state under the unlimited control of every holder of a military commission." Despan v. Olney, 7 F. Cas. 534, 535 (C.C.D. R.I. 1852).

27. Curtis, *Executive Power*, 25.

28. Joel Parker, *Habeas Corpus and Martial Law* (Cambridge, Mass., 1861), 32.

29. Curtis, *Executive Power*, 13; *CWAL* 6:265.

30. 17 F. Cas. at 152; 71 U.S. at 127; Curtis, *Executive Power*, 26.

31. Curtis, *Executive Power*, 24, 25, 26.

32. Ibid., 24.

33. *CWAL* 6:264; Curtis, *Executive Power*, 18; Hyman, *More Perfect Union*, 94-98; Hyman and Wiecek, *Equal Justice under Law*, 239.

34. Curtis, *Executive Power*, 13; J. G. Randall, *Constitutional Problems under Lincoln*, rev. ed. (Urbana, Ill., 1951), 186–89; Charles Fairman, *The Law of Martial Rule*, 2d ed. (Chicago, 1943), 280–82.
35. Sherman quoted in George Clarke Sellery, "Lincoln's Suspension of Habeas Corpus as Viewed by Congress," *Bulletin of the University of Wisconsin, History Series* 1 (1907): 237; Horace Binney, *The Privilege of the Writ of Habeas Corpus under the Constitution*, pt. 2 (Philadelphia, 1862), 18; see also [Charles Ingersoll], *An Undelivered Speech on Executive Arrests* (Philadelphia, 1862), 61.
36. *CWAL* 4:430.
37. Congress declared that "all the acts, proclamations, and orders of the President . . . respecting the army and navy of the United States, and calling out or relating to the militia or volunteers from the States, are hereby approved and in all respects legalized and made valid, to the same intent and with the same effect as if they had been issued and done under the previous express authority and direction of the Congress of the United States." *Stats. at Large of USA* 12 (1865): 326. Commentators have mostly concluded that congressmen did not intend to endorse Lincoln's suspension of habeas corpus. Paludan, *Presidency of Abraham Lincoln*, 82; *Presidential Power and the Constitution: Essays by Edward S. Corwin*, ed. Richard Loss (Ithaca, N.Y., 1976), 163; Randall, *Constitutional Problems under Lincoln*, 128.
38. For details on the legislative process, see Sellery, "Lincoln's Suspension of Habeas Corpus," 223–45.
39. Curtis, *Executive Power*, 16, 13.
40. *CWAL* 5:434.
41. Lincoln made an earlier appeal to the border states. *CWAL* 5:317–19.
42. James M. McPherson, *The Struggle for Equality: Abolitionists and the Negro in the Civil War and Reconstruction* (Princeton, N.J., 1964), 118; David Herbert Donald, *Lincoln* (New York, 1995), 379.
43. *The Complete Works of Ralph Waldo Emerson* 11 (1904; reprint, New York, 1979): 315–16.
44. Curtis, *Executive Power*, 10; Gillette, "Curtis," 906. Considering Curtis's actions, Herbert Wechsler suggested that the issues of black citizenship in *Dred Scott* were logically distinguishable from the questions surrounding the Emancipation Proclamation. Herbert Wechsler, "Toward Neutral Principles of Constitutional Law," *Harvard Law Review* 73 (1959): 13–14.
45. In re Jane, 5 Western L.J. 202 (Ill. Cir. Ct. 1848).
46. *CWAL* 3:145–46.
47. *Memoir* 1:341; *CWAL* 4:270.
48. Curtis said that the Constitution "should contain a provision absolutely securing each slave-holding State from all interference with this institution within the State by the Federal government." Less emphatically, the president said that he did not object to making the implied principle of federal noninterference "express" and "irrevocable" by amending the Constitution. *Memoir* 1:342; *CWAL* 4:270.
49. *CWAL* 7:49, 433; Gideon Welles, "The History of Emancipation," 14 *Galaxy* (1872): 843.
50. *CWAL* 6:30, 428.

51. Donald, *Liberty and Union*, 145.
52. Curtis, *Executive Power*, 28, 26, 14. For the legal theory of secession, see Randall, *Constitutional Problems under Lincoln*, 61.
53. Curtis, *Executive Power*, 12, 28. President Lincoln acknowledged in December 1862 that a longer period of adjustment would spare "both races from the evils of sudden derangement." *CWAL* 5:531.
54. *Stats. at Large of USA* 12 (1865): 589–92; see also Patricia M. L. Lucie, "Confiscation: Constitutional Crossroads," *Civil War History* 23 (1977): 307–21.
55. Curtis, *Executive Power*, 15.
56. Hyman and Wiecek, *Equal Justice under Law*, 251–52; Randall, *Constitutional Problems under Lincoln*, 359.
57. McPherson, *Struggle for Equality*, 112.
58. Curtis, *Executive Power*, 31. After the war Curtis appeared before the U.S. Supreme Court representing persons litigating over property (not slaves) taken under the confiscation act. Curtis did not attack the constitutionality of this legislation. In one case he offered a statutory interpretation to show that the act did not apply to his client. McVeigh v. United States, 78 U.S. (11 Wall.) 259, 261–63 (1870). In another he only addressed procedural issues. Garnett v. United States, 78 U.S. (11 Wall.) 256 (1870).
59. Curtis, *Executive Power*, 12–13.
60. Swisher, *Taney Period*, 918.
61. *CG*, 37th Cong., 3d sess., 1862, 33, pt. 1:22, 67.
62. For example, ibid., 1863, 33, pt. 1:529–34.
63. Ibid., 1862, 33, pt. 1:14; Curtis, *Executive Power*, 13.
64. *Stats. at Large of USA* 12 (1865): 756. For further discussion of this legislation, see Sellery, "Lincoln's Suspension of Habeas Corpus," 265; Neely, *Fate of Liberty*, 69; Randall, *Constitutional Problems under Lincoln*, 189. Harold Hyman pointed to the statute's multiple purposes when he referred to it as the "habeas-corpus-indemnity-removal statute." Hyman, *More Perfect Union*, 245.
65. Grosvenor P. Lowrey, *The Commander-in-Chief; A Defence upon Legal Grounds of the Proclamation of Emancipation; and an Answer to Ex-Judge Curtis's Pamphlet, Entitled* Executive Power (New York, 1862), 7; Kirkland, *Letter*, 19, 12; [Charles Mayo Ellis], *The Power of the Commander-in-Chief . . . as Shown from B. R. Curtis* (Boston, 1862), 12. As another critic suggested, "Judge Curtis would have us believe that the President's power is confined to a lot, spot or tract of land, not too large." *Boston Advertiser*, 3 Nov. 1862. See generally Fairman, *Law of Martial Rule*, 165; Edward S. Corwin, *Total War and the Constitution* (New York, 1947).
66. In re Kemp, 16 Wis. 382, 417 (1863).
67. 71 U.S. at 121, 127. For further details on the Milligan case, see Frank L. Klement, "The Indianapolis Treason Trials and *Ex Parte Milligan*," in *American Political Trials*, 101–27; Fairman, *Reconstruction and Reunion, 1864–88*, pt. 1, 185–237; Warren, *Supreme Court in United States History* 2:418–54.
68. 71 U.S. at 122; ibid. at 136–41 (Chase, C.J., concurring). The chief justice concurred in the result based upon his interpretation of the Indemnity Act, which in his view expressly provided for the release of prisoners in Milligan's circumstances. Ibid., 133–35 (Chase, C.J., concurring).

69. Davis quoted in Stanley I. Kutler, *Judicial Power and Reconstruction Politics* (Chicago, 1968), 67.
70. Curtis to Davis, 17 Jan., 25 Feb. 1867, and n.d., David Davis Family Papers, Illinois State Historical Library, Springfield.
71. Warren, *Supreme Court in United States History* 2:427; Rossiter, *Supreme Court and the Commander in Chief*, 31–39; Neely, *Fate of Liberty*, 175–84; Ex parte Quirin, 317 U.S. 1, 45–46 (1942).
72. Curtis to Davis, 17 Jan. and 25 Feb. 1867, Davis Family Papers, Illinois State Historical Library.
73. Morgan D. Dowd, "Lincoln, the Rule of Law, and Crisis Government: A Study of His Constitutional Law Theories," *University of Detroit Law Journal* 39 (1962): 645; Gillette, "Curtis," 906.
74. Curtis, *Executive Power*, 29; Curtis to Davis, 25 Feb. 1867, Davis Family Papers, Illinois State Historical Library.
75. Curtis, *Executive Power*, 11, 12.
76. Lowrey, *Commander-in-Chief*, 16; *Boston Advertiser*, 24 Oct. 1862.
77. Curtis, *Executive Power*, 27, 28.
78. Ibid., 30.
79. Ibid., 31.
80. Curtis to Davis, 17 Jan. 1867, Davis Family Papers, Illinois State Historical Library.

7. THE JOHNSON IMPEACHMENT TRIAL

1. *Memoir* 1:408, 409. Orville Hickman Browning, Johnson's secretary of the interior, wrote that the cabinet "unanimously agreed" that the attorney general would be lead counsel with "two other eminent counsel"; "we all agreed that Judge Curtis should be one." *The Diary of Orville Hickman Browning . . .* 2 (Springfield, Ill., 1933): 183.
2. Colfax quoted in Gene Smith, *High Crimes and Misdemeanors: The Impeachment and Trial of Andrew Johnson* (New York, 1977), 244; Michael Les Benedict, *The Impeachment and Trial of Andrew Johnson* (New York, 1973), 134; *Diary of Gideon Welles . . .* (Boston, 1911), 3:324; *New York Tribune*, 2 Mar. 1868; Hans L. Trefousse, *Impeachment of a President: Andrew Johnson, the Blacks, and Reconstruction* (Knoxville, Tenn., 1975), 156–57.
3. *New York Tribune*, 9, 10 Apr. 1868; *Trial of Andrew Johnson* 1:377.
4. *New York Tribune*, 10 Apr. 1868.
5. *Trial of Andrew Johnson* 1:377; *New York Herald*, 10 Apr. 1868.
6. Browning was the sole exception. *Diary of Orville Hickman Browning* 2:192.
7. Records of the Harvard College Class of 1829, p. 197, HUD 229.714, Harvard University Archives; *Memoir* 1:417.
8. *CWAL* 7:54–56.
9. Eric Foner, *Reconstruction: America's Unfinished Revolution, 1863–1877* (New York, 1988), 35–37, 60–61; Michael Les Benedict, *A Compromise of Principle: Congressional Republicans and Reconstruction, 1863–1869* (New York, 1974), 70–99; Hyman and Wiecek, *Equal Justice under Law*, 271–76; Paludan, *Presidency of Abraham Lincoln*, 280–81, 306–9; David Donald, *Charles Sum-*

ner and the Rights of Man (New York, 1970), 162, 185–86, 188. For divisions among the Republicans in Congress, see Benedict, *Compromise of Principle*, 22–29.

10. "George W. Julian's Journal—The Assassination of Lincoln," *Indiana Magazine of History* 9 (1915): 335.

11. Foner, *Reconstruction*, 177, 178, 183; Hans L. Trefousse, *Andrew Johnson: A Biography* (New York, 1989), 198.

12. *Trial of Andrew Johnson* 3:247; Sumner to John Bright, 24 Apr. 1865, *The Selected Letters of Charles Sumner*, ed. Beverly Palmer, 2 (Boston, 1990): 297.

13. Foner, *Reconstruction*, 199–225; Kenneth M. Stampp, *The Era of Reconstruction, 1865–1877* (New York, 1982), 79–81; Hyman and Wiecek, *Equal Justice under Law*, 319–22; Michael Perman, *Reunion without Compromise: The South and Reconstruction, 1865–1868* (Cambridge, 1973), 77–81; Leon F. Litwack, *Been in the Storm So Long: The Aftermath of Slavery* (New York, 1979), 366–71.

14. Foner, *Reconstruction*, 142–70; Litwack, *Been in the Storm So Long*, 379–82; Civil Rights Act of 1866, *Stats. at Large of USA* 14 (1868): 27.

15. Foner, *Reconstruction*, 243–51; Eric L. McKitrick, *Andrew Johnson and Reconstruction* (Chicago, 1960), 287–92, 310–18; W. R. Brock, *An American Crisis: Congress and Reconstruction, 1865–1867* (1963; reprint, New York, 1966), 105–17.

16. Benedict, *Compromise of Principle*, 169–87; Brock, *American Crisis*, 148, 173–74; Foner, *Reconstruction*, 251–61; McKitrick, *Andrew Johnson and Reconstruction*, 349–51. President Johnson had endorsed the adoption of the Thirteenth Amendment even though several states were not represented in Congress. He believed that the Thirteenth Amendment was uniquely justified to end the practice of slavery that had put the Union in jeopardy. James E. Sefton, *Andrew Johnson and the Uses of Constitutional Power* (Boston, 1980), 135.

17. *Stats. at Large of USA* 14 (1868): 428–29.

18. Hyman, *More Perfect Union*, 491–97; David Donald, "Why They Impeached Andrew Johnson," *American Heritage* 8 (1956): 21–25, 102–3; Donald, *Sumner and the Rights of Man*, 255–56; Foner, *Reconstruction*, 251.

19. Trefousse, *Impeachment of a President*, 48; Howard P. Nash Jr., *Andrew Johnson: Congress and Reconstruction* (Rutherford, N.J., 1972), 130.

20. Trefousse, *Impeachment of a President*, 55, 57–58, 70–71, 107–12; Benedict, *Impeachment and Trial*, 73–81; *CG*, 40th Cong., 2d sess., 1867, 39, pt. 2:68.

21. Trefousse, *Impeachment of a President*, 109–10; Benedict, *Impeachment and Trial*, 81–85; U.S. Constitution, art. 2, sec. 4.

22. Story, *Commentaries on the Constitution* 2:262–70; Hyman and Wiecek, *Equal Justice under Law*, 450; Benedict, *Impeachment and Trial*, 26–36.

23. Benedict, *Impeachment and Trial*, 46–49; *Stats. at Large of USA* 14 (1868): 432.

24. Benjamin P. Thomas and Harold M. Hyman, *Stanton: The Life and Times of Lincoln's Secretary of War* (New York, 1962), 585; *New York Tribune*, 22, 24 Feb. 1868; *CG*, 40th Cong., 2d sess., 1868, 39, pt. 2:1400; Benedict, *Impeachment and Trial*, 112.

25. As to the conspiracy charges, Curtis argued that there can be no conspiracy between the commander in chief and a subordinate officer. He also called the attempted use of the conspiracy statute "one of the extraordinary things" in this

case, as the legislation did not apply to acts within the District of Columbia. *Trial of Andrew Johnson* 1:199, 406; *Stats. at Large of USA* 12 (1863): 284.

26. *Trial of Andrew Johnson* 1:8-10.

27. Ibid., 1:89, 90, 94, 3:256, 1:377.

28. Ibid., 1:20, 28, 26.

29. David Miller DeWitt, *The Impeachment and Trial of Andrew Johnson* (1903; reprint, Madison, Wis., 1967), 422-23; Hans L. Trefousse, *Ben Butler: The South Called Him BEAST!* (New York, 1957).

30. *Trial of Andrew Johnson* 1:89, 90, 93, 94.

31. Story, *Commentaries on the Constitution* 2:235.

32. *Trial of Andrew Johnson* 1:410, 377, 409; see U.S. Constitution, art. 1, sec. 3, and art. 3, sec. 2.

33. Curtis to Ticknor, 10 Apr. 1868, *Memoir* 1:416-17.

34. *Trial of Andrew Johnson* 1:407.

35. Charles J. Cooper, "A Perjurer in the White House? The Constitutional Case for Perjury and Obstruction of Justice as High Crimes and Misdemeanors," *Harvard Journal of Law and Public Policy* 22 (1999): 619-46; Cass R. Sunstein, "Impeachment and Stability," *George Washington Law Review* 67 (1999): 699-711; Laurence H. Tribe, "Defining 'High Crimes and Misdemeanors': Basic Principles," *George Washington University Law Review* 67 (1999): 712-34; Michael J. Gerhardt, *The Federal Impeachment Process: A Constitutional and Historical Analysis* (Princeton, N.J., 1996), 102-11; Tribe, *American Constitutional Law* 1:155-56; Benedict, *Impeachment and Trial*, 30, 34-35; Raoul Berger, *Impeachment: The Constitutional Problems* (Cambridge, Mass., 1973), 53-102; Charles L. Black Jr., *Impeachment: A Handbook* (New Haven, 1974), 39. When the House Judiciary Committee considered impeaching President Richard M. Nixon, its legal staff concluded that "to limit impeachable conduct to criminal offenses would be incompatible with the evidence concerning the constitutional meaning of the phrase 'high Crimes and Misdemeanors' and would frustrate the purpose that the framers intended for impeachment." House Committee on the Judiciary, *Constitutional Grounds for Presidential Impeachment: Report by the Staff of the Impeachment Inquiry*, 93d Cong., 2d sess., 1974, 25.

36. *The Records of the Federal Convention of 1787*, ed. Max Farrand, 2 (New Haven, 1937): 550.

37. *The Federalist* no. 65. Interestingly, Blackstone defined "high misdemeanors" to include "mal-administration" by public officers. Blackstone, *Commentaries on the Laws* 4:121. On the historical understanding of impeachment, see Sunstein, "Impeachment and Stability," 700-704; Gary L. McDowell, "'High Crimes and Misdemeanors': Recovering the Intentions of the Founders," *George Washington University Law Review* 67 (1999): 626-49; Edwin Brown Firmage, "The Law of Presidential Impeachment," *Utah Law Review*, 1973, no. 4:687-94; Philip B. Kurland, "Watergate, Impeachment, and the Constitution," *Mississippi Law Journal* 45 (1974): 540-48; Berger, *Impeachment*, 59-73.

38. *Trial of Andrew Johnson* 1:8, 9.

39. Ibid., 408, 88, 409.

40. Kurland, *Watergate and the Constitution*, 105; *Trial of Andrew Johnson* 1:410.

41. *Trial of Andrew Johnson* 1:409, 410.
42. U.S. Constitution, art. 3, sec. 2; *Trial of Andrew Johnson* 1:409; Benedict, *Impeachment and Trial*, 32–33.
43. *Trial of Andrew Johnson* 1:409.
44. Ibid., 411; *New York Tribune*, 11 Apr. 1868.
45. *Trial of Andrew Johnson* 1:116, 413.
46. *CG*, 40th Cong., 2d sess., 1868, 39, pt. 2:1361; Benedict, *Impeachment and Trial*, 108–13.
47. *Trial of Andrew Johnson* 1:378, 383.
48. Ibid., 102.
49. Ibid., 379; *Stats. at Large of USA* 14 (1868): 430.
50. *Trial of Andrew Johnson* 1:379.
51. Ibid., 3:264.
52. Ibid., 1:379.
53. U.S. Constitution, art. 2, sec. 1; Benedict, *Impeachment and Trial*, 149.
54. U.S. Constitution, art. 2, sec. 2.
55. *Trial of Andrew Johnson* 1:380, 381. A similar argument had been advanced when the Senate considered the bill. *CG*, 39th Cong., 2d sess., 1867, 37, pt. 1: 382–83.
56. *Trial of Andrew Johnson* 1:382; *CG*, 39th Cong., 2d sess., 1867, 37, pt. 2:1340.
57. *Trial of Andrew Johnson* 1:383, 384.
58. Ibid., 384.
59. Ibid., 96.
60. In *Myers v. United States* (1926), the Court declared unconstitutional legislation that required Senate approval of the president's removal of postmasters. 272 U.S. 52 (1926). Nine years later a majority of justices limited *Myers* in ruling that Congress may limit the president's removal powers over officers performing quasi-legislative or quasi-judicial functions in independent agencies, in this case the Federal Trade Commission. Humphrey's Executor v. United States, 295 U.S. 602 (1935). The issue reappeared in various forms in the late twentieth century involving the power to remove the independent counsel, comptroller general, and members of the U.S. Sentencing Commission. See, for example, Bowsher v. Synar, 478 U.S. 714, 762 (1986) (Congress cannot "reserve for itself the power" to remove officers "charged with the execution of the laws"; a legislative officer, the comptroller general, cannot perform executive functions).
61. U.S. Constitution, art. 2, sec. 2; *The Federalist* no. 77; Louis Fisher, *Constitutional Conflicts between Congress and the President* (Princeton, N.J., 1985), 61–66.
62. Kent, *Commentaries on American Law* 1:310; Story, *Commentaries of the Constitution* 3:394–96; Fisher, *Constitutional Conflicts*, 66–68; Berger, *Impeachment*, 281–82.
63. *Papers of Daniel Webster*, ser. 4, *Speeches* 2:90; In re Hennen, 38 U.S. (13 Pet.) 230, 259 (1839).
64. *Trial of Andrew Johnson* 1:97.
65. Ibid., 388.
66. Ibid., 385, 391–92.
67. Ibid., 388, 389.

68. It has been suggested that a majority of the congressmen did not actually support the position that the president had the power over removal solely, but this position prevailed through a "brilliant parliamentary maneuver." Benedict, *Impeachment and Trial*, 161; Edward S. Corwin, *The President's Removal Power under the Constitution* (New York, 1927), 10–23. The justices of the Supreme Court tangled over this history in *Myers v. United States*. Compare 272 U.S. at 111–26 (Taft, C.J.) with ibid., 194–98 (Holmes, J., dissenting).

69. *Trial of Andrew Johnson* 1:389, 390, 391.

70. Ibid., 389–90, 385.

71. Ibid., 1:357–59, 547–89, 2:247–48; Benedict, *Impeachment and Trial*, 162–64.

72. *Trial of Andrew Johnson* 1:392.

73. Ibid., 2:167.

74. Ibid., 1:387.

75. Ibid., 387, 386.

76. Ibid., 387.

77. Ibid., 388.

78. Benedict, *Impeachment and Trial*, 20.

79. The U.S. Army was prepared to try William McCardle with a military tribunal authorized by the Reconstruction Acts. He was a Mississippi newspaper editor arrested for publishing "incendiary" articles. Ex parte McCardle, 74 U.S. 506, 508 (1869).

80. Fairman, *Reconstruction and Reunion*, pt. 1, 459–65; Kutler, *Judicial Power and Reconstruction Politics*, 78–86.

81. *Trial of Andrew Johnson* 1:394.

82. Ibid., 123, 414.

83. Curtis to Ticknor, 10 Apr. 1868, *Memoir* 1:416; Frederick Trevor Hill, *Decisive Battles of the Law . . .* (New York, 1907), 162; *Diary of Gideon Welles* 3:330, 331–32.

84. Benedict, *Impeachment and Trial*, 100; *Trial of Andrew Johnson* 1:521, 525, 529. Defense counsel had lined up several cabinet members to testify that Johnson consulted with them on the Tenure of Office Act, that they advised him the legislation was unconstitutional, and that Johnson dispatched Seward and Stanton to prepare a response. The Senate held the testimony inadmissible. *Trial of Andrew Johnson*, 676–701.

85. Curtis to Ticknor, 10 Apr. 1868, *Memoir* 1:416.

86. Benedict, *Impeachment and Trial*, 130–37; Foner, *Reconstruction*, 336.

87. For an alternative interpretation of party alignment, see Claude Albright, "Dixon, Doolittle, and Norton: The Forgotten Republican Votes," *Wisconsin Magazine of History* 59 (1975–76): 91–100.

88. *Trial of Andrew Johnson* 2:486; Trefousse, *Impeachment of a President*, 169; *Chicago Tribune*, 18 May 1868; John B. Henderson, "Emancipation and Impeachment," *Century Magazine* 85 (1912): 207.

89. *Trial of Andrew Johnson* 2:496–97.

90. See, for example, *Nation*, 16 Apr. 1868.

91. Generally speaking, the business community had concerns over the financial policies embraced by Radicals. Benedict, *Impeachment and Trial*, 65–67; Tre-

fousse, *Impeachment of a President*, 149–50. See also Ralph J. Roske, "Republican Newspaper Support for the Acquittal of President Johnson," *Tennessee Historical Quarterly* 11 (1952): 263–73.

92. Benedict, *Impeachment and Trial*, 137–38; Trefousse, *Impeachment of a President*, 157–59.

93. Randall, *Civil War and Reconstruction*, 611; Milton Lomask, *Andrew Johnson: President on Trial* (New York, 1960), 311; McKitrick, *Andrew Johnson and Reconstruction*, 507.

94. *Nation*, 23 Apr. 1868; George S. Boutwell, "The Impeachment of Andrew Johnson: From the Standpoint of One of the Managers of the Impeachment Trial," *McClure's Magazine* 14 (1899): 180; *Harper's Weekly*, 25 Apr. 1868; Benjamin F. Butler, *Butler's Book: Autobiography and Personal Reminiscences of Major-General Benj. F. Butler* (Boston, 1892), 930.

95. *Trial of Andrew Johnson* 2:172, 411, 243.

96. At first Bingham contrasted Curtis's precise analysis with that of Evarts, who was "not so careful of his words." Ibid., 411. This was a promising beginning. Bingham could have exploited the differences to show that whatever restrictions Curtis had in mind, the president's power was not so easily cabined. Bingham missed the opportunity to do that, however. Ibid., 391, 397, 407, 464.

97. Ibid., 95–106, 221.

98. Ibid., 3:123 (Vickers), 169 (Davis), 220 (Buckalew), 301 (Henderson), 321 (Trumbull).

99. Ibid., 69 (Howe), 232 (Buckalew), 273 (Sumner).

100. Records of the Harvard College Class of 1829, p. 197, HUD 229.714, Harvard University Archives; *Memoir* 1:409.

101. George F. Edmunds, "Ex-Senator Edmunds on Reconstruction and Impeachment," *Century Magazine* 85 (1913): 863–64; Benedict, *Impeachment and Trial*, 130–41; Boutwell, "Impeachment of Andrew Johnson," 180. Fessenden's biographer believed that the senator from Maine based his decision on the legal issues. Charles A. Jellison, *Fessenden of Maine: Civil War Senator* (Syracuse, N.Y., 1962), 233–34.

102. Eugene H. Berwanger, "Ross and the Impeachment: A New Look at a Critical Vote," *Kansas History* 1 (1978): 239; Charles A. Jellison, "The Ross Impeachment Vote: A Need for Reappraisal," *Southwestern Social Science Quarterly* 41 (1960): 150–55. For Edmund G. Ross's retrospective account, see *History of the Impeachment of Andrew Johnson . . .* (Santa Fe, N.Mex., 1896).

103. One historian suggested that Senator Van Winkle voted to acquit because of deficiencies in the articles. R. W. Bayless, "Peter G. Van Winkle and Waitman T. Willey in the Impeachment Trial of Andrew Johnson," *West Virginia History* 13 (1952): 85, 88. Trumbull's biographer concluded that the senator from Illinois based his judgment on legal issues, although his vote was made easier after the *Chicago Tribune* expressed fears over a Wade presidency. Mark M. Krug, *Lyman Trumbull: Conservative Radical* (New York, 1965), 268.

104. *Trial of Andrew Johnson* 3:323 (Trumbull), 19–22 (Fessenden), 199 (Fowler), 332 (Grimes), 303 (Henderson), 199 (Fowler).

105. Ibid., 193 (Fowler), 16 (Fessenden), 193 (Fowler), 319 (Trumbull), 340 (Grimes); see also ibid., 82 (Edmunds), 157 (Davis), 233 (Buckalew).
106. On the Clinton impeachment, see Michael J. Gerhardt, "The Historical and Constitutional Significance of the Impeachment and Trial of President Clinton," *Hofstra Law Review* 28 (1999): 349–92.
107. Michael Les Benedict, "A New Look at the Impeachment of Andrew Johnson," *Political Science Quarterly* 88 (1973): 351; William H. Rehnquist, "The Impeachment Clause: A Wild Card in the Constitution," *Northwestern University Law Review* 85 (1991): 904; Arthur M. Schlesinger Jr., "Reflections on Impeachment," *George Washington Law Review* 67 (1999): 697; Berger, *Impeachment*, 295.
108. Curtis to Evarts, 8 May 1868, William Maxwell Evarts Papers, DLC.

CONCLUSION

1. Curtis to Davis, 17 Jan. 1867, David Davis Family Papers, Illinois State Historical Library.
2. Curtis to Andrew Johnson, 8 June 1868, *The Papers of Andrew Johnson*, ed. Paul H. Bergeron, 14 (Knoxville, Tenn., 1997): 182; Curtis to Reverdy Johnson, 23 May 1873, *Memoir* 1 : 444. In 1874 the Democrats in the Massachusetts state legislature nominated Curtis for the U.S. Senate, but he was not elected. *Boston Advertiser*, 21 Mar. 1874.
3. Foner, *Reconstruction*, 260; Benedict, *Compromise of Principle*, 192–96; McKitrick, *Andrew Johnson and Reconstruction*, 397–420; Thomas Wagstaff, "The Arm-in-Arm Convention," *Civil War History* 14 (1968): 101–19; *Diary of Gideon Welles* 2 : 540.
4. Curtis to Ticknor, 27 July 1866, *Memoir* 1 : 389; Curtis to Walter Curtis, 22 July 1866, Curtis Papers, DLC; Curtis to Orville Hickman Browning, n.d., Papers of Orville Hickman Browning, Illinois State Historical Library.
5. Curtis to Ticknor, 27 July 1866, *Memoir* 1 : 389.
6. Texas v. White, 74 U.S. 700 (1869).
7. Hyman and Wiecek, *Equal Justice under Law*, 296; Benedict, *Compromise of Principle*, 122–26; McKitrick, *Andrew Johnson and Reconstruction*, 93–119; John C. Hurd, "Theories of Reconstruction," *American Law Review* 1 (1867): 238–64; U.S. Constitution, art. 4, sec. 4.
8. "Letter from Judge B. R. Curtis," *National Intelligencer*, 24 July 1866.
9. Ibid.
10. Benedict, *Compromise of Principle*, 413; McKitrick, *Andrew Johnson and Reconstruction*, 113–17, 229.
11. Curtis to Andrew Johnson, 8 June 1868, *Papers of Andrew Johnson* 14 : 182; Curtis to Ticknor, 10 Apr. 1868, *Memoir* 1 : 417.
12. Curtis to Ticknor, 5 Feb. 1869, *Memoir* 1 : 421.
13. Virginia v. West Virginia, 78 U.S. (11 Wall.) 39 (1871).
14. Quoted in Fairman, *Reconstruction and Reunion*, pt. 1, 623, 622. See Randall, *Constitutional Problems under Lincoln*, 433–76.
15. McVeigh v. United States, 78 U.S. (11 Wall.) 259, 265, 267 (1871).

16. Curtis to Ticknor, 5 Feb. 1869, *Memoir* 1:421; Brief for the Complainant, Willard v. Tayloe, File Copies of Briefs, U.S. Supreme Court, vol. 1, Dec. Term 1868; Hepburn v. Griswold, 75 U.S. (8 Wall.) 603 (1870).

17. Curtis to Evarts, 8 May 1868, Evarts Papers, DLC.

18. Randall Kennedy, *Nigger: The Strange Career of a Troublesome Word* (New York, 2002), 5.

19. *CG*, 39th Cong., 1st sess., 1866, 36, pt. 2:1776.

20. *CWAL* 2:403; *Proceedings of the Bench and Bar of the Circuit Court of the United States, District of Massachusetts*, 16; 87 U.S. (20 Wall.) ix (1875).

21. Taney to Curtis, 11 June 1857, Curtis Papers, DLC; Cardozo, *Law and Literature*, 36.

22. Cf. Neal K. Katyal and Laurence H. Tribe, "Waging War, Deciding Guilt: Trying the Military's Tribunals," *Yale Law Journal* 111 (2002): 1259–1307; Jack Goldsmith and Cass R. Sunstein, "Military Tribunals and Legal Culture: What a Difference Sixty Years Makes," *Constitutional Commentary* 19 (2002): 261–89.

23. Curtis, *Executive Power*, 11.

24. Scott v. Sandford, 60 U.S. (19 How.) 393, 589 (1857); Curtis, *Executive Power*, 9; *Trial of Andrew Johnson* 1:410, 412.

25. *Selected Historical Essays of F. W. Maitland*, ed. Helen M. Cam (Cambridge, 1957), 132.

26. Curtis to Ticknor, 3 July 1857, *Memoir* 1:247.

27. *CWAL* 7:23; Curtis to Maria Malleville Allen Curtis, 26 Dec. 1862, *Memoir* 1:353.

INDEX

abolitionists and abolitionist movement:
on confiscation act, 165; on conscience
as guide, 46; on Constitution as
proslavery, 2, 40–41, 63, 125; Curtis
on, 25–34, 43, 49–50; Curtis's reputation among, 4, 25, 29, 39, 52, 64; on
disunion, 40–41, 49–51; on *Dred
Scott*, 120; on due process, 112; on
Emancipation Proclamation, 162–63;
on Fugitive Slave Act, 41–42, 44, 49–
50; on Mass. court actions, 53–54; on
natural law and slavery, 26–27; radical-
ization of, 33–34; territorial question
and, 134
Adams, Charles Francis, 9, 34, 42, 50, 149
Adams, Henry, 210, 235–36n58
Adams, John, 188
Adams, John Quincy, 12
adequacy constitutionalism theory, 155,
169
admiralty law, 87
agrarian society, 23–24
Amar, Akhil Reed, 99
American Anti-Slavery Society, 26,
33–34
American Revolution, 16–17
Amistad (ship), 29
Antelope, The (case), 30
Anti-Federalists, 81
antikidnapping laws, 40
antimiscegenation statute (Mass.), 124,
126
antislavery societies, 26, 33–34, 41. See
also *Commonwealth v. Aves*
Appleby, Joyce, 23
Appleton, Nathan, 34
Aristotle, 14
Arkansas Supreme Court, 130
Articles of Confederation, 125–27, 137
Ashley, James M., 176, 184

Aves, Thomas, 28. See also *Commonwealth
v. Aves*

Badger, George E., 145
banking system, 9, 12, 90, 141, 142
Bank of the United States, 9
bankruptcy, 92
Barbour, Philip P., 81
Baring Brothers & Company, 23
Barron v. Baltimore, 109
Benedict, Michael Les, 197
Benton, Thomas Hart, 139
Bill of Rights: drafting of, 100–101; on
due process, 98; impetus for, 117; incorporation of, 109–11; Lincoln's
proclamation as overriding, 158. *See
also specific amendments*
Bingham, John A., 172, 194, 195, 205,
251n96
Binney, Horace, 161
Black, Charles L., Jr., 92, 142
Black, Hugo L., 88, 109, 111
black citizenship: Curtis on, 125–34,
149, 150, 199, 206; emancipation issues
compared with, 244n44; Lincoln on,
163; seamen acts in context of,
239n50; Taney on, 119, 123–25;
voting rights as issue in, 119–20,
125, 131, 206
Black Codes, 175–76
blacks: as excluded from constitutional
protection, 44; laws regulating move-
ments of, 72–73, 79, 133; northern vs.
southern courts' treatment of, 43–44;
rights of, 65, 128–29, 131–32, 150,
175, 205; voting in southern states of,
176. *See also* black citizenship; free
blacks; slaves
Blackstone, Sir William, 21, 26, 248n27
Bloomer v. McQuewan, 235n56

reform of, 13; role of, 6–7, 86, 144; sources of law for, 87; standard of morality for, 30–31; subjectivity of, 20–21, 88, 111. *See also* judicial power; judicial review; Supreme Court, U.S.
jurors and juries: law vs. fact and, 57; law vs. morality as basis for decisions of, 39, 55–56, 59; oaths of, 49, 52; powers of, 56–59, 65; uniformity undermined by, 58–59, 226n82
jury nullification, 39, 49, 55–59
justice: law's relationship to, 30, 48–49; popular conception of, 65

Kane, John K., 224–25n65
Kansas-Nebraska Act, 62, 135, 145
Kent, James: on codification, 20; on comity, 28–29; on due process, 100, 104; on lawyers, 218n63; on president's removal power, 188
Kentucky court of appeals, 26
King, Martin Luther, Jr., 50
Kings' Chapel (Boston), 12
Kirkland, Charles P., 152, 167
Kurland, Philip B., 181

labor legislation, 112–13, 118
Latimer, George, 40–41
law and laws: admiralty, 87; authority to decide questions of, 56–59, 65; evaluating constitutionality of, 174; executive prerogative in overriding, 153; of forum vs. domicile, 28–29, 30; as framework for change, 134; as human arrangement, 49; morality's relationship to, 30–31, 45, 55–56, 59, 65; politics' relationship with, 18, 143–44; reason vs. passion in considering, 48, 63; resistance to, as civic virtue, 191; as science vs. custom, 20, 21; on seamen, 72–73, 79, 239n50; tort, 87; wartime uses of existing, 160–61. *See also* common law; law of the land; martial law; natural law; state laws; *and specific laws*
law of the land: application of, 102–7; definition of, 103, 233n17, 234n37; due process juxtaposed to, 99–102; equality under law linked to, 116; text of, 232n3

Lawrence, Abbott, 34
Lawrence, Amos A., 62
lawyers: elitist notions of, 22, 218n63
Laycock, Douglas, 103
legal process: obstruction of, 62–64
Legal Tender Cases, 204, 235–36n58
legislative power: habeas corpus and, 154; limits to, 102–5, 107, 111–15, 207, 209; "needful" as line between judicial and, 140, 144. *See also* Congress, U.S.; state laws
Levy, Leonard W., 25
Liberator, 33, 42, 52, 61, 64
liberty: English "ancestry" of, 17; Mass. law on, 40–41
liberty of contract: definition of, 112–13; early recognition of, 114, 118; support for, 235n52; upheld, 115
License Cases, 71, 83, 90, 94
Lilburne, John, 57
Lincoln, Abraham: on commander in chief clause, 154, 156; constitutional interpretation of, 2, 7, 140, 169; Curtis's disappointment with, 151–52; on Curtis's *Dred Scott* dissent, 4, 120, 127, 206; Declaration of Independence and Constitution linked by, 3; end of term for, 186; on *Executive Power*, 152; "malice toward none" theme of, 202; martial law proclamation of, 156–62; on race relations, 205; on spread of slavery, 134; on suspension of habeas corpus, 155–56; on Taney's *Dred Scott* opinion, 137–38; Taney's efforts to discredit, 154–55; 10 Percent Plan of, 174; as Whig leader, 9. *See also* commander in chief clause; Emancipation Proclamation; executive war powers
Lochner v. New York, 113, 117
Locke, John, 14, 153
Logan, John A., 173
Loring, Edward G.: Anthony Burns's case and, 60, 62–63
Loring, Ellis Gray: legal arguments of, 29–30, 31
Louisiana: anti-discrimination law in, 96; citizenship in, 129; due process case in, 112

Constitutionalism and Democracy

Kevin T. McGuire
The Supreme Court Bar: Legal Elites in the Washington Community

Mark Tushnet, ed.
The Warren Court in Historical and Political Perspective

David N. Mayer
The Constitutional Thought of Thomas Jefferson

F. Thornton Miller
*Juries and Judges versus the Law: Virginia's Provincial
Legal Perspective, 1783–1828*

Martin Edelman
Courts, Politics, and Culture in Israel

Tony Freyer
Producers versus Capitalists: Constitutional Conflict in Antebellum America

Amitai Etzioni, ed.
New Communitarian Thinking: Persons, Virtues, Institutions, and Communities

Gregg Ivers
To Build a Wall: American Jews and the Separation of Church and State

Eric W. Rise
The Martinsville Seven: Race, Rape, and Capital Punishment

Stephen L. Wasby
Race Relations Litigation in an Age of Complexity

Peter H. Russell and David M. O'Brien, eds.
*Judicial Independence in the Age of Democracy: Critical Perspectives from
around the World*

Gregg Ivers and Kevin T. McGuire, eds.
Creating Constitutional Change

Stuart Streichler
*Justice Curtis in the Civil War Era: At the Crossroads of
American Constitutionalism*